Praise for *Policy as Code*

This book fills a gap I frequently see in many organizations looking to adopt modern software development practices and the cloud—how to think about automated policy enforcement in a coherent and actionable way. The first chapter alone is worth the price of the book and it should be mandatory reading for any leader thinking about or struggling with cloud adoption.

—*Mark Donovan, Director,*
WW Technologists, AWS

Policy as Code is transforming SecOps, just as infrastructure as code has transformed DevOps! In this book, Jimmy Ray provides a fantastic foundation of PaC principles and a comprehensive tour of solutions for platform engineers looking to build secure self-service for developers and data scientists.

—*Jim Bugwadia, Cochair,*
CNCF Kubernetes Policy Working Group,
Cofounder and CEO, Nirmata

Jimmy Ray has really poured his heart and soul into this book, covering the journey of Policy as Code in the OSS community from humble beginnings to wider adoption as a key guardrail in protecting and governing the end state. I found it full of practical examples and technical details that provide insight into the various Policy as Code solutions.

—*Jesse Loudon, Tech Stream Lead (Azure), Arinco, and*
Microsoft MVP (Azure)

Governance as code is a deep subject which every CIO or CTO will need to implement. Jimmy Ray breaks down the subject matter, making it easy to understand, and gives the reader all the tools necessary to be successful in its roll out.

—*Darien Ford, CTO, Madhive*

Policy as Code

Improving Cloud Native Security

Jimmy Ray

Beijing · Boston · Farnham · Sebastopol · Tokyo

Policy as Code

by Jimmy Ray

Published by O'Reilly Media, Inc., 1005 Gravenstein Highway North, Sebastopol, CA 95472.

O'Reilly books may be purchased for educational, business, or sales promotional use. Online editions are also available for most titles (*http://oreilly.com*). For more information, contact our corporate/institutional sales department: 800-998-9938 or *corporate@oreilly.com*.

Acquisitions Editor: Simina Calin
Development Editor: Melissa Potter
Production Editor: Elizabeth Faerm
Copyeditor: Shannon Turlington
Proofreader: Brandon Hashemi

Indexer: Ellen Troutman-Zaig
Interior Designer: David Futato
Cover Designer: Karen Montgomery
Illustrator: Kate Dullea

July 2024: First Edition

Revision History for the First Edition
2024-07-02: First Release

See *http://oreilly.com/catalog/errata.csp?isbn=9781098139186* for release details.

978-1-098-13918-6

[LSI]

Table of Contents

Preface

In 2016, I was tasked with writing cloud computing controls as part of a large cloud-migration effort. These controls were based on standards adopted by—and created within—our organization, and they prevented unwanted and potentially dangerous changes within our cloud environments. I started writing the controls using what I thought was the best tool in my toolbox, Java; I was a Java subject matter expert (SME), and the cloud service provider (CSP) offered a mature Java software development kit (SDK).

The first and, as it turns out, last control I wrote in Java enforced encryption of data at rest on object storage. There are certain control types within cloud computing that I consider fundamental for secure computing, and encryption of data at rest and data in transit tops my list.

I quickly realized that building and running individual programs or modules to implement controls for the vast collection of cloud computing services and their respective features was not scalable or easily supportable. Writing code to consume the SDK was too low level. I was moving too slow, and it was challenging for me to share my approach in a way that facilitated broad adoption. The standards and controls SMEs were not Java programmers, and I couldn't expect them to learn Java just to build new controls or even support those already built.

I Needed Policy as Code

I needed a more abstract solution—maybe underpinned by a domain-specific language (DSL)—that provided a common lexicon that was more familiar to the folks specifying the cloud computing controls. Regardless of the underlying implementation, users defining the controls should be experts in cloud computing controls, not the technology used to implement the controls. The solution I chose was Cloud Custodian (c7n) (*https://cloudcustodian.io*).

C7n was developed by a colleague of mine, and over time, it has been broadly adopted by cloud computing users and providers. With c7n we deployed rules engines to our cloud environments and wrote policies using a controls-friendly YAML DSL. Moreover, the DSL did not require any knowledge of the underlying Python code used to build c7n. C7n was the first Policy as Code (PaC) tool I used.

 As a point of reference, *Policy as Code* (PaC)—the focus of this book—is the use of code artifacts to manage and apply rules and conditions. Policy engines are the programs that interpret policy artifacts to apply policy decisions. The rules and conditions defined in policy artifacts help us implement standards and policies that we have created or adopted. These implementations—known as *controls*—apply security, compliance, governance, and best-practices decisions that are designed to prevent and react to unwanted changes within the systems we support and use.

From that experience I learned that security, compliance, and governance did not need to hinder progress. We wrote policies that served as boundaries between which our cloud engineers worked. These boundaries did not stop them; moreover, our engineers learned the controls they needed to follow, and we reduced unwanted changes into our cloud environments. We managed c7n policies like other code artifacts, employing continuous integration (CI) and continuous delivery (CD) tools to keep our policies and cloud environments updated.

PaC solutions allow users to write policies to enforce behaviors. These behaviors are scoped into security, compliance, and governance controls as well as best practices. PaC—with appropriate policies—can reduce or even eliminate nondeterministic behaviors within your artifacts and systems. And when it comes to securing systems, fewer surprises are generally considered a good thing.

Who Should Read This Book

This book is for DevOps practitioners, Kubernetes cluster operators, security engineers, and anyone charged with ensuring secure operations in cloud native and everything-as-code environments. In this book, I introduce PaC concepts and use cases, and expose you to patterns and solutions to help you successfully use PaC for your security, compliance, and governance needs. I think this book can serve as a reference for those of you needing to understand PaC and choose the right solution for your use cases. You can also use this book to discover techniques and patterns that you can apply immediately. I think some of you will reread this book to gain a deeper understanding of the different aspects of PaC.

For the purposes of this book, I mean to cover PaC and PaC solutions that are, for the most part, vendor neutral and CSP agnostic. By the end of this book, you should better understand PaC theory and capabilities as well as use cases, patterns, and best practices for security, compliance, and governance controls. In Chapter 1, I introduce a process you can use to choose the correct PaC solution for your needs and capabilities. As you read this book, refer back to the process to better understand each solution and its potential fit for your needs.

Conventions Used in This Book

The following typographical conventions are used in this book:

Italic
Indicates new terms, URLs, email addresses, filenames, and file extensions.

`Constant width`
Used for program listings, as well as within paragraphs to refer to program elements such as variable or function names, databases, data types, environment variables, statements, and keywords.

`Constant width bold`
Shows commands or other text that should be typed literally by the user.

`Constant width italic`
Shows text that should be replaced with user-supplied values or by values determined by context.

This element signifies a tip or suggestion.

This element signifies a general note.

This element indicates a warning or caution.

Using Code Examples

Supplemental material (code examples, etc.) is available for download at *https://github.com/Policy-as-Code-Book*.

If you have a technical question or a problem using the code examples, please send email to *support@oreilly.com*.

This book is here to help you get your job done. In general, if example code is offered with this book, you may use it in your programs and documentation. You do not need to contact us for permission unless you're reproducing a significant portion of the code. For example, writing a program that uses several chunks of code from this book does not require permission. Selling or distributing examples from O'Reilly books does require permission. Answering a question by citing this book and quoting example code does not require permission. Incorporating a significant amount of example code from this book into your product's documentation does require permission.

We appreciate, but generally do not require, attribution. An attribution usually includes the title, author, publisher, and ISBN. For example: "*Policy as Code* by Jimmy Ray (O'Reilly). Copyright 2024 Jimmy Ray, 978-1-098-13918-6."

If you feel your use of code examples falls outside fair use or the permission given above, feel free to contact us at *permissions@oreilly.com*.

O'Reilly Online Learning

 For more than 40 years, *O'Reilly Media* has provided technology and business training, knowledge, and insight to help companies succeed.

Our unique network of experts and innovators share their knowledge and expertise through books, articles, and our online learning platform. O'Reilly's online learning platform gives you on-demand access to live training courses, in-depth learning paths, interactive coding environments, and a vast collection of text and video from O'Reilly and 200+ other publishers. For more information, visit *https://oreilly.com*.

How to Contact Us

Please address comments and questions concerning this book to the publisher:

O'Reilly Media, Inc.
1005 Gravenstein Highway North
Sebastopol, CA 95472
800-889-8969 (in the United States or Canada)
707-827-7019 (international or local)
707-829-0104 (fax)
support@oreilly.com
https://www.oreilly.com/about/contact.html

We have a web page for this book, where we list errata, examples, and any additional information. You can access this page at *https://oreil.ly/policy-as-code*.

For news and information about our books and courses, visit *https://oreilly.com*.

Find us on LinkedIn: *https://linkedin.com/company/oreilly-media*.

Watch us on YouTube: *https://youtube.com/oreillymedia*.

Acknowledgments

Although I am the only author listed on this book, and I set out alone to write this book, I immediately found myself seeking the guidance of those who have gone before me and other industry SMEs. I started this effort while still at AWS, and Michael Hausenblas—my colleague and a prolific author whose books I usually read from cover to cover—helped me get started with O'Reilly and the writing process. It would have been much harder to launch this effort without Michael's experience and knowledge as my wayfinder.

I was lucky enough to receive technical reviews, subject matter expertise, critical feedback, and encouragement from several individuals during the process; I am indebted to them, even if they do not realize it. Anders Eknert, Jesse Loudon, and Rosemary Wang were my first technical reviewers. They were tough, they challenged me to think beyond my perspective and consider the needs of my readers, and they set the bar and my expectations high. They went on to help me throughout the writing of this book with general policy, Kubernetes, and Open Policy Agent (OPA) topics; when it comes to OPA, Rego, and PaC, Anders provided a wealth of valuable information. Within the OPA community Slack channel, Stephan Renatus stands out for helping me answer questions just in time to finish topics.

For MagTape and OPA topics, Joe Searcy was quite helpful. Even though the project is somewhat dormant, that chapter is one of my favorites in this book, as it challenges the status quo of PaC and Kubernetes integration and illustrates the art of the possible.

I have known Jim Bugwadia for years, dating back to when I was at Capital One; he and I collaborated on a couple of AWS blogs, efforts for which I also enlisted the help of Chip Zoller. Jim and Chip provided much needed insight into Kubernetes and Kyverno as well as technical reviews on related topics. Together, they helped correct and smooth what I thought I knew.

Michael LaPane helped with several complex Terraform topics, and we discussed the book over several sessions at the Crazy Rooster in Powhatan, Virginia, and at his house, consuming BBQ.

I spent several hours over the course of writing this book in the Gatekeeper Slack channel, and Sertaç Özercan and Rita Zhang were quite helpful there.

Eve Ben Ezra, Michael Hume, and Thomas Lawson provided valuable help and understanding about Conftest in the form of timely KubeCon talks and blog posts.

When it came time to write about Cloud Custodian for infrastructure as a service (IaaS) and Kubernetes, Kapil Thangavelu (creator of Cloud Custodian) and David Shepherd—both colleagues from my Capital One days—and AJ Kerrigan readily answered all my questions and helped me stay on the right path. It's one thing to use a technology; it's altogether different to be able to write about it with authority.

Rich Burroughs—with Loft Labs—helped me with jsPolicy, and Christopher Phillips—another former Capital One colleague, now with Anchore—helped me with SBOMs and the Anchore Syft and Grype tools.

When it came to software supply chain topics, I received considerable help from the folks at Liatrio, including Oliver Eikenberry, Robert Kelly, Jonathan Dorsey, Ahmed Alsabag, and Eric Chapman. Liatrio has a wealth of knowledge and experience in the software supply chain space. And, as my chapter on PaC and the software supply chain was one of my last chapters, I received just-in-time help from Cassie Crossley and her newly minted—at the time—book *Software Supply Chain Security* (O'Reilly). Dan Lorenc helped me distill simplicity from the complex topic of how public key infrastructure is used to apply signatures to artifacts and attestations to create software supply chain statements.

I appreciate the experience of building Kubernetes the hard way—using Bash and Go—with my then Capital One colleagues Andrew Myhre and Zach Abrahamson. Lessons I learned then I still use today.

I want to thank Mark Donovan, Jeremy Cowan, and Jesse Butler, three outstanding colleagues from AWS—Mark and I go back to my earliest days at Capital One. I am not sure they know how much I rely on their mentorship.

Writing—like working—is not without sacrifice. Writing a book is a whole other level of sacrifice, and my family was good at not complaining or showing disappointment when I worked to stay on schedule. I learned new techniques to navigate the quiet and dark house as I worked late into the night. Regardless of how I tried not to, I always seemed to wake my wife. I appreciate her forbearance.

Finally, none of this would be possible without my O'Reilly team. Melissa Potter is a fantastic content development editor and one of the main reasons I was able to deliver the content for this book. She and I met regularly, and she helped me understand how to write for O'Reilly, reminding me how best to build content. As I navigated several health- and work-related issues, Melissa was there to encourage me and help with scheduling. Liz Faerm is a production editor, and she routinely rewarded me with my early releases and additional recommendations to improve the structure of my content. Simina Calin—senior acquisition editor—was my primary initial contact with O'Reilly, and she helped me build a strategy and outline for the entire book.

## CHAPTER 1

Policy as Code: A Gentle Introduction

By some estimates (*https://oreil.ly/x6poa*), more than 2.7 trillion lines of code have been written in the last 60-plus years. How many lines have you written? I don't know how many lines I've written, but I've been writing code for almost 30 years. Only in the last eight years have I used Policy as Code (PaC) to control changes better, guide me through complex systems and solutions, and ensure that what I write is what I mean to write, execute, and distribute.

Regardless of system or artifact, PaC has emerged as the standard for how we reduce unwanted and nondeterministic changes and behaviors across the systems and solutions we use, build, and support. PaC allows us to codify the guidelines we specify, follow, and impose. PaC inherits its utility from coding standards and best practices as well as the controls to implement them.

PaC shows up in and improves many systems and solutions today, ranging from cloud computing and Kubernetes to Authorization (AuthZ) (*https://oreil.ly/xSkM8*), continuous integration/continuous delivery (CI/CD (*https://oreil.ly/84zqG*)), DevOps (*https://oreil.ly/1bFw3*), DevSecOps (*https://oreil.ly/y3bgw*), GitOps (*https://www.gitops.tech*), and software supply chain security (*https://oreil.ly/vDEro*). In this book, I examine PaC more closely and present ideas, patterns, and examples of how to use PaC to policy-enable your solutions. For now, in this chapter I introduce PaC concepts, how PaC should trace from your standards, and the characteristics of PaC that can be used to help you choose the right solution for your needs. By chapter's end, you will have a process and a checklist that you can apply throughout this book to gauge how additional PaC solutions fit your needs.

What Is Policy?

You follow policies every day. Policies help you make decisions within the context of the situations in which you operate. Usually, these policies are based on documented rules and guidelines. You agree to these rules and guidelines as part of employment or membership in organizations in which you function. Policy is not new to you. Simply put, *policy* is a planned system of rules and guidelines that directs users and automation to execute within purposeful boundaries. Policy sets guardrails that both enlighten and limit.

I would add that with policy we try to achieve *desired* results or outcomes. At work, getting you to follow company policy is management's way of achieving desired results or outcomes, like making sure that you properly document and report your time away from work.

Regulatory policy has emerged as a driving force for the IT systems that service businesses. According to the Organisation for Economic Co-operation and Development (OECD) (*https://oreil.ly/q4XzD*), "Regulatory policy is about achieving government's objectives through the use of regulations, laws, and other instruments to deliver better economic and social outcomes and thus enhance the life of citizens and business."

The General Data Protection Regulation (GDPR) (*https://gdpr-info.eu*) is one of the most well known emerging data-privacy regulatory policies in the European Union (EU). As such, the GDPR should be considered a driving force, along with regulatory policies in general.

Since policies in this book will be focused on information technology (IT) systems, we need a more IT-focused policy definition. According to Torin Sandall in his 2017 *Medium* article "What Is Policy? Part One: Enforcement" (*https://oreil.ly/EACKS*), "In the context of software systems, policies are the rules that govern how the system behaves."

I would add that policies also govern how actors behave within those systems. Policies define rules, and these rules specify how systems behave as well as how they are configured, used for their defined purpose, and secured.

A major theme of this book is using policy and policy tools to prevent unwanted changes and enforce best practices in our systems and artifacts. It just makes sense that we adopt a policy definition that better covers the scope of our needs.

Now that we understand the basic idea and purpose of policy, let's define Policy as Code.

What Is Policy as Code?

As mentioned in the Preface, PaC is the use of code artifacts—policies—to manage and apply rules and conditions. Policy engines are the programs that interpret policy artifacts to apply policy decisions, using the aforementioned rules and conditions. The rules and conditions defined in policy artifacts help us implement organizational standards and policies that we have created or adopted. These implementations—known as *controls*—apply security, compliance, governance, and best-practices decisions that are designed to prevent and react to unwanted changes within the systems we support and use.

At the fundamental level, during execution to arrive at decisions, PaC answers questions—questions about systems, artifacts, scenarios, and situations that need to be controlled. More questions answered means more controls implemented. More controls implemented means more deterministic behaviors, fewer unwanted behaviors, and fewer surprises.

In the next section, we'll examine policy structure and characteristics.

What Is a Policy?

We can easily model a policy by decomposing it into parts that make sense for our use. At a high level, our policy model is made up of the following parts:

Policy name
> Used to label the policy for future reference

Policy purpose
> The reason this policy exists and what it tries to enforce or address

Policy situation
> The context (including system and environment) in which the policy will be used

Policy rules
> Individual controls or prescribed behaviors; policies can have multiple rules

Policy actions
> Actions taken if a policy rule is violated (not always part of the policy engine)

Next, we will more closely examine the characteristics of policies that make them so useful and the policy languages they use.

PaC Policy Characteristics

In the context of PaC, policies have other characteristics that make them useful in IT systems. First, PaC policies are written, stored, managed, and interpreted as code artifacts. This makes them easier to manage and deploy to systems with the same automated tools and processes you may already use for application delivery.

Another important aspect of PaC policies, regardless of the underlying implementation, is their *syntactical familiarity*. As you will see later when you explore the individual PaC solutions in more detail, different policy languages enhance the adoption of PaC. For example, if your organization has deep JavaScript capabilities, then you might choose a PaC solution underpinned by the JavaScript language.

The familiar nature of PaC policies, or their configuration wrappers, aid in their adoption. For me, the more familiar the PaC policy language or configuration wrapper is, the more intuitive the solution tends to be. However, how familiar or intuitive a language—or lexicon thereof—is to me is subjective, based on my knowledge and experience. You may have different ideas about the familiar and intuitive natures of the languages you use or prefer. You may choose PaC solutions with policy languages that are declarative, or you may choose languages that are more imperative or even assertion based.

Regardless of the policy language you choose, the inputs that PaC handles, evaluates, and outputs tend to be more declarative and structured. In fact, the more declarative and structured artifacts are, the more reliably PaC can evaluate them. To that end, we will explore why JSON and YAML are so popular in PaC solutions.

The Role of JSON and YAML

I think we can all agree that JSON (*https://oreil.ly/xth6b*) and YAML (*https://yaml.org*) are examples of two of the most declarative and intuitive data formats widely used in modern IT systems. In fact, many cloud computing and Kubernetes engineers use these data formats on a daily basis to define and declare their configurations in structured formats.

It's not by accident that PaC tools have embraced these two data formats to deliver policies to systems, process inputs, and provide outputs. To some in the industry, PaC policies written or wrapped in JSON or YAML tend to be more declarative, expressive, and even self-documenting (*https://oreil.ly/uncmR*). Even if the PaC policy language, used within a policy engine, is not based on or wrapped by JSON or YAML data formats, artifacts that policies evaluate are usually JSON or YAML. Structured data is simply easier to handle.

PaC naturally parses and evaluates JSON and YAML artifacts as part of policy matching and evaluation. Data, regardless of what it represents, is better suited for PaC evaluations when it can be structured in JSON or YAML. JSON and YAML can be converted to and from each other very easily. Finally, other nonstructured or less structured artifacts can be parsed into JSON and YAML for further processing by PaC.

Next, let's see how we can avoid unwanted actions or changes by using PaC to erect guardrails.

Guardrails: Preventing the Unwanted

As I mentioned in the Preface of this book, in the past I worked with organizations that used PaC to build boundaries for cloud computing operations. When it comes to preventing unwanted changes or behaviors by users or automation, these boundaries act as guardrails. If operations stay within the guardrails, like you normally drive along a highway, then those operations are not restricted. Once those operations stray from the prescribed path, violate the rules and conditions set by policies, and try to operate outside the guardrails, then those operations are restricted by controls, which are enforced and implemented by policies.

Guardrails allow unrestricted flow between their edges. In the case of cloud computing, infrastructure changes fast to meet business needs. Practitioners who manage security, compliance, and governance erect guardrails, in the form of controls, to prevent unwanted behaviors that could put the business at risk. Regardless of the implemented control, there is a strong desire to not hinder allowed progress.

Many organizations put controls in place to determine how compute instances are provisioned. This helps prevent unwanted changes, regardless of the users' intentions or experience and knowledge levels. For example, it is common to see controls that prevent compute instances from existing if they are associated with public IP addresses. The controls act as guardrails. Given our earlier policy model, you can visualize the policy for disallowing compute with a public IP address, shown in Figure 1-1.

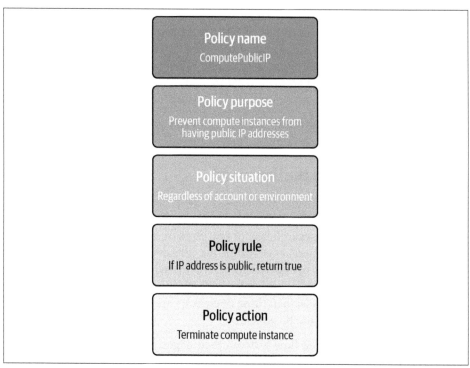

Figure 1-1. Policy model: ComputePublicIP

In this example, when you are provisioning compute, your actions proceed unrestricted as long as you stay within the guardrails. However, if you create compute with a public IP, your progress is stopped, and the compute you provisioned is disabled or even terminated. Figure 1-2 shows a simple activity diagram of the flow.

Over time, guardrails teach you the correct flow and how to proceed without restrictions. Organizations, as a whole, move faster and more securely when they operate between prescribed boundaries with low friction.

Now let's see how we can use PaC to prevent the unwanted by reacting to the unplanned.

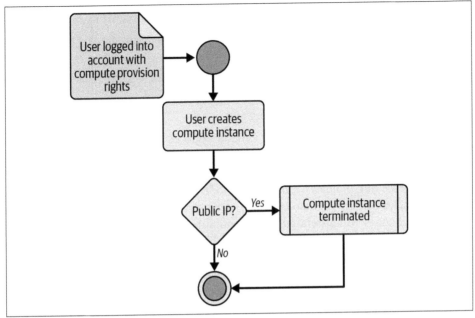

Figure 1-2. ComputeNoPublicIP policy activity diagram

Plans: Reacting to the Unplanned

Users are constantly making changes to systems and artifacts. It's next to impossible to judge what they will try next. Curtailing the actions of bad actors is even more difficult. However, it's not impossible to determine what both are *allowed* to do next. Policies, enforced by PaC engines, construct a defense-in-depth (DiD) strategy (*https://oreil.ly/f5jpJ*), adding a layer of countermeasures regardless of the source of change.

For example, let's consider a scenario where you operate and maintain a Kubernetes cluster or collection thereof. Even if users who deploy to your cluster(s) are in your organization, you won't always have the control over their code or container images that you need to prevent their containers from compromising the integrity of your cluster(s). You can specify certain practices to prevent their containers from behaving badly, such as security settings, network settings, or even from where container images are allowed to be sourced. However, you cannot rely on users to follow your instructions; moreover, they may not have the requisite Kubernetes knowledge. Instead, you need guardrails.

To counteract the possibility of rogue code or containers overwhelming your cluster(s), you need policies in place, underpinned by policy engines that integrate with Kubernetes. We will explore this topic in more detail in later chapters, but for now, the following examples of baseline policies could be implemented:

- Limit sourcing of container images from only approved registries
- Enforce appropriate Kubernetes security context elements at the Pod and container levels
- Prevent unwanted network egress and ingress from and to Pods by enforcing appropriate Kubernetes network policies
- Prevent Pod use of host networking and ports
- Prevent Pod use of host processes and namespaces
- Enforce container resource requests and limits

All of the preceding policies fit the policy model defined earlier. Combining the preceding policies with policy actions like deny or modify can prevent the related unwanted changes to clusters and the possibility of rogue code causing problems. Even if rogue code, or unwanted or drifted binaries, exists within a container, the chances of it causing harm are reduced, if not eliminated. This is part of a DiD strategy with a focus on least privilege (*https://oreil.ly/S635j*). With these policies, the containers get only the permissions and resources they need to function correctly. With this approach, you actually react to the unplanned.

 PaC is just one part of a successful DiD strategy. For more information about DiD, please start with NIST SP 800-53 (*https://oreil.ly/b6vs5*).

Now that we have defined *policy* and *policies*, and discussed how they can help prevent the unwanted and react to the unplanned, we need to shift gears and explore how open source software plays a key role in PaC.

Adopting Open Source Software

When I hear the term *open source software* (OSS), I think of software that is publicly accessible, such that anyone can review the code or even modify it. Of course, this is subject to OSS licenses and contributor guides and agreements. I also think of community, and with a larger project development community comes the possibility of greater stability and security.

The majority of PaC solutions are open source projects. Have you ever worked on or contributed to an OSS project? Have you ever wanted or had to adopt an OSS project for your needs? There are certain advantages and disadvantages to OSS in the context of PaC, and not all OSS projects are created equally.

In my opinion, the two biggest advantages of OSS are the potential cost savings it can provide and its scale of contributions. Many OSS projects and libraries are used by organizations to reduce overall development effort. Someone else already wrote it, and if it works for your needs, then why should you duplicate the effort? All things being equal, you can move faster with OSS. Moving faster by reducing development effort usually means cost reductions.

By their nature, mature OSS projects can have a larger number of maintainers and contributors. This means that there are more eyes on the project and contributions come from different perspectives. OSS project maintainers run and guide the project, keeping to the defined project charter and direction. Contributors provide suggestions and potential changes and are force multipliers for OSS projects; they increase the effectiveness of project activities.

More involvement means more control and less chance of something being missed. While this doesn't mean that you will not need to review and manage the project artifacts, like you would with any other software project, it does increase the likelihood that major issues will be caught and fixed sooner.

 For more information about OSS maintainers and contributors, please see the article "How Open Source Maintainers Keep Contributors—and Themselves—Happy" (*https://oreil.ly/GulEa*) by Klint Finley at The ReadME Project (*https://github.com/readme*).

Along with OSS project maturity, continued and steady project momentum is key to successful OSS PaC projects. PaC solutions succeed best when they can solve multiple use cases. Solving use cases requires new and updated policies and integrations. In other words, the projects must continue to grow, solving more problems for more users. Without momentum, PaC projects—and OSS projects in general—stagnate, and users look elsewhere for solutions.

Now that we know why we should use OSS, let's balance the equation by considering some of the disadvantages of OSS.

Disadvantages of OSS

OSS projects are certainly not without disadvantages and risks. In fact, if I let it take over, the topic of OSS risk could consume most, if not all, of this book. Far and away, the biggest disadvantage with OSS is the potential lack of support. I am not saying that OSS maintainers and contributors don't support their community of users; my experience has been quite the opposite. However, OSS maintenance and contributions are usually done as side efforts; maintainers and contributors have day jobs outside of the projects they support.

While there are exceptions, this conflict between jobs and projects naturally limits how quickly maintainers and contributors can respond to requests. This may not work for organizations that are used to enterprise support agreements or that require more deterministic response times for support requests. While third-party enterprise support does exist for some OSS projects, this is not the norm.

When you use an OSS project and you're not a maintainer, you lack definitive control over the direction of the project. You have to decide if that lack of control, supplanted by a limited sphere of influence, fits your needs. In a lot of instances, it is a manageable compromise.

 Risk is another possible disadvantage of OSS projects. For more information about OSS risk, please see OWASP's recently released Top 10 Risks for Open Source Software (*https://oreil.ly/BkmNy*). This list outlines the significant risk of OSS projects and is based in part on findings from the *Open Source Security and Risk Analysis Report* (*https://oreil.ly/DXdVT*) by Synopsys. The Synopsys report called out the following general OSS risk data:

> - 89% of codebases contain OSS that is more than four years out of date
> - 91% of codebases contain components that have had no new development in more than two years
>
> Together, these two reports provide valuable insight into OSS project risk.

OSS is not perfect, but used correctly, it is still an enabler, if not a force multiplier. Now, let's look closer at some of the OSS aspects we should consider when deciding if we should use OSS projects.

The Care and Feeding of OSS

Although OSS offers advantages over internally developed projects, the use of OSS requires a certain care and feeding. The following OSS issues should be considered:

Licensing
> Make sure that the OSS project you want to use has a license that permits the way you want to use it. Can you fork it, if need be? Most organizations have an open source program office (OSPO) that defines what licenses can be used internally.

Security
> Is security engineered into the project? The OpenSSF Scorecard (*https://oreil.ly/scorecard*) is an emerging tool to gauge the security of the OSS project.

Maturity

How mature is this project? How many and what types of releases have been cut? Is it generally available (GA)? What is the rate of bugs and requested enhancements? How does the project handle changes?

Dependencies

What dependencies does the OSS project have? Are those dependencies documented? Are they safe?

Active support

How active are the maintainers of the OSS project you are considering? When was the last time contributions were made to this project? Are contributions regular? How soon will bugs or vulnerabilities be corrected? Could you continue to support it if you needed to? Does your organization require a more formalized support agreement for external software?

Project direction

Where is the project headed? Does your use case make sense for the project direction, or is it just an edge case?

In-house capability

Are you or your team familiar with the technology or languages used in the OSS project? Can you all review the code and accurately decide on its reliability and fitness for your use? Do you have the systems in place to store, manage, and vend the OSS project artifacts for secure and reliable use within your organization? Do you have the tools to thoroughly and reliably scan and detect vulnerabilities in OSS?

Beyond the short-lived forks used for pull-request contributions, OSS projects should only be forked as a last resort. Forking an OSS project is usually done to steer the project in a different direction and eventually replace it.

While necessity may be the "mother of invention" (Plato), desperate decisions lead to mistakes and misunderstandings. If you choose to use OSS for any reason, PaC or otherwise, choose to embrace the holistic effort involved in managing the OSS artifacts as if you developed them yourself. If you need more influence over the OSS project, plan on contributing to the project or even maintaining it, if need be.

Project and contributor sponsorship are ways to support OSS projects beyond active contributor or maintainer involvement in the project. Considering how many OSS projects are used in software products and projects within corporations, there is little giveback in the way of financial support to these projects. Sponsorship (*https://oreil.ly/OE4G7*) of projects and contributors is a good way to give back to the OSS project community and to the projects which your products or projects depend on.

If your organization has an OSPO, leverage its knowledge and experience to better guide you along the path of least resistance when it comes to consuming OSS projects. The OSPO has been there and done that, and it is charged with helping your organization successfully and securely use OSS.

 For more information about OSPOs and the community of practitioners, please see the Talk Openly Develop Openly (TODO) organization (*https://todogroup.org*).

Moving on from OSS concerns, let's look at how PaC is linked to your organization's standards and controls.

Standards and Controls

Most organizations have groups that manage policies and standards, such as cybersecurity. These groups create their own standards and adopt recognized standards and best practices from organizations like the Cloud Security Alliance (CSA) (*https://oreil.ly/ypght*), the Center for Internet Security (CIS) (*https://oreil.ly/Ym2MV*), and the National Institute of Standards and Technology (NIST) (*https://www.nist.gov*). Additional standards bodies like the Payment Card Industry (PCI) (*https://oreil.ly/5WhOY*) are referenced as needed, based on business focus.

Standards are normally traceable upstream to organizational policies. The difference between organizational policies and standards is that policies are usually more focused on communicating organizational or managerial intent, where standards are usually focused on the specific measurable requirements implied in and needed by the policies.

Requirements defined by standards are followed by the organization. To govern, manage, and measure compliance to standards, organizations use internal—and sometimes external—governance, risk, and compliance (GRC) teams. GRC teams focus on specific areas of the business and, in some cases, specific IT systems. In the case of IT, GRC teams work with systems and technology SMEs to define the controls needed to enforce requirements.

For example, your company's cloud engineering team manages the use of public cloud services. To provide a secure and well-managed cloud computing experience, the team works with GRC to define a set of controls that matches the requirements set by organizational standards. The SMEs advise GRC about what is possible in the cloud. The working group, formed by the collaboration of GRC and cloud engineering SMEs, tracks the standards and associated controls through a matrix. In the example Controls Traceability Matrix shown in Table 1-1, the cardinality between standards and controls is one-to-many. Standards can have multiple controls.

Table 1-1. GRC Controls Traceability Matrix

Standard	Focus area	ID	Control	Status
Non-customer-facing compute should not directly access endpoints beyond the corporate network.	Information Security— Cloud Computing	ISCC-1	Prevent public IP addresses from being assigned to compute	Approved
	Information Security— Cloud Computing	ISCC-2	Prevent NAT from being associated with private subnets	Under development

The SMEs on the cloud engineering team agree to implement the controls and manage internal efforts to build, test, and deploy the respective controls. The GRC teams are project stakeholders that guide cloud engineering on the requirements. GRC reviews the controls and confirms that the controls meet requirements.

The cloud engineering team uses PaC to implement the controls agreed to by the GRC working group. The PaC controls emit logs and messages that serve as auditable artifacts that are used by the SMEs to prove to GRC that the implemented controls are enforcing behaviors defined in the requirements. Similarly, GRC uses the auditable artifacts to satisfy management and internal and external auditors.

In the model given in this example, there is traceability from broad organizational policies to focused PaC policies used to implement controls. The pyramid model in Figure 1-3 depicts the hierarchy as well the narrowing of focus.

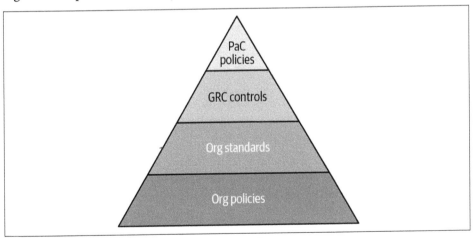

Figure 1-3. Policy traceability and focus pyramid

PaC policies enforce controls by preventing unwanted changes and behaviors and by reinforcing desired behaviors and practices. Simply put, PaC implements controls. Usually, controls implemented by PaC will originate from standards created or adopted by your organization. These controls should also be traceable and auditable.

Next, we will explore how PaC is changing how we leverage and extend code artifacts.

Policy as Code for Everything as Code

During the last several years, we have witnessed a transformation of sorts with respect to how we provision and use IT resources: we moved and are still moving to *everything as code* (EaC). Many of the processes we now use to provision, mutate, or validate IT resources use *-as-code artifacts. For many of us, gone are the days of waiting weeks or months to receive compute capacity. Now we just dial it up, so to speak, by applying *infrastructure-as-code* (IaC) (*https://oreil.ly/5bxPv*) artifacts, like JSON or YAML, or even Terraform (*https://www.terraform.io*) plans, through our public or private cloud services. We can even provision bare-metal resources now using tools like Tinkerbell (*https://docs.tinkerbell.org*).

While there's usually a console that we can still use to provision our resources, using IaC affords us the opportunity to manage our infrastructure resources the same as we do our application code. We now use source code management tools, as well as CI tools and even GitOps, to manage and apply infrastructure. And while we usually apply IaC declaratively, we have now even blurred the lines between the imperative and declarative, and combined the two with tools like the Cloud Development Kit (CDK) (*https://aws.amazon.com/cdk*) from Amazon Web Services (AWS) (*https://aws.amazon.com*) or the Cloud Development Kit for Terraform (CDKTF) (*https://oreil.ly/BPhXK*) from HashiCorp (*https://www.hashicorp.com*).

Regardless of what you are doing or using, if you can do it with code, then you gain several tangible benefits that are lost when you perform tasks manually. For example, you can utilize the same single source of truth (SSOT) that centralized source code management provides. You can also take advantage of the collaboration opportunities that EaC offers. The tools and processes have been honed by years of source code management.

Using and deploying artifacts as code leads to improvements in repeatability, as the automated processes reduce variability between integrations and deployments; since the artifacts and deployments are code, understood by underlying systems, scalability with deterministic behaviors is also improved.

Source code management and CI tools provide automation to manage your *-as-code artifacts. You can automate testing as well as source code scanning. With automated tests and PaC, you apply policies to code to evaluate changes before they are allowed to be merged. More automation leads to quicker issue detection and allows you to fail and succeed faster, with more deterministic outcomes. In other words, you get more repeatability and reproducibility–and, as I have said before, fewer surprises are generally a good thing.

Applying PaC to your source code also helps you implement *compliance as code* (CaC). With CaC, compliance policies are used as tests and are often used in CI pipelines to validate *-as-code artifacts before they can be used for downstream changes.

Security as code (SaC) is related to CaC and can also benefit from PaC. According to Jim Bird, in his book *DevOpsSec* (O'Reilly), "Security as code is the practice of building security into DevOps tools and workflows by mapping out how changes to code and infrastructure are made and finding places to add security checks, tests, and gates without introducing unnecessary costs or delays."

Codifying security and policies thereof frees the security settings from human-only readable documents and converts them to human- and machine-readable artifacts, making the SaC artifacts executable, traceable, and auditable.

In my opinion, SaC, as defined by Jim Bird, implies PaC. PaC can be used to evaluate the artifacts and produce the attestations that are needed by DevOps gates. As long as the attestations (evidence) are parseable (JSON, YAML, etc.) by the PaC policy engine, then PaC suits this use case.

Over time, the PaC policies, used for CaC and SaC, form guardrails, just like test cases did for test-driven development (TDD). Ongoing automation of tests and PaC evaluations increases reliability of your codebases and reduces unwanted variances from reaching your production environments. As a point of reference, Figure 1-4 depicts how CaC and SaC use PaC for EaC.

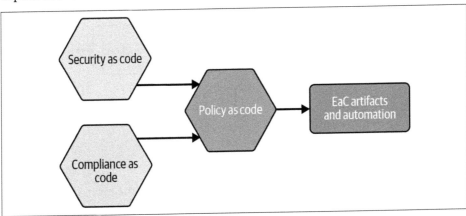

Figure 1-4. CaC and SaC using PaC for applying policies to EaC

Now that we have explored the use of PaC within the evolving EaC landscape, let's move on to the engines and languages that run and build policies for our needs.

Policy Engines and Languages

As part of a PaC solution, *policy engines* perform the heavy lifting by interpreting the policy language and evaluating the data. According to Bruce A. Fette in his book *Cognitive Radio Technology* (*https://oreil.ly/Gae_1*), Second Edition (Academic Press), "A policy engine is a program or process that is able to ingest machine-readable policies and apply them to a particular problem domain to constrain the behavior of network resources."

I like this definition as it surfaces three features that I think correctly characterize PaC policy engines:

- Ingesting machine-readable policies (PaC)
- Applying policies to specific problem domains (data)
- Constraining behaviors (outcomes)

A policy engine ingests the policy to be used in the evaluation, the data to be evaluated, and the query to be used. Then, the policy engine evaluates the supplied data against the supplied policy and produces an answer, used by the system to which the policy engine is integrated or serves. Policies are written to match the data they evaluate; moreover, that matching happens before the policy evaluates the data and after any input processes, such as parsing. Figure 1-5 shows a flow diagram of a policy engine's typical evaluation process.

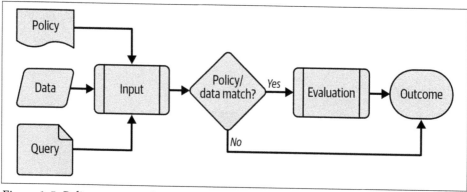

Figure 1-5. Policy engine evaluation flow

In the flow shown in Figure 1-5, if a policy does not match the given data, the policy engine might return an undefined or empty object, an error, or even a false value. Some policy engines support the ability to load policies and supporting data asynchronously, not just during evaluation cycles. And there are policy engines that will even look up external data as part of the evaluation cycle.

In the context of a policy engine, *policy language* is the language in which the policy is written, not necessarily the language in which the engine is written. Not all policy engines use the same policy languages, however. I cover the following policy engines, along with others, in this book, along with their associated policy languages:

- Cloud Custodian (c7n) (*https://cloudcustodian.io*)—YAML
- jsPolicy (*https://www.jspolicy.com*)—JavaScript
- Kyverno (*https://kyverno.io*)—YAML
- MagTape (*https://github.com/tmobile/magtape*)—Rego
- Open Policy Agent (OPA) (*https://www.openpolicyagent.org*)—Rego (*https://oreil.ly/SCjak*)
- OPA/Gatekeeper (*https://oreil.ly/ZT5W_*)—Rego and YAML

I will describe each of these later in more detail, but for now, let's look at how we can choose the right PaC solution for our needs, based on language as well as other factors.

Choosing the Right PaC Solution

Which policy engine should you use? The answer to that question depends on several factors. In fact, you may have to read most of this book and try multiple PaC solutions before you are ready to make that choice. The good news is that choosing the correct PaC solution, the one that best suits your needs, is not necessarily a one-way door decision (*https://oreil.ly/Wfvv_*). More to the point, it's not unheard of for users to deploy multiple PaC solutions; they can coexist in the systems they serve.

The best practice for choosing the right PaC solution starts with honesty. Be honest with yourself, your team, and your organization. Don't just choose what you think is the coolest solution, or even the most marketed, adopted, or well known. Choose the solution that best fits your selection criteria—all (or at least the majority) of your selection criteria. Understand and define your must-haves versus your should-haves or even your nice-to-haves. Weighting selection criteria is good for this classification process. Base your selection criteria on true representations of the needs and capabilities of your organization.

Know your use cases intimately. Arguably, the next step in choosing the correct PaC solution for your needs is matching your use cases. This is followed closely by matching the user experience (UX) (*https://oreil.ly/b0XBL*) you will need to foster the broadest acceptance and adoption within your organization. Obviously, part of the UX match is defining your users and understanding their needs. The use case and UX matching exercises help you avoid erroneous choices that result in solution mismatch.

Don't try to boil the ocean with your chosen PaC solution. Be wary of edge cases. Even if the PaC solution you are considering satisfies a specific use case that is troubling your organization, that solution still may not be the right fit if your case is an edge case that is not broadly adopted or supported.

In the next couple of sections, I will discuss in detail the factors for PaC selection, how to construct your criteria, and how you can make data-driven decisions based on how well the factors meet your criteria. Even though the choice is relatively reversible, reversing the decision is not without cost or business impact. So it's important to align the PaC selection factors, related to the choices, with your selection criteria.

The following section provides a nonexhaustive list of possible PaC selection factors. These factors, along with use cases and organizational-specific drivers, are used to define your relative selection criteria and create a corresponding scorecard. Your scorecard enables you to make informed, data-driven decisions. Keep in mind that your decisions may mean using multiple solutions; PaC solutions are not necessarily mutually exclusive. For example, you may decide on one PaC solution for cloud computing IaC while you use a different PaC solution for CI/CD or Kubernetes.

Example PaC Selection Factors

You need to consider the following factors before deciding on which PaC solution to adopt:

Alignment—organizational capabilities
> How well do the technologies (languages, etc.) used by the PaC solution match the technical capabilities of the team(s) that will launch and manage the solution?

Alignment—organizational strategies
> How well does the PaC solution match the internal strategies for how tools and applications are to be adopted and managed?

Alignment—organizational standards
> How well do the controls to be built with the PaC solution fit the needs, at least partially, of the internal standards driving this decision?

Analytics/logging/metrics
> How well does the PaC solution provide adequate logging, metrics, and analytics to support internal requirements, including audits?

Automation (CI/CD)
> Can the PaC solution be used in CI/CD pipelines, shifting left from the target system? If so, how? Can deployment of the engine and policies be automated?

Available examples and patterns

Given your desired use cases, are there sufficient examples and patterns available for testing, evaluation, and proofs of concept?

Community adoption

Who is using and supporting this PaC solution? How much adoption has the project seen?

Complexity

How difficult is it to install and manage this solution within your environments?

Documentation

How well is the solution documented? How understandable is the documentation?

Operation modes

PaC solutions differ in how they can be used (server, libraries, CLI, etc.). What modes of operation are supported, and do they fit your needs and even enhance your practices?

Project recency

How recent are contributions and changes to the project? Is the project still viable?

Reporting

Does the solution provide a reporting feature? Does it use or integrate to standard reporting tools? How well does it support data exchange standards, such as OSCAL (*https://oreil.ly/EaVAA*)?

Security

What risks and vulnerabilities are present in the OSS project? How soon do risks and vulnerabilities usually get solved? What automated tools and processes are used to discover security issues? Is there a proactive security stance? Are commits signed? What security controls are in the actual software, such as multifactor authentication (MFA) and the like?

Solution extensibility

Can you extend the solution with scripts, languages, or modules? How easy is this process?

Solution/project maturity

Has the solution/project gone through enough iterations? Is it mature enough to be operationalized? Are there examples or documentation for operationalizing the solution?

Support model

How well is the solution supported? Can you purchase enterprise support, if need be?

Use cases (IaC, Kubernetes, etc.)

What are the primary use cases supported by the solution? Do they match your use cases?

User experience

How easy is it to use the PaC solution? Is it intuitive and familiar? How much training will be required to deploy it?

Now that we have selection factors, let's look at how we can use them to create our selection criteria and score PaC solutions.

PaC Selection Scorecard

Once you have defined and understood the selection factors, you can derive your selection criteria and create your scorecard (see Figure 1-6). Selection criteria are composed of the selection factors relative to your situation, annotated with a weight. The factor weight indicates how important each individual factor is to your organization. For factors of zero importance, you can either weight the factor accordingly (with a zero) or leave it off the scorecard entirely. The fit score is self-explanatory; it indicates how well the PaC solution selection criterion fits your needs.

In the scorecard shown in Figure 1-6, the Weight column contains values 1–3, indicating which of the three classifications (must-have, should-have, nice-to-have) are applied to the selection factors to form the selection criteria chosen for the evaluation. The scorecard includes evaluations for two solutions side by side. You multiply the Fit columns in each evaluation section by the common Weight column to determine the individual Score for each selection criterion. The Fit column uses values 1–5. To indicate a bigger difference in the evaluations, you could change the ranges in the Weight and Fit columns to be larger or even replace the base-10 numbers with Fibonacci numbers (*https://oreil.ly/3DB4X*).

With this scorecard approach, you can evaluate and choose the right solution for your needs. You use the scorecard to record your data-driven decisions, based on your evaluations. Your evaluations derive from active testing and/or proofs of concept. For OSS projects, the respective project communities can provide valuable assistance and insight about potential use cases and project direction.

Selection criteria		PaC solution 1		PaC solution 2	
Selection factors	Weight	Fit	Score	Fit	Score
Alignment—organizational capabilities	3	3	9	1	3
Alignment—organizational strategies	3	2	6	3	9
Alignment—organizational standards	3	5	15	2	6
Analytics/logging/metrics	2	3	6	5	10
Automation (CI/CD)	2	4	8	4	8
Available examples and patterns	2	4	8	5	10
Community adoption	1	5	5	2	2
Complexity	2	3	6	4	8
Documentation	3	3	9	5	15
Operation modes	3	5	15	3	9
Project recency	2	5	10	5	10
Reporting	2	3	6	3	6
Security	3	3	9	2	6
Solution extensibility	3	5	15	2	6
Solution/project maturity	1	4	4	5	5
Support model	1	4	4	2	2
Use cases (IaC, Kubernetes, etc.)	3	3	9	5	15
User experience (UX)	3	2	6	4	12
			150		142

Figure 1-6. PaC Solution Selection Scorecard

Finally, you can use charts to visualize and communicate your decisions. Figure 1-7 is an example of a lollipop chart that clearly shows your aggregate evaluation without exposing your selection criteria details. This is ideal when presenting to stakeholders with limited time or attention spans. For more detail, I would suggest a radar chart, an area chart, or even a radial-lollipop chart.

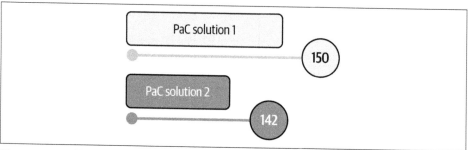

Figure 1-7. Lollipop chart depicting overall scores

Now that we are equipped with a method to evaluate different PaC solutions, I want to introduce the Cloud Native Computing Foundation (CNCF) (*https://www.cncf.io*) and touch on how it indicates the maturity of its "accepted" OSS projects.

The Cloud Native Computing Foundation

The CNCF is part of the Linux Foundation (*https://linuxfoundation.org*). The CNCF is a hub for open source, vendor-neutral projects that have been accepted by the CNCF. Part of its focus is to drive cloud native adoption.

According to the CNCF charter, CNCF was created with a mission: to "make cloud native ubiquitous" (*https://www.cncf.io*). What is cloud native computing (CNC)? You are free to review the CNCF definition of *cloud native computing* (*https://oreil.ly/DEFI NITIONmd*) at your leisure.

For me, the CNCF definition of CNC describes technologies that we use for sustainable, modern application development and delivery. Some of the CNCF characteristics I find most important and relevant to this book are:

- Automation
- Cloud computing (public, private, and hybrid)
- Frequent and deterministic changes
- Immutability

- Manageability
- Observability
- Scalability
- Security

CNC technologies are desirable for most organizations. Even with the CNC definition, organizations may struggle to identify CNC projects and technologies that are ready for immediate consumption. This is where the CNCF comes in. Only projects that meet the CNCF's rigorous CNC guidelines are considered for membership in the CNCF. With this membership comes a label indicating the level of readiness to be used in CNC use cases that each member project has.

Project maturity is an important aspect of evaluating OSS projects, and as I mentioned earlier, solution/project maturity is one of my recommended PaC selection factors. In the context of the CNCF, the de facto indication of project maturity is found in the three levels of CNCF projects: sandbox (*https://oreil.ly/dZpV7*), incubating, and graduated (*https://oreil.ly/7DGC_*). As we progress through the following chapters, I will point out the CNCF projects and their corresponding CNCF project level.

 I did not set out to write an exhaustive tome covering all the possible IT rules and policy tools available today. In fact, I purposefully descoped the rules and policy tools that are CSP specific. Some of the tools and services that I explicitly do not cover in this book are:

- AWS service control policies
- AWS Config
- Azure Policy
- Google Cloud Platform (GCP) organization policy service
- Identity and access management (IAM) policies

For the purposes of this book, I cover PaC and PaC solutions that are, for the most part, vendor neutral and CSP agnostic.

Summary

We've covered a lot of information in this introduction to PaC, but we have just scratched the surface. In this chapter, you were exposed to policy, policies, and Policy as Code (PaC). We discussed policy engines and languages, some uses of PaC (such as guardrails), and how to select the best PaC solution for your needs. With a general understanding of PaC and against the backdrop of OSS and the CNCF, we can now dive deeper into PaC solutions for the systems you use, build, and support.

Throughout the remainder of this book, I will present, in considerably more detail, specific PaC solutions and their respective use cases, technology, and overall functionality. As you progress through this book, please take with you the PaC Solution Selection Scorecard to apply along the way. I introduced it in this first chapter so that you could use it throughout the rest of this book as a preliminary guide to evaluate the multiple PaC solutions that follow. Finally, in the interest of not regurgitating already published documentation, I will focus on the practical knowledge of the PaC solutions and reference the documentation only as needed.

In Chapter 2, I will begin my detailed presentation of PaC solutions with a deeper dive into Open Policy Agent.

Open Policy Agent

I started using Open Policy Agent (OPA) (*https://www.openpolicyagent.org*) in 2018, almost two full years after the project launched and just after it was accepted into the CNCF. OPA is now a graduated CNCF project, which is an attestation of its overall maturity as a PaC solution.

OPA is a very mature OSS project with a strong and active community of developers and users. The following links provide more information about OPA:

- GitHub project (*https://oreil.ly/opa*)
- Documentation website (*https://oreil.ly/kFoJd*)
- Policy library (*https://oreil.ly/library*)
- Slack community (*https://oreil.ly/IACpT*)

When I think of OPA, the two things that immediately come to mind are *general purpose* and *unification*. OPA is domain agnostic, which means it's not focused on a single data domain or stack. In fact, OPA doesn't come with built-in, ready-to-use Kubernetes or cloud computing policies. You pass it policies, data, and queries. It matches policies to the data you send it and evaluates said data with the policies based on queries you provide.

Because OPA is domain agnostic, it is general purpose. And because of OPA's general-purpose utility, you can pass input (data) and policies (data) regardless of the domain or stack you are evaluating. This general purpose leads to PaC unification across domains and stacks. In other words, since OPA is domain agnostic, it can be used across many domains and stacks, thereby unifying the different policy needs using one PaC solution.

As we explore OPA in this chapter, we will start with the requisite Hello World example. Then, we will put OPA through its paces using its different operational modes with the OPA CLI. Along the way, we will discover bundles, bearer tokens, and WebAssembly. Where applicable, I will show examples of running OPA as a container using Docker Desktop for Mac. Then we will discuss Rego, OPA's powerful policy language. Finally, we will survey the different means by which OPA can be extended and integrated.

Now, it's on to Hello World!

Hello World

Usually, the quickest way to familiarize yourself with a new technology is to install it and try a Hello World example. However, I have found that the easiest way to understand how OPA evaluates data with policies and queries is to use the Rego Playground (*https://oreil.ly/tHrnH*). We will dive deeper into Rego (OPA's policy language) and the Rego Playground later in this chapter, but for now, this example should help you understand where we're headed.

In the Hello World example in Figure 2-1, I wrote the Rego policy in the left pane of the interface. I entered the JSON data to be evaluated into the upper-right INPUT pane. The evaluation produced the outcome of the evaluation and deposited it into the lower-right OUTPUT pane. The output indicates that the input data we provided was matched and evaluated by the policy we wrote. The output was "hello": true.

You may also notice that the Rego Playground was built by Styra (*https://www.styra.com*), the creators of OPA; this is noted in the lower left corner of the screen. In the lower-right corner of the screen is the version of OPA that is currently running in the Rego Playground, shown as of the time of this writing.

Now that we have looked at the requisite Hello World example for OPA, let's see how we can install OPA and run its different modes of operation.

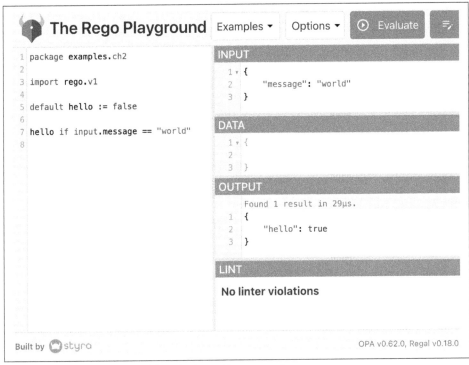

The Rego Playground

```
1 package examples.ch2
2
3 import rego.v1
4
5 default hello := false
6
7 hello if input.message == "world"
8
```

INPUT
```
1 {
2     "message": "world"
3 }
```

DATA
```
1 {
2
3 }
```

OUTPUT
```
  Found 1 result in 29µs.
1 {
2     "hello": true
3 }
```

LINT

No linter violations

Built by styra   OPA v0.62.0, Regal v0.18.0

Figure 2-1. OPA Hello World in the Rego Playground

OPA Installation and Modes

The easiest way to install OPA on my Mac was via Homebrew (*https://brew.sh*), using the following command:

```
# Install OPA with Homebrew
$ brew install opa
```

I am using an ARM64-based Mac, and Homebrew auto-detected the architecture and installed the correct binary:

```
# Get OPA version
$ opa version
Version: 0.62.0
Build Commit:
Build Timestamp:
Build Hostname:
Go Version: go1.22.0
Platform: darwin/arm64
WebAssembly: unavailable
```

You'll notice that the build information is missing from the output of the `opa version` command. This is typical for the ARM64 architecture binaries, as they are statically built.

To see build information, I pulled the Linux/AMD64 OPA container image from Docker Hub.

Then, I ran the version command using the container and Docker. I pulled the Linux/AMD64 platform image so that I could run it in Rosetta emulation mode (*https://oreil.ly/nazaU*) on my M2 MacBook Pro:

```
# Pull linux/amd64 OPA image
$ docker pull --platform linux/amd64 openpolicyagent/opa:0.62.0
0.62.0: Pulling from openpolicyagent/opa
6bc2b10798c4: Pull complete
d9b078b6e67f: Pull complete
Digest: sha256:3b9b224dd782a81b592ffc245cc328aa400e3e8007abaad170331e9259b758af
Status: Downloaded newer image for openpolicyagent/opa:0.62.0
docker.io/openpolicyagent/opa:0.62.0

$ docker run --rm --platform linux/amd64 openpolicyagent/opa:0.62.0 version
Version: 0.62.0
Build Commit: 1d0ab93822e83a4165c78372a7fb4c05e14a8bca
Build Timestamp: 2024-02-29T17:07:11Z
Build Hostname: 70e4f345ecf5
Go Version: go1.22.0
Platform: linux/amd64
WebAssembly: available ❶
```

❶ WebAssembly is available in the OPA images for the Linux/AMD64 platform.

You'll notice that along with the build information now present in the output, WebAssembly is also available in the Linux/AMD64 image.

As soon as I downloaded the OPA image, I ran Docker Scout (*https://oreil.ly/kJsY3*) on the image to see if any common vulnerabilities and exposures (CVEs) (*https://cve.mitre.org*) existed for the image:

```
# Use docker scout to check for CVEs
$ docker scout quickview openpolicyagent/opa:0.62.0
    ✓ Image stored for indexing
    ✓ Indexed 93 packages
  Target    | openpolicyagent/opa:0.62.0 |    0C    0H    0M    0L
```

As seen in the preceding commands, no CVEs were reported by Docker Scout.

You can also get started with OPA on your machine by downloading and installing the latest release from the OPA GitHub project (*https://oreil.ly/opa*), using a script similar to the one in the following console output:

```
# Download arm64 OPA binary
$ curl https://github.com/open-policy-agent/opa/releases/download/v0.62.0/\
opa_darwin_arm64_static -o opa -sL && chmod +x opa
```

In the curl command, the -o flag was used to select the filename and the -sL flag to
download the file silently and tell cURL to follow any HTTP redirects.

 Always verify the checksum of downloaded files. On my Mac, I
could use the shasum -a 256 opa command and compare that
output to the SHA-256 checksum stored with the OPA binary file.

Before we dive into OPA modes, let's explore the OPA CLI.

OPA Command-Line Interface

Once the OPA binary is installed, you can run OPA to see its CLI commands:

```
# Run OPA for command list
$ opa
An open source project to policy-enable your service.

Usage:
  opa [command]

Available Commands:
  bench        Benchmark a Rego query
  build        Build an OPA bundle
  capabilities Print the capabilities of OPA
  check        Check Rego source files
  completion   Generate the autocompletion script for the specified shell
  deps         Analyze Rego query dependencies
  eval         Evaluate a Rego query
  exec         Execute against input files
  fmt          Format Rego source files
  help         Help about any command
  inspect      Inspect OPA bundle(s)
  parse        Parse Rego source file
  run          Start OPA in interactive or server mode
  sign         Generate an OPA bundle signature
  test         Execute Rego test cases
  version      Print the version of OPA
Flags:
  -h, --help   help for opa

Use "opa [command] --help" for more information about a command.
```

I won't cover every CLI command, but you can see that the OPA CLI comes with many functions to run the different OPA operational modes as well as to manage policies. Different versions of OPA have different capabilities. For this book, I used the latest versions of OPA available to me; I started with v0.44.0 and progressed to v0.62.1. If you want to see the capabilities of the OPA version you have installed, then you can run the `capabilities` command as shown in the following example:

```
# Get OPA capabilities
$ opa capabilities --current > opa.json
```

In the preceding command, I directed the current OPA capabilities output to a (rather large) JSON file for easier reading. The following snippet starts with listing the built-in functions that are included in the OPA version I installed:

```
{
  "builtins": [
    {
      "name": "abs",
      "description": "Returns the number without its sign.",
      "categories": [
        "numbers"
      ],...
```

We'll cover built-in functions later in the section "Rego Policy Language" on page 41.

Next up, we will use the OPA CLI to run OPA in read-eval-print loop mode.

OPA Read-Eval-Print Loop

The OPA CLI includes a read-eval-print loop (REPL) (*https://oreil.ly/wsQCP*) tool that is similar to those in Python, Ruby, or Java (JShell). With the OPA REPL interactive shell, you can run OPA commands for experimentation or even policy prototyping and development. You invoke the OPA REPL with the `run` subcommand, as shown in the following console output:

```
# Run the OPA repl environment
$ opa run
OPA 0.62.0 (commit , built at )

Run 'help' to see a list of commands and check for updates.

>
```

Once inside the OPA REPL, you can check your system version:

```
# OPA repl version command output
> data.system.version
{
  "build_commit": "",
  "build_hostname": "",
```

```
    "build_timestamp": "",
    "version": "0.62.0"
}
```

It's always good to know how to get your version if you need to troubleshoot issues or understand capabilities.

As shown in the preceding console output, when using the statically built OPA binaries—like the Darwin ARM64 version I am using—build information is not made available again. However, running OPA as a container (Linux/AMD64) using Docker Desktop for Mac—with the following command—you see the build information in the output:

```
# Docker run command
$ docker run -it --rm --platform linux/amd64 openpolicyagent/opa:0.62.0

# OPA repl version output
# Output
> data.system.version
{
  "build_commit": "1d0ab93822e83a4165c78372a7fb4c05e14a8bca",
  "build_hostname": "70e4f345ecf5",
  "build_timestamp": "2024-02-29T17:07:11Z",
  "version": "0.62.0"
}
>
```

The show debug command is also very important as it exposes your current REPL settings, as shown in the following example:

```
# OPA repl debug output
> show debug
{
        "explain": "off",
        "metrics": false,
        "instrument": false,
        "profile": false,
        "strict-builtin-errors": false
}
```

To use our previous Hello World example in the REPL, you can start the REPL and preload the Rego policy and the input document. As shown in the following example, I used a YAML input document instead of JSON this time:

```
# Run OPA repl with input document
$ opa run helloworld.rego repl.input:helloworld.yaml
```

The preceding command loads the Rego policy and input YAML document to be evaluated by the following Rego policy:

```
# Rego hello-world policy
package examples.ch2
hello if {
        msg := input.message
        msg == "world"
}
```

The way to read the preceding policy is if the input.message field exists and its value is "world", then the hello rule will return true:

```
# YAML input document
---
message: world
```

Once the REPL starts, you can view the loaded policy and input using the data command. The policy and input were loaded as documents, rooted under the data global variable and displayed as JSON:

```
# Read data in OPA repl
> data
{
  "examples": {
    "ch2": {
      "hello": true
    }
  },
  "repl": {
    "input": {
      "message": "world"
    }
  }
}
```

You can execute the following query to apply the policy against the input data:

```
# Run query in OPA repl
> data.examples.ch2.hello
true
```

In the preceding query, we executed data.examples.ch2.hello against the input document containing the message field. The rule matched the input with the input.message field. The statement of msg == "world" was evaluated, and the rule returned true. If the input.message field was not located in the input document or the input.message field value was not "world", then the query would have returned as undefined.

To avoid undefined returns from policy evaluations, you can write your rule to specify a default value, such as `default hello := false` or `default hello := "good bye"`. Both default values are "truthy," meaning that the return from the `hello` rule will not be undefined. However, rules produce decisions, and in the case of the `hello` rule, the decision should be boolean (true or false). Setting a default to `goodbye` may seem like the correct approach, but if `goodbye` is the default value returned by the `hello` rule, the mixed data types—boolean and string—will result in a nondeterministic value of true. To avoid this and make your rules more deterministic, data types—rule returns and default values—should be the same. Regardless of language, undefined outputs or returns are generally considered a bad practice and should be avoided if possible.

To run the example as an OPA container in Docker, you could use the following command:

```
# Run OPA repl command with docker container
$ docker run -it --rm -v $(pwd):/helloworld --platform linux/amd64 \
openpolicyagent/opa:0.62.1 run helloworld/helloworld.rego \
repl.input:helloworld/helloworld.yaml  ❶

Run 'help' to see a list of commands and check for updates.

> data.examples.ch2.hello
true
>
```

❶ The Docker command includes mapped volumes.

The preceding `docker` command required that we used volumes, so I mapped the */helloworld* path to the present working directory, from where I called the `docker run` command. I then prefixed the files with the *helloworld* directory:

```
# Docker volume mapping to allow loading on files into OPA repl
-v $(pwd):/helloworld

# Prefixed paths
helloworld/helloworld.rego repl.input:helloworld/helloworld.yaml
```

The OPA REPL is useful for prototyping and learning OPA, as it allows you to create on the fly with immediate feedback. Next, we will explore OPA server.

OPA Server

I use OPA server mode the most. OPA server mode can be used to run so-called OPA agents for policy daemons across multiple platforms for multiple use cases. In fact, most of my use cases involve running the OPA server as a container in Docker or Kubernetes.

The simplest way to run the OPA server, using my Hello World example, is with the following run -s subcommand:

```
# Run OPA in server mode, loading a bundle in the server directory
$ opa run -s --bundle server --addr localhost:8181    ❶
{"addrs":["localhost:8181"],"diagnostic-addrs":[],"level":"info",
"msg":"Initializing server.","time":"2024-03-03T14:10:44-05:00"}
```

❶   Bind OPA server to localhost and not default 0.0.0.0.

In the preceding command, I explicitly bound the OPA server to the localhost address. This is considered a best practice. Without doing so, I would have received the following warning message upon server initialization:

```
# OPA public binding warning message
OPA is running on a public (0.0.0.0) network interface. Unless you intend
to expose OPA outside of the host, binding to the localhost interface
(--addr localhost:8181) is recommended.
See https://www.openpolicyagent.org/docs/latest/security/#interface-binding
```

 When the OPA server starts, it compares its version to the latest available, as seen in the following example using previous versions:

```
{"current_version":"0.44.0","download_opa":
"https://openpolicyagent.org/downloads/v0.45.0/...
...opa_darwin_arm64",
"latest_version":"0.45.0","level":"info","msg":"OPA is
out of date.",
"release_notes":
"https://github.com/open-policy-agent/opa/...
...releases/tag/v0.45.0",
"time":"2022-10-17T22:02:34-04:00"}
```

To run this example as an OPA container in Docker, you could use the following command:

```
# Run OPA server with using a Docker container
$ docker run -it --rm -p 8181:8181 -v $(pwd):/examples --platform \
linux/amd64 openpolicyagent/opa:0.62.1 run -s --bundle /examples/server \
--addr localhost:8181
```

You may notice that I added the port mapping with the -p flag.

Running the preceding commands from the directory containing my Rego policy, *helloworld.rego*, uses the bundle flag to load my local Rego and data files as an OPA bundle (*https://oreil.ly/sXDuF*). What is an OPA bundle? Let's check that out in the next section.

Bundles

Bundles are used to bundle data and policies to be loaded into OPA, as opposed to using the REST API to load them. While I didn't need to build a bundle, as the bundle flag took care of that inline with the `opa run -s` command, the `opa build` command can be used to build a bundle if need be, as shown in the following example:

```
# Build OPA bundle
$ opa build --ignore '.*' --ignore '*.yaml' --ignore '*.json' .
```

The preceding command builds an OPA bundle in the current directory while ignoring specific files, such as YAML and JSON files, as well as hidden files. The bundle file, *bundle.tar.gz*, can be inspected with the `tar` command:

```
# Use tar tvf to view tar file contents
$ tar tvf bundle.tar.gz
-rw------- 0 0        0          3 Dec 31  1969 /data.json
-rw------- 0 0        0        108 Dec 31  1969 /helloworld.rego
```

For reference, the *data.json* file is created even if no data files are included in the bundle. In the case of no data, only empty curly braces, {}, are present in the file.

Additionally, OPA has its own `inspect` command for bundles:

```
# Inspect bundle
$ opa inspect bundle.tar.gz
NAMESPACES:
+-------------------+--------------------+
|     NAMESPACE     |        FILE        |
+-------------------+--------------------+
| data              | /data.json         |
| data.examples.ch2 | /helloworld.rego   |
+-------------------+--------------------+
```

Notice that our policy and the data placeholder file were placed in namespaces. Our policy namespace matches the package name that we supplied earlier in the Rego Playground, prefixed with `data`. Since we didn't supply any additional data for our bundle, the *data.json* file was rooted in the data global variable.

Once we have bundles, we can verify that they come from a trusted source. For that purpose, we can sign our bundles so that bundle consumers can verify the bundles with a cryptographic signature.

> Though they are a great way to deploy data and policies to OPA servers, bundles are not necessary to run OPA. They are normally not used in local OPA development.

Now that we can run an OPA server with bundles, we will explore how to query the server.

Querying the server

Once the server is running, you can view the uploaded data with the following `curl` command:

```
# Query the data API
$ curl localhost:8181/v1/data
{"result":{"examples":{"ch2":{"hello":"false"}}}}
```

You might notice that the hello rule now has a default `false` return. Now, with any missing or wrong fields in the input document, false is returned instead of undefined:

```
# New helloworld example with default value to avoid undefined returns
package examples.ch2

default hello := false ❶

hello := "world" {
    msg := input.message
    msg == "world"
}
```

❶ The `hello` rule now has a default value of false.

To see the actual policy, you can use the following `curl` command to query the Policy API:

```
# Query policies
$ curl localhost:8181/v1/policies
{"result":[{"id":"bundle/bundle/helloworld.rego","raw":
"package examples.ch2\n\nimport rego.v1\n\n#
default hello := \"false\"\n\nhello …
```

> An easy way to construct and manage your HTTP request commands and response outputs is to use *.http* files in Visual Studio (VS) Code along with the REST Client extension (*https://oreil.ly/R1Biq*), as shown in Figure 2-2.

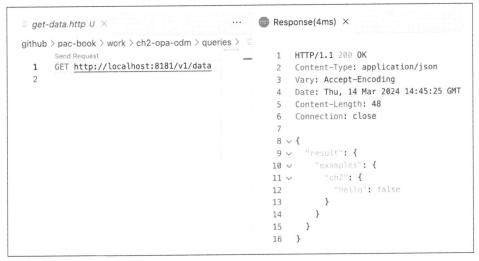

Figure 2-2. Using *.http files in VS Code

To run the query to my Hello World example, you can use the following `curl` command to send an HTTP POST to the OPA server Data API:

```
# Run OPA server query with input
$ curl localhost:8181/v1/data/examples/ch2/hello -d @opa-input.json
{"result":true}
```

The *opa-input.json* file contains the following content:

```
{
    "input":{
        "message":"world"
    }
}
```

Notice that the `input` element must be added when making a call via the REST API.

The HTTP request/response flow is shown in Figure 2-3. The key thing to remember here is that the request to OPA to evaluate data, based on policies stored in OPA, is an HTTP POST request, where the URL contains the query (refers to package and policy rules) and the *input* base document (discussed later in the section "Rego Policy Language" on page 41), sent as the JSON payload. The result of the HTTP POST is also JSON. So JSON-in and JSON-out are key to how and why OPA is domain and stack agnostic. As long as you can represent your domain, stack, artifact, and so on as JSON, send and receive JSON, and write policies that match and evaluate JSON, OPA can fulfill your PaC needs.

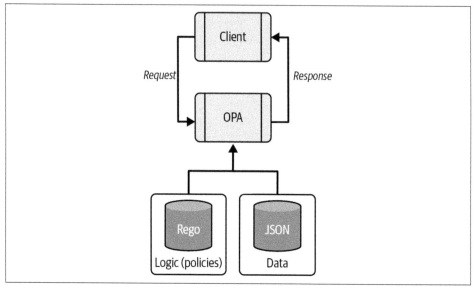

Figure 2-3. OPA request-response diagram

OPA REST API

OPA includes a mature REST API (*https://oreil.ly/acNFy*), with seven API endpoints. We have already used the Data and Policy APIs. The OPA Data API supports several parameters. One that I use often is the `metrics` parameter:

```
# Call OPA data API with metrics parameter
$ curl "localhost:8181/v1/data/examples/ch2/hello?metrics" -d @opa-input.json
{"metrics":{"counter_server_query_cache_hit":1,"timer_rego_input_parse_ns":
305750,"timer_rego_query_eval_ns":365375,"timer_server_handler_ns":871833},
"result":true}
```

With the `metrics` parameter, the OPA Data API returns the following performance metrics from my sample query:

counter_server_query_cache_hit
    Number of cache hits for the query

timer_rego_input_parse_ns
    Time taken (in nanoseconds) to parse the input

timer_rego_query_eval_ns
    Time taken (in nanoseconds) to evaluate the query

timer_server_handler_ns
    Time taken (in nanoseconds) to handle the API request

The metrics returned indicate the execution time of the operations performed by the OPA server—as a result of my request—measured in nanoseconds. Performance metrics are a good method of validating system design, and OPA has them built into its REST API.

Other OPA modes support the `metrics` parameter as well, in the form of command flags. For example, the `opa eval` command produces the following metrics:

```
# OPA eval with metrics parameter
$ opa eval -i data/helloworld.json -d rego/helloworld.rego \
"data.examples.ch2.hello" --metrics
...
  "metrics": {
    "timer_rego_load_files_ns": 650917,
    "timer_rego_module_compile_ns": 1006375,
    "timer_rego_module_parse_ns": 389667,
    "timer_rego_query_compile_ns": 60292,
    "timer_rego_query_eval_ns": 221625,
    "timer_rego_query_parse_ns": 65750
  }
}
```

Ad hoc queries

Though I don't use them as much, you can submit ad hoc queries (*https://oreil.ly/ LTmI3*) to the OPA server via the Query API. Unlike previous examples where I had to specify the package (*examples.ch2*) and rule (`hello`), with ad hoc queries I write the rules and submit them to the server. The following JSON doc contains the Hello World query along with my input data:

```
{
    "query": "msg := input.message\nmsg == \"world\"",
    "input": {
        "message": "world"
    }
}
```

Then I use a `curl` POST command to send the query and the input data to the OPA server:

```
# Run OPA ad hoc query
$ curl "localhost:8181/v1/query" -d @query-input.json
{"result":[{"msg":"world"}]}
```

The OPA server Query API also supports HTTP GET methods, using the `"q"` parameter, where the query and input data would need to be URL encoded. As this could get unwieldy for larger payloads, POST is usually recommended.

Next, let's explore one-shot methods for running Rego policies, starting with OPA eval.

OPA eval

OPA `eval` is another CLI subcommand that is used to evaluate a Rego query and print the result. I think of `eval` as a "one-shot" OPA tool that is handy in bash scripts and automation steps to apply policies to data and return a machine-readable result at runtime. This makes `eval` useful for CI/CD and DevOps processes.

Our Hello World example can be used with `eval`, using the following CLI command:

```
# Run OPA eval to evaluate JSON with a Rego policy
$ opa eval -i helloworld.json -d helloworld.rego "data.examples.ch2.hello"
{
  "result": [
    {
      "expressions": [
        {
          "value": true,
          "text": "data.examples.ch2.hello",
          "location": {
            "row": 1,
            "col": 1
          }
        }
      ]
    }
  ]
}
```

The `-i` flag sets the input document for the evaluation, and the `-d` flag sets the policy and/or additional data. The `-d` flag can be repeated.

The preceding `eval` command outputs machine-readable JSON, which makes it useful for automation purposes. To run this example as an OPA container in Docker, you could use the following command, again with volume mapping:

```
# Run OPA eval using a Docker container
$ docker run -it --rm -v $(pwd):/helloworld --platform linux/amd64 \
openpolicyagent/opa:0.62.1 eval -i helloworld/helloworld.json \
-d helloworld/helloworld.rego "data.examples.ch2.hello"
```

OPA exec

OPA exec was added to OPA toward the end of 2021 and can be seen as the possible successor to OPA `eval`. Like `eval`, `exec` is a "one-shot" approach to using OPA that returns JSON and is useful for automation. However, `exec` can use advanced features that are unavailable to `eval`, such as OPA config files (*https://oreil.ly/1xx_a*). With config files, you can configure advanced OPA features, such as pulling remote bundles (*https://oreil.ly/-Biuo*) and sending decision logs to remote endpoints. In that context, OPA exec can be seen as the one-shot version of OPA `run`, making it more flexible and better suited for production-ready, one-shot use cases. The following exec command for the Hello World use case uses an OPA bundle built earlier in the section "OPA Server" on page 33:

```
# Run OPA exec with a policy/data bundle
$ opa exec ./helloworld.json --decision examples/ch2/hello -b ./bundle.tar.gz
{
  "result": [
    {
      "path": "./helloworld.json",
      "result": true
    }
  ]
}
```

Again, if you wanted to run this example as an OPA container, the following command can be used:

```
# Run OPA exec using a Docker container
$ docker run -it --rm -v $(pwd):/helloworld --platform linux/amd64 \
openpolicyagent/opa:0.62.1 exec helloworld/helloworld.json --decision \
examples/ch2/hello -b helloworld/bundle.tar.gz
```

> Conftest (*https://oreil.ly/conftest*) is similar to OPA eval and exec. It uses Rego to write assertions against structured configuration data, like that used in IaC. We will discuss Conftest later in this book when we cover PaC and IaC solutions.

We have touched on Rego as we exercised the different OPA modes with our Hello World examples. Now, let's dive deeper into the Rego language that powers OPA's decisions.

Rego Policy Language

While OPA is a general-purpose policy engine, it is also purpose built. According to the documentation, "OPA is purpose built for reasoning about information represented in structured documents."

Rego (*https://oreil.ly/OKCIO*) is OPA's declarative assertion language that provides that reasoning. As a point of reference, *declarative languages* declare what you want to do, instead of imperatively how you want to do it. How it is done for you is an implementation detail of Rego. So, in a way, Rego is a domain-specific language (DSL) for applying reasoning and assertions to domain-agnostic, structured data.

In this section, I will cover the basics of how to use Rego. For a deeper understanding of Rego, I strongly recommend the Rego Style Guide (*https://oreil.ly/rego-style-guide*) from Styra and the Rego Policy Language documentation (*https://oreil.ly/UK0yd*).

To start us on our Rego learning path, we will begin by understanding the OPA document model and how it's referenced in Rego.

OPA Document Model

Before we start with Rego, we must first understand the OPA document model (*https://oreil.ly/Hw8oF*). We got a glimpse of it in earlier examples. As we saw in our previous server examples, data and policies that we loaded from bundles at server startup were placed (namespaced) into the data global variable. When working with data, OPA models data into two documents: base documents and virtual documents. *Base documents* are data loaded from external sources to OPA, and *virtual documents* are data created by OPA, like policy decisions.

Base documents are placed into two global variables, determined by how they are added to OPA. Data added from bundles or HTTP PUT requests are long-lived and placed into the data global variable. For example, the following command and data illustrate how the HTTP PUT command can be used to put data into the OPA server using the REST API:

```
# Projects data JSON file
$ cat data.json
{
    "projects": [
        {
            "method": "GET",
            "project": "book",
            "lead": "jimmy"
        }
    ]
}

# Upload data
$ curl -vX PUT http://localhost:8181/v1/data -d @data.json \
--header "Content-Type: application/json"

# Query data
$ curl localhost:8181/v1/data
{"result":{"projects":[{"lead":"jimmy","method":"GET","project":"book"}]}}

# Query data/projects
$ curl localhost:8181/v1/data/projects
{"result":[{"lead":"jimmy","method":"GET","project":"book"}]}
```

Data added via HTTP POST requests, normally as part of policy queries, are short-lived and stored in the input global variable. Regardless of how these data are stored, they are referenced by dot notation using data.<DATA> or input.<DATA>.

We have seen these references used in our prior examples, and we will see them again as we explore the Rego syntax and logic structures in the next section.

Rego Syntax and Logic

I have always thought that one of the challenges with learning Rego was the idea that the syntax resembled imperative languages like C and Java, but the Rego assertion behavior was sufficiently different from these imperative languages. So, I'll try to walk you through Rego examples to give you an introductory understanding, but you should plan to use the OPA Rego documentation to dive deeper as needed.

Rules

In OPA's document model, rules define the "content of virtual documents" through rule evaluation. Policies are made up of rules, and rules contain expressions. OPA tries to bind variables in rules so that all the internal rule expressions are true. The following Hello World policy has one rule, `hello`. That rule has a default value of false that is returned in a `false` condition. When OPA evaluates the rule, the virtual document produced will either be {`"hello": true`} or {`"hello": false`}:

```
# Policy with defaults
package examples.ch2

default hello := false        ❶

hello := "world" {            ❷
        msg := input.message  ❸
        msg == "world"        ❹
}
```

❶ Default rule value

❷ Rule head

❸ Rule body expression: load value from input

❹ Rule body expression: compare input value to desired value

The preceding rule has a default value, a head, and a body. The head element specifies the name of the rule and, in our case, the value (optional) of the rule to be returned in a true condition. Without the explicit `"world"` value, the rule will return a boolean true when all the rule statements are true, even though the default return is a string.

The body element contains the expressions of the rule. A logical ANDing of rule expressions is applied, so every expression that is a comparison must be true for the rule to be true.

The `hello` rule default value of false is returned if:

- The input document doesn't exist.

- The input.message field doesn't exist.

- The input.message field doesn't match the value of "world".

The hello rule will return true if all the statements in the rule are true. If we add more statements, then we can see the logical AND being applied:

```
# Rego policy, hello rule
hello := "world" {
    msg := input.message  ❶
    msg == "world"         ❷
    from := input.from
    from == "jimmy"        ❸
}
```

❶ This is an assignment.

❷ This is an equality comparison.

❸ This must also be true for hello to return true, using implied AND logic.

In the preceding example, hello is true and returns "world" if all statements in the rule are true. The comparison statements with the == syntax must both be true. As a side note, the assignment statements using := must be present, or the variables msg and from will be marked "unsafe" and produce a policy compile error. And while using the Strict mode with the Rego Playground or the CLI, the msg and from variables must also be used, or a policy compile "unused variable" error is produced.

To apply a logical OR condition, we need multiple rules with the same name in the head:

```
hello if {
    msg := input.message
    msg == "world"
    from := input.from
    from == "jimmy"
}

hello if {   ❶
    msg := input.message
    msg == "me"
    from := input.from
    from == "jimmy"
}
```

❶ The second rule creates a logical OR scenario, while each rule has its own logical AND expressions.

This new version of the policy will return true if the msg field equals "world" and the from field equals "jimmy" OR the msg field equals "me" and the from field equals "jimmy".

As we learned earlier, rules that are not evaluated true will return an undefined value unless the rule or rule set has a default value defined. Only one default value can be defined per rule set.

Functions

Rego functions are a great way to apply the "don't repeat yourself" (DRY) principle (*https://oreil.ly/T1INz*) to your Rego and deduplicate your code while also applying modularity. In our Hello World example, we could change the code to use a function to build our return message. The following version uses the build_return_msg function to build a return message:

```
# Function example
package examples.ch2

import future.keywords.in    ❶

default hello := ""

hello := output {
    input.method == "POST"
    input.message in {"world", "planet"}
    output := build_return_msg("Hello",input.from)
}

build_return_msg (msg, from) := result {   ❷
    result := sprintf("%s, %s", [msg, from])
}
```

❶ I imported keywords to be used later in the policy.

❷ Functions take parameters.

Notice that in the preceding modified code, I imported the *future.keywords.in* (*https://oreil.ly/NJRs9*) package. This allowed me to use newer OPA operators like in while maintaining backward compatibility. I also used a documented best practice of passing arguments to a function instead of using the input and data global variables, thereby reducing ambiguous dependencies.

The true condition result appears in the following JSON:

```
{
    "hello": "Hello, jimmy"
}
```

Finally, I assigned the `hello` rule value to the "output" of the `build_return_msg` function. In doing so, I wanted to demonstrate that rules and functions can return any value, not just boolean or scalar values. For example, if I wanted to return an object with key/value pairs, I could reconstruct the `build_return_msg` as seen in the following Rego:

```
# Rego function
build_return_msg (msg, from) := result {
    result := {"msg":msg,"to":from}
}
```

The new output of the `hello` rule evaluation appears in the following JSON:

```
{
    "hello": {
        "msg": "Hello",
        "to": "jimmy"
    }
}
```

Functions are rules

If functions look similar to rules, it is because they are; functions are just rules that take arguments. Like rules, functions have a head and a body, and they can be duplicated (same head) for logical ORing. For example, I could write functions to validate the `input.method`, as shown in the following Rego code:

```
is_write_method (method) {
    method == "POST"
}

is_write_method (method) {
    method == "PUT"
}
```

The `PUT` or `POST` methods would result in a true condition. Like rules, functions have a default true in the head that can be left out.

Built-in functions

Beyond writing your own functions, Rego includes many built-in functions (*https://oreil.ly/XZ75X*). These functions are arranged into functional categories, like aggregates and strings, and can be easily identified by their syntax: `<name>(<arg-1>, ..., <arg-n>)`. The `count`, `sum`, `product`, `min`, and `max` functions (aggregates) and the `sprintf` function (string) are shown in the following example for a given input JSON array of numbers:

```
{
    "nums": [0,1,2,3,4,5]
}
```

```
# Rego policy using built-in functions
msg := sprintf("For the given array, %v, the count is %v, the sum is %v,
the product is %v, the minimum is %v, and the maximum is %v.",
[input.nums,count(input.nums), sum(input.nums), product(input.nums),
min(input.nums), max(input.nums)])

// JSON output
{
    "msg": "For the given array, [0, 1, 2, 3, 4, 5], the count is 6,
    the sum is 15, the product is 0, the minimum is 0, and the maximum is 5."
}
```

The Rego language has many more built-in functions that make Rego more expressive and provide a better user experience, though I have not covered them here in detail. Next, let's explore compound variable data types.

Objects, collections, and comprehensions

Like other languages, Rego supports compound values. For example, objects are unordered key/value pairs, like maps, as shown in the following example:

```
# Rego maps, keys must be unique
animals := {"a":"deer", "b":"moose", "c":"bear"}
```

Unlike some languages where arrays are strictly typed, Rego arrays can hold multiple types:

```
# Rego arrays hold multiple types
stuff := [1,"hello",null,{"a":"b"}]
```

Sets hold unique values and are also unordered:

```
# Set values are unique
material := {"metal","wood","cloth"}
```

Sets can also be unkeyed documents:

```
k := {"metal","wood","cloth"} == {"cloth","wood","metal"}
```

Comprehensions can be used to create compound values. For example, you can use a set comprehension to convert an array of duplicate values into a unique-valued set:

```
m := ["metal","wood","cloth","metal"]  ❶
u := {z | z = m[_]}  ❷
```

❶ I first created an array of duplicate values.

❷ I then used set comprehension to convert the array into a set of unique values.

This yields:

```
"u": [
    "cloth",
    "metal",
    "wood"
]
```

With the preceding set comprehensions, we built set collections using subqueries, in the form of { <term> | <body> }. The m[_] syntax is used to loop through every element in the array.

We use set comprehension often in Kubernetes policies:

```
# using a set comprehension to construct set from input
provided_labels := {k |
input.request.object.metadata.labels[k]}
```

Like any language, using composite data types—objects and collections—allows you to group, aggregate, and process related data. Rego comprehensions are useful for converting between these data types. Next, we will look at Rego unification and how it differs from assignment and comparison.

Unification versus assignment and comparison

Rego has several operators that can be used for different purposes. For example, in Rego, the == operator is used for equal-to comparisons. Comparison operators also include, !=, >, >=, <, and <=.

The assignment operator is := and must be used on a variable assignment before the variable is referenced. Assignments to variables with the assignment operator can happen only once for that variable.

Beyond the comparison and assignment operators, Rego throws us a curveball with the unification operator, =. Unification combines comparison and assignment by assigning values to variables that make the comparison true. In other words, by using the unification operator in your policies, you are asking for variable values that make your unification expression true. If those values are present, your expression will be true:

```
# Rego unification policy example
package examples.ch2
default allow := false
allow {
    some person
    input.path = ["users", person] ❶
    input.method == "GET"
```

```
        person == input.user_id
}
```

❶ I am using the unification operator to assign and compare values.

```
// input
{
    "user_id": "jimmy",
    "method":"GET",
    "path":["users","jimmy"]
}
```

```
// output
{
    "allow": true
}
```

In the preceding example, when the `input.user_id` and the second element in the `input.path` array both equal `"jimmy"`, then the `person == input.user_id` expression is true.

> If you are confused about the unification operator, don't worry—you are not alone. In fact, the published best practice (*https://oreil.ly/S9gIN*) is to not use the unification operator in most cases; you should instead explicitly use the assignment and comparison operators. While this may make your policies slightly longer, it also minimizes ambiguity. It just so happens that my preceding example is a good use case for unification.

I just touched on Rego, its syntax, rules, functions, collections, and objects. As it turns out, Styra, the creators of OPA, offer an Essential Foundations of OPA Policy (*https://oreil.ly/8I3iC*) course from their Styra Academy. It's a good starter course for Rego. Next, let's learn how we can write and test Rego policies.

Writing and Testing Rego

You can use multiple tools (*https://oreil.ly/eHfDO*) to write your Rego policies. For prototyping policies, I recommend the Rego Playground or the REPL. The Rego Playground provides a coding interface that includes syntax highlighting and error checking as well as a means to manage OPA documents, like *data*, *input*, and *output*. I touch on it more directly later in this section.

For editing, I also find the OPA VS Code integration to be very useful. In the VS Code screenshot in Figure 2-4, the extra "=" sign in the policy is detected when I use the Format Document command in the context-aware actions menu.

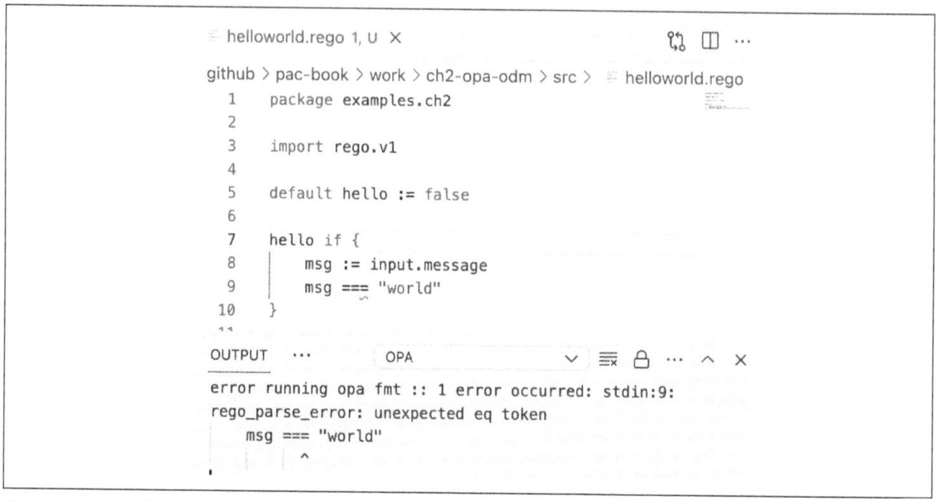

Figure 2-4. OPA VS Code Format Document integration

You can also use the OPA CLI check command for the same purpose:

```
# Using OPA check on a policy with a syntax error
$ opa fmt helloworld.rego
failed to format Rego source file: 1 error occurred: helloworld.rego:9:
rego_parse_error: unexpected eq token
        msg === "world"
            ^
```

OPA provides a unit testing framework, and you use the OPA CLI test command to apply unit tests (*https://oreil.ly/fHcQN*) to your Rego policies. These tests are written as *_test.rego* files, with each test case prefixed by *test_*. My tests appear in the following Rego:

```
# Rego policy
package examples.ch2

import rego.v1     ❶

default hello := false

hello if {
        msg := input.message
        msg == "world"
}
```

❶   The *rego.v1* import is recommended (*https://oreil.ly/Anp1m*) here.

```
# Policy tests
package examples.ch2_test     ❶
```

```
import data.examples.ch2  ❷
import rego.v1

test_hello_pass if {
        ch2.hello with input as {"message": "world"}  ❸
}

test_hello_fail if {
        ch2.hello with input as {"message": "goodbye"}  ❹
}
```

❶ It's a best practice to test outside of the policy-under-test package, and the _test suffix is the convention normally used.

❷ Because packages are different, I had to import the policy package into the test Rego.

❸ I also had to prefix the calls to the hello function to be able to reach it from a different package.

❹ This test will fail as the message input field does not equal "world".

The following command will execute the tests for our Hello World example:

```
# Execute Rego policy tests with the OPA CLI
$ opa test . -v  ❶
FAILURES
--------------------------------------------------------------------------
data.examples.ch2_test.test_hello_fail: FAIL (82.5µs)

  query:1                      Enter data.examples.ch2_test.test_hello_fail = _
  helloworld_test.rego:11      | Enter data.examples.ch2_test.test_hello_fail
  helloworld.rego:7            | | Enter data.examples.ch2.hello
  helloworld.rego:9            | | | Fail msg = "world"
  helloworld_test.rego:12      | | Fail data.examples.ch2.hello with input as
                                     {"message": "goodbye"}  ❷
  query:1                      | Fail data.examples.ch2_test.test_hello_fail = _

SUMMARY
--------------------------------------------------------------------------
helloworld_test.rego:
data.examples.ch2_test.test_hello_pass: PASS (177.083µs)
data.examples.ch2_test.test_hello_fail: FAIL (82.5µs)
--------------------------------------------------------------------------
PASS: 1/2
FAIL: 1/2
```

❶ This test was executed in verbose mode.

❷ The failed test includes the input that caused the failure.

The `opa test` command parses the Rego files (policies and tests) and checks for errors. You can also use the `-f json` flag to create machine-readable output from the test executions, which is useful for automation. The following command includes a snippet of the JSON output:

```
# Test Rego and produce JSON output
$ opa test . -v -f json   ❶
[
  {
    "location": {
      "file": "helloworld_test.rego",
      "row": 6,
      "col": 1
    },
    "package": "data.examples.ch2_test",
    "name": "test_hello_pass",
    "duration": 1380291
  },
  {
    "location": {
      "file": "helloworld_test.rego",
      "row": 10,
      "col": 1
    },
    "package": "data.examples.ch2_test",
    "name": "test_hello_fail",   ❷
    "fail": true,
    "duration": 68083
  }
]
```

❶ Output JSON from the test.

❷ This was a failed test.

With writing and testing Rego now under our belts, we can dive deeper into the Rego Playground and explore its rich feature set.

The Rego Playground

I find the Rego Playground to be easier to use when I am prototyping Rego, especially from scratch. I develop new policies in the Rego Playground and then move my work to VS Code and Git repositories. The Examples drop-down menu in the Rego Playground provides several useful example policies to help start you on your way.

I especially like the Strict and Coverage modes of the Rego Playground. In our ongoing Hello World example, the Coverage mode, seen in Figure 2-5, shows us which statements were evaluated (green) and which ones were not (red)—in grayscale, red highlights are darker than green—for a given input document.

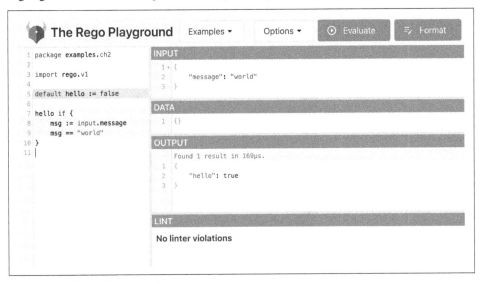

Figure 2-5. Rego Playground coverage

You use Strict mode to make sure that your variables match your definitions. This is similar to Option Declare in LotusScript or Option Explicit in VB.NET.

In Figure 2-6, I used another Rego Playground feature to highlight the statements that I wanted to execute without executing other statements. When isolating that statement for execution, Strict mode produced the "unsafe variable" error in the OUTPUT pane; the statement that assigned a value to the variable was not executed.

As shown in Figures 2-5 and 2-6, the Rego Playground includes a Format button that works like the `opa fmt` CLI command mentioned earlier.

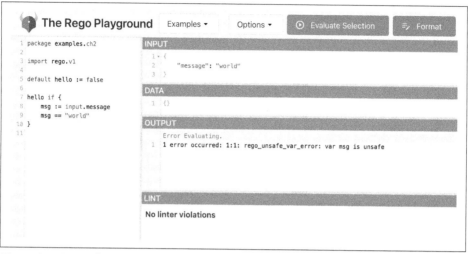

Figure 2-6. Rego Playground Strict mode

While writing this book, two new features were added to the Rego Playground as options:

Built-in error behavior

This option allows you to change the default ignore behavior of errors in built-in functions to strict (exit immediately) or show all.

Live linting

Rego linting is done as you type, using the Regal tool (*https://oreil.ly/0v4IS*) from Styra.

With live linting enabled, I changed the Hello World example to use the imports compatible with the future OPA v1 release and the `if` keyword in my rule:

```
# Linted hello-world example
package examples.ch2

import rego.v1

default hello := false

hello := "world" if {
        msg := input.message
        msg == "world"
}
```

Finally, the Publish button publishes the Rego and provides a shareable link that changes with updates. The Publish screen, shown in Figure 2-7, includes additional instructions for using the policy.

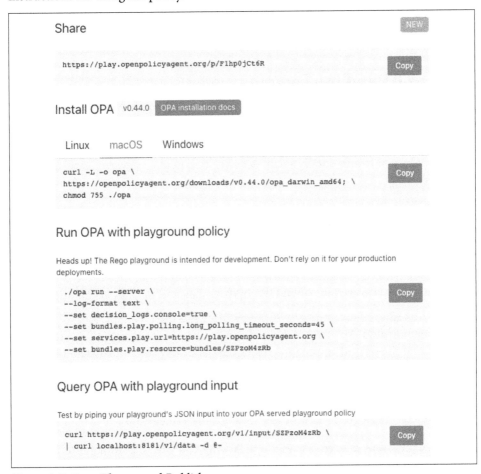

Figure 2-7. Rego Playground Publish screen

One of the coolest things about publishing is that now we can run the OPA server with the policy and data bundle that we just published, which improves prototyping and testing:

```
# Run OPA server with policies published by Rego Playground
$ opa run -s --set services.play.url=https://play.openpolicyagent.org \
--set bundles.play.resource=bundles/SZPzoM4zRb

{"addrs":[":8181"],"diagnostic-addrs":[],"level":"info","msg":
"Initializing server.","time":"2022-11-18T23:03:34-05:00"}
{"level":"info","msg":"Starting bundle loader.","name":"play",
"plugin":"bundle","time":"2022-11-18T23:03:34-05:00"}
```

```
{"level":"info","msg":"Bundle loaded and activated successfully.
Etag updated to \"d6caf...58a00\".","name":"play","plugin":"bundle",
"time":"2022-11-18T23:03:34-05:00"}
```

Now that we've explored writing and testing Rego and have test-driven the Rego Playground, let's switch gears and take a quick look at how we can extend and integrate OPA to better meet our needs.

Advanced Bundling Topics

Earlier in this chapter—in the section "OPA Server" on page 33—I introduced the concept of OPA bundles. Bundles are used with the OPA server as well as the REPL and other OPA commands. In this section, I will explore advanced topics with OPA bundles. Since software supply chain security is a major concern, I will start with bundle signing.

Bundle Signing

Bundles are signed (*https://oreil.ly/aZBkk*) using the opa sign subcommand or by including the --signing-key flag with the opa build command. Signing bundles (*https://oreil.ly/cXyU_*) helps to ensure their integrity and that they come from a trusted source. This is important when OPA updates data and policies via bundles.

To sign a bundle, I first created a PEM key file. I use the OpenSSL tool to create my bundle-signing keys. The first command creates the private key that I use to sign the bundles, and the second command creates the public key that I distribute to the OPA instances to consume signed bundles:

```
# Use openssl commands to create private and public keys
$ openssl genrsa -out key.pem 2048
$ openssl rsa -in key.pem -outform PEM -pubout -out key.pem.pub
```

Once the keys were created, I used the following opa build command to build and sign the bundle:

```
# Build bundles with signatures
$ opa build -b . --signing-key ../keys/key.pem -o signed-bundle.tar.gz
```

I have found that this is the easiest way to build and sign the bundle while simultaneously storing the signatures in the bundle tarball.

Using the following `tar` command, I can see that the *.signatures.json* file is included in the bundle:

```
# Bundle file with signatures
$ tar tvf bundle.tar.gz
-rw------- 0 0        0       69 Dec 31  1969 /data.json
-rw------- 0 0        0      147 Dec 31  1969 /policy.rego
-rw------- 0 0        0      961 Dec 31  1969 /.signatures.json
```

The *.signatures.json* file contains a JSON Web Token (JWT) (*https://jwt.io*) that can be decoded:

```
{
  "signatures": [
    "eyJhbGciOiJSUzI1NiJ9 …"
  ]
}
```

I decoded the signatures JWT on jwt.io (*https://jwt.io*). The following listing contains the decoded output:

```
HEADER:ALGORITHM & TOKEN TYPE
{
  "alg": "RS256"
}

PAYLOAD:DATA
{
  "files": [
    {
      "name": "authz-bearer.rego",
      "hash": "4cedc703d3e851c8c8ae…",
      "algorithm": "SHA-256"
    },
    {
      "name": "employees.json",
      "hash": "0f97573c90635f16dc62…",
      "algorithm": "SHA-256"
    },
    {
      "name": "helloworld.rego",
      "hash": "2b8c01dde0acb3962d8e…",
      "algorithm": "SHA-256"
    }
  ]
}
```

The decoded JWT contained SHA-256 checksums for the files in the bundle. The public key from my PEM key pair would be shared with the OPA server to verify signatures of bundles upon update operations.

Once the bundle is signed with a private key, we can use a public key to verify the bundle signature. In fact, when using a signed bundle, we must verify the signature or tell OPA to skip verification; otherwise, we see the following error:

```
# Error for not verifying bundle signature
error: load error: bundle signed-bundle.tar.gz: verification key not provided

# Verify bundle signature
$ opa run -b signed-bundle.tar.gz --verification-key ../keys/key.pem.pub

# Skip bundle signature verification
$ opa run -b signed-bundle.tar.gz --skip-verify
```

Bundle signing is just one step in improving software supply chain security with OPA bundles. Signing is designed to help ensure provenance of artifacts. As you will see in Chapter 14, there are other concerns to make sure that artifact authenticity and integrity are not forged.

In the next session, I will explore OPA bundles and WebAssembly usage.

Bundles for Extension: WebAssembly

Bundles can also be used for extending OPA. For example, the following opa build command builds a bundle to be used with WebAssembly (Wasm) (*https://webassembly.org*):

```
# Build OPA bundle with Wasm
$ opa build -t wasm -e examples/ch2/hello ./bundle/helloworld.rego
```

The target is wasm, and the entrypoint is *examples/ch2/hello*.

With the opa inspect command, you can see the *policy.wasm* binary in the bundle:

```
$ opa inspect bundle.tar.gz
NAMESPACES:
+-----------------------------+-------------------------+
|          NAMESPACE          |          FILE           |
+-----------------------------+-------------------------+
| data                        | /data.json              |
| data.examples.ch2           | /bundle/helloworld.rego |
| data.examples.ch2.hello     | /policy.wasm            |
+-----------------------------+-------------------------+
```

An example of how to use this approach can be had from the Open Policy Agent WebAssembly NPM Module project (*https://oreil.ly/nodejs-app*).

The OPA Wasm functionality is currently not available in the statically compiled OPA ARM64 architecture binaries. While Wasm can be added to ARM64 binaries, the OPA project currently has no automated means to test the Wasm in ARM64 binaries, so without those tests, it was correctly decided to leave Wasm out of the ARM64 binaries.

Next, let's explore more ways to extend OPA and OPA integration.

Extending and Integrating with OPA

As you might guess, from a mature project like OPA there are several means by which OPA can be extended or integrated into your solutions. Since OPA is an OSS project, you can contribute to the project. According to the documentation (*https://oreil.ly/xbA5Y*), you can extend OPA via its Golang API with custom built-in functions and plug-ins. For example, the opa-envoy-plugin project (*https://oreil.ly/opa-envoy-plugin*) uses the OPA Golang API.

You should also remember that OPA is just one project under the Open Policy Agent (*https://oreil.ly/0oph_*) GitHub organization, an umbrella of 22 repositories (at the time of this writing). Within this organization, you will find several existing projects, such as Conftest, Gatekeeper, and the OPA WebAssembly NPM Module (mentioned earlier in this chapter).

You can easily integrate to OPA via its APIs and SDKs. These integration interfaces are categorized by purpose:

Evaluation
Using OPA's policy evaluation functionality:

- REST API (seen earlier in this chapter)
- Golang API
- WebAssembly (seen earlier in this chapter)
- Golang SDK

Management
Managing policies (deploying, uploading logs, metrics, etc.):

- Bundle API
- Status API
- Decision Log API
- Health API
- Prometheus API

We have seen that even though OPA provides a powerful set of tools to meet our PaC needs, we can also gain tighter integration to OPA via its SDKs and APIs.

 At the time of this writing, OPA v1.0 is due out shortly. This document (*https://oreil.ly/pWQ6I*) outlines the preparedness steps that users should consider.

OPA is not just a CLI and a server. OPA offers mature APIs and SDKs that make it easier to integrate OPA with your applications.

Summary

Open Policy Agent (OPA) is a very mature PaC solution, evidenced by its CNCF graduated-project status (*https://oreil.ly/P1H8E*).

As we discovered in this chapter, OPA offers several operational modes to fit our various needs as well as many different means by which we can extend OPA or integrate OPA to our systems. The OPA policy language, Rego, may be a departure from the imperative languages you may be used to, but Rego is very powerful and flexible for evaluation and reasoning of structured data.

If we consider the PaC Solution Selection Scorecard from Chapter 1, OPA ticks many of the boxes in a positive way. There is a learning curve with OPA, especially if you haven't used Rego before, but OPA should be able to support and satisfy many of your use cases and solutions while providing a good user experience.

In this chapter, we focused on the general purpose utility of OPA and its toolset, and we lightly explored the Rego language that is used in OPA policies. In Chapter 3, we will use OPA to solve modern authorization problems using access control techniques, such as role-based and attribute-based access control.

Policy as Code and Access Control

In Chapter 2, we discovered how OPA offers several operational modes to fit our different needs. We explored Rego, the OPA policy language, and learned how it can be used for evaluation and reasoning of structured data.

Regardless of the system you operate, the application you support, or the data you maintain, access control is an essential component. In fact, access control is not an afterthought—at least, it shouldn't be—when building new solutions. Access control determines who or what can perform operations in your systems, what operations they can perform, and when—under what circumstances or in what contexts—they can perform those operations.

Access control is divided into two main processes: authentication (AuthN) and authorization (AuthZ). *AuthN* is used to determine that users or systems are who they claim to be and provide proof in the form of identity principals and attributes. Once identity is verified, *AuthZ* is used to decide what privileges an actor has within a system.

In this chapter, we start with a primer on privileged access management, why it exists, and the types of PAM that are commonly used. I will introduce you to role-based and attribute-based access control models, and show you how PaC can be used with these models to provide more dynamic AuthZ services. We will also explore tooling that reduces the operational burden of managing policy engines and the artifacts used by them to make AuthZ decisions.

Privileged Access Management

Every properly secured system controls access to permissions and provides users with different levels of access. *Privileged access management* (PAM) is an amalgam of technologies and cybersecurity approaches designed, implemented, and integrated to control who can do what in systems under access control. The idea behind PAM is to control who and what can get privileged access and for when and how long they can get that access. PAM also includes logging of access decisions for auditability.

The *principle of least privilege* (PoLP) is a well-known PAM standard for allocating access to authenticated system principals (a.k.a. system actors). Under PoLP, a system actor receives only the permissions that the actor needs and is authorized to have, and gets that access only for the time they need it for system interaction. For example, under a role-based access control (RBAC) model, the permissions granted to system actors are based on a persona or role that the actor has within the secured system. In this context, permissions are the rules in the system that define the actions a principal can perform. The credentials returned as part of the role assumption are good for only a limited time. With PoLP, the actor is assigned a role, and the role is associated with a finite set of permissions for a finite time. The actor then gets only the permissions that the assigned role is allowed.

Let's start our journey into access control with an example of OPA AuthN and AuthZ.

OPA Bearer Token AuthN and AuthZ

In Chapter 2, we explored the OPA server. To secure an OPA server, I have sometimes used bearer tokens. I find bearer tokens simple to use; you don't have to sign each request. And even though the tokens are unencrypted plaintext, as long as I use them over HTTPS or in an isolated or even air-gapped development environment, bearer tokens fit my needs.

To use bearer tokens, I must add the following to my OPA server:

1. Add a policy in the *system.authz* package to handle the authorization for token presenters. Load this as part of the bundle when the server starts.

2. Add the `authentication=token` flag to the server command.

3. Add the `authorization=basic` flag to the server command.

4. Add an Authorization header to inbound requests.

The following command runs the server with token-based AuthN and basic AuthZ schemes enabled; I also added the debug flag:

```
# Start local OPA server with AuthN/AuthZ schemes
$ opa run -s -l debug --bundle . --authentication=token \
--authorization=basic --addr localhost:8181
```

In this AuthZ policy, I hard-coded the single token I am using for the purposes of this demo. In a real-world scenario, I would most likely store the allowed bearer tokens in a separate secured vault and load them as data into OPA as needed.

 This is a contrived example meant to illustrate a simple AuthZ approach. For a more realistic solution, I could use a JWT as the bearer token. Then I could include JWT payloads and claims as well as secrets to be used in my AuthZ policy. An example of this approach is available in the Rego Playground under the Examples for JWT Decoding.

The default return for the `allow` rule is false. Roles are associated with tokens. The `lookup_permissions` function looks up permissions for roles associated with the token passed in through the `input.identity` field, which gets its value from the request Authorization header:

```
# OPA AuthZ policy
package system.authz

permissions := {
    "admin": {
        "path": "*"
    }
}

tokens := {
    "21ad4323-f187-4237-9b88-1e0aa6a4599d": {    ❶
        "roles": ["admin"]
    }
}

default allow := false

allow {
    some permission
    lookup_permissions[permission]
    permission.path == "*"
}

lookup_permissions[permission] {
    token := tokens[input.identity]
    role := token.roles[_]
    permission := permissions[role]
}
```

❶ The Rego AuthZ policy expects to see this token in the `input.identity`.

Without a bearer token in the request, the request failed with a deny error:

```
# Unauthorized data API request
$ curl localhost:8181/v1/data
{
  "code": "unauthorized",
  "message": "request rejected by administrative policy"
}
```

With the correct bearer token in the request Authorization header, I successfully made the request:

```
# Authorized data API request
$ curl localhost:8181/v1/data -H "Authorization: Bearer 21ad4323..."
{"result":{"examples":{"ch2":{"hello":"goodbye"}}}}
```

In the preceding example, I configured the server with authentication and authorization flags so that I could use a bearer token as an AuthN principal. However, it's important to remember that OPA is not an AuthN identity provider (IDP). The bearer token I used was not issued as proof of my identity by OPA. Moreover, according to the documentation, "OPA does not handle authentication." Users do not register with OPA, and OPA does not issue credentials. Once the IDP has authenticated the user principal, artifacts from that authentication, such as a JWT or bearer token, can be passed to OPA in the input for parsing and authorization.

In Chapter 5—when we discuss OPA integration to Kubernetes—we will use Transport Layer Security (TLS) certificates to allow the Kubernetes API server to communicate securely with the OPA service.

OPA servers are normally used within systems or within close proximity of policy-enforcement points on the same localhost network. Given these common deployment scenarios—where OPA is located on the same machine or instance of the policy-enforcement point and localhost networking is used to connect to the OPA server—AuthN/AuthZ policies are not normally used. They are considered added complexity that is not needed. Instead, using the --addr localhost:8181 argument with the OPA server startup will restrict OPA server network reachability to only those clients on the same localhost network, where both localhost and 127.0.0.1 addresses will work.

According to my friend Anders Eknert, an industry colleague and OPA expert whom I trust implicitly and routinely consult:

- OPA exposed to the public should be protected with authentication requirements and an AuthZ policy.
- OPA exposed only to services on localhost normally won't need that.

While I generally recommend that zero-trust architecture (*https://oreil.ly/9PCT_*) be considered, OPA running on the same localhost network as the application or system calling OPA precludes the need for local AuthN/AuthZ policies. If a bad actor can infiltrate the local machine and localhost network where OPA and the application both reside, that same actor would have little difficulty also compromising the token used by the application to access OPA. The added complexity is not warranted. Instead, compensating controls should be used to isolate the system where the application and OPA are running.

Now, let's explore RBAC and how it is implemented in OPA.

Role-Based Access Control

As mentioned earlier, we use RBAC to provide permissions to system actors based on their respective roles within a secured system. This works well in an organization with a hierarchical structure. Under RBAC, the semantics of a system role are different, depending on the respective system and context of the actor. Users within an organization normally have different roles that require different permissions across the multiple systems with which they interact. These differences imply an overhead of role and permission management.

With RBAC, we create and manage "entitlements" in the form of roles and associated permissions. More precisely, users are entitled to certain permissions based on the roles they are assigned. Entitlement management is often the biggest overhead of implementing a successful RBAC model. Auditors routinely examine entitlement systems to verify how roles are managed and provisioned.

RBAC is very useful; it ties permissions to actor personas and roles, making it easier to understand the scope of permissions and why certain users get those permissions. Roles are used to scope permissions, which facilitates the application of PoLP. Onboarding of folks to systems is also easier when you can assign them a role, or accumulative set thereof, and intuitively understand which permissions the system actors will have.

An example of RBAC is used within Kubernetes (*https://oreil.ly/N1M9F*) to define permissions that actors have within a cluster. As you might imagine, different actors have different roles within different clusters. In general, Kubernetes uses ClusterRoles to specify cluster-wide permissions and Roles to specify namespace-specific permissions. Permissions are given to actors by binding the ClusterRoles and Roles to specific principals.

 When the same permissions are needed in multiple Kubernetes namespaces but are scoped to namespace-specific actors, it is a best practice to create ClusterRoles for uniformity of permissions across the cluster. Then namespace-scoped Role Bindings can be used to bind permissions to namespace-scoped actors. With this approach, you get uniform permissions across the cluster, with access that is scoped (isolated) to namespace resources.

The following snippet contains the Kubernetes view ClusterRole that provides read-only access, via the `get`, `list`, and `watch` verbs, to specific Kubernetes resources:

```
# Kubernetes ClusterRole resource
apiVersion: rbac.authorization.k8s.io/v1
kind: ClusterRole
metadata:
  name: view
rules:
- apiGroups:
  - ""
  resources:
  - configmaps
  - endpoints
  - persistentvolumeclaims
  - persistentvolumeclaims/status
  - pods
  - replicationcontrollers
  - replicationcontrollers/scale
  - serviceaccounts
  - services
  - services/status
  verbs:
  - get
  - list
  - watch … (edited for brevity)
```

To assign the preceding permissions, the example following Kubernetes ClusterRole-Binding resource binds the view ClusterRole to the readonly-users group:

```
# Kubernetes ClusterRoleBinding resource
apiVersion: rbac.authorization.k8s.io/v1
kind: ClusterRoleBinding
metadata:
  name: cluster-readonly
roleRef:
  apiGroup: rbac.authorization.k8s.io
  kind: ClusterRole
  name: view
subjects:
- apiGroup: rbac.authorization.k8s.io
  kind: Group
  name: readonly-users
```

Given the preceding ClusterRole and ClusterRoleBinding resources, any authenticated principal that is part of the readonly-users group in the respective Kubernetes cluster will get read-only permissions defined in the view ClusterRole. Using the kubectl who-can plug-in (*https://oreil.ly/kubectl-who-can*), we can implement an RBAC best practice by auditing permissions. The following command lists principals that can watch Pods:

```
# Audit permissions with who-can
$ kubectl who-can watch pods
No subjects found with permissions to watch pods assigned through RoleBindings

CLUSTERROLEBINDING      SUBJECT         TYPE
cluster-admin           system:masters  Group
cluster-readonly        readonly-users  Group      (edited for brevity)
```

In the previous example, the role permissions were explicitly defined in the role (ClusterRole). However, this is not always the case. Some RBAC models separate the permissions from the roles; moreover, the permissions are contained in policies that are attached to roles when necessary. This layer of indirection allows policies to be used across multiple roles.

For example, IAM roles in AWS do not contain permissions. Instead, permissions are defined in IAM policies, and those policies are associated with roles, as shown in Figure 3-1. Policies used this way can be shared among roles. AWS roles can also contain inline policies that are role specific. Users assume those roles and gain permissions defined in the associated policies.

 Please see the NIST documentation (*https://oreil.ly/j7Ia4*) for more info about RBAC.

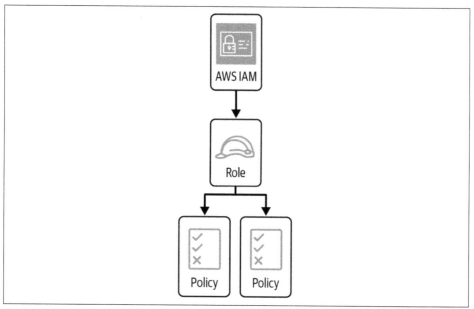

Figure 3-1. AWS IAM roles with policies

Now that we have a basic understanding of RBAC, let's explore how OPA can be used to implement RBAC more dynamically.

OPA and RBAC

Earlier in this chapter, we learned that while OPA can handle AuthZ, it doesn't handle credentials or AuthN. AuthN is not the same as AuthZ. AuthN is about verifying the identity of system actors based on provided evidence. AuthZ happens after AuthN and is the process of defining and enforcing permissions that authenticated actors have within systems.

OPA policies can be written to interrogate input data and apply policies for AuthZ. As it turns out, the Rego Playground (*https://oreil.ly/tHrnH*)—which we explored in Chapter 2—has a good example of prototyping RBAC policies. As shown in Figure 3-2, you can explore an RBAC example from the Examples menu in the Rego Playground.

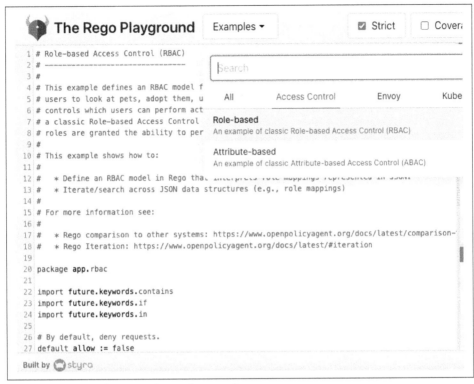

Figure 3-2. Rego Playground RBAC example

The following policy from the RBAC example excludes some of the comments:

```
package app.rbac

import future.keywords.contains
import future.keywords.if
import future.keywords.in

# By default, deny requests.
default allow := false    ❶

# Allow admins to do anything.
allow if user_is_admin    ❷
# Allow the action if the user is granted permission to perform the action.
allow if {
    # Find grants for the user.
    some grant in user_is_granted

    # Check if the grant permits the action.
    input.action == grant.action
    input.type == grant.type
}
```

```
# user_is_admin is true if "admin" is among the user's roles as per
# data.user_roles
user_is_admin if "admin" in data.user_roles[input.user]

# user_is_granted is a set of grants for the user identified in the request.
# The `grant` will be contained if the set `user_is_granted` for every...
user_is_granted contains grant if {   ❸
    # `role` assigned an element of the user_roles for this user...
    some role in data.user_roles[input.user]

    # `grant` assigned a single grant from the grants list for 'role'...
    some grant in data.role_grants[role]
}
```

❶   Set default deny.

❷   Check if the user is an admin.

❸   Check if the user has required grants.

This policy defaults to not allow users to access the underlying application:

```
# Default disallow
default allow := false
```

The policy then allows users if (1) they are admins or (2) they have the requisite roles and permissions (grants) to perform the actions they are trying. Roles and permissions are loaded into the OPA engine via data provided in the following JSON:

```
{
    "user_roles": {
        "alice": [
            "admin"
        ],
        "bob": [
            "employee",
            "billing"
        ],
        "eve": [
            "customer"
        ]
    },
    "role_grants": {
        "customer": [
            {
                "action": "read",
                "type": "dog"
            },
            {
                "action": "read",
```

```
                "type": "cat"
            },
            {
                "action": "adopt",
                "type": "dog"
            },
            {
                "action": "adopt",
                "type": "cat"
            }
        ],
        "employee": [
            {
                "action": "read",
                "type": "dog"
            },
            {
                "action": "read",
                "type": "cat"
            },
            {
                "action": "update",
                "type": "dog"
            },
            {
                "action": "update",
                "type": "cat"
            }
        ],
        "billing": [
            {
                "action": "read",
                "type": "finance"
            },
            {
                "action": "update",
                "type": "finance"
            }
        ]
    }
}
```

As we learned in Chapter 2, we could load this data via OPA bundles, server flags, or even the REST API.

Given the policy and roles/permissions data, we can now test the input. In the default test input, alice is trying to perform a read operation on the dog type:

```
{
    "user": "alice",
    "action": "read",
    "object": "id123",
```

```
    "type": "dog"
}
```

Since `alice` is an `admin` in the system, this is an easy policy evaluation. The user is determined to be an admin, and the policy does not even try to evaluate if additional grants are needed:

```
{
    "allow": true,
    "user_is_admin": true,
    "user_is_granted": []
}
```

This is an example of OPA's policy evaluation optimization.

Figure 3-3 shows the Rego Playground with the Coverage option enabled. Statements that were executed are marked in green, and statements not executed are marked in red; in grayscale, red highlights are darker than green.

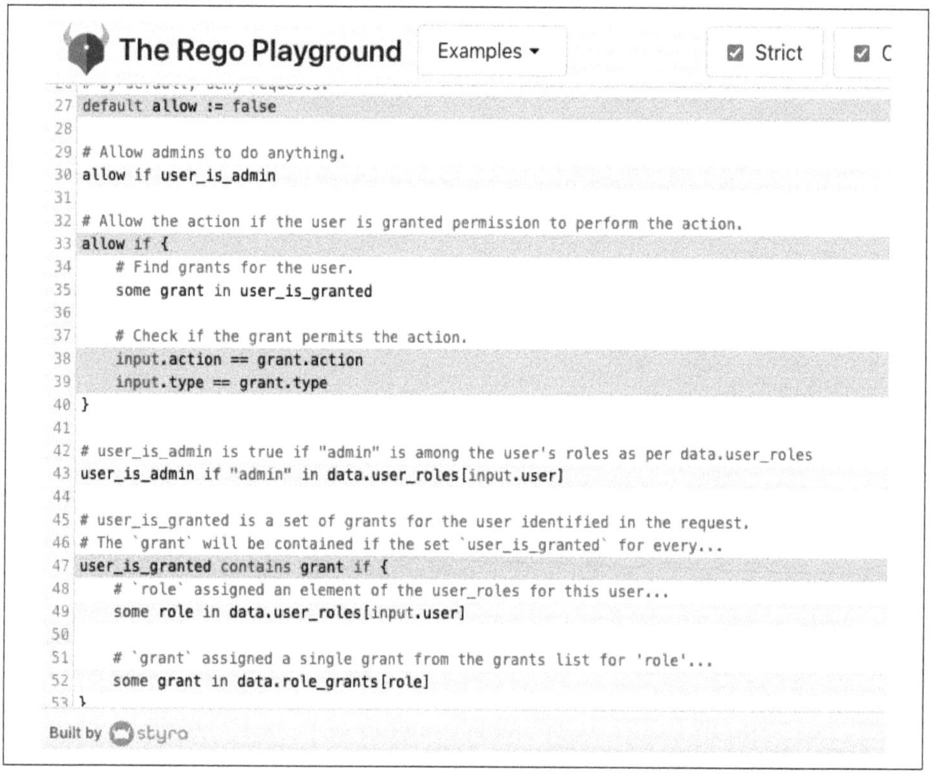

Figure 3-3. Rego Playground optimized policy evaluation: user alice

If we switch the input user to bob, then we see a different output. This time, the policy did not detect an admin and had to evaluate roles and grants to see if bob could perform the read operation on the dog type:

```
{
    "user": "bob",
    "action": "read",
    "object": "id123",
    "type": "dog"
}
```

The Rego Playground coverage is shown in Figure 3-4. This time, the policy had to evaluate rules to apply roles and grants.

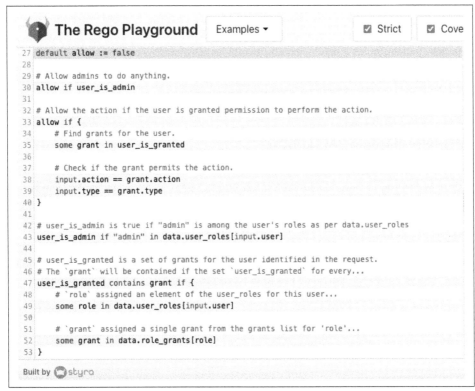

Figure 3-4. Rego Playground optimized policy evaluation: user bob

In the following JSON, you can see that while bob is not an admin, he has several grants related to his two roles, employee and billing:

```
{
    "allow": true,
    "user_is_granted": [
...
```

```
    {
        "action": "read",
        "type": "dog"
    },
...
    ]
}
```

The permissions bob receives via his roles are cumulative. Given the grants, bob can perform read operations on the dog type.

RBAC is a well-established access control model, and most organizations start with some sort of RBAC approach since it is easier to implement, especially in smaller environments. However, as organizations grow and larger volumes of personas, roles, and permissions need to be managed, RBAC can become cumbersome to maintain without automated processes and routine monitoring and auditing. It may also be necessary to augment RBAC with additional layers of access control.

Organizations looking to augment or replace RBAC sometimes turn to attribute-based access control (ABAC) as a more dynamic alternative. As we will see in the next section, OPA can be used to create ABAC policies as well.

Attribute-Based Access Control

ABAC uses attributes, a.k.a. characteristics, to dynamically determine access privileges. According to NIST (*https://oreil.ly/Ljqqk*), ABAC is "an access control approach in which access is mediated based on attributes associated with subjects (requesters) and the objects to be accessed."

ABAC is considered more dynamic because you do not manage point-in-time entitlements in an entitlement management system. With ABAC, you need not manage roles, trying to match permissions to actor types, personas, or organizational structure. Instead, you modify attributes of system actors and system resources to be accessed. ABAC uses policies to compare and match attributes or characteristics of actors and resources to determine permissions.

With ABAC, you design your architecture with attributes associated with your users and the resources they are trying to access. Then, you write policies that use those attributes to define access based on the relationships you modeled. Given that the ABAC policies use actor and resource data, ABAC is also considered to be more data driven than RBAC is.

One of the most important aspects of ABAC is the decoupling of actor and resource metadata from each other as well as from the policies that produce AuthZ decisions. Actor metadata is usually managed in different systems than resource metadata. ABAC policies are separate from both. All three come together in an ABAC policy decision point. The implied decoupling in ABAC acts as a pace-layering mechanism, where actor metadata is allowed to change independently and at different cadences than resource metadata or policies. As long as the relative data models do not change, ABAC continues to function. When data models or characteristic types used for decisions change, policies need to change.

Now, let's explore ABAC using OPA.

OPA and ABAC

For our ABAC example, we are again going to use OPA to handle the policy evaluations. As shown in Figure 3-5, we are storing attributes and policies in the OPA engine.

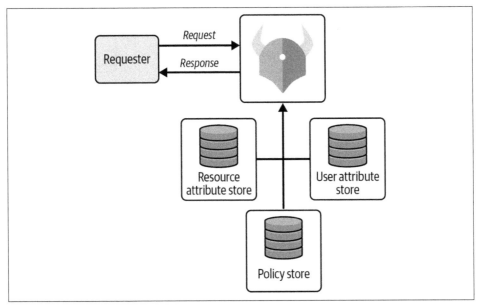

Figure 3-5. OPA and ABAC policy evaluation

As seen in Figure 3-5, when an ABAC AuthZ decision is received, OPA matches policies from its Policy Store to the inbound request. Then, the OPA policy uses data from the Resource Attribute Store and the User Attribute Store to decide if the request should be authorized or denied.

It's important to remember that the requestor in the preceding diagram is most likely another system or part of the same system where the policy decision point is embedded. In this model, OPA is the policy mediator that returns the AuthZ decisions.

If you consider the OASIS XACML Policy Architecture (*https://oreil.ly/ncuTA*) from the Kubernetes Policy Management Whitepaper (*https://oreil.ly/policy*) referenced in Chapter 1, OPA functions as the policy enforcement point (PEP), policy decision point (PDP), policy administration point (PAP), and policy information point (PIP) modules in the architecture diagram depicted in Figure 3-6.

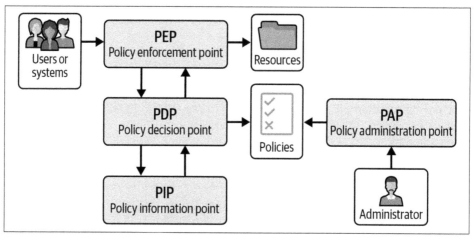

Figure 3-6. XACML policy architecture (Source: Kubernetes Policy Management Whitepaper (https://oreil.ly/policy))

In Figure 3-6, PEPs integrate to applications and send policy decision requests to PDPs. PDPs retrieve—and normally cache—policies from PAPs. Additional information needed for policy evaluation is obtained from the PIPs. It's important to understand that these are logical areas of functionality and may be combined as one physical policy engine.

To start my ABAC example, I chose the Examples > Access Control > Attribute-based example within the Rego Playground. The example is modeled similarly to the RBAC example, but this time we are not using roles or grants. Instead, we are using attributes stored in the policy engine data and passed into the policy engine via the input data, evaluated by the following policy:

```
# ABAC policy snippet
package app.abac

import future.keywords.if
import future.keywords.in

default allow := false

allow if user_is_owner

allow if {
        user_is_employee
        action_is_read
        user_is_on_shift
}
```

```
allow if {
        user_is_employee
        user_is_senior
        action_is_update
        user_is_on_shift
}

allow if {
        user_is_customer
        action_is_read
        not pet_is_adopted
}
user_is_owner if data.user_attributes[input.user].title == "owner"

user_is_employee if data.user_attributes[input.user].title == "employee"

user_is_customer if data.user_attributes[input.user].title == "customer"

user_is_senior if data.user_attributes[input.user].tenure > 8

action_is_read if input.action == "read"

action_is_update if input.action == "update"

pet_is_adopted if data.pet_attributes[input.resource].adopted == true

...
```

In the preceding policy snippet, the owner user is always allowed to perform their operations. The employee users can perform read operations if they are on shift. The employee users can also perform update operations if they are senior and they are on shift. Finally, customer users can perform read operations on nonadopted pets.

The preceding policy is written to use the attributes passed into OPA via the input request as well as the attribute data about the users, pets, and shifts stored in OPA. The data model is seen in the following JSON:

```
{
    "user_attributes": {
        "alice": {
            "tenure": 20,
            "title": "owner",
            "shift": "D"
        },
        "bob": {
            "tenure": 15,
            "title": "employee",
            "shift": "N"
        },
...
```

```
        },
        "shifts": {
            "D": {
                "start": 9,
                "end": 17
            },
            "N": {
                "start": 15,
                "end": 23
            }
        },
        "pet_attributes": {
            "dog123": {
                "adopted": true,
                "age": 2,
                "breed": "terrier",
                "name": "toto"
            },
...
    }
}
```

In the preceding example, I added the logic to detect if nonowner employees were actually on shift, to make sure that no operations can be done by an employee not on shift. To do this, I added the following time-handling logic that uses OPA's built-in time functions:

```
# Time handling logic
tz := "America/New_York"

now := time.now_ns()

clock := time.clock([now, tz])

day := time.weekday(now)

shift := data.user_attributes[input.user].shift

user_is_on_shift if {
    is_weekday
    is_valid_time
}

is_valid_time if {
    clock[0] >= data.shifts[shift].start
    clock[0] < data.shifts[shift].end
}

is_valid_time if {
    clock[0] >= data.shifts[shift].start
    clock[0] == data.shifts[shift].end
    clock[1] == 0
```

```
    clock[2] == 0
}

is_weekday if day in ["Monday", "Tuesday", "Wednesday", "Thursday", "Friday"]
```

In the preceding policy snippet, I set the time zone to America/New York, and I get the clock time using that timezone and the epoch time from the OPA `time.now_ns()` function. Then, I check that the returned time is on a weekday and that the time of the operation occurs between the start and end of the nonowner employee's shift.

Given the following input and the stored data attributes, the following output is produced in the Rego Playground:

```
// Input Data
{
    "user": "bob",
    "action": "read",
    "resource": "dog123"
}

// Output Data
{
    "action_is_read": true,
    "allow": true,
    "clock": [
        22,
        4,
        10
    ],
    "day": "Thursday",
    "is_valid_time": true,
    "is_weekday": true,
    "now": 1663207450305625000,
    "pet_is_adopted": true,
    "shift": "N",
    "tz": "America/New_York",
    "user_is_employee": true,
    "user_is_on_shift": true,
    "user_is_senior": true
}
```

With the right policy, ABAC is considerably more dynamic than RBAC. Modifying attributes promotes adaptability as well. If we leave the policy alone, the employee, customer, and pet data will be used by the policy to dynamically generate access control decisions. We don't have to fuss with roles or grants as long as we ensure that employee attributes are changed when employees change roles in the company. This is augmented by pulling employee data from a human resources or employee information system. Correctly modeled, the employee and resource attributes can be sourced from human resources and inventory systems, respectively. So once the policies are written, data drives the decisions going forward.

When implementing ABAC—especially in a cloud computing environment—tags and labels are used to apply resource metadata evaluated by ABAC policies. Because tags and labels are used to grant access via ABAC policies, it's important that you tightly control who or what can create or modify these tags or labels and under what conditions. Cloud Custodian (*https://cloudcustodian.io*)—discussed in Chapter 13—can help solve this requirement.

RBAC and ABAC are two AuthZ models that are used to implement least-privileged access in multiple systems. With these models, PaC is used to evaluate roles and attributes with policies when granting access. RBAC and ABAC are not mutually exclusive and are sometimes used as complementing approaches to build fine-grained access models.

Regardless of what type of AuthZ model we use, we need to plan for how we will manage those policies across the enterprise and multiple systems. Policy automation should provide context-rich authorization and a unified way to manage authorization, allowing policy decisions to be decoupled from the underlying application code.

In the next section, we will explore tooling that makes it easier to manage and deploy our policies and data across different systems and use cases while easing—if not eliminating—the common heavy lifting that is policy and data management.

Administering Policies and Data

As we saw in Chapter 2, OPA policies and data can be bundled and signed and then distributed via these signed bundles to OPA instances. To make this bundle approach work, we need a bundle server that can be reached by our OPA instances. Conversely, we need to configure our OPA instances to download bundles from the bundle server. Let's explore a Golang-based bundle server.

Bundle Server

To illustrate how a bundle server works, I built this example bundle server (*https://oreil.ly/bundle-server*) using Golang. The main portion of the server uses the gorilla/mux project (*https://oreil.ly/mux*) to create routers, handlers, and middleware to handle inbound HTTPS requests.

Most HTTP servers—Apache, NGINX, and so on—will work just fine to serve OPA bundles. Bundles are also easily served via object storage, like Amazon Simple Storage Service (S3) (*https://oreil.ly/kX1XI*).

When the server starts in debug mode, it listens on socket 10.0.2.2:8443 and produces the following startup logs:

```
{"level":"info","time":"2022-12-11T20:05:26.159931-05:00","message":
"Service started successfully."}
{"level":"info","time":"2022-12-11T20:05:26.16005-05:00","message":
"Flags: map[], Args: [./main.bin]"}
{"level":"info","time":"2022-12-11T20:05:26.163098-05:00","message":
"Listening on socket 10.0.2.2:8443"}
```

I use the 10.0.2.2 loopback address alias so that my OPA server—running in Docker—can connect to my local HTTPS server outside of Docker. The context of localhost and 127.0.0.1 are different between apps running in the Docker virtual machine and my desktop. The server log entries indicate the server startup settings.

To test the server, I ran the following `curl` command to hit the server's *info* endpoint with an HTTPS GET request, passing a bearer token for AuthZ:

```
# Bundle server info request
$ TOKEN=`cat token`
$ curl -k -H 'Accept: application/json' -H "Authorization: Bearer \
${TOKEN}" https://10.0.2.2:8443/info
{"service-name":"opa-bundle-api","service-id":"078f5...d2954"}
```

You should notice the `-k` flag with the `curl` command; it is used to ignore the self-signed TLS certificate configuration I used for this example.

Once I verified that the *info* endpoint was working with a bearer token, I tried the bundle download, again with the `-k` flag. The file server handler of my bundle server allows clients to download bundles as gzipped tarballs:

```
# Bundle download request
$ TOKEN=`cat token`
$ curl -k -H "Authorization: Bearer ${TOKEN}" https://10.0.2.2:8443/bundles/\
signed-main.tar.gz -o signed-main.tar.gz
  % Total    % Received % Xferd  Average Speed   Time    Time     Time  Current
                                 Dload  Upload   Total   Spent    Left  Speed
100   265  100   265    0     0  38646      0 --:--:-- --:--:-- --:--:--  258k
```

With a successful file download test, we can now configure our OPA server to connect to the bundle server:

```
# OPA server to bundle server config
keys:
  project-bundle-key:
    key: |
      -----BEGIN PUBLIC KEY-----
      <PUBLIC_KEY>
      -----END PUBLIC KEY-----

services:
```

```
  - name: opa-bundle-api
    url: https://10.0.2.2:8443/v1/bundles
    allow_insecure_tls: true
    credentials:
      bearer:
        token: "eyJ…"

bundles:
  project:
    service: opa-bundle-api
    resource: signed-main.tar.gz
    persist: true
    polling:
      min_delay_seconds: 10
      max_delay_seconds: 20
    signing:
      keyid: project-bundle-key
```

Now we can start the OPA server with the preceding configuration file to connect to the bundle server:

```
# Start OPA server with config file
$ opa run -s --config-file opa-conf.yaml
```

Although it is not necessarily needed, I have enabled persisting the downloaded bundle via the `bundles[_].persist` setting. When `persist` is enabled, the OPA server creates the *.opa/bundles* working directory to persist bundles.

Instead of adding the bundle-verification public key directly to the OPA config file, I could use the `--set-file` flag, as shown in the following command, to load the key at runtime directly from the key file:

```
# Start server and supply public key
$ opa run -s --config-file opa-conf.yaml --set-file \
"keys.project-bundle-key.key=keys/key.pem.pub"
```

This setting works inline with the existing configuration file. For those following the Twelve-Factor App methodology (*https://12factor.net*), this is a good approach to separating secrets from code and configurations.

To run the server in Docker with the preceding config file, I mapped two volumes to provide config files and bundle storage for the OPA container to download and persist bundles:

```
# Run OPA server, passing a config file, using Docker and volumes
$ docker run -it --rm -p 8181:8181 -v $(pwd):/config -v $(pwd)/.opa:/.opa \
--platform linux/amd64 openpolicyagent/opa:0.62.0 run -s \
--config-file=config/opa-conf.yaml
```

The OPA server produced the following output:

```
# Start server and review bundle settings
$ opa run -s --config-file opa-conf.yaml
{"addrs":[":8181"],"diagnostic-addrs":[],"level":"info","msg":
"Initializing server.","time":"2022-11-25T23:32:17-05:00"}
{"level":"info","msg":"Starting bundle loader.","name":"project",
"plugin":"bundle","time":"2022-11-25T23:32:17-05:00"}
{"level":"info","msg":
"Bundle loaded and activated successfully. Etag updated to 6...c.",
"name":"project","plugin":"bundle","time":
"2022-11-25T23:32:17-05:00"}
```

We can see that the bundle settings we provided worked and that the bundle was downloaded and activated successfully. Based on the config file, the OPA server will check for an updated bundle every 10–20 seconds. We can also see that an ETag (*https://oreil.ly/nrgoK*) was used to determine changes to bundle files.

 ETags—also known as *entity tags*—are used to reduce server bandwidth requirements by allowing cached content to be checked for changes before being redownloaded from servers. For more information about ETags, please review the Mozilla developers documentation (*https://oreil.ly/Cf9ny*).

In my bundle server logs—in debug mode—we can see the OPA bundle request being served:

```
{"level":"debug","time":"2022-11-25T23:50:54.627103-05:00","message":\
"HTTP request URI: /v1/bundles/signed-main.tar.gz, HTTP request
headers: map[Accept-Encoding:[gzip] Authorization:[Bearer eyJ…]
If-None-Match:[6...c]
Prefer:[modes=snapshot,delta] User-Agent:[Open Policy Agent/0.46.1
(darwin, arm64)]]"}
```

Bundle servers and the OPA bundle configuration work well to provide bundles—policy and data—to OPA. However, given the number of AuthZ decisions that systems need to handle—possibly millions—and the number of policy changes that need to occur, manually managing and distributing policies does not scale well. Instead, we need solutions that allow us to centrally manage policies and scale policy distribution to many policy engine instances, in a secure and frictionless manner.

There are several tools and services that can scale. In the following sections, I introduce four solutions to help scale your bundle management and delivery. As you explore these tools, you need to consider which best fit your needs and what trade-offs you are willing to accept. Some solutions offer enterprise support, considerable ease of use, and mature management tools. Others are OSS and require more work on your part. You should also consider whether you want to manage these tools—in your datacenter or cloud—or if a software-as-a-service (SaaS) model would better fit your needs. Selecting a bundle management solution is similar to selecting PaC tools using the selection criteria from Chapter 1.

The first tool we will examine is from Styra, the creators of OPA.

Styra DAS and Policy-Based Access Management

Access control policies—evaluated in real time—and the systems we use to manage and distribute said policies are together referred to as *policy-based access management* (PBAM). Additionally, *PBAM* is used to describe an authorization strategy characterized by the following approaches:

- Use PaC to grant access through evaluation of roles and policies.
- Decouple policy decisions from underlying application code.
- Unify AuthZ management across multiple systems.
- Make event-driven updates to policies and data.

Styra (*https://www.styra.com*), the creator of OPA, has created a SaaS product for PBAM called Declarative Authorization Service (DAS). DAS provides a unified and centralized management and distribution platform for your systems, policies, libraries, and stacks. From DAS you can instrument multiple systems with OPA agents, such as Kubernetes, Istio, Envoy, IaC, and several more.

With Styra DAS, you can centrally create and manage resources that help you instrument and manage your applications and systems. You can also model and manage reusable stacks and libraries to keep your access management, mutation, and validation DRY. Let's explore DAS with the free version: Styra DAS Free.

Styra DAS Free allows you to get started with DAS at no cost, save for time. Once you create a free account on *Styra.com* (*https://signup.styra.com*), you can immediately jump in and start creating systems, stacks, libraries, and so on. Even though DAS may be new to you, the interface intuitively guides you through the processes of creating and managing resources after you log in. Styra Academy (*https://academy.styra.com*) hosts a collection of free courses—which I can personally recommend—designed to get you up and running with easy-to-follow instructions and examples. The DAS interface is shown in Figure 3-7.

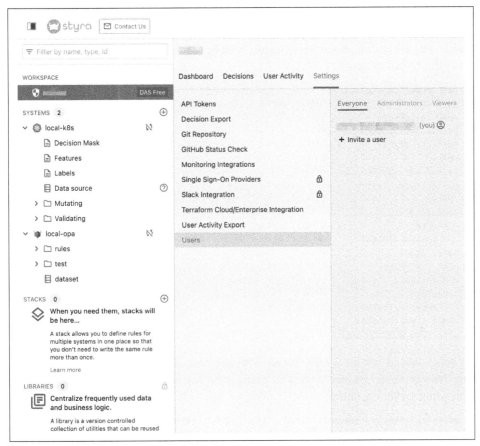

Figure 3-7. Styra DAS workspace

As you can see in Figure 3-7, my DAS workspace contains two systems: a local Kubernetes (minikube (*https://oreil.ly/8-wpN*)) system and a local (custom) OPA system. On the far right, the DAS workspace displays recommendations, tutorials, and helpful links to courses and communities.

The Settings tab is system-context aware and provides guidance for system settings, including how to install components, such as OPA agents, and have them securely connect back to your DAS workspace. For example, on the Settings tab of my local-opa system, I was shown how to start my local OPA server, referencing my workspace with a downloaded configuration file that was generated for my system configuration:

```
# Run OPA with Styra configuration
$ opa run --server --config-file=opa-conf.yaml
```

The config file is easy to understand. The major difference between the bundle-server example and this DAS example is that instead of configuring name bundles to download, we are using discovery (*https://oreil.ly/f2Amc*) to discover bundles made available to our system:

```
# OPA server config file to connect to Styra DAS
discovery:
  name: discovery
  prefix: <DISCOVERY_PREFIX>
  service: styra
labels:
  system-id: <SYSTEM_ID>
  system-type: custom
services:
- credentials:
    bearer:
      token: <TOKEN>
  name: styra
  url: <DAS_URL>
- credentials:
    bearer:
      token: <TOKEN>
  name: styra-bundles
  url: <DAS_BUNDLES_URL>
```

When I started my local OPA server with the preceding command, it connected to my remote DAS instance over TLS using a bearer token credential, as seen in the following server log entries:

```
{"addrs":[":8181"],"diagnostic-addrs":[],"level":"info","msg":
"Initializing server.","time":"2022-10-17T21:27:50-04:00"}
{"level":"info","msg":"Starting bundle loader.","name":
"systems/a13dbce…","plugin":"bundle","time":"2022-10-17T21:27:51-04:00"}
{"level":"info","msg":"Starting decision logger.","plugin":
"decision_logs","time":"2022-10-17T21:27:51-04:00"}
{"level":"info","msg":"Starting status reporter.","plugin":"status",
"time":"2022-10-17T21:27:51-04:00"}
{"level":"info","msg":"Status update sent successfully in response to
plugin update.","plugin":"status","time":"2022-10-17T21:27:52-04:00"}
{"level":"info","msg":"Discovery update processed successfully.
Etag updated to \"971261…\".","plugin":"discovery","time":
"2022-10-17T21:27:52-04:00"}
{"level":"info","msg":"Bundle loaded and activated successfully…
```

With my local OPA server now connected to my DAS workspace, I authored policies that were bundled and sent directly to my local OPA instance via a secure network connection.

As shown in Figure 3-8, the Styra DAS Free rules IDE has a rich set of tools that allows me to edit, validate, and test my rules.

Figure 3-8. Styra DAS Free rules IDE

In addition to rules, I can edit datasets and publish them to the remote OPA server configured for the system with which I am currently working. The dataset editor is shown in Figure 3-9.

Figure 3-9. Styra DAS Free dataset editor

DAS will also monitor the systems to which it is supposed to be connected. In Figure 3-10, my local OPA server is down and no longer communicating to my DAS workspace—indicated by the error.

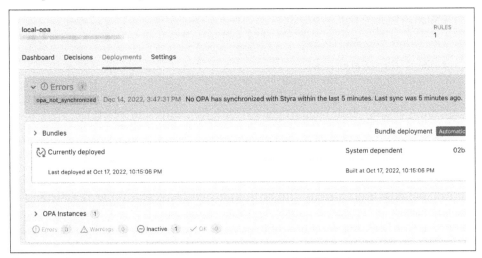

Figure 3-10. Styra DAS Free error connecting to remote OPA instance

Once the system connection is restored, DAS will automatically resume operations and ensure that published artifacts—policies, datasets, tests—are synchronized to the respective system via bundles automatically created and managed in my workspace.

DAS can be used to centrally manage policy and data and to offload that management for remote OPA instances, thereby reducing the operational burden of OPA engines. DAS provides near-real-time updates to remote OPA agents. It expands on the notion of bundle servers and provides a centralized hub to organize your systems, stacks, logs, policies, and data. This centralized management aids in auditing, which can be a challenge for ABAC.

Next, we will look at a solution that eliminates the need to run OPA locally by integrating to remote APIs for AuthZ.

Styra Run

Styra Run is the newest SaaS offering from Styra that is used to directly instrument applications for AuthZ and data filtering without needing local OPA instances. Applications integrated to Run use the Run SDK to connect to the Run API. The API exposes the ability to remotely manage policies, data, and AuthZ decisions via SDK calls that can be added directly to application code. In this model, the PEPs remain local to applications using the SDK, but the PDP resides in the Run SaaS platform.

The Styra Run SDKs are split into two categories: backend and frontend. The backend SDKs facilitate server-side integrations and common applications. These SDKs currently support the following languages and frameworks:

- Golang (*https://oreil.ly/RTqwX*)
- Java (*https://oreil.ly/192Wg*)
- Node.js (*https://oreil.ly/wh2wf*)

The frontend SDKs are for AuthZ in web browsers—for dynamic AuthZ-based UI rendering—and currently support plain HTML/JavaScript and React:

- HTML/JavaScript (*https://oreil.ly/cuA_t*)
- React (*https://oreil.ly/lVVUJ*)

To help developers get started with Styra Run, Styra has created the TicketHub sample application (*https://oreil.ly/AqzNX*), which eases onboarding via tutorials. Run is positioned to help organizations offload local management of policies and policy engines. Instead, applications call Run to get decisions. Other than the local application development and SDK integration, everything—policy, data, policy engine—is managed remotely.

The folks at Styra created OPA and Styra tools that augment the OPA experience to help organizations better manage policies and data and build enterprise-grade AuthZ systems. Next, we will explore alternative tools used to manage the common heavy lifting of AuthZ policy and data management. The first tool we will look at is Open Policy Administration Layer.

Open Policy Administration Layer

Open Policy Administration Layer (OPAL) (*https://oreil.ly/opal*) is an open source project—backed by Permit.io (*https://www.permit.io*)—for administering authorization policies and data. OPAL connects to your policy and data stores, detects changes in policy and data resources, and responds to those changes by pushing updates to remote specific OPA agents.

To get started with OPAL, I downloaded the example Docker Compose file and modified it to monitor the *main* branch of my OPAL example repo. The new *docker-compose.yaml* file is shown in the following YAML:

```
# OPAL config Docker Compose file (line breaks to fit margins)
version: "3.8"
services:
  broadcast_channel:
    image: postgres:alpine
    environment:
```

```
      - POSTGRES_DB=postgres
      - POSTGRES_USER=postgres
      - POSTGRES_PASSWORD=postgres
  opal_server:
    image: permitio/opal-server:latest
    environment:
      - >
      OPAL_BROADCAST_URI=postgres://postgres:postgres@broadcast_channel:5432/
      postgres
      - UVICORN_NUM_WORKERS=4
      - OPAL_POLICY_REPO_URL=https://github.com/Policy-as-Code-Book/
      pac-ch3-opal-repo
      - OPAL_POLICY_REPO_MAIN_BRANCH=main
      - OPAL_POLICY_REPO_POLLING_INTERVAL=30
      - >
      OPAL_DATA_CONFIG_SOURCES={"config":{"entries":[{"url":
      "http://opal_server:7002/policy-data","topics":["policy_data"],
      "dst_path":"/static"}]}}
      - OPAL_LOG_FORMAT_INCLUDE_PID=true
    ports:
      - "7002:7002"
    depends_on:
      - broadcast_channel
  opal_client:
    image: permitio/opal-client:latest
    environment:
      - OPAL_SERVER_URL=http://opal_server:7002
      - OPAL_LOG_FORMAT_INCLUDE_PID=true
      - OPAL_INLINE_OPA_LOG_FORMAT=http
    ports:
      - "7000:7000"
      - "8181:8181"
    depends_on:
      - opal_server
    command: sh -c "./wait-for.sh opal_server:7002 --timeout=20 -- ./start.sh"
```

When I ran the `docker-compose` up command from the directory containing the Docker Compose file, the OPAL environment started, as shown in the following log entries:

```
$ docker-compose up
Creating opal_broadcast_channel_1 ... done
Creating opal_opal_server_1       ... done
Creating opal_opal_client_1       ... done
Attaching to opal_broadcast_channel_1, opal_opal_server_1,
opal_opal_client_1
…
opal_server_1 | 2022-09-18T05:49:40.201419+0000 | 10 | opal_server.server \
| INFO | *** OPAL Server Startup ***
opal_server_1 | 2022-09-18T05:49:40.201560+0000 | 10 | \
opal_common.topics.publisher          | INFO | started topic publisher
…
```

When the Docker Compose orchestration of OPAL starts, it starts an OPAL server, a PostgreSQL server (for the publisher/subscriber communication), and an OPAL client. The OPAL client then starts an OPA server. Once the OPAL server starts, it publishes a topic that is subscribed to by the OPAL client.

As shown in the diagram in Figure 3-11, the OPAL server connects to the GitHub repository and polls for changes in policy and data. The OPAL client instance subscribes to the topic published by the OPAL server. Once a change is made to policy and/or data in the Git repo, the OPAL server detects the change in the next polling interval (default 30 seconds), downloads the change, and publishes a new topic message on the broadcast channel for the OPAL client.

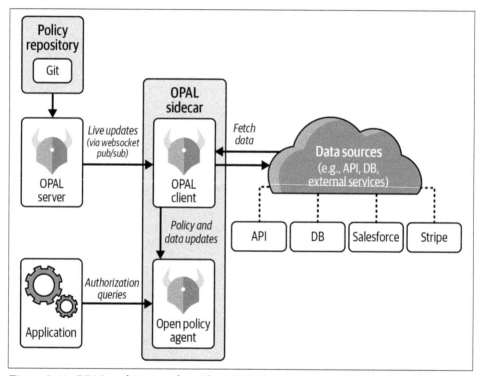

Figure 3-11. OPAL architecture from the OPAL documentation (Source: https://github.com/permitio/opal)

The OPAL client reaches out to the OPAL server pub/sub model via an outbound websocket connection, which makes it effective for positioning behind a firewall. This outbound network request is similar to the model used by Syra DAS. The OPAL client gets the topic message and calls the OPAL server to get the newly acquired policy and/or data. The OPAL client then creates an OPA bundle and pushes the bundle to the OPA server via the REST API with PUT commands. In this model, the OPAL client acts as a sidecar container, providing data to the OPA agent. As we'll see later in this book, the idea of using sidecar containers to update OPA data and policies is a common pattern.

With the OPAL model, near-real-time updates to your remote OPA agents are possible with an event-driven GitOps approach. Shortly after policy and/or data are updated in your Git repository, OPAL will detect, download, and propagate the changes to OPA.

Next, we will explore using container images to deliver the same policy and data for which we used bundles in previous examples.

Using OCI Images with OPA and Open Policy Containers

Open Policy Containers (OPCR) (*https://oreil.ly/hI7yL*) is a combination of an Open Container Initiative (OCI) registry (*https://oreil.ly/zAvl8*) and a CLI to package and store OPA policies and data. OPCR was accepted into the CNCF as a Sandbox project on December 12, 2022. With OPCR, you can build, version, and publish policy and data as OCI images. Given the wide adoption of containerization and the open standards created and shared by OCI, it makes sense that policy and data be available for consumption and propagated to OPA agents via OCI-compatible container images. And since version 0.40.0, OPA has been able to use policy/data bundles packaged as OCI images.

To get started with OPCR, I created a GitHub personal access token (PAT)—with minimal privileges—to allow me to log in to my GitHub Container Registry (GHCR) account via the OPCR CLI. Once I had my account and credentials, I installed the CLI and logged into the OPCR with the CLI:

```
# Install the OPCR CLI
$ brew install opcr-io/tap/policy

# use GitHub PAT for password to login into remote account
$ GH_PAT=`cat <PATH_TO_GH_PAT_FILE>`
policy login -u jimmyraywv -p "$GH_PAT"
Logging in.
server: ghcr.io
user: jimmyraywv
OK.
```

Next, I built a policy OCI image from the following bundle material, using the CLI:

```
# OPCR OCI image contents
-rw-r--r-- .manifest
-rw-r--r-- data.json
-rw-r--r-- policy.rego
```

Along with data and Rego files, I added the optional manifest file. The manifest file is a JSON file with a specific format and items (*https://oreil.ly/yEipk*).

The main reason that I use manifest files is for data scoping inside OPA. If OPA is configured to download data from bundles, its default behavior is to load its entire policy and data cache from the bundle. For use cases where multiple data sources may be used to load policy and data, scoping that data is made easier with namespaces defined in bundle manifests.

The following bundle manifest provides a roots entry that scopes bundle data into namespaces:

```
{
    "roots": ["normal","pacbook"]
}
```

When this bundle is loaded, only data from that roots entry is written or overwritten, thereby allowing OPA to load data from multiple sources without data collisions.

When I build artifacts—of any kind, regardless of type or CLI—I use Make (*https:// oreil.ly/Bqg_i*) so that I can repeat the process without variation:

```
# Build bundle material
$ make build
[METADATA]
timestamp: [2022-12-11_05:54:07PM]
git commit: [793309a9eaf0ad39a61c5c964e813299752da8ee]
Image version: [v0.1.0-793309a9ea]

policy build ./bundle-material -t ghcr.io/jimmyraywv/pacbook:v0.1.0-793309a9ea

Created new image.
digest: sha256:cabd3a636541622cde59b92bf22033627bc137840cefc57ed6265f000a12e187

Tagging image.
reference: ghcr.io/jimmyraywv/pacbook:v0.1.0-793309a9ea
```

I also add help targets in Makefile to provide help about the different available targets:

```
# Example Makefile help output
$ make help
Usage:
  make <target>

General
  help              Display this help.
  meta              Provides metadata for other commands; good for DevOps \
                    logging. Can be called as a target, but is mostly used \
                    by other targets as a dependency.

Build and deploy
  build             Build container with Docker buildx, based on PLATFORM \
                    argument (default linux/amd64)
  login             Login to remote image registry
  push              Push to remote image registry
```

```
pull            Pull from remote image registry
clean           Clean by removing image and tarball
run             Run the OPA repl with the bundle image
bundle          Create bundle
```

On my M2 MacBook Pro, the images were stored locally under my user directory as tarballs:

```
$ ls ~/.policy/policies-root/blobs/sha256
cabd3a636541622cde59b92bf22033627bc137840cefc57ed6265f000a12e187
```

The created images are viewed and inspected similarly to how the Docker CLI is used:

```
# List images
$ policy images
  REPOSITORY                      TAG             IMAGE ID        CREATED      SIZE
  ghcr.io/jimmyraywv/pacbook   v0.1.0-793309a9ea  cabd3a636541  1 hour ago   348B

#Inspect image
$ policy inspect ghcr.io/jimmyraywv/pacbook:v0.1.0-793309a9ea

digest: sha256:cabd3a636541622cde59b92bf22033627bc137840cefc57ed6265f000a12e187
size: 348
created_at: 2022-12-11 17:54:07.502764 -0500 EST
updated_at: 2022-12-11 17:54:07.502764 -0500 EST
Annotations
  ANNOTATION                        VALUE
  org.opencontainers.image.created  2022-12-11T22:54:07Z
  org.opencontainers.image.ref_name ghcr.io/jimmyraywv/pacbook:v0.1.0-793309a9ea
  org.opencontainers.image.title    ghcr.io/jimmyraywv/pacbook
  org.openpolicyregistry.type       policy
```

The policy CLI keeps a local index in my user directory:

```
# cat ~/.policy/policies-root/index.json

{
    "schemaVersion": 2,
    "manifests": [
        {
            "mediaType":
            "application/vnd.oci.image.layer.v1.tar+gzip",
            "digest": "sha256:cabd3...2e187",
            "size": 348,
            "annotations": {
                "org.opencontainers.image.ref.name":
                "ghcr.io/jimmyraywv/pacbook:v0.1.0-793309a9ea"
            }
        }
    ]
}
```

Just like in Chapter 2, we can use the `tar` command to view the actual files contained within the tarball:

```
# View tar files
$ tar tvf ~/.policy/policies-root/blobs/sha256/\
cabd3a636541622cde59b92bf22033627bc137840cefc57ed6265f000a12e187
-rw-------  0 0       0          72 Dec 31  1969 /data.json
-rw-------  0 0       0         160 Dec 31  1969 /bundle-material/policy.rego
-rw-------  0 0       0          45 Dec 31  1969 /.manifest
```

To use the image I created, I called the `policy repl` command and specified the policy. I then viewed the data:

```
# Run OPA repl with newly-created policy/data bundle
$ policy repl ghcr.io/jimmyraywv/pacbook:v0.1.0-793309a9ea
running policy [ghcr.io/jimmyraywv/pacbook:v0.1.0-793309a9ea]

# View data in OPA repl
> data
{
  "normal": {
    "stuff": [
      {
        "lead": "jimmy",
        "method": "GET",
        "project": "book"
      }
    ]
  },
  "pacbook": {
    "things": {
      "allow": false
    }
  }
}
```

Next, I pushed the image to the remote registry:

```
# Push image
$ make push
[METADATA]
timestamp: [2022-12-11_05:58:23PM]
git commit: [793309a9eaf0ad39a61c5c964e813299752da8ee]
Image version: [v0.1.0-793309a9ea]

policy push ghcr.io/jimmyraywv/pacbook:v0.1.0-793309a9ea

Resolved ref [ghcr.io/jimmyraywv/pacbook:v0.1.0-793309a9ea].
digest: sha256:cabd3a636541622cde59b92bf22033627bc137840cefc57ed6265f000a12e187

Pushed ref [ghcr.io/jimmyraywv/pacbook:v0.1.0-793309a9ea].
digest: sha256:7a6b6d5187bb6de682609f671dc3012499726f407b1fcb08e2f06fae007801bc
```

Once pushed, I ran my local OPA with the OCI image downloaded from the remote registry using an OPA config file.

According to the GitHub project, OPCR is still a work in progress. My personal experience with OPCR is that the CLI user experience is easy to learn, as it resembles the Docker CLI as well as the OPA CLI. The project—the OCI image delivery vector—looks promising.

Summary

In this chapter, we discussed privileged access management (PAM) and the principle of least privilege (PoLP). We explored role-based access control (RBAC) and attribute-based access control (ABAC) as well as how PaC could be used to dynamically manage these access control models.

RBAC is often used to control access in organizations where users are arranged into groups or organizational structures. Because of the central management of entitlements, RBAC is easier to audit. However, as RBAC permissions across the organization become more granular, the RBAC roles and policies grow, becoming more complex and difficult to manage.

ABAC works well in flatter organizations or even in customer-facing applications, where users are not arranged into hierarchies. However, given the nature of ABAC and its reliance on data about resources and users, which is spread across systems, it is usually less transparent than RBAC and more difficult to audit.

Using PaC, we realized the difference between RBAC and ABAC and the scenarios where they would be used. Understanding the different AuthZ models will help you choose the right option when adding AuthZ to your applications and services. RBAC is well known; however, ABAC offers a potentially more dynamic AuthZ model.

We then moved on to manage PaC policies and data with bundle servers. We learned how to connect OPA servers to bundle servers with bearer token AuthZ, ETag support, and TLS to auto-load signed bundles with signature verification. These features are table stakes for automated support of PaC policy and data management. Please use the example bundle management server to help you understand the processes needed to manage and serve bundles, and decide if another solution would be better for you.

Finally, we explored policy-based access management (PBAM) tooling with Strya DAS, Styra Run, Open Policy Administration Layer (OPAL), and OCI images with Open Policy Containers. These tools are meant to offload much of the operational overhead of policy and data management, and they even provide SDKs and APIs for application integration to SaaS environments. Given what we learned in Chapter 2 about building, signing, and using bundles, it's easy to understand the utility of these solutions when we consider AuthZ across multiple systems or an enterprise.

After seven years of experience with PaC, I am a firm believer in the value proposition that PaC offers organizations. AuthZ use cases are no exception. The tooling that is now available—that which we explored in this chapter—makes it easier to manage policies and data across the enterprises and multiple OPA agents.

Now that we have a thorough understanding of PaC, AuthZ, and PBAM, we are going to shift gears in Chapter 4 and begin our exploration of how PaC is used with Kubernetes to enhance AuthZ, security, and best practices. Chapter 4 is a primer on multiple PaC use cases in Kubernetes. Once we have that foundational knowledge, we will start our survey of specific PaC solutions in subsequent chapters.

Policy as Code and Kubernetes

In 2018, I took over leading a team that was building tooling to provision Kubernetes, similar to Kubernetes the hard way (*https://oreil.ly/t8nQZ*). We were building tooling, mostly using Bash shell scripts, to provision and manage clusters. I had been working with Kubernetes (*https://kubernetes.io*) part-time for almost two years at that point. We had considered tools like kOps (*https://oreil.ly/kops*) to help build and upgrade clusters, but at the time, kOps did not meet our cloud computing needs.

 Even with the automated services, platforms, APIs, and tools available today to help folks build and manage Kubernetes, I recommend that you investigate and try running Kubernetes the hard way. That experience was invaluable to my learning curve.

One of my first tasks was to implement controls inside Kubernetes to prevent unwanted cluster changes. We held an internal hackathon to help generate ideas about Kubernetes controls. That is when I first used PaC for Kubernetes and discovered how I could integrate policies into the Kubernetes API.

In this chapter, we will explore how PaC is used with Kubernetes to build controls that prevent unwanted changes, to erect guardrails that guide best practices, and to perform authorization. I will introduce concepts about PaC and Kubernetes integration, using examples where necessary. In subsequent chapters, we will dive deeper into each PaC solution.

I will start by briefly reviewing the CNCF and introducing Kubernetes community organization; then I will ask you to hit the ground running with me as we go on a quick tour of use cases and solutions that PaC can offer Kubernetes. We will set the stage for deeper dives into each PaC solution later in this book.

CNCF and Policy Management

In Chapter 1, I introduced the Cloud Native Computing Foundation (CNCF) and its project structure. Here, I want to briefly cover how Kubernetes fits in. Kubernetes was accepted into the CNCF in 2016 and is now a graduated project. However, the CNCF is still heavily involved in the direction of Kubernetes and the Kubernetes project community (*https://oreil.ly/community*).

Within the Kubernetes project community, management of activities is arranged into special interest groups (SIGs). These SIGs encompass a broad spectrum of efforts meant to improve Kubernetes. Each SIG is a community of practice focused on specific and related efforts in the Kubernetes project. In particular, the Auth Special Interest Group (*https://oreil.ly/C57H8*), a.k.a. sig-auth, focuses on ongoing efforts related to Kubernetes authentication (AuthN), authorization (AuthZ), and security policy.

When a narrower focus is needed for a temporary effort, working groups (WGs) are formed. SIGs sponsor WGs and are also stakeholders of WG efforts.

The Policy WG (*https://oreil.ly/wg-policy*) focuses on policy management architecture and policy proposals for Kubernetes. Sig-auth sponsors the Policy WG and is a listed stakeholder. In Chapter 3, you were introduced to the Kubernetes Policy Management Whitepaper that is stored in the sig-security project.

> For more information about the lifecycle of Kubernetes SIGs, WGs, and user groups (UGs), please refer to this Kubernetes community documentation (*https://oreil.ly/wan95*).

With this synopsis of the Kubernetes SIG and WG organization behind us, let's look at how we can enhance and control Kubernetes operations with PaC.

Implementing Security Controls and Controlling Behaviors

The rich feature set provided by Kubernetes reduces or outright eliminates common tasks and heavy lifting involved in running containers at scale. Among those features are security configurations, along with settings that can be made to follow best practices. Just as security is not simply something bolted on at the end of a software project, planning a Kubernetes cluster—or collection thereof—requires security designs and decisions at the onset—Day 0, if you will—of your Kubernetes journey.

Even with all the levers that you can pull to secure your Kubernetes applications and strengthen the robustness of their execution, Kubernetes does not force you to follow best practices or recommended security settings. That gap can be filled with PaC. And to understand how PaC enhances Kubernetes and helps control behavior within clusters, we must first examine how changes are made within a running Kubernetes cluster via API server requests.

API Server Requests

Kubernetes components are divided into those that run on the control plane (CP) and those that run on nodes in the data plane (DP). CP components manage the cluster. Without diving too deep into Kubernetes architecture, Figure 4-1 shows the relationship between the CP components and the DP (node) components.

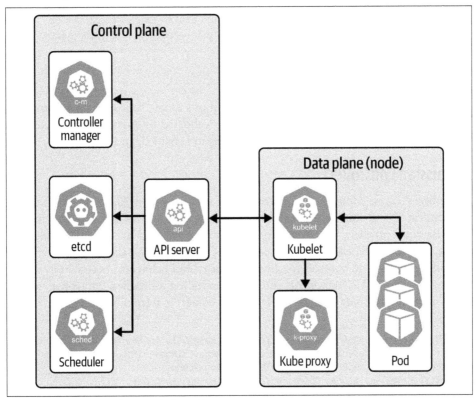

Figure 4-1. Control plane and data plane components

The key component that ties things together is the Kubernetes API server. The API server handles requests from external clients, such as kubectl, as well as internal clients, such as node kubelet agents and controllers.

Kubectl (*https://oreil.ly/39F3b*) is the CLI used to manage and interact with Kubernetes clusters.

As you can see in Figure 4-1, communication between the node kubelet agents and the CP goes through the API server. No kubelet agent talks directly to the CP components. Additionally, no components—save for the API server—talk directly to etcd, the Kubernetes key-value store that houses cluster configurations. The idea behind this architecture is that changes that come through the API server are persisted into etcd. Then, those changes are sent to the CP components to make changes to the cluster.

Please refer to the Kubernetes component overview documentation (*https://oreil.ly/8VjZe*) for a more in-depth view of Kubernetes architecture.

Kubernetes API server requests can be mutated or validated via admission controllers that are compiled into the API server code or validated by AuthZ services. Next, we will explore the admission controllers, how they are enabled, and their types.

Admission Controllers

In Kubernetes, an *admission controller* is code that runs after API server requests are authenticated and authorized but before the request results in a change to etcd. Admission controllers are compiled into Kubernetes and are meant to intercept inbound requests. These controllers can be of type mutating, validating, or even both, and they add built-in controls for cluster security and behavior. As shown in the following minikube API server log entries, 12 mutating admission controllers and 11 validating admission controllers are loaded by default in minikube 1.27.1:

```
# Mutating Admission Controllers
Loaded 12 mutating admission controller(s) successfully in the following
order: NamespaceLifecycle,LimitRanger,ServiceAccount,NodeRestriction,
TaintNodesByCondition,Priority,DefaultTolerationSeconds,
DefaultStorageClass,StorageObjectInUseProtection,RuntimeClass,
DefaultIngressClass,MutatingAdmissionWebhook.

# Validating Admission Controllers
Loaded 11 validating admission controller(s) successfully in the
following order: LimitRanger,ServiceAccount,PodSecurity,Priority,
PersistentVolumeClaimResize,RuntimeClass,CertificateApproval,
CertificateSigning,CertificateSubjectRestriction,
ValidatingAdmissionWebhook,ResourceQuota.
```

Admission controllers do not respond to Kubernetes read operations, like get, watch, and list. To prevent these operations, you need to use AuthZ like RBAC.

As you can see in the preceding admission controller lists, LimitRanger and Service-Account are both mutating and validating admission controllers. You may also notice that two "webhook" admission controllers are listed:

- MutatingAdmissionWebhook
- ValidatingAdmissionWebhook

These two "webhook" admission controllers are actually used to call configured dynamic admission controllers, like the aforementioned policy engine services. In the next section, we will dive deeper into dynamic admission controllers and how their runtime utility enhances Kubernetes.

Dynamic Admission Controllers

Virtually every change introduced to a Kubernetes cluster enters through the API server. This means that changes progress through the same API-server request flow—depicted in Figure 4-2—on their way to be persisted into etcd. *Dynamic admission controllers* allow cluster users to add custom controllers to this API server request flow to change how requests are allowed to proceed without having to customize the API server. In this way, dynamic admission controllers are an extension to the API server. If the contents of a request are not persisted into etcd, that change is not made to the cluster. In fact, one of the most important purposes of the Kubernetes components is to maintain the state of the cluster based on what is successfully stored in etcd.

In the request flow shown in Figure 4-2, there are two steps at which PaC can be used to affect the inbound request. The *mutating admission webhook* calls out to a configured policy engine service running on nodes in the cluster DP. The request payload is sent to this service, and if a mutating policy matches the request, then the service mutates the payload before it continues to object schema validation.

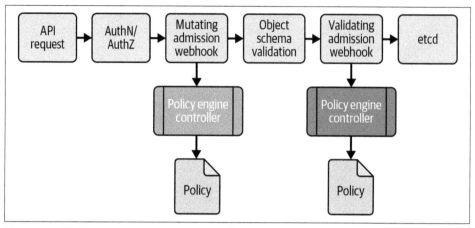

Figure 4-2. Kubernetes API server request flow

After object schema validation, there is a second step in the flow where a DP service can affect the inbound request. The *validating admission webhook* calls out to a configured service to have the current payload validated. In the case where the DP service is connected to a policy engine, the validation is done by any policies that match. If the validation returns true, then the change is persisted to etcd, and downstream processes change the cluster. However, if the validation results in a false (invalid) return, then the request stops, and the status is immediately returned back to the calling client by the API server. An example of a returned failure message for using the latest container image tag can be seen in the following console output:

```
Error from server ("DEPLOYMENT_INVALID": "GOOD_REGISTRY/read-only-container:
latest" container image "latest" tag/version is not allowed. Resource ID
(ns/name/kind): "opa-test/test/Deployment"): error when creating "test.yaml":
 admission webhook <WEBHOOK_NAME>" denied the request: "DEPLOYMENT_INVALID":
 "GOOD_REGISTRY/read-only-container:latest" container image "latest"
 tag/version is not allowed. Resource ID (ns/name/kind):
 "opa-test/test/Deployment"
```

Now that we have a high-level understanding of why dynamic admission controllers exist, let's dive deeper into their operation by examining how they communicate with the API server.

API server request payload

The Kubernetes API server sends an AdmissionReview API object (*https://oreil.ly/ ScWww*) to the configured webhook services. This object contains the request payload sent to the API server by the client requesting the change to the cluster. Mutating and validating webhook services are sent API server requests via POST requests as Content-Type: "application/json". These post requests deliver the AdmissionReview API object to be matched and handled by the webhook services. Depending on the PaC solution being used, these AdmissionReview objects can be captured from the policy engine logs.

One of the easiest ways to see what this AdmissionReview object looks like is to create one from a source Kubernetes resource YAML file. The kube-review GitHub project (*https://oreil.ly/kube-review*) is a utility that is used to model an AdmissionReview object from a source YAML file. This is also very handy when you want to prototype or test policies for admission.

The following Pod YAML file will be used to create an AdmissionReview object—out of band from an API server request—using the kube-review create command:

```
# test-pod.yaml
apiVersion: v1
kind: Pod
metadata:
  name: test-pod
  namespace: policy-test
spec:
  containers:
    - name: test-pause
      image: <IMAGE_URL>
      imagePullPolicy: Always
      securityContext:
        allowPrivilegeEscalation: false
        runAsUser: 1000
        readOnlyRootFilesystem: true
```

After installing the kube-review utility, the following command can be used to create an AdmissionReview object that reflects what the Kubernetes API server would send to the admission webhook services:

```
# Use kube-review to create AdmissionReview object
$ kube-review create test-pod.yaml > kube-review.json

{
    "kind": "AdmissionReview",
    "apiVersion": "admission.k8s.io/v1",
    "request": {
        "uid": "d44c6009-1a75-428d-80ac-ba2ad13b985e",
        "kind": {
            "group": "",
            "version": "v1",
            "kind": "Pod"
        },
        "resource": {
            "group": "",
            "version": "v1",
            "resource": "pods"
        },
        "requestKind": {
```

```
            "group": "",
            "version": "v1",
            "kind": "Pod"
        },
        "requestResource": {
            "group": "",
            "version": "v1",
            "resource": "pods"
        },
        "name": "test-pod",
        "namespace": "test",
        "operation": "CREATE",
        "userInfo": {
            "username": "kube-review",
            "uid": "66befdaa-1097-4249-9279-4fe5ed2fa4f3"
        },
        "object": {
            "kind": "Pod",
            "apiVersion": "v1",
            "metadata": {
                "name": "test-pod",
                "namespace": "test",
                "creationTimestamp": null
            },
            "spec": {
                "containers": [
                    {
                        "name": "test-pause",
                        "image": "<IMAGE_URL>",
                        "resources": {},
                        "imagePullPolicy": "Always",
                        "securityContext": {
                            "runAsUser": 1000,
                            "readOnlyRootFilesystem": true,
                            "allowPrivilegeEscalation": false
                        }
                    }
                ]
            },
            "status": {}
        },
        "oldObject": null,
        "dryRun": true,
        "options": {
            "kind": "CreateOptions",
            "apiVersion": "meta.k8s.io/v1"
        }
    }
}
```

The preceding JSON AdmissionReview object would be interpreted and perhaps logged by services integrated to the API server and running on nodes in the DP. Unless stopped by admission control, the request will ultimately result in an etcd update and a Pod created (test-pod) in the `policy-test` Namespace.

Admission response

The webhook services respond to the API server request with AdmissionReview objects containing response elements. This is a contract they must fulfill. The following responses range from minimal to advanced responses with status codes, messages, patches (mutating), and warnings:

```
// minimal response - allowed and uid
{
  "apiVersion": "admission.k8s.io/v1",
  "kind": "AdmissionReview",
  "response": {
    "uid": "<value from request.uid>",
    "allowed": true
  }
}

// Response with error code and message
{
  "apiVersion": "admission.k8s.io/v1",
  "kind": "AdmissionReview",
  "response": {
    "uid": "<value from request.uid>",
    "allowed": false,
    "status": {
      "code": 403,
      "message": "something wasn't allowed"
    }
  }
}

// Mutating webhook response with base64 encoded patch
{
  "apiVersion": "admission.k8s.io/v1",
  "kind": "AdmissionReview",
  "response": {
    "uid": "<value from request.uid>",
    "allowed": true,
    "patchType": "JSONPatch",
    "patch": "base64 encoded Patch"
  }
}

// Response with warnings
{
  "apiVersion": "admission.k8s.io/v1",
```

```
  "kind": "AdmissionReview",
  "response": {
    "uid": "<value from request.uid>",
    "allowed": true,
    "warnings": [
      "<WARNING_1>",
      "<WARNING_2>"
    ]
  }
}
```

Every response must return the `allowed` element and the `uid` element. The `uid` element must match the `uid` of the original API server POST request.

PaC engines will use the properties in the AdmissionReview object to match policies to inbound requests and mutate or validate requests. The primary method for integrating PaC to the Kubernetes API server is through admission controllers. We will explore these components next.

Configuring dynamic admission controllers

Kubernetes dynamic admission controllers (*https://oreil.ly/xm2af*) are made possible by loading the MutatingAdmissionWebhook and ValidatingAdmissionWebhook compiled admission controllers when the API server starts. With these two admission controllers running, we can configure extensions to the API server request flow at runtime using services running on DP nodes. This means that after the API server is up and the cluster is running, we can add policy engine services to the DP at runtime and configure them to be called by API server webhooks. This approach reduces the need to customize API server settings from cluster to cluster.

Mutating webhook configuration. The dynamic admission webhooks are categorized as *mutating* and *validating*, just like the compiled admission controllers. The webhook configurations are used to configure how DP services—installed after the cluster starts and the API server is configured—can be used to communicate with and extend the API server. Let's start with an example of a mutating webhook configuration. Using the following `kubectl` command, we can explore an example `mutating webhookconfiguration` resource:

```
# Get mutating webhook configuration
$ kubectl get mutatingwebhookconfiguration <WEBHOOK_CONFIGURATION_NAME> \
-o yaml

apiVersion: admissionregistration.k8s.io/v1
kind: MutatingWebhookConfiguration
metadata:
  name: <WEBHOOK_CONFIGURATION_NAME>
webhooks:
```

```
- admissionReviewVersions:
  - v1
  clientConfig:
    caBundle: <x509_CERT>
    url: https://127.0.0.1:23443/mutate
  failurePolicy: Ignore
  matchPolicy: Equivalent
  namespaceSelector: {}
  objectSelector: {}
  reinvocationPolicy: IfNeeded
  rules:
  - apiGroups:
    - ""
    apiVersions:
    - v1
    operations:
    - CREATE
    resources:
    - pods
    scope: '*'
  sideEffects: None
  timeoutSeconds: 10
```

Let's look closer at some of the settings:

admissionReviewVersions
> Array of supported versions for the webhook integration. The API server will send a request with the first version in the list and traverse the list until a suitable (if any) version succeeds.

clientConfig.caBundle
> An x509 certificate used to authenticate the Kubernetes API server (client) to the webhook service over TLS for secure communication.

clientConfig.url
> Internal cluster address of the webhook service.

failurePolicy
> The webhook failure policy determines what happens when a call from the API server to the webhook fails to return in the configured timeout.

rules
> Rules for what Kubernetes resource requests should be sent by the API server to the webhook service.

Given the preceding settings, this mutating webhook will receive authenticated requests from the API server when Pods are created. The API server will wait a max of 10 seconds for a response from the mutation service. The API server will ignore failures and proceed to the step in the request flow, regardless of success or failure.

Validating webhook configuration. Validating webhooks are configured similarly to mutating webhooks. Let's explore an example with the following `kubectl` command:

```
# Get validating admission webhook configuration
$ kubectl get validatingwebhookconfiguration <WEBHOOK_CONFIGURATION_NAME> -oyaml

apiVersion: admissionregistration.k8s.io/v1
kind: ValidatingWebhookConfiguration
metadata:
  name: <WEBHOOK_CONFIGURATION_NAME>
webhooks:
- admissionReviewVersions:
  - v1
  clientConfig:
    caBundle: <x509_CERT>
    Service:   ❶
      name: <WEBHOOK_SERVICE_NAME>
      namespace: <WEBHOOK_SERVICE_NAMESPACE>
      port: 443
  failurePolicy: Fail
  matchPolicy: Equivalent
  name: <WEBHOOK_NAME>
  namespaceSelector:   ❷
    matchExpressions:
    - key: <LABEL_NAME>
      operator: NotIn
      values:
      - ignore
  objectSelector: {}
  rules:
  - apiGroups:
    - '*'
    apiVersions:
    - '*'
    operations:
    - CREATE
    - UPDATE
    resources:
    - '*'
    scope: '*'
  sideEffects: None
  timeoutSeconds: 10
```

❶ Internal Kubernetes service address of the validating webhook service called by the API server

❷ Namespace select rule for including/excluding Namespaces from processing with this validating webhook

---

Given the preceding settings, this validating webhook will receive authenticated requests from the API server when any Kubernetes resource with any API group or version is created or updated. The exception to this rule is that no request for resources being created or updated in Namespaces with the following label will be sent to the validating webhook service:

```
# Label to ignore a namespace
metadata.label.<LABEL_NAME>=ignore
```

 It is usually seen as a best practice to exclude system Namespaces and Namespaces in which the webhook services are running. This is done so that cluster operations are not compromised by overly restrictive or incorrect policy settings. Compensating controls would be to use RBAC to restrict access to these Namespaces. If dynamic mutating or validating admission controllers are causing issues with the cluster, the corresponding configurations can be disabled to regain cluster control.

The API server will wait a max of 10 seconds for a response from the validation service. If the API server does not receive a response from the service within the configured timeout period, then the request, valid or otherwise, will fail.

 Kubernetes dynamic admission controllers use webhook integration to call validating and mutating services. These calls have timeout settings (max 30 seconds, default 10 seconds) for how long the call will wait before a timeout occurs. The webhook configurations also include a `failurePolicy` setting to configure how the API server should respond when the webhook call doesn't return within the configured timeout period. The webhook will either fail open (where the API server request is allowed to proceed) or fail closed (where the API server request is blocked). The default is to fail closed.

There are trade-offs for each failure scenario. While a fail-open scenario could be seen as a potential security issue, a fail-closed scenario could cause operational issues for the cluster. Further information about failure policies can be found in the Kubernetes documentation (*https://oreil.ly/4BGnk*).

Data beyond AdmissionReview

With the AdmissionReview object, policy validations are context aware, with the context being within the boundaries of the API server request under evaluation. This means that the policy validations' primary data source is the AdmissionReview object. However, there are scenarios where additional—external—data is useful, if not required. A few of those use cases are:

Container image signature verification

External data provides the container image signature and the required public key used to verify the image.

Cluster-aware validation

When an API server request validation needs to consider existing cluster resources to render a decision.

Non-Kubernetes data needed for validation

Occasionally, there are dependencies that need to be modeled for correct validation to occur.

External data can find its way into PaC solutions in multiple ways. The following are just a few of these that we will cover later in this book:

- External data is pulled at evaluation time, as needed.
- External cluster data is collected by a sidecar container that listens to cluster change and is updated into the policy engine on a regular cadence.
- External data from outside the cluster is pushed into the policy engine at startup and when data changes.

Now, let's look at the first operation that can be done in the Kubernetes API server request flow: mutation.

Mutating Resources

Kubernetes mutating admission controllers can mutate inbound server requests—via in-place patching—before requests are validated and used to change the cluster. This is a well-known pattern in application development, where client-side data is translated, coerced, or changed using server-side actions before the data is validated and saved into server-side data storage. To see how this works, you can try it using kubectl. First, we will apply the following Namespace and Pod resources:

```
apiVersion: v1
kind: Namespace
metadata:
  name: test
---
apiVersion: v1
kind: Pod
metadata:
  name: test-pod
  namespace: test
spec:
  containers:
    - name: test-pause
      image: <IMAGE_URL>
```

```
    imagePullPolicy: Always
    securityContext:
      allowPrivilegeEscalation: false
      runAsUser: 1000
      readOnlyRootFilesystem: true
```

Next, we can add a label to the Pod with the following `kubectl patch` command:

```
# Add a label to a Pod via the kubectl patch command
$ kubectl -n test patch pod test-pod --patch-file patch.yaml -o yaml

# patch.yaml
metadata:
  labels:
    owner: jimmy
```

The following YAML contains the new Pod configuration:

```
# Patched Pod
apiVersion: v1
kind: Pod
metadata:
  name: test-pod
  namespace: test
  labels:
    owner: jimmy
...
```

Kubernetes API server request mutation is used all the time, mostly unnoticed. Some of the use cases I have used and seen include:

- Inject sidecar containers into Deployments for instrumentation, such as service mesh proxies, observability, and PaC solutions
- Add labels or annotations to resources
- Change security settings in Pods and containers
- Add tolerations and node-affinity settings to Pods for multitenancy solutions
- Change container image registries

You can also review some of the mutating admission controllers in the preceding list.

 After mutation, it's still good zero-trust and DiD practices to validate inbound Kubernetes API server requests, ensuring that the desired settings are present in the request payload even after mutation.

There is a difference of opinion among the Kubernetes community when it comes to using mutation of inbound API server requests. Some believe that it helps reduce the number of validation errors and makes life easier for Kubernetes users. Others believe that it introduces drift into the API server request and should not be used. I can see both sides of this argument as valid, though I tend to use mutation infrequently.

Next, let's explore validating inbound API server requests.

Validating Resources

Validating Kubernetes API server requests prevents unwanted changes to your clusters. As mentioned before, this is a valid approach for implementing additional security and best practices.

Validation use cases span security controls and best practices. Some of the validation use cases I have seen—and for which I have written PaC policies—are:

- Enforce Pod and container security configurations
- Enforce container resource settings
- Restrict from where container images are sourced
- Prevent use of `latest` tag or no version tags on container images
- Enforce multitenancy settings (node-affinity, taints, tolerations, etc.)
- Validate container image signatures
- Validate ingress and provide collision protection
- Enforce Namespace quotas and limit ranges
- Enforce Pod priority classes
- Enforce Pod disruption budgets
- Prevent external IP addresses from being used in ClusterIP services
- Prevent resource creation or modifications in specific Namespaces (this is also an AuthZ use case)

Let's take a look at an example validation policy used in the jsPolicy PaC solution:

```
# Example jsPolicy validating policy
apiVersion: policy.jspolicy.com/v1beta1
kind: JsPolicy
metadata:
  name: "no-default-ns.jimmyray.io"
spec:
  operations: ["CREATE","UPDATE"]
  resources: ["*"]
  scope: Namespaced
  javascript: |
    if (request.namespace === "default") {
      deny("Create and Update in the default namespace is not allowed!");
    }
```

As you can see, the preceding policy applies to CREATE and UPDATE operations on any resource in the default Namespace. Properties from the AdmissionReview object—Namespace and operation—are used by this policy to evaluate the incoming Kubernetes API server request and prevent these unwanted changes, as defined by the policy.

 It's a best practice to not use the default Namespace in a Kubernetes cluster. Because the default behavior of the kubectl CLI is to select the default Namespace when no Namespace is specified in the command or the kubeconfig file, the default Namespace is easily polluted and potentially compromised. Using a validating admission policy to prevent the use of the default Namespace substantially reduces the chances of errant use of this Namespace and nondeterministic behavior.

In the following section, we will briefly explore API server request latency.

API Server Request Latency and Webhook Order

In Chapter 6 of *Site Reliability Engineering* (O'Reilly), authors Betsy Beyer, Chris Jones, Niall Richard Murphy, and Jennifer Petoff introduced the monitoring concept of the "Four Golden Signals": latency, traffic, errors, and saturation. In this section, we are going to briefly examine latency and how it affects API server requests in the context of admission control.

In the case of the Kubernetes API server, *latency* is how long the API server takes to respond to, or serve, a request. That latency is directly affected by the number of admission controllers and dynamic admission controller webhooks that perform processing of inbound API server requests. To prevent API server issues due to latency, you should consider the number of admission controllers and admission webhooks as well as the aggregate timeout settings of all of them.

The order in which admission controllers execute is also important for controlling API server latency. For example, in the case of dynamic admission controllers, the API server calls mutating and validating webhooks differently. Mutating webhooks are called serially—in random order—to avoid collisions. Validating webhooks are called concurrently—in parallel. So, in the case of mutating webhooks, individually configured timeout settings can increase the aggregate timeout of the mutation phase and contribute to overall API server request latency.

The default timeout setting for Kubernetes API server requests is 60 seconds. Changing this setting can result in not enough time for API server requests to successfully execute or too much allowed time, leading to possible denial-of-service attacks (*https://oreil.ly/2nQC4*). Given that the maximum timeout for admission controllers is 30 seconds, processing API server requests by multiple admission controllers can cause API server requests to time out, resulting in failed requests.

It is a best practice to tune your API server timeout settings while considering the PaC webhooks that will potentially execute in your clusters. This tuning may change as your clusters become busier. Part of tuning includes setting respective timeouts to the lowest possible duration without introducing timeout errors.

We have looked at how Kubernetes API server requests can be mutated and validated and how admission controllers affect API server latency; however, what do we do with resources that existed before new policies were added or when the PaC engines don't catch violations? Let's take a look at PaC auditing and background scanning.

Auditing and Background Scanning Existing Resources

As mentioned earlier, mutating and validating dynamic admission controllers can be configured to fail open or closed. In the previous mutating and validating examples, the mutating webhook configuration was set to fail open while the validating webhook configuration was set to fail closed. Setting the webhook configuration to fail open—`failurePolicy: Ignore`—errors on the side of caution. If for any reason the webhook fails to respond, the changes will proceed regardless of missing mutation or validation. However, this setting also provides the biggest chance of permitting unwanted changes to update the cluster. It is considered less secure.

If you decide to set the webhooks to fail closed—`failurePolicy: Fail`—changes will not be allowed to progress if the webhooks don't successfully respond. Although this is more secure, you can also compromise the operation of your cluster by preventing any changes. You must remember that many changes to a cluster originate from within the cluster, as opposed to external client requests. Compromising the operation of your cluster in this way is also known as "bricking" your cluster.

To avoid gaps in your security and best practices controls, some Kubernetes PaC solutions support auditing (e.g., Gatekeeper) or background scanning (e.g., Kyverno). With auditing or background scanning, PaC solutions augment the event-driven nature of API server requests and log or report on missed violations. This helps prevent unwanted changes that slipped through when webhook services did not respond in the allotted time period and the request proceeded. Another great use case for auditing and background scanning is to perform impact testing and analysis when releasing new policies to clusters, without adversely affecting existing cluster resources with potentially disrupting enforcement policies. As we dive deeper into individual Kubernetes PaC solutions, we will explore these features and their respective settings and operations.

Next, let's look at how we can reduce the heavy lifting of Kubernetes and policy management by using PaC automation to generate resources and policies.

Generating Resources and Policies

The best part about PaC integration to the Kubernetes API server requests is that the controls we implement are primarily preventive. We can modify and even prevent unwanted changes from happening in our clusters with PaC before they happen. However, use cases exist that require us to react to events in the cluster. For example, the Kubernetes Cluster Autoscaler responds to unschedulable Pod events by provisioning additional cluster compute nodes.

PaC solutions can also be used to respond to cluster events. For example, some Kubernetes PaC solutions provide the ability to generate Kubernetes resources and policies on the fly, in response to the application of other Kubernetes resources. Given a compatible PaC solution, you can reduce your policy-management overhead by using resource and policy generation. Resource and policy generation increases the expressive nature of policies and reduces the effort to maintain policies for all resources.

For example, with Kyverno (*https://kyverno.io*) you can write policies for Pods and use the Kyverno Auto-Gen (*https://oreil.ly/7TgEg*) feature to generate policies for corresponding controller resources that create Pods, such as Deployment resources. With policy Auto-Gen, you can reduce the need to manage policies for multiple resource types. Gatekeeper has a similar feature through policy expansion. I cover Gatekeeper and Kyverno in Chapters 7 and 8, respectively.

 Kyverno Auto-Gen also works with the Kyverno CLI (*https://oreil.ly/YFEXp*). With the CLI, you can apply policies to YAML—outside of the Kubernetes cluster—before API server requests are made. For the record, Kyverno Auto-Gen works in the CLI as well.

Another Kyverno feature, generate resources (*https://oreil.ly/NSSQu*), uses generate-policy types to build policies in response to applied Kubernetes resources. Given a multitenancy use case where applications are isolated into their respective Namespaces, generate policies can be used to prepare the Namespace for use after it is created and before applications are deployed.

For example, using a generate policy, you can generate a deny-all network policy resource for each provisioned Namespace as part of the provisioning process. This will lock down egress and ingress network traffic for all Pods in the Namespace. When the application is finally deployed to the Namespace, network policies with appropriate egress and ingress rules can be used to provide the least-privileged network access needed for the respective application. This would then be followed up with the appropriate mutation or validation policies to ensure that unauthorized network access is not configured in the applied network policies.

jsPolicy has the controller policy feature—similar to generate resources—that reacts to cluster events. In Chapter 9, I cover jsPolicy.

PaC solutions are not always from the Kubernetes ecosystem. Next, we will look at "native" Kubernetes PaC solutions.

Kubernetes Native Policy Features

Until now, we have focused on PaC solutions that are added to clusters to decorate them with additional functionality to enforce best practices and security controls. However, Kubernetes includes native tools that can also be used to apply similar controls. Now we will explore these native tools.

Pod Security

Pods are the atomic unit-of-compute in Kubernetes; they contain containers. When creating Pods, security is primarily configured using the securityContext (*https:// oreil.ly/A6Grl*) elements at the Pod and container levels. The Pod-level securityContext, found in the Pod specification, is less granular than its container counterpart and is overridden by the container-level securityContext when settings overlap. Otherwise, Pod-level securityContext settings are used by all containers within the Pod and are often combined with container-level settings.

An example of a container-level securityContext with settings that are considered container security best practices is shown in the following YAML snippet:

```
# Container-level securityContext element - best practice settings
securityContext:
  allowPrivilegeEscalation: false
  runAsUser: 1000
  readOnlyRootFilesystem: true
  runAsNonRoot: true
  capabilities:
    drop: ["ALL"]
  seccompProfile:
    type: "RuntimeDefault"
```

The preceding container-level securityContext settings are designed to run a container with least-privilege access while also preventing the container from escalating privileges and making unwanted calls to the node operating system kernel.

In the Linux world, containers contain applications—code, libraries, and interpreters—that run in user space. *User space* refers to the area outside of the operating system kernel. The space inside the kernel is called *kernel space*. For applications to successfully operate in user space, they need resources—CPU, memory, disk, network, and so on—obtained from kernel space. Containers contain user space and make system calls to kernel space. Container security is used to limit what a container can do in user space to only that which it needs to operate. It is also meant to limit the system calls that can be made from a container to the kernel.

In the earlier days of Kubernetes, PodSecurityPolicy (PSP) resources were used to secure Pods and prevent unwanted behaviors from emanating from containers therein. PSPs enforced container security settings found in the Pod and container securityContext elements. However, PSPs were notoriously difficult to configure and use, and this resulted in many misconfigurations that lessened desired security or even hampered cluster operations.

Many Kubernetes administrators added PaC solutions to their clusters to enhance security, enforce desired behaviors, and prevent undesired behaviors. This often meant that default PSPs were left wide open, in privileged mode. PSP resources were deprecated (*https://oreil.ly/qFK7q*) in Kubernetes 1.21 and removed in Kubernetes 1.25.

Pod Security Admission

PSPs were a Kubernetes in-tree feature, and so it was highly desirable to replace them with another in-tree solution. The Pod Security Admission (PSA) (*https://oreil.ly/xFGbF*) controller is that Kubernetes in-tree replacement for PSP. This admission controller went beta in Kubernetes v1.23 and stable in v1.25. PSA implements the Kubernetes Pod Security Standards (PSS) (*https://oreil.ly/rYvfn*), which define 17 security controls for Pod configurations organized into three levels:

- Privileged (unsecure)
- Baseline (secure)
- Restricted (highly secure)

The term *in-tree*, when used with Kubernetes, refers to where Kubernetes functionality resides. When a feature is shipped within a Kubernetes release and available for use without installing additional software, that component is known as *in-tree*. As a reference, PSPs were an in-tree feature. PaC solutions are made available from the Kubernetes ecosystem and installed into or integrated with Kubernetes; PaC solutions are considered *out-of-tree*.

To be clear, the in-tree moniker is not necessarily an indicator of how simple to configure or user-friendly a feature is. In fact, PSPs were removed from Kubernetes in large part because of their complexity and difficult UX.

PSA implements PSS using three modes of operation. The modes, coupled with the PSS levels, create logical security policies that are used to control Pod security within a Kubernetes cluster by enforcing settings in the Pod and container securityContext elements. The PSA modes are:

Enforce
Policy violations will prevent Pods from provisioning.

Warn
Policy violations will cause the Kubernetes API server to respond with warnings.

Audit
Policy violations will cause audit annotations on events recorded in the Kubernetes API server audit logs.

PSA is an admission controller that is loaded when the Kubernetes API server starts. As seen in k8s-psa-pss-testing (*https://oreil.ly/osxpv*)—an OSS project that I created when I was on the AWS Kubernetes team and for which I am a maintainer—PSA can be customized at API server start. Without such customization, cluster-wide Pod security settings, using PSA and PSS, are set to the privileged PSS level by default for all three PSA modes. These default settings result in unsecure Pod security settings in the respective cluster.

To apply more secure PSA and PSS settings, Kubernetes Namespaces must opt into more security using Kubernetes Namespace labels. As shown in the following code snippet from the k8s-psa-pss-testing project, labels are used to opt the Namespace into specific PSA modes and PSS levels:

```
# Namespace labels for PSA and PSS settings
apiVersion: v1
kind: Namespace
metadata:
  name: policy-test
  labels:
    # pod-security.kubernetes.io/enforce: privileged
```

```
# pod-security.kubernetes.io/audit: privileged
# pod-security.kubernetes.io/warn: privileged

pod-security.kubernetes.io/enforce: baseline
pod-security.kubernetes.io/audit: baseline
pod-security.kubernetes.io/warn: baseline

# pod-security.kubernetes.io/enforce: restricted
# pod-security.kubernetes.io/audit: restricted
# pod-security.kubernetes.io/warn: restricted
```

Additionally, multiple combinations of PSA modes and PSS levels can be used. In the following example, PSA enforce mode is set for the PSS baseline level, while PSA audit and warn are set to PSS restricted. This satisfies the use case where you would want to enforce a baseline Pod security but also understand the potential impact of moving to PSS restricted:

```
# Mixed PSA modes and PSS levels
apiVersion: v1
kind: Namespace
metadata:
  name: policy-test
  labels:
    pod-security.kubernetes.io/enforce: baseline
    pod-security.kubernetes.io/audit: restricted
    pod-security.kubernetes.io/warn: restricted
```

PSA enforce is the only PSA mode that prevents changes from physically happening in a Kubernetes cluster. At the time of this writing, PSA enforce reacts only to Pod changes; it does not prevent other Kubernetes resources that create or update Pods from being created or updated—or any other resource, for that matter. For example, if a Kubernetes Deployment resource is applied to a cluster, and the Pod specifications violate the current PSA/PSS settings for the Namespace in which the Pods reside, the Pods would be rejected and prevented from being provisioned. However, the Deployment would be created with no outward indication that anything was wrong. The Pods just wouldn't start because the changes to provision the Pods would not be validated and allowed to reach etcd.

Since PSA enforce mode would not stop the Kubernetes Deployment, you would need to examine the status of the Deployment resource to determine why the Pods didn't start:

```
# Examine Deployment status to determine Pod start issues
$ kubectl -n policy-test get deploy test -oyaml

...
status:
  conditions:
...
```

```
- lastTransitionTime: "2022-07-12T23:56:10Z"
  lastUpdateTime: "2022-07-12T23:56:10Z"
  message: >
        'pods "test-59955f994-wl8hf" is forbidden: violates
        PodSecurity "restricted:latest":
        allowPrivilegeEscalation != false (container "test"
        must set securityContext.allowPrivilegeEscalation=false),
        unrestricted capabilities (container "test" must set
        securityContext.capabilities.drop=["ALL"]),
        runAsNonRoot != true (pod or container "test" must set
        securityContext.runAsNonRoot=true),
        seccompProfile (pod or container "test" must set
        securityContext.seccompProfile.type
        to "RuntimeDefault" or "Localhost")'
  reason: FailedCreate
  status: "True"
  type: ReplicaFailure
...
```

This is a difficult user experience and another reason why you would want to use all the PSA modes, not just enforce. The PSA warn and audit modes do react to Pod controllers like Kubernetes Deployment and DaemonSet resources. So, even though the Deployments would not be prevented, at least the Kubernetes API server client and API server audit logs would receive indications that there was a possible security violation. An example warning, sent to Kubernetes API server clients, can be seen in the following console output:

```
Warning: would violate PodSecurity "restricted:latest":
allowPrivilegeEscalation != false (container "test" must
set securityContext.allowPrivilegeEscalation=false),
unrestricted capabilities (container "test" must set
securityContext.capabilities.drop=["ALL"]), runAsNonRoot != true
(pod or container "test" must set securityContext.runAsNonRoot=true),
seccompProfile (pod or container "test" must set
securityContext.seccompProfile.type to "RuntimeDefault" or "Localhost")
deployment.apps/test created
```

For folks replacing PSP or implementing Pod security, PSA is a relatively simple migration, as long as the PSS levels meet their security needs. However, when Kubernetes users need more granularity and flexibility for their Pod security schemes or even want to enforce other behaviors of additional Kubernetes resources, PaC solutions are a better choice.

It's also important to understand that PaC can be run on the same cluster as PSA and PSS; they are not mutually exclusive. In fact, there are use cases where PaC enhances PSA and PSS security and user experience. For example, PaC can enhance the use of PSA and PSS by enforcing the PSA/PSS opt-in model. Using Kubernetes dynamic admission controllers, which were covered earlier in this chapter, PaC can enforce the PSA/PSS labels on Namespaces, via policies, and on mutating and validating webhook configurations.

 For more information and examples of using PaC solutions with Kubernetes PSA/PSS, please review this blog post that I coauthored with Jim Bugwadia of Nirmata, "Managing Pod Security on Amazon EKS with Kyverno" (*https://oreil.ly/_YgAJ*).

Not all PaC solutions come from outside of Kubernetes; in other words, not all PaC is out-of-tree and from the Kubernetes ecosystem. In this section, we reviewed PSA, an in-tree feature, which when coupled with PSS, provides the ability to apply policies for Pod security. We have only lightly explored Pod security in Kubernetes, though; we will dive deeper in subsequent chapters as we look at specific PaC solutions and their use with Kubernetes.

Now let's discover a new Kubernetes in-tree feature that is internalizing PaC as part of a Kubernetes in-tree offering.

Validating Admission Policy

As of Kubernetes v1.28, a new in-tree PaC solution, Validating Admission Policy (VAP) (*https://oreil.ly/D106S*), is in beta state. VAP is a native (in-tree) PaC solution embedded into Kubernetes that is "highly configurable." With VAP, cluster administrators and operators can build policies to enforce best practices and security controls.

Unlike PSA, VAP works on both Pod and non-Pod resources. VAP functionality resembles the PaC solutions that I will cover in the next several chapters. However, unlike those PaC solutions, VAP is built in to Kubernetes and requires no additional installed software.

To use this feature, you must apply the correct configurations to enable it in your cluster:

- Enable the ValidatingAdmissionPolicy feature gate.
- Enable the admissionregistration.k8s.io/v1alpha1 API.

The Kubernetes resources needed for VAP are:

ValidatingAdmissionPolicy
   Contains the rule logic for the policy, including which resources and operations the policy is applied to, as well as the Common Expression Language (CEL) expressions

ValidatingAdmissionPolicyBinding

Binds the policy to a specific scope, like a Namespace, and binds parameter resources to the policy

ParameterResource

Enables policy configuration to be separate from policy definition

VAP goes beyond Pod security and offers a PaC solution built into Kubernetes, based on CEL (*https://oreil.ly/cel-spec*) from Google. CEL syntax resembles that of C or Java and is embedded into YAML resources, as shown in the following VAP resource examples:

```
# ValidatingAdmissionPolicy resource
apiVersion: admissionregistration.k8s.io/v1alpha1
kind: ValidatingAdmissionPolicy
metadata:
  name: "deploy-history-policy.jimmyray.io"
spec:
  failurePolicy: Fail
  paramKind:
    apiVersion: rules.jimmyray.io/v1
    kind: HistoryLimit
  matchConstraints:
    resourceRules:
    - apiGroups:    ["apps"]
      apiVersions:  ["v1"]
      operations:   ["CREATE", "UPDATE"]
      resources:    ["deployments"]
  validations:
    - expression: "object.spec.revisionHistoryLimit <= params.historyLimit"
      reason: Invalid
```

The preceding ValidatingAdmissionPolicy resource applies to Deployments that are created or updated. The CEL syntax looks for the revisionHistoryLimit setting in the Deployment specification. The `failurePolicy` field can be set to Fail or Ignore. Fail means that if the CEL expression is false, then the API operation fails and doesn't change the cluster.

The `paramKind` field sets up the parameter resource that the ValidatingAdmission Policy will use to get the parameter(s) it needs to evaluate the API server request. That parameter resource is shown in the following YAML:

```
# Resource parameter
apiVersion: rules.jimmyray.io/v1
kind: HistoryLimit
metadata:
  name: "deploy-history-limit.jimmyray.io"
historyLimit: 3
```

To connect everything together, we need the ValidatingAdmissionPolicyBinding, shown in the following YAML:

```
# Binding
apiVersion: admissionregistration.k8s.io/v1alpha1
kind: ValidatingAdmissionPolicyBinding
metadata:
  name: "deploy-history-binding.jimmyray.io"
spec:
  policy: "deploy-history-policy.jimmyray.io"
  paramsRef:
    name: "deploy-history-limit.jimmyray.io"
  matchResources:
    namespaceSelectors:
    - key: environment,
      operator: In,
      values: ["policy-test"]
```

The ValidatingAdmissionPolicyBinding links the policy and parameter resources and then scopes the policy application to the `policy-test` Namespace.

To test this policy, we will use two Deployments:

- Known good spec with revisionHistoryLimit <= 3

- Known bad spec with revisionHistoryLimit > 3 (including a missing revision HistoryLimit field that defaults to 10)

The error message, triggered by validation failure, is shown in the following console output:

```
# VAP error message
ValidatingAdmissionPolicy 'deploy-history-policy.jimmyray.io' with binding
'deploy-history-binding.jimmyray.io' denied request: failed expression:
object.spec.revisionHistoryLimit <= 3
```

After years of working with PaC, I am cautiously optimistic about the potential of the ValidatingAdmissionPolicy feature underpinned by CEL. ValidatingAdmissionPolicy has the potential to reduce the burden of managing infrastructure for PaC solutions that have to be installed in Kubernetes after clusters are provisioned. I am also excited to finally dive deeper into CEL, with use cases that make it easy for me to apply my PaC experience.

In addition to the ValidatingAdmissionPolicy feature, the Kubernetes project is working on a new Kubernetes Enhancement Proposal (KEP) (*https://oreil.ly/keps*) for a MutatingAdmissionPolicy feature. KEP-3962 (*https://oreil.ly/kep-3962*) covers this new MutatingAdmissionPolicy feature. At the time of this writing, the feature is targeted for initial release in Kubernetes version v1.31

Now, let's briefly leave admission control behind and shift to access control as we look into how PaC can be used for AuthZ use cases in Kubernetes.

AuthZ Webhook Mode

At this point, I want to shift focus from admission control and look at another possibility for integrating PaC to Kubernetes for AuthZ. AuthZ in Kubernetes is designed to control access to the Kubernetes API server from external and internal clients. Kubernetes supports multiple modes of AuthZ, including node-level access, client AuthZ via webhook integration, and RBAC and ABAC, which we had explored in Chapter 3.

Unlike PaC for admission control—which is primarily integrated to dynamic admission controllers—the AuthZ webhook (*https://oreil.ly/iToz8*) integration is configured at the API server during cluster startup. This type of AuthZ is not used as much as RBAC, but it can be combined with RBAC for more granular security. Webhook mode can be very effective in integrating to external AuthN providers. The AuthZ webhook is not used as much as RBAC, mainly because of the need to configure the Kubernetes API server to integrate to cluster or remote services to handle AuthZ decisions. Additionally, Kubernetes multitenancy design decisions, like using granular Namespaces with RBAC and augmenting AuthZ with mutating and validating admission services—integrated via dynamic admission controllers—have traditionally been easier to configure and support.

As with admission controls, the Kubernetes API server posts JSON payloads to the AuthZ webhook services and receives allowed or denied decisions. The following example payload is sent from the API server:

```
// SubjectAccessReview
{
    "apiVersion": "authorization.k8s.io/v1beta1",
    "kind": "SubjectAccessReview",
    "spec": {
        "resourceAttributes": {
            "namespace": "kube-system",
            "verb": "get",
            "resource": "pods",
            "version": "v1"
        },
        "user": "jimmy",
        "groups": [
            "system:authenticated",
            "devops"
        ]
    }
}
```

The first thing to notice is that the SubjectAccessReview example payload is smaller than the AdmissionReview example payload from earlier in this chapter. This is mainly due to the fact that the AdmissionReview contains within it the actual cluster resource changes that are desired, and the SubjectAccessReview primarily contains desired actions and AuthN principle information, such as group membership.

Now that we understand the idea of AuthZ webhook mode, let's look closer at how AuthZ decisions are made with this approach.

AuthZ Decisions

The configuration YAML for the AuthZ Webhook reuses the kubeconfig (*https://oreil.ly/UmNjo*) format, where the *clusters* node is used to configure AuthZ services—also known as *authorizers*—called by the API server. The *users* node is used to configure the API server to securely communicate with the webhook service. This means that multiple—chained—authorizers can be used for AuthZ decisions by the API server.

Decisions returned by the authorizers are either allowed or denied, and these decisions are not always mutually exclusive. Since multiple authorizers can be configured to return AuthZ decisions, it's possible that not all authorizers can "allow" or authorize a user to perform an action. And if an authorizer cannot allow the access, that doesn't necessarily mean that the same authorizer can actually deny the access. It could be that the authorizer that cannot allow the access simply doesn't have deterministic rules to deny the access.

In the case of multiple authorizers, an authorizer that cannot allow an access, for whatever reason, may pass the decision on to subsequent authorizers by returning an `allowed=false` condition without returning a `denied=true` condition. An authorizer with the appropriate rules to act on the information passed in via SubjectAccessReview—with deterministic logic—may also deny the request. With multiple authorizers, access decisions become very granular. Table 4-1 explains how allow and deny decisions can be combined.

Table 4-1. Possible authorizer decisions

allowed = true		Authorizer can allow.
allowed = false		Authorizer cannot allow but also cannot deny.
allowed = false	denied = true	Authorizer can deny.

The authorizers return a SubjectAccessReview JSON object with the `status` field containing the decision and applicable messages:

```
// Decision to allow access, message not necessary
{
  "apiVersion": "authorization.k8s.io/v1",
```

```
  "kind": "SubjectAccessReview",
  "status": {
    "allowed": true
  }
}

// Decision to disallow access, but not deny, additional authorizers can deny
{
  "apiVersion": "authorization.k8s.io/v1",
  "kind": "SubjectAccessReview",
  "status": {
    "allowed": false,
    "reason": "Non-admin users cannot access admin namespaces."
  }
}

// Decision to disallow and deny
{
  "apiVersion": "authorization.k8s.io/v1",
  "kind": "SubjectAccessReview",
  "status": {
    "allowed": false,
    "denied": true,
    "reason": "Non-admin users cannot access admin namespaces."
  }
}
```

When a `denied=true` response is sent back from an authorizer, it bypasses any need to reach out to additional configured authorizers for a decision.

Now that we understand what authorizers do, let's look at how they do it, with PaC integration.

AuthZ Webhook and PaC

Given the fact that JSON is exchanged between the API server and the AuthZ services, it's easy to imagine how PaC tools can be used to make the AuthZ decisions for the API server. The trick is to start the API server and configure the AuthZ webhook without preventing any needed changes before the AuthZ webhook is configured.

The Kubernetes documentation seems to indicate that an external service is used to create the AuthZ webhook integration. However, a PaC best practice is to localize the decision engines as close to the decision points as possible. Adding additional network hops by calling services external to the cluster can make the response slower and the solution brittle. Running PaC engines within the cluster, with multiple Pods, creates partition tolerance as well.

An example of such a configuration that uses kind (*https://kind.sigs.k8s.io*), OPA, and kubeadm (*https://oreil.ly/Z8mpp*) to demonstrate this solution can be found as an OPA contribution (*https://oreil.ly/0t02-*). This solution runs OPA on the Kubernetes control plane nodes using DaemonSet resources. The configuration (Figure 4-3) sets a static IP on the Kubernetes Service resource that fronts the multiple OPA Pods created by the DaemonSet.

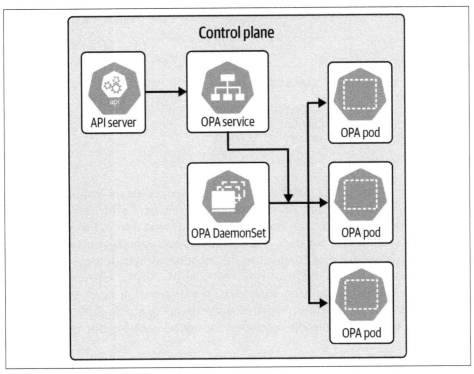

Figure 4-3. AuthZ webhook configuration using OPA

Using Kubernetes taints and tolerations, the Pods shown in Figure 4-3 are isolated to the Kubernetes CP nodes. In fact, any services that are sensitive to cluster operations—such as the API server AuthZ service—should be isolated to the CP nodes.

Example Policy

To create the preceding authorizer decisions, given the SubjectAccessReview object, the following example OPA policy will deny nonadmin users from accessing admin Namespaces:

```
# OPA policy to restrict admin Namespace access
package k8s.authz

import future.keywords.in
```

```
# Admin namespaces
admin_nss := ["kube-system","admin","opa"]

# Non-admin users cannot access admin namespaces.
deny[reason] {
        input.spec.resourceAttributes.namespace in admin_nss
        not "admin" in input.spec.groups
        reason := "Non-admin users cannot access admin namespaces."
}

decision = {
        "apiVersion": "v1",
        "kind": "SubjectAccessReview",
        "status": {
                "allowed": count(deny) == 0,
                "deny": count(deny) > 0,
                "reason": concat(" | ", deny),
        },
}
```

The purpose of the AuthZ webhook is to allow or deny access to Kubernetes API server actions based on information about the authenticated principle trying to perform the action. To be clear, this AuthN information is not seen in the AdmissionReview object used during mutating and validating admission via dynamic admission controllers, unless like data is added to the inbound request in a nonauthoritative manner. So even though PaC can easily be used to validate inbound API server requests via dynamic admission controllers, the information needed to authorize requests—as done by the AuthZ webhook authorizers—is not available. At this time, Kubernetes dynamic admission controllers cannot be used for this type of AuthZ use case.

The AWS Kubernetes (EKS) team delivered what they referred to as "simplified Amazon EKS access management controls" in December 2023. This approach is based on the Kubernetes authorizer functionality. While I was at AWS on the Kubernetes team, I helped test the feature and contributed to this blog post (*https://oreil.ly/lJzcX*) introducing it. My name was left off the post as an author, as I left AWS before the feature was released.

Before we close out this chapter, we need to explore how PaC reporting can be implemented and utilized.

Policy Reporting

Different PaC solutions provide different means for reporting and logging. While all the PaC solutions I have used have different levels of logging, logging is not reporting, as much as metrics gathering is not logging. PaC reporting is used to verify that your PaC solution is providing the desired result; moreover, PaC reporting can create informational and auditable artifacts to satisfy internal and external regulatory requirements.

When it comes to PaC reporting inside Kubernetes, the implementation—upon which I would base a standard—is the open format defined by the Kubernetes Policy WG. This PolicyReport is underpinned by a Kubernetes custom resource definition (CRD) (*https://oreil.ly/QeQQW*):

```
# policyreports.wgpolicyk8s.io CRD
$ kubectl get crd policyreports.wgpolicyk8s.io -oyaml

apiVersion: apiextensions.k8s.io/v1
kind: CustomResourceDefinition
metadata:
...
  name: policyreports.wgpolicyk8s.io
spec:
  conversion:
    strategy: None
  group: wgpolicyk8s.io
  names:
    kind: PolicyReport
    listKind: PolicyReportList
    plural: policyreports
    shortNames:
    - polr
    singular: policyreport
  scope: Namespaced
  versions:
...
    name: v1alpha2
```

As seen in the abbreviated output—CRDs are notoriously long and convoluted—the current version of the PolicyReport CRD is v1alpha2. Given the adoption pattern of Kuberrnetes, adoption of new features usually doesn't increase until the feature is promoted to at least beta status. That said, I have used PolicyReports with the Kyverno Policy Engine.

Kubernetes (*https://oreil.ly/QeQQW*) CRDs are used to extend the Kubernetes API. The following kubectl `api-resources` command can be used to view existing API resources in your cluster:

```
$ kubectl api-resources | grep pod
NAME        SHORTNAMES   APIVERSION   NAMESPACED   KIND
pods        po           v1           true         Pod
...
```

The following kubectl `explain` command can be used to explore the APIs:

```
$ kubectl explain pod.spec.containers.name
KIND:     Pod
VERSION:  v1

FIELD:    name <string>

DESCRIPTION:
    Name of the container specified as a DNS_LABEL.
    Each container in a Pod must have a unique name
    (DNS_LABEL). Cannot be updated.
```

PolicyReports can be Namespaced scoped and cluster scoped. The following example includes a Namespace-scoped PolicyReport from the kyverno Namespace:

```
# List PolicyReports in the kyverno namespace
$ kubectl -n kyverno get policyreports.wgpolicyk8s.io
NAME           PASS   FAIL   WARN   ERROR   SKIP   AGE
cpol-example   2      0      0      0       0      1h10m

# Review PolicyReport
$ kubectl -n kyverno get policyreports.wgpolicyk8s.io cpol-example \
-o yaml

apiVersion: wgpolicyk8s.io/v1alpha2
kind: PolicyReport
metadata:
...
  labels:
    app.kubernetes.io/managed-by: kyverno
  name: cpol-example
  namespace: kyverno
results:
- message: Validation rule 'autogen-example' passed.
  policy: example
  resources:
  - apiVersion: apps/v1
    kind: Deployment
    name: kyverno
    namespace: kyverno
  result: pass
  rule: autogen-example
```

```
  scored: true
  source: kyverno
...
summary:
  error: 0
  fail: 0
  pass: 2
  skip: 0
  warn: 0
```

The preceding PolicyReport is for the cpol-example Kyverno ClusterPolicy that was auto-generated for Deployment resources from a defined Pod policy. The report also indicates that the policy had two passed validations. The PolicyReport is a useful artifact for human consumption, and since it's YAML, it is also machine readable, like policies themselves.

Not all PaC solutions include reporting, and we will explore that feature and others as we dive deeper into specific PaC solutions in subsequent chapters.

Summary

If there is one thing I have learned from working with Kubernetes for the last seven years, it is that Kubernetes is ever evolving, spurred on by its community of developers and stakeholders. As Kubernetes continues to change, it's inevitable that PaC will as well. We are witnessing that evolution now, with new PaC features from the Kubernetes ecosystem as well as new in-tree solutions.

In this chapter, I surfaced several Kubernetes use cases that can be satisfied using PaC. You should now have foundational knowledge about admission controllers and their purpose in your clusters. I covered how you can mutate and validate inbound API server requests with dynamic admission controllers as well as use policies to respond to events in your cluster, such as resource modifications (CREATE and UPDATE).

We explored new in-tree solutions like Pod Security Admission and Validating Admission Policy. I took you on a short detour to explore how PaC can be used for AuthZ using Kubernetes webhook mode. Finally, we reviewed the emerging policy-reporting standards from the Policy WG.

With all this information that I have asked you to digest in this chapter, I want to remind you of my original recommendation from Chapter 1 on how to choose the right PaC solution for your needs. There are several use cases in this chapter that you should consider for your PaC Solution Selection Scorecard if you run and secure Kubernetes clusters. As we look at each solution throughout the next several chapters, you should consider how well the solution fits the described use case as well as your needs and capabilities. I will guide you along the way, discussing suitability, exposing issues and challenges, and making recommendations.

We will start our survey of specific PaC solutions in Chapter 5, as we explore how OPA is installed and used with Kubernetes for better security, control, and user experience.

Open Policy Agent and Kubernetes

So far, we have explored PaC as a general subject, with a focus on foundational knowledge. In Chapter 2, I introduced you to Open Policy Agent (OPA), and we examined the OPA suite of tools. We explored how to write, test, and manage policies as well as how to extend and integrate with OPA. In Chapter 3, we looked into PaC and AuthZ, and again we reviewed examples of how OPA can be used in those use cases. Finally, in Chapter 4, I covered the different features, components, and use cases with which PaC is used within Kubernetes clusters.

Over the next several chapters, we will explore specific PaC solutions and how they are used within Kubernetes clusters to satisfy mutating and validating use cases. Along the way, I will expose you to best practices and potential challenges. In these chapters, you should learn how each PaC solution that I cover in this book best fits your needs and capabilities.

In this chapter, I will cover OPA and Kubernetes. As described in Chapter 2, OPA is a domain-agnostic PaC solution that evaluates Rego policies against submitted and stored data. I will start with the installation and components; then, I will dive deeper into Kubernetes-specific OPA policies, libraries, tools, and techniques.

 In this book, I may refer to OPA—not OPA/Gatekeeper—as *OPA classic*. I add the *classic* moniker to differentiate OPA from OPA/ Gatekeeper.

OPA is a very mature OSS project with a strong and active community of developers and users. The following links will help you gain more information about OPA:

- GitHub project (*https://github.com/open-policy-agent/opa*)
- Main website (*https://www.openpolicyagent.org*)
- Slack community (*https://slack.openpolicyagent.org*)
- CNCF page (*https://www.cncf.io/projects/open-policy-agent-opa*)

As you read through this chapter, remember that—as in other chapters—all the examples will either be included in referenced material that I surface or will be made available from examples in the companion GitHub repositories in the Policy as Code Book organization (*https://github.com/policy-as-code-book*).

Now, let's start by installing OPA into Kubernetes—my local minikube—and we'll see how it fits the mutating and validating webhook use cases.

OPA Installation

As we learned in Chapter 4, mutating and validating admission controllers are loaded when the Kubernetes API server starts. Two of the most common admission controllers—which also enable dynamic admission control—are the mutating admission webhook and the validating admission webhook. These admission controllers enable us to configure OPA and other PaC solutions as admission control services without having to load them as admission controllers—with custom API server settings—when the API server starts.

 The official installation instructions for installing OPA into a Kubernetes cluster can be found in this tutorial (*https://oreil.ly/kOpw9*). In the following section, I use automated install/uninstall solutions that I have found to be reliable and that help others learn how OPA connectivity works.

Figure 5-1 illustrates how OPA installs into a Kubernetes cluster and interacts with other Kubernetes resources.

As shown in Figure 5-1, the OPA server installs into Kubernetes fronted by a service that is called by the Kubernetes API server via dynamic admission control. As part of the installation, the kube-mgmt sidecar container is also installed. I will cover the kube-mgmt sidecar in the next section. For now, let's look at how we can configure Kubernetes validating webhooks using OPA.

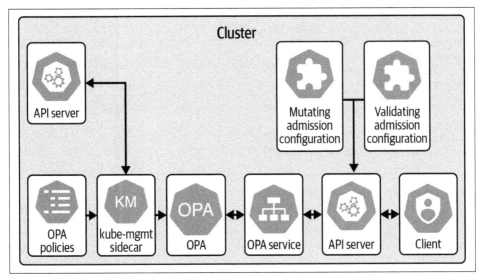

Figure 5-1. OPA-Kubernetes installation

Validating Admission Webhook

To install OPA properly into Kubernetes as an admission controller solution, you must configure a webhook configuration for the type of admission control you need. The following example ValidatingWebhookConfiguration resource is configured to allow the API server to call the OPA service to validate inbound requests. With this configured resource, the API server is configured as a client to the OPA server for validation purposes:

```
# Get validating webhook configurations
$ kubectl get validatingwebhookconfigurations opa-validating-webhook \
-oyaml

# Example validatingwebhookconfigurations resource
apiVersion: admissionregistration.k8s.io/v1
kind: ValidatingWebhookConfiguration
metadata:
…
  name: opa-validating-webhook
webhooks:
- admissionReviewVersions:
  - v1
  clientConfig:
    caBundle: LS0…
    service:
      name: opa
      namespace: opa
      port: 443
  failurePolicy: Fail   ❶
```

```
  matchPolicy: Equivalent
  name: validating-webhook.openpolicyagent.org
  namespaceSelector:  ❷
    matchExpressions:
    - key: openpolicyagent.org/webhook
      operator: NotIn
      values:
      - ignore
  objectSelector: {}
  rules:
    - operations: ["CREATE", "UPDATE"]
      apiGroups: ["*"]
      apiVersions: ["v1"]
      resources: ["pods","deployments","services"]
      scope: '*'
  sideEffects: None
  timeoutSeconds: 10  ❸
```

❶ Prevent change to cluster if webhook calls fail.

❷ Use labels to exclude Namespaces from processing.

❸ Time out webhook call at 10 seconds.

In the preceding YAML, I configured the validating webhook to time out after 10 seconds and fail—prevent cluster changes—upon timeout. I also set validation to occur only for resources that are in Namespaces that are not labeled openpolicyagent.org/ webhook=ignore; Namespaces labeled thusly are excluded.

 When using dynamic admission controls to call validating and mutating services, the webhook calls have timeout settings (default 10 seconds). The webhook failurePolicy setting configures how the API server should respond when the webhook call times out. According to the documentation, failurePolicy defines how the webhook configuration should react to "unrecognized errors and timeout errors." If set to Ignore, the webhook will fail open, and the inbound change—regardless of validity—will proceed to the next step in the flow. If set to Fail, the webhook will fail closed, and the inbound change will stop, again regardless of the validity of the change.

The timeoutSeconds, failurePolicy, and namespaceSelector settings are used to tune the webhook configuration so that the cluster remains operative regardless of failure mode. For example, it's not a good idea to use a fail-closed scenario without excluding system Namespaces like kube-system and opa.

In Chapter 4, we learned that validating and mutating webhook services receive AdmissionReview objects from the Kubernetes API server. In the preceding configuration, I set the version of the AdmissionReview to v1. This version must match the version that OPA policies expect, as seen in the following policy snippet:

```
# Main policy - snippet
  main = {
    "apiVersion": "admission.k8s.io/v1",
    "kind": "AdmissionReview",
    "response": response,
  }
```

The API server uses the internal OPA service address and the Base64-encoded certificate—clientConfig.caBundle—to communicate with the OPA server over TLS with a self-signed certificate. However, this does not prevent other clients within the cluster from connecting to OPA, even without the caBundle field. For example, as you can see in the following console outputs, I was able to run an Alpine Pod and connect to the OPA service, even with a self-signed TLS cert:

```
# Connecting to OPA service within Kubernetes
$ kubectl run -n opa -it debugger \
--image jimmyraywv/debugger:v0.1.0 --restart=Never

/ # curl -k https://opa.opa.svc/v1/data
{"decision_id":"c9278638-9c26-43c2-9f…
```

> The Kubernetes API server can be configured to authenticate (*https://oreil.ly/9WPvn*) to admission controllers. This requires custom configuration files added to the API server startup process as well as OPA server AuthN and AuthZ settings (*https://oreil.ly/undwk*) like we used in Chapter 2. Another layer of security could be implemented with network policy resources (*https://oreil.ly/xQq34*), used to control ingress to the OPA server.

Under the rules section on the webhook configuration, I configured the validating webhook to review resources with the following characteristics:

- All API groups
- All API versions
- CREATE and UPDATE operations
- Pod resources only
- Cluster and Namespace scopes

I restricted the reviewed resources to Pods to make it easier for demonstration. However, in a real-world production environment, I would most likely expand the rules to all resources, as shown in the following configuration:

```
# Rules snippet
rules:
  - operations: ["CREATE", "UPDATE"]
    apiGroups: ["*"]
    apiVersions: ["*"]
    resources: ["*"]
```

Next, let's explore reusable automation to install OPA and configure the resources needed for a validating webhook.

Automated install and uninstall

To make it easier to install—and uninstall—OPA and reduce the chances of errors, I automated the processes via a set of shell scripts that I call with a Makefile. I will step through the automation I used to reliably install OPA into a Kubernetes cluster. First, I configured the kubectl command. This layer-of-indirection approach allows me to customize the kubectl command if need be. Options for the kubectl command can be found with the kubectl options command. Then, I configured labels and the OPA Namespace:

```
# shell install OPA script - up.sh
#!/usr/bin/env bash

# error handling
set -e
trap 'catch $? $LINENO' ERR
catch() {
  if [ "$1" != "0" ]; then
    echo "Error $1 occurred on $2"
  fi
}

OWNER="jimmy"
ENV="dev"
BILLING="lob-cc"
KUBECTL="kubectl"
CA_BUNDLE=""
CONFIGS_DIRECTORY="generated/configs"
SECRETS_DIRECTORY="generated/secrets"
TEMPLATES_DIRECTORY="templates"
POLICY_CM_DIRECTORY="../policy-configmaps/deploy"

if [ ! -d "$TEMPLATES_DIRECTORY" ]; then    ❶
  echo "$TEMPLATES_DIRECTORY not found, install aborted"
  exit 99
fi
```

```
if [ ! -d "$CONFIGS_DIRECTORY" ]; then
  mkdir -p $CONFIGS_DIRECTORY
fi

if [ ! -d "$SECRETS_DIRECTORY" ]; then
  mkdir -p $SECRETS_DIRECTORY
fi

rm -f $CONFIGS_DIRECTORY/*
rm -f $SECRETS_DIRECTORY/*

cat $TEMPLATES_DIRECTORY/ns-template.yaml | sed -e  ❷
"s/__OWNER_VALUE__/${OWNER}/g" \
| sed -e "s/__ENV_VALUE__/${ENV}/g" \
| sed -e "s/__BILLING_VALUE__/${BILLING}/g" \
> "$CONFIGS_DIRECTORY/ns.yaml"
${KUBECTL} apply -f $CONFIGS_DIRECTORY/ns.yaml
```

❶ Verify that the *templates* directory exists; the install cannot continue without it.

❷ Create the Namespace from a template using sed commands.

Next, I labeled the system Namespaces—opa and kube-system—that I did not want
the admission control policies to affect:

```
${KUBECTL} label --overwrite namespace kube-system \
openpolicyagent.org/webhook=ignore
${KUBECTL} label --overwrite namespace opa \
openpolicyagent.org/webhook=ignore
```

Then, I generated the TLS material needed to operate OPA with TLS and allow the
API server to connect to OPA running with self-signed certificates. I also created a
TLS secret containing the server certificate and the server private key. This secret is
mapped to volume mounts used by the OPA server Pod:

```
openssl genrsa -out $SECRETS_DIRECTORY/opa-ca.key 2048  ❶
openssl req -x509 -new -nodes -sha256 -key $SECRETS_DIRECTORY/opa-ca.key \
-days 100000 -out $SECRETS_DIRECTORY/opa-ca.crt -subj /CN=admission_ca 2>&1
openssl genrsa -out $SECRETS_DIRECTORY/opa-server.key 2048
openssl req -new -key $SECRETS_DIRECTORY/opa-server.key -sha256 -out \
$SECRETS_DIRECTORY/opa-server.csr -subj /CN=opa.opa.svc -config \
$TEMPLATES_DIRECTORY/opa-server.conf 2>&1
openssl x509 -req -in $SECRETS_DIRECTORY/opa-server.csr -sha256 -CA \
$SECRETS_DIRECTORY/opa-ca.crt -CAkey $SECRETS_DIRECTORY/opa-ca.key \
-CAcreateserial -out $SECRETS_DIRECTORY/opa-server.crt -days 100000 \
-extensions v3_ext -extfile $TEMPLATES_DIRECTORY/opa-server.conf

echo "Trying to delete \"opa-server\" secret..."  ❷
${KUBECTL} -n opa delete secret opa-server --ignore-not-found 2>&1
${KUBECTL} -n opa create secret tls opa-server \
```

```
--cert=$SECRETS_DIRECTORY/opa-server.crt \
--key=$SECRETS_DIRECTORY/opa-server.key
```

❶ Create the TLS artifacts.

❷ Store the TLS cert and key into a Kubernetes secret.

 It's important that OpenSSL commands that create cryptography artifacts—opa-ca.key, opa-server.csr, and opa-server.crt—use the SHA-256 secure-hash algorithm, as the OpenSSL default, SHA-1, is no longer supported.

Next, I applied the Kuberneters resources to create the OPA server and needed RBAC permissions:

```
cat $TEMPLATES_DIRECTORY/admission-controller-template.yaml | \
sed -e "s/__OWNER_VALUE__/${OWNER}/g" | sed -e "s/__ENV_VALUE__/${ENV}/g" \
| sed -e "s/__BILLING_VALUE__/${BILLING}/g" > \
"$CONFIGS_DIRECTORY/opa-admission-controller.yaml"
${KUBECTL} apply -f $CONFIGS_DIRECTORY/opa-admission-controller.yaml

CA_BUNDLE="$(base64 -i $SECRETS_DIRECTORY/opa-ca.crt)"

Sleep 10
```

I waited for 10 seconds for OPA and the kube-mgmt sidecar to start communicating. Then, I applied the Rego main policy configmap so that OPA would operate correctly:

```
${KUBECTL} apply -f $POLICY_CM_DIRECTORY/.

CA_BUNDLE="$(base64 -i $SECRETS_DIRECTORY/opa-ca.crt)"

cat $TEMPLATES_DIRECTORY/validating-webhook-configuration-template.yaml | \
sed -e "s/__OWNER_VALUE__/${OWNER}/g" | sed -e "s/__ENV_VALUE__/${ENV}/g" \
| sed -e "s/__BILLING_VALUE__/${BILLING}/g" | sed -e \
"s/__CA_BUNDLE_VALUE__/${CA_BUNDLE}/g" > \
"$CONFIGS_DIRECTORY/opa-validating-webhook-configuration.yaml"
${KUBECTL} apply -f \
$CONFIGS_DIRECTORY/opa-validating-webhook-configuration.yaml
```

Only after OPA was up and running and clients could communicate with it did I apply the validating webhook configuration—to connect the Kubernetes API server to OPA—for the purpose of validating API server requests.

In the preceding shell script, you may have noticed that I used a simple templating approach with the sed utility (*https://oreil.ly/AJ_2j*). I considered using kustomize (*https://oreil.ly/m5ofI*) to create bases and overlays for different configurations; however, kustomize is not really a templating tool as much as it is a multiple configuration management and build tool. Since I didn't know the OpenSSL artifacts until script runtime, kustomize was not the best choice, at least not alone. I could have used kustomize for the common labels and configurations, but for simplicity, I opted to continue with sed alone. The shell-script and Makefile approach also makes it very easy for me to tweak settings when I am prototyping. As with many things related to Kubernetes, there are multiple ways to perform a task.

The following console output contains the output from the install automation:

```
# Make command to install OPA
$ make up
./up.sh 2>&1
namespace/opa created
namespace/kube-system labeled
namespace/opa labeled
Certificate request self-signature ok
subject=CN=opa.opa.svc
Trying to delete "opa-server" secret...
secret/opa-server created
serviceaccount/kube-mgmt created
clusterrolebinding.rbac.authorization.k8s.io/opa-kube-mgmt-viewer created
role.rbac.authorization.k8s.io/opa-configmap-ingester created
rolebinding.rbac.authorization.k8s.io/opa-configmap-ingester created
service/opa created
deployment.apps/opa created
configmap/opa-policy-main created
configmap/lib-k8s-helpers created
configmap/deployment-labels created
configmap/deployment-spec-temp-labels created
configmap/deployment-security-context created
configmap/deployment-registry-allowed created
configmap/pod-registry-allowed created
configmap/deployment-allowed-role-ns created
configmap/deployment-resources created
configmap/deployment-valid-image-version created
configmap/clusterip-svc-ext-ips created
configmap/clusterip-svc-ext-ips-allowed created
validatingwebhookconfiguration.admissionregistration.k8s.io/
opa-validating-webhook created
```

The install automation configures the OPA server container with the following settings:

```
# OPA server settings
- name: opa
  image: openpolicyagent/opa:0.62.0-static   ❶
  securityContext:
    allowPrivilegeEscalation: false
    runAsUser: 1000
    readOnlyRootFilesystem: true
    runAsNonRoot: true
    capabilities:
      drop: ["ALL"]
    seccompProfile:
      type: "RuntimeDefault"
  args:
    - "run"
    - "--server"
    - "--tls-cert-file=/certs/tls.crt"
    - "--tls-private-key-file=/certs/tls.key"
    - "--addr=0.0.0.0:8443"
    - "--addr=http://127.0.0.1:8181"   ❷
    - "--log-format=json"
    - "--set=status.console=true"
    - "--set=decision_logs.console=true"
```

❶   Use a static OPA image that supports Linux/ARM64 platforms.

❷   Bind the OPA server to a local networking address—best practice.

As you can see, I used a static image because my Kubernetes test cluster runs on an ARM 64 machine (*https://oreil.ly/poPYK*), my M2 MacBook Pro.

In the preceding YAML configuration, you should notice that I bound the OPA server to the local Pod address space with the `--addr=http://127.0.0.1:8181` argument. As I mentioned in Chapters 2 and 3, this normally prevents the OPA server from being accessed by clients not on the local Pod network. However, working together, the Kubernetes Service and Endpoint resources in the OPA Namespace expose network access to OPA to resources outside of the OPA Namespace and OPA Pod.

The installation process that I used is based on years of experience with OPA and Kubernetes as well as the official documentation. In fact, I used parts of the shell script in 2018 when I first started with OPA and Kubernetes. That said, there is also a Helm chart (*https://oreil.ly/jkrCT*) that can be used to install OPA and its kube-mgmt sidecar. In fact, if you would rather just install OPA without the kube-mgmt sidecar, you can do that with the *values.yaml* settings:

```
# Helm values snippet to disable kube-mgmt sidecar
mgmt:
    enabled: false
```

I used my custom installation in this book to help readers better understand how the OPA install works.

Once OPA was installed, I verified that it was functional through a couple of checks. First, I verified that the OPA policy configmaps that I installed were compiled and ingested without issues. The following `kubectl` commands checked the status annotation of each configmap, using JSONPath expressions (*https://oreil.ly/YQ5JL*):

```
# OPA policy configmap checks
$ kubectl get cm opa-policy-main \
-o=jsonpath=\
'{.metadata.annotations.openpolicyagent\.org\/kube-mgmt-status}'
{"status":"ok"}

$ kubectl get cm lib-k8s-helpers \
-o=jsonpath=\
'{.metadata.annotations.openpolicyagent\.org\/kube-mgmt-status}'
{"status":"ok"}%
```

Another check that I found helpful was simply reviewing the OPA server logs, looking for REST API health checks:

```
# Review logs for health-checks
$ kubectl -n opa logs opa…
{"client_addr":"172.17.0.1:36366","level":"info","msg":"Received request.",
"req_id":82,"req_method":"GET","req_path":"/health","time":
"2022-12-20T18:42:11Z"}
{"client_addr":"172.17.0.1:36366","level":"info","msg":"Sent response.",
"req_id":82,"req_method":"GET","req_path":"/health","resp_bytes":2,
"resp_duration":1.964084,"resp_status":200,"time":"2022-12-20T18:42:11Z"}
```

Now that we know how to install and configure OPA in Kubernetes, let's uninstall it.

Uninstalling OPA

I uninstalled OPA in my test cluster using a similar shell script:

```
# OPA uninstall script
#!/usr/bin/env bash

# error handling
set -e
trap 'catch $? $LINENO' ERR
catch() {
  if [ "$1" != "0" ]; then
    echo "Error $1 occurred on $2"
  fi
}

KUBECTL="kubectl"
${KUBECTL} delete MutatingWebhookConfiguration -l app=opa --ignore-not-found
${KUBECTL} delete ValidatingWebhookConfiguration -l app=opa --ignore-not-found
${KUBECTL} delete ns opa --ignore-not-found
${KUBECTL} delete ns policy-test --ignore-not-found
${KUBECTL} delete clusterrolebinding opa-kube-mgmt-viewer --ignore-not-found
${KUBECTL} label namespace kube-system openpolicyagent.org/webhook-
```

I also used make for the uninstall process:

```
$ Make command to uninstall OPA
$ make down
./down.sh 2>&1
No resources found
validatingwebhookconfiguration.admissionregistration.k8s.io
"opa-validating-webhook" deleted
namespace "opa" deleted
clusterrolebinding.rbac.authorization.k8s.io "opa-kube-mgmt-viewer" deleted
namespace/kube-system unlabeled
```

> In this book, I write a lot of bash scripts for automation purposes. For my bigger scripts, I use the ShellCheck utility (*https://oreil.ly/shellcheck*) to verify syntax and semantics.

In this section, I have alluded to the kube-mgmt sidecar used by OPA. Next, we will take a deeper dive into kube-mgmt and see how it helps us use OPA in Kubernetes.

Kubernetes Management Sidecar

As we learned in Chapter 2, OPA has a mature CLI and REST API to help manage policies and data needed for decisions. We also saw how bundles were used to manage policies and data for the different OPA modes. In Chapter 3, we explored tools that we could use to manage OPA policies and data across multiple systems.

When you install OPA into a Kubernetes cluster, you have the option of how you want to manage OPA policies and data, just like running OPA outside of Kubernetes. You can use bundles, and you can also use the OPA REST API. In fact, as I installed OPA, the Kubernetes Management sidecar used the OPA REST API to load data and policies into the OPA server.

The Kubernetes Management sidecar—also known as *kube-mgmt* (*https://oreil.ly/ kube-mgmt*)—runs within the same Kubernetes Pod and is used to manage OPA policies and data for the OPA container. The following YAML configures the kube-mgmt container:

```
# kube-mgmt config
- name: kube-mgmt
  image: openpolicyagent/kube-mgmt:8.5.5
  securityContext:
    allowPrivilegeEscalation: false
    runAsUser: 1000
    readOnlyRootFilesystem: true
    runAsNonRoot: true
    capabilities:
      drop: ["ALL"]
    seccompProfile:
      type: "RuntimeDefault"
  args:
    - "--replicate-cluster=v1/namespaces"     ❶
    - "--replicate=networking.k8s.io/v1/ingresses"
    - "--namespaces=opa"     ❷
```

❶ Replicate Kubernetes Namespace resource data into the OPA.

❷ Configure the Namespaces from which to load policy configmaps.

Now that we know how to configure kube-mgmt, let's explore how it functions, including how it loads OPA policies and data into OPA.

Kubernetes Policy Management

The kube-mgmt sidecar loads Rego-based policies into OPA via HTTP PUT methods to the OPA REST API. Kube-mgmt receives Rego policies for loading into OPA from configmaps loaded into the opa Namespace. When configmaps are applied to the opa Namespace, kube-mgmt processes the Rego therein, if the configmap is labeled with openpolicyagent.org/policy: rego. Configmaps not labeled thusly are ignored by kube-mgmt. The label and value are defaults when kube-mgmt boots. Kube-mgmt compiles the Rego in the policy and, upon successful compilation, loads the policy into OPA. The following console outputs are examples of both failed and successful compile and load operations:

```
# kube-mgmt cannot connect to OPA
openpolicyagent.org/kube-mgmt-status: '{"status":"error","error":
{"Op":"Put","URL":
"http://localhost:8181/v1/policies/opa/opa-default-system-main/main",
"Err":{"Op":"dial","Net":"tcp","Source":null,"Addr":{"IP":"127.0.0.1",
"Port":8181,"Zone":""},"Err":{"Syscall":"connect","Err":111}}}}'

# Policy could not be successfully compiled
openpolicyagent.org/kube-mgmt-status: '{"status":"error","error":
{"code":"invalid_parameter","message":
"error(s) occurred while compiling module(s)","errors":[{"code":
"rego_parse_error","message":"unexpected minus token: expected number",
"location":{"file":"opa/opa-default-system-main/main","row":13,"col":7},
"details":{"line":"uid---= input.request.uid","idx":6}}]}}'

# kube-mgmt successful compile and put
openpolicyagent.org/kube-mgmt-status: '{"status":"ok"}'
```

Kube-mgmt can also help us with loading Kubernetes data into OPA, which we'll explore next.

Kubernetes Data Management

Clients with authorized access can put and modify data in the OPA server. For example, as we saw in Chapter 2, this can be done via HTTP PUT. As with policies, kube-mgmt can be configured to load Kubernetes data from the local cluster. Kube-mgmt data sources for OPA are from configmaps and Kubernetes cluster data.

In the case of policy decisions that need more data than what is provided by the API server request—posted to OPA by the API server—kube-mgmt can be set to gather cluster resource data and replicate it into OPA. For example, if you wanted to write policies to prevent duplicate Kubernetes resources, you would need resource data from the cluster to know which resources already existed.

When kube-mgmt comes online, it boots its configmap processor, tries to read data from Kubernetes—as configured by replication settings—and then tries to load policy and data into OPA. It takes a few seconds before OPA is online and kube-mgmt can successfully connect, evidenced by the kube-mgmt logs in the following console output:

```
# kube-mgmt logs - configmap loader and Kubernetes
$ kubectl logs opa-7f5f5f645-xqsv4 -c kube-mgmt
time="2024-03-08T20:09:27Z" level=info msg="Policy/data ConfigMap processor
```

```
connected to K8s: namespaces=[opa]"
time="2024-03-08T20:09:27Z" level=info msg="Initial informer sync for
v1/namespaces completed, took 103.300667ms"
time="2024-03-08T20:09:27Z" level=info msg="Syncing v1/namespaces."
time="2024-03-08T20:09:27Z" level=info msg="Initial informer sync for
networking.k8s.io/v1/ingresses completed, took 103.519875ms"
time="2024-03-08T20:09:27Z" level=info
msg="Syncing networking.k8s.io/v1/ingresses."
time="2024-03-08T20:09:27Z" level=info
msg="Loaded 5 resources of kind v1/namespaces into OPA. Took 502.791µs"
time="2024-03-08T20:09:27Z" level=info
msg="Loaded 0 resources of kind networking.k8s.io/v1/ingresses into OPA.
Took 556.458µs"
time="2024-03-08T20:09:37Z" level=info msg="Added policy
opa/opa-policy-main/main, err=<nil>"
time="2024-03-08T20:09:37Z" level=info msg="Added policy
opa/lib-k8s-helpers/main, err=<nil>"
time="2024-03-08T20:09:37Z" level=info msg="Added policy
opa/deployment-labels/main, err=<nil>" …
```

As you can see in the preceding logs, kube-mgmt was able to load policies and data into OPA with no errors. By querying the v1/data API, I verified that the Kubernetes resources were replicated. To get at the data API, I used port forwarding to the OPA container; then, I used cURL to query the OPA data API:

```
# Forward local port to OPA container port
$ kubectl -n opa port-forward pods/opa-7689cd4bd7-tlrhq 8080:8181
Forwarding from 127.0.0.1:8080 -> 8181

# Query the OPA data API
$ curl localhost:8080/v1/data
…{"kubernetes":{"ingresses":{},"namespaces":{"default":{"apiVersion":"v1",
"kind":"Namespace","metadata":{"creationTimestamp":"2024-03-02T05:37:27Z",
"labels":{"kubernetes.io/metadata.name":"default"}...
```

To include the Kubernetes service address in this check, I used kubectl run to run a separate Pod from which I could execute the cURL command against the Kubernetes service:

```
# Run a Pod to access the OPA service
$ make run-debugger-pod
kubectl run -n opa -it debugger --image=jimmyraywv/debugger:v0.1.0 \
--restart=Never
If you don't see a command prompt, try pressing enter.
/ #
```

The container image for the single container in the Pod is one that I built from an Alpine base image, into which I layered the cURL package.

In the following cURL example, I queried the OPA data API using the Kubernetes OPA service address:

```
# Query OPA data API from different Pod
$ curl -k https://opa.opa.svc/v1/data
...{"kubernetes":{"ingresses":{},"namespaces":{"default":{"apiVersion":
"v1","kind":"Namespace","metadata":{"creationTimestamp":"2024-03-02T05:37:27Z",
"labels":{"kubernetes.io/metadata.name":"default"}...
```

Since I used the OPA service with TLS ports, I used the `curl -k` option so that I would not have to worry about the self-signed TLS certificate being used by the OPA server.

To query the OPA server to see the policies that were loaded from the kube-mgmt sidecar container ingesting policy configmaps, I called the *v1/policies* endpoint:

```
# Query OPA policies endpoint to see policies loaded by kube-mgmt sidecar
$ curl -k https://opa.opa.svc/v1/policies
{"result":[{"id":"opa/lib-k8s-helpers/main","raw":
"package lib.k8s.helpers\n\n#
import data.kubernetes.admission\n\nallowed_operations = allowed_ops
{\n  allowed_ops := {\"CREATE\", \"UPDATE\"} ...
```

With these approaches, I verified not only that the OPA data and policies were loaded but also that the OPA service was reachable in the cluster.

 In a production OPA installation in Kubernetes, I would also include Kubernetes NetworkPolicy resources (*https://oreil.ly/dKjXY*) around the OPA Pod to prevent unwanted network access to the OPA Pod.

Kube-mgmt data replication is not the only way to load data into OPA. In the next section, we will explore additional methods for loading data beyond the replication.

Data from Configmaps

Configmaps can be used to specify data—beyond replicated cluster resources—to be loaded into OPA by kube-mgmt. The following data configmap example is used to load projects data:

```
# Configmap containing project data to be loaded into OPA
kind: ConfigMap
apiVersion: v1
metadata:
  name: opa-data-projects
  namespace: opa
  labels:
    app: opa
    billing: lob-cc
    env: dev
    owner: jimmy
    openpolicyagent.org/data: opa
```

```
data:
  main: |
    {"projects":[{"lead":"jimmy","method":"GET","project":"book"}]}
```

In the preceding YAML example, the `openpolicyagent.org/data:` opa label is used to mark configmaps that kube-mgmt should ingest and load as data. If kube-mgmt can load the data successfully, then it will set the `openpolicyagent.org/kube-mgmt-status` annotation as it did with policy ConfigMap resources:

```
# Apply data resource
$ kubectl -n opa apply -f data-configmaps/0-data-json.yaml
configmap/opa-data-projects configured

# Review configmap status
$ kubectl get cm opa-data-projects \
-o=jsonpath=\
'{.metadata.annotations.openpolicyagent\.org\/kube-mgmt-status}'
{"status":"ok"}

# Query OPA server for data
$ curl -k https://opa.opa.svc/v1/data/opa
{"decision_id":"65218a05-2681-46dc-a3a0-919cf1208e04","result":
{"opa-data-projects":{"main":{"projects":[{"lead":"jimmy","method":
"GET","project":"book"}]}}}}
```

Now that we have explored kube-mgmt data management, let's look at how to secure OPA while still allowing Kubernetes and kube-mgmt to access OPA as needed.

OPA AuthZ and kube-mgmt

When OPA is used in Kubernetes only for the purposes of mutating and validating API server requests, then it should be secured with an AuthZ policy. The AuthZ policy ensures that clients—other than the Kubernetes API server—are not able to access the OPA server. This protects OPA policies and data from unwanted access.

The following policy is from the kube-mgmt *README.md* file (*https://oreil.ly/ LNyYz*); it is used to allow minimal anonymous access to OPA while granting privileged access to kube-mgmt to be able to put, patch, and delete data—including policies—in OPA:

```
# Rego policy to secure OPA
package system.authz

# Deny access by default.
default allow := false

# Allow anonymous access to decision `data.example.response`
#
# NOTE: the specific decision differs depending on your policies.
# NOTE: depending on how callers are configured, they may only require
```

```
# this or the default decision below.
allow {
  input.path == ["v0", "data", "example", "response"]
  input.method == "POST"
}

# Allow anonymous access to default decision.
allow {
  input.path == [""]
  input.method == "POST"
}

# This is only used for health check in liveness and readiness probe
allow {
  input.path == ["health"]
  input.method == "GET"
}

# This is only used for prometheus metrics
allow {
  input.path == ["metrics"]
  input.method == "GET"
}

# This is used by kube-mgmt to PUT/PATCH against /v1/data and PUT/DELETE
# against /v1/policies.
#
# NOTE: The $TOKEN value is replaced at deploy-time with the actual value
# that kube-mgmt will use. This is typically done by an initContainer.
allow {
  input.identity == "$TOKEN"
}
```

In the preceding policy, access is authorized under the following multiple conditions:

- Anonymous POST to configured—or default—decision entry point
- Anonymous GET to the health endpoint
- Anonymous GET to the metrics endpoint
- kube-mgmt access to OPA API with correctly supplied AuthZ token

To use the aforementioned AuthZ policy, OPA and kube-mgmt must have additional configuration items to load the policy and token needed for access. The following YAML configuration from the kube-mgmt docs (*https://oreil.ly/kvGOy*) shows how to configure AuthZ using the `authentication=token` and `authorization=basic` settings that we first saw in Chapter 2:

```
# OPA Pod spec with AuthZ settings
spec:
  containers:
```

```
  - name: opa
    image: openpolicyagent/opa:0.47.3-rootless
    args:
      - "run"
      - "--server"
      - "--tls-cert-file=/certs/tls.crt"
      - "--tls-private-key-file=/certs/tls.key"
      - "--addr=0.0.0.0:443"
      - "--addr=http://127.0.0.1:8181"
      - "--authentication=token"   ❶
      - "--authorization=basic"    ❷
      - "/policies/authz.rego" # authorization policy used on startup
      - "--ignore=.*"          # exclude hidden dirs created by Kubernetes
    volumeMounts:
      - readOnly: true
        mountPath: /certs
        name: opa-server
      - readOnly: true
        mountPath: /policies
        name: inject-policy
- name: kube-mgmt
  image: openpolicyagent/kube-mgmt:7.3.0
  args:
    - "--replicate-cluster=v1/namespaces"
    - "--replicate=extensions/v1/ingresses"
    - "--opa-auth-token-file=/policies/token"  ❸
  volumeMounts:
    - readOnly: true
      mountPath: /policies
      name: inject-policy
volumes:
  - name: opa-server
    secret:
      secretName: opa-server
  - name: inject-policy
    secret:
      secretName: inject-policy
```

❶ Configure token AuthN setting.

❷ Configure basic AuthZ setting.

❸ Set auth token file.

With the preceding AuthZ policy—and OPA and kube-mgmt settings—your OPA mutating and validation service can be used securely by Kubernetes and kube-mgmt.

In the next section, we will explore OPA Kubernetes policies and how they are used and configured.

Kubernetes Policies

As mentioned in the previous section, OPA Rego policies that are stored in correctly labeled Kubernetes configmaps are loaded into OPA via the kube-mgmt sidecar. The following example shows how such a policy is used for resource validation and stored within a configmap:

```
# Configmap with deny-all Pods policy that returns the AdmissionReview object
kind: ConfigMap
apiVersion: v1
metadata:
  name: deny-all-pods
  namespace: opa
  labels:
...
    openpolicyagent.org/policy: rego
data:
  main: |
    package kubernetes.admission

    import future.keywords.in

    deny[msg] {
        input.request.kind.kind == "Pod"
        input.request.operation in ["CREATE", "DELETE", "UPDATE"]
        msg = sprintf("Request object: %q", [input.request.object])
    }
```

The preceding Rego policy matches to Pod resources, with specific operations and denies all requests where the operation is CREATE, DELETE, or UPDATE.

> The deny-all policy is handy when troubleshooting OPA inside Kubernetes. The policy will deny all Pod operations and then return the `input.request.object` to be examined. You can write this policy for any Kubernetes resource:
>
> ```
> # Failed request to create and run Pod in default
> Namespace
> $ kubectl -n default run --image=alpine -it \
> alpine-shell -- /bin/sh
> Error from server (Request object: "{\"apiVersion\":
> \"v1\", \"kind\": \"Pod\", \"metadata\":
> {\"creationTimestamp\": \"2022-12-21T02:25:51Z\",
> \"labels\": {\"run\": \"alpine-shell\"}, ...
> ```

Kubernetes webhook policies are divided into mutation and validation types. Let's first look at validation types.

Validation Policies

Even though the aforementioned policy just denies all requests, it is an example of an OPA validation policy. Validation policies use the Kubernetes AdmissionReview object as input data to validate API server requests. In the following code listings, we will examine an OPA validation policy and how it matches to—and then evaluates—inbound request data.

The validation policy—delivered in a ConfigMap resource—begins with the `package` and `import` statements, followed by the deny rule:

```
# Configmap for image registry validation
kind: ConfigMap
apiVersion: v1
metadata:
  name: pod-registry-allowed
  namespace: opa
  labels:
    app: opa
    billing: lob-cc
    env: dev
    owner: jimmy
    openpolicyagent.org/policy: rego
data:
  main: |
    package kubernetes.admission

    import future.keywords.in

    deny[msg] {
      req_kind = "Pod"
      req_op in allowed_ops
      image = pod_containers[_].image
      not reg_matches_any(image, valid_registries)
      msg = sprintf("POD_INVALID: %q image is not sourced from an authorized \
      registry. Valid registries are %q. Resource ID (ns/name/kind): %q",
      [image, allowed_regs, req_id])
    }
```

The first part of the deny rule is used to match the policy to the inbound requests data. If the request is used to create or update a Pod, the match is made. Once the match is made, the rest of the deny rule is used to evaluate the inbound data. This policy evaluates whether or not an inbound Pod request sources its container images from approved registries. Rules and statements, used by the deny rule to complete evaluation, comprise the rest of the policy:

```
# Rego snippet with rules
req_op = op {
      op := input.request.operation
}
```

```
pod_containers = c {
        c := input.request.object.spec.containers
}

req_id = value {
        value := sprintf("%v/%v/%v", [
                req_namespace,
                req_name,
                req_kind,
        ])
}

req_name = value {
        value := input.request.object.metadata.name
}

else = value {
        value := "NOT_FOUND"
}

req_namespace = value {
        value := input.request.object.metadata.namespace
}

else = value {
        value := "NOT_FOUND"
}

req_kind = value {
        value := input.request.kind.kind
}

else = value {
        value := "NOT_FOUND"
}

allowed_ops := ["CREATE", "UPDATE"]

allowed_regs := ["GOOD_REGISTRY", "VERY_GOOD_REGISTRY"]

valid_registries = {registry |
        registry = allowed_regs[_]
}

reg_matches_any(str, patterns) {
        reg_matches(str, patterns[_])
}

reg_matches(str, pattern) {
        contains(str, pattern)
}
```

When the policy evaluates an inbound request and the request is invalid, the following error is returned to the client:

```
# Policy validation error message
Error from server (POD_INVALID:
"public.ecr.aws/eks-distro/kubernetes/pause:3.2" image is not sourced
from an authorized registry. Valid registries are
"[\"GOOD_REGISTRY\", \"VERY_GOOD_REGISTRY\"]".
Resource ID (ns/name/kind): "opa-test/test-pod/Pod"):
error when creating "tests/99-test-pod.yaml"
```

As seen in the preceding validation policy, OPA policy rules are used to match policies to and then evaluate inbound data. This pattern—first mentioned in Chapter 1—repeats across different PaC solutions and policy types. Now, let's look at how OPA is configured to allow webhook calls to reach Rego policies.

OPA Policy Entry Point

OPA uses a policy entry point to operate as a Kubernetes dynamic webhook service. Without this policy entry point—and matching policy packages and objects—OPA will not respond correctly to the API server. Depending on the webhook configurations, this could potentially compromise your Kubernetes cluster. As seen in the following errors, the missing policy entry point prevents normal cluster operations from completing successfully:

```
# Cannot review opa logs
$ Kubectl -n opa logs opa-795c4cd467-htg9v
Defaulted container "opa" out of: opa, kube-mgmt
Error from server (InternalError): Internal error occurred:
Authorization error (user=kube-apiserver-kubelet-client, verb=get,
resource=nodes, subresource=proxy)

# Cannot create Pod in opa Namespace (even though opa Namespace is labeled
# to be ignored)
$ kubectl -n opa run --image=alpine -it alpine-shell -- /bin/sh
If you don't see a command prompt, try pressing enter.
warning: couldn't attach to pod/alpine-shell, falling back to streaming logs:
unable to upgrade connection: Authorization error
(user=kube-apiserver-kubelet-client, verb=create, resource=nodes,
subresource=proxy)
Error from server (InternalError): Internal error occurred: Authorization
error (user=kube-apiserver-kubelet-client, verb=get, resource=nodes,
subresource=proxy)

$ kubectl apply -f generated/config/kubelet-api-admin.yaml
Error from server (InternalError): error when creating
"generated/config/kubelet-api-admin.yaml": Internal error occurred:
failed calling webhook "validating-webhook.openpolicyagent.org":
failed to call webhook: the server could not find the requested resource
```

As shown in the previous examples, not having the main OPA entry point correctly configured can lead to multiple errors with different symptoms, none of which intuitively indicate that the missing main entry point is the issue.

When OPA receives the API server request containing the AdmissionReview object, it binds the AdmissionReview object to the OPA input document. The OPA entry-point policy must generate the AdmissionReview.response to satisfy the contract we learned about in Chapter 4. This contract stipulates the following conditions:

- Response uid must match request uid.
- The allowed field must be true or false.
- The status object should be provided for validation failures.

As you can see, the AdmissionReview.response is constructed to be sent back to the Kubernetes API server. You may notice that the data.kubernetes.admission import is also part of this in this main policy; this import is not required in other policies added to OPA:

```
# Main OPA entry point policy
apiVersion: v1
kind: ConfigMap
metadata:
  name: opa-default-system-main
  namespace: opa
...
data:
  main: |  ❶
    package system

    import data.kubernetes.admission

    main = {
      "apiVersion": "admission.k8s.io/v1",
      "kind": "AdmissionReview",
      "response": response,
    }

    default uid = ""

    uid = input.request.uid

    response = {
        "allowed": false,
        "uid": uid,
        "status": {
            "reason": reason,
        },
    } {
        reason = concat(", ", admission.deny)
```

```
            reason != ""
    }
    else = {"allowed": true, "uid": uid}
```

❶ This Rego configures the main policy entry point and AdmissionReview .response.

In the preceding entry-point policy, the `system.main` object must be present for the validating admission webhook to function with default settings. Without this package and object, the Rego policies may still correctly compile, but the validation will fail for the missing *system.main* document, as seen in the following error:

```
# Error message - missing main entry point
...
"error": {
        "code": "undefined_document",
        "message": "document missing: data.system.main"
    }
...
```

Querying the OPA server in the cluster can retrieve this *system.main* document:

```
# Get main entry point policy from OPA query
# OPA query run from Alpine container inside cluster
$ curl -k https://opa.opa.svc/v1/data/system/main
{"decision_id":"06ea19e3-de9c-4fe3-a34d-3a58cab39403","result":
{"apiVersion":"admission.k8s.io/v1","kind":"AdmissionReview","response":
{"allowed":true,"uid":""}}}
```

The entry-point policy with the `system.main` object constructs the scaffolding for the AdmissionReview.response. With this model, the other policies loaded into OPA do not need to do the same. This also reduces potential errors. The response includes the `allowed`, `status`, and `uid` fields. As a reminder, the `uid` must match the `uid` sent to OPA in the AdmissionReview.request; this is done by the `uid = input.request.uid` line.

Next, we will explore how we can write reusable Rego, usable across multiple policies.

Custom Helper Libraries

Rego—like other languages—supports code libraries to reduce common coding and improve DRY (don't repeat yourself). Using DRY methods also reduces errors. When I use OPA (classic) in Kubernetes, I almost always use my so-called *helpers* libraries to reduce common coding that I must write to make policies functional and more expressive. In the OPA installation examples, I could have installed my *helpers* library with the following command:

```
# Apply helpers library policy
$ kubectl apply -f policy-configmaps/0-lib.yaml
```

The *helpers* library contains several functions that I reuse in multiple policies to reduce code duplication. As you can see in the following Rego, most of the helpers are focused on getting fields and objects from the inbound AdmissionReview object:

```
# Rego Kubermetes helper library
kind: ConfigMap
apiVersion: v1
metadata:
  name: library-k8s-helpers
  namespace: opa
  labels:
    app: opa
    billing: lob-cc
    env: dev
    owner: jimmy
    openpolicyagent.org/policy: rego
data:
  main: |
    package lib.k8s.helpers

    allowed_operations = allowed_ops {
      allowed_ops := {"CREATE", "UPDATE"}
    }

    request_operation = op {
      op := input.request.operation
    }

    request_metadata_labels = labels {
      labels := input.request.object.metadata.labels
    }

    request_spec_template_metadata_labels = labels {
      labels := input.request.object.spec.template.metadata.labels
    }

    deployment_error = e {
      e := "DEPLOYMENT_INVALID"
    }

    deployment_containers = c {
      c := input.request.object.spec.template.spec.containers
    }

    required_deployment_labels = l {
      l := {"app", "owner"}
    }

    deployment_role = dr {
      dr := input.request.object.spec.template.metadata.annotations["iam..."]
    }
```

```
service_error = e {
  e := "SERVICE_INVALID"
}

allowed_ext_ips = l {
  l := ["1.1.1.1","2.2.2.2","3.3.3.3","4.4.4.4"]
}

ips_allowed(a,x) {
  allowedIPs := {ip | ip := a[_]}
  externalIPs := {ip | ip := x[_]}
  forbiddenIPs := externalIPs - allowedIPs
  count(forbiddenIPs) > 0
}

request_object = o {
  o := input.request.object
}

request_id = value {
  value := sprintf("%v/%v/%v", [
    request_namespace,
    request_name,
    request_kind
  ])
}

request_name = value {
  value := input.request.object.metadata.name
}

request_namespace = value {
  value := input.request.object.metadata.namespace
}

else = value {
  value := "NOT_FOUND"
}

request_kind = value {
  value := input.request.kind.kind
}

else = value {
  value := "NOT_FOUND"
}
```

In the following policy—a Deployment version of the prior policy to restrict from where container images are sourced—I used the helper functions to go after inbound request data, such as operations, kind, images, and request ID. I constructed the request ID from a combination of the resource name, namespace, and kind:

```
# Configmap with Deployment registry validation policy
kind: ConfigMap
apiVersion: v1
metadata:
  name: deployment-registry-allowed
  namespace: opa
  labels:
...
    openpolicyagent.org/policy: rego
data:
  main: |
    package kubernetes.admission

    import data.lib.k8s.helpers as helpers

    deny[msg] {
      helpers.request_kind == "Deployment"
      helpers.allowed_operations[helpers.request_operation]
      image = helpers.deployment_containers[_].image
      not reg_matches_any(image,valid_deployment_registries_v2)
      msg = sprintf("%q: %q image is not sourced from an authorized registry. \
      Resource ID (ns/name/kind): %q", [helpers.deployment_error,image,
      helpers.request_id])
    }

    valid_deployment_registries_v2 = {registry |
      allowed = "GOOD_REGISTRY"
      registries = split(allowed, ",")
      registry = registries[_]
    }

    reg_matches_any(str, patterns) {
      reg_matches(str, patterns[_])
    }

    reg_matches(str, pattern) {
      contains(str, pattern)
    }
```

In the preceding policy, I imported the *helpers* library and referenced it as *helpers* with the following statement:

```
# Rego import statement for helpers library
import data.lib.k8s.helpers as helpers
```

With helpers, we can reduce code duplication and errors, leveraging reusable libraries.

We are now going to shift gears a bit and explore how OPA can be used with mutating webhooks.

Mutating Configuration and Policies

Configuring OPA for mutating admission control in Kubernetes is like configuring validating admission, which we explored earlier in this chapter; I used a similar shell script and make process. The following console output contains the installed MutatingWebhookConfiguration resource YAML:

```
# Get the mutating webhook configurations in the cluster
$ kubectl get mutatingwebhookconfigurations opa-mutating-webhook -oyaml
apiVersion: admissionregistration.k8s.io/v1
kind: MutatingWebhookConfiguration
metadata:
  labels:
    app: opa
    billing: lob-cc
    env: dev
    owner: jimmy
  name: opa-mutating-webhook
webhooks:
- admissionReviewVersions:
  - v1
  clientConfig:
    caBundle: LS0…
    service:
      name: opa
      namespace: opa
      port: 443
  failurePolicy: Fail
  matchPolicy: Equivalent
  name: mutating-webhook.openpolicyagent.org
  namespaceSelector:
    matchExpressions:
    - key: openpolicyagent.org/webhook
      operator: NotIn
      values:
      - ignore
  objectSelector: {}
  reinvocationPolicy: Never
  Rules:  ❶
  - apiGroups:
    - '*'
    apiVersions:
    - '*'
    operations:
    - CREATE
    - UPDATE
    resources:
    - pods
    scope: '*'
  sideEffects: None
  timeoutSeconds: 10
```

❶ Configure rules to handle Kubernetes resource types.

Again, the admission webhook will only affect Pods during CREATE or UPDATE operations and only in Namespaces not labeled with `openpolicyagent.org/webhook=ignore`. Mutation of inbound resources—contained within API server requests—is done using the JSON patch schema that is defined in RFC 6902 (*https://oreil.ly/rfc6902*).

As I mentioned earlier in this book, the OPA community is vast, and the GitHub OPA organization is host to at least 22 repositories. To demonstrate how mutating admission works, I used a portion of an older GitHub project, the OPA Library (*https://oreil.ly/YyW6I*). I installed the *kubernetes/mutating-admission/main.rego* policy via a configmap to build the entry-point policy that creates the contract fields for the Kubernetes AdmissionReview.response object. Since the Rego package was not *system*, I decided to change the OPA server `default_decision` argument, as shown in the following YAML; another option would have been to change the packages to *system*:

```
# OPA admission controller server arguments
args:
  - "run"
  - "--server"
  - "--tls-cert-file=/certs/tls.crt"
  - "--tls-private-key-file=/certs/tls.key"
  - "--addr=0.0.0.0:8443"
  - "--addr=http://127.0.0.1:8181"
# - "--set=bundles.default.resource=bundle.tar.gz"
  - "--log-format=json"
  - "--set=status.console=true"
  - "--set=decision_logs.console=true"
  - "--set=default_decision=/library/kubernetes/admission/mutating/main"
```

Another matching option would have been to not modify the `default_decision` argument for the OPA server but instead add a path field to the webhook configuration, as shown in the following YAML:

```
# Mutating webhook service configuration
service:
  namespace: opa
  name: opa
  path: /v0/data/library/kubernetes/admission/mutating/main
  port: 443
```

In Chapter 2, I introduced you to the OPA REST API */v1/...* endpoint. The v1 API endpoint—when used with post queries—expects a defined input JSON document, as seen in the following JSON:

```
// Example input document
{
    "input":{
        "message":"world"
    }
}
```

When the Kubernetes API server posts the AdmissionReview document to OPA—for a mutating or validating decision—it does not use the input document structure. The v0 API endpoint expects no such structure; it handles raw input, and the subsequent rules handle the POST request.

Since the default decision path for OPA is */system/main*, I needed to update either the entry-point package and main rule to match the default OPA decision path, the `default_decision` argument to match the entry-point package and main rule, or the webhook `service.path` field to match the entry-point package and main rule. Without this match, I would see the following error in the OPA decision logs:

```
# Main entry-point policy mismatch error
{"decision_id":"1739aacc-48e3-4346-a19a-6ba479dd6b26","error":{"code":
"undefined_document","message":"document missing: data.system.main"},"...
```

Next, I used the policy patterns from the aforementioned OPA Library project to patch Pods with labels, if the labels did not yet exist. My policy uses several helper functions that are contained in the entry-point Rego. To use them, I defined my policy Rego in the same package as the entry-point Rego:

```
# Configmap with mutating policy
kind: ConfigMap
apiVersion: v1
metadata:
  name: label-pods
  namespace: opa
  labels:
...
    openpolicyagent.org/policy: rego
data:
  main: |
    package system

    ############################################################
    # PATCH rules
    #
    # Note: All patch rules should start with `isValidRequest` and
    # `isCreateOrUpdate`
```

```
##########################################################

# add billing,env,owner labels to pods
patch[patchCode] {  ❶
  isValidRequest
  isCreateOrUpdate
  input.request.kind.kind == "Pod"
  not hasLabelValue(input.request.object, "billing", "lob-cc")
  patchCode = makeLabelPatch("add", "billing", "lob-cc", "")
}
patch[patchCode] {  ❷
  isValidRequest
  isCreateOrUpdate
  input.request.kind.kind == "Pod"
  not hasLabelValue(input.request.object, "env", "dev")
  patchCode = makeLabelPatch("add", "env", "dev", "")
}
patch[patchCode] {  ❸
  isValidRequest
  isCreateOrUpdate
  input.request.kind.kind == "Pod"
  not hasLabelValue(input.request.object, "owner", "jimmy")
  patchCode = makeLabelPatch("add", "owner", "jimmy", "")
}
```

❶ This patch adds the billing label.

❷ This patch adds the env label.

❸ This patch adds the owner label.

The mutating process uses functions from the entry-point Rego to create a flattened array of patches, marshal the array into JSON, and then Base64-encode the patches to be sent back to the Kubernetes API server:

```
# marshaling JSON from patch array, then base64 encoding
x := {
  "allowed": true,
  "uid": response_uid,
  "patchType": "JSONPatch",
  "patch": base64.encode(json.marshal(fullPatches)),}
```

If we grab the decision logs from OPA when a Pod is created and decode the Base64-encoded string, we can see all three patches that were applied to the Pod request before it continued in the flow to validation and, potentially, etcd:

```
// AdmissionReview response returned to the API server
…"result": {
        "apiVersion": "admission.k8s.io/v1",
        "kind": "AdmissionReview",
        "response": {
            "allowed": true,
            "patch": "W3sib…fV0=",
            "patchType": "JSONPatch",
            "uid": "32c8e37c-8f01-4787-bf47-58e70d07fed1"
        }
    },...
```

```
# base64 decoded JSON patches
$ echo "W3si…fV0=" | base64 -d
[{"op":"add","path":"/metadata/labels","value":{}},{"op":"add","path":
"/metadata/labels/billing","value":"lob-cc"},{"op":"add","path":
"/metadata/labels/env","value":"dev"},{"op":"add","path":
"/metadata/labels/owner","value":"jimmy"}]
```

As you can see in the preceding example, the patches sent back to the API server are an array of JSON patch objects.

Now that we have explored how validating and mutating webhooks use OPA, let's look at how we can centralize the management of OPA resources.

Centralized OPA Management with Styra DAS

In Chapter 3, we explored using Styra DAS to centrally manage OPA agents and policy bundles. In fact, using OPA (classic) for Kubernetes validating and mutating webhook services enables you to use OPA management features, such as bundles and decision logs.

To use Styra DAS with my local minikube environment, I created a system in my Styra DAS (Free) workspace. Then I used install commands from my configured Styra system to create the Styra resources in my local cluster. This can be seen in Figure 5-2.

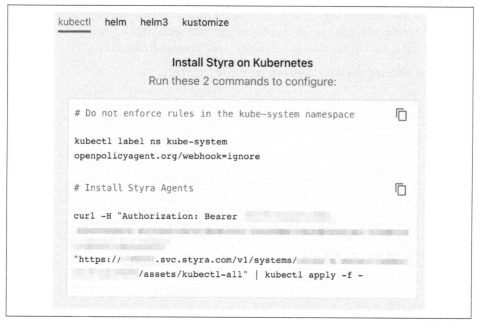

Figure 5-2. Styra system agent install

I used the following automated install script, built with the install commands I received from my Styra DAS workspace:

```
# Styra automated install scripts
$ ./up-styra.sh
clusterrolebinding.rbac.authorization.k8s.io/kubelet-api-admin created
namespace/kube-system labeled
  % Total    % Received % Xferd  Average Speed   Time    Time     Time  Current
                                 Dload  Upload   Total   Spent    Left  Speed
100 20408    0 20408    0     0  24350      0 --:--:-- --:--:-- --:--:-- 24440
namespace/styra-system created
secret/opa-server created
configmap/opa-config created
secret/das-slp-token created
clusterrolebinding.rbac.authorization.k8s.io/opa-viewer created
service/opa created
statefulset.apps/opa created
secret/styra-access created
configmap/datasources-agent-config created
clusterrole.rbac.authorization.k8s.io/read-all-global created
clusterrolebinding.rbac.authorization.k8s.io/datasources-agent-read-all created
deployment.apps/datasources-agent created
validatingwebhookconfiguration.admissionregistration.k8s.io/
opa-validating-webhook created
mutatingwebhookconfiguration.admissionregistration.k8s.io/
opa-mutating-webhook created
```

Once the Strya OPA resources are installed, I can view the Pods running in the `styra-system` Namespace:

```
# Get OPA Pods from Stray system
$ kubectl -n styra-system get pod
NAME                                READY   STATUS    RESTARTS   AGE
datasources-agent-7c556dfdf6-49p6w  1/1     Running   0          5m33s
opa-0                               2/2     Running   0          5m33s
opa-1                               2/2     Running   0          5m17s
opa-2                               2/2     Running   0          5m
```

With OPA agents installed and connected to my Styra workspace, I can now create policies that will be propagated to remote agents. Next, let's explore the Styra tools to write, store, and deploy policies across your environments.

Policy Management

To exercise the centralized policy management features of Styra DAS with my local minikube environment, I created and published a rule in my workspace, shown in Figure 5-3. The rule IDE validates rules (syntax, etc.) and provides an interface to preview execution with mocks, input, and output documents, much like we experience with the Rego Playground.

Figure 5-3. Editing and publishing rules in Styra DAS

As shown in Figure 5-3, the rule is set to enforce; it can also be set to monitor or ignore. Within Styra DAS (free), I can create up to one hundred rules. Monitor is handy, should you need to send notifications to Slack channels and so forth without enforcing denials.

If you would rather store and manage your policies in a Git repository, Styra DAS can be configured as a Git client. Figure 5-4 depicts the Git client settings.

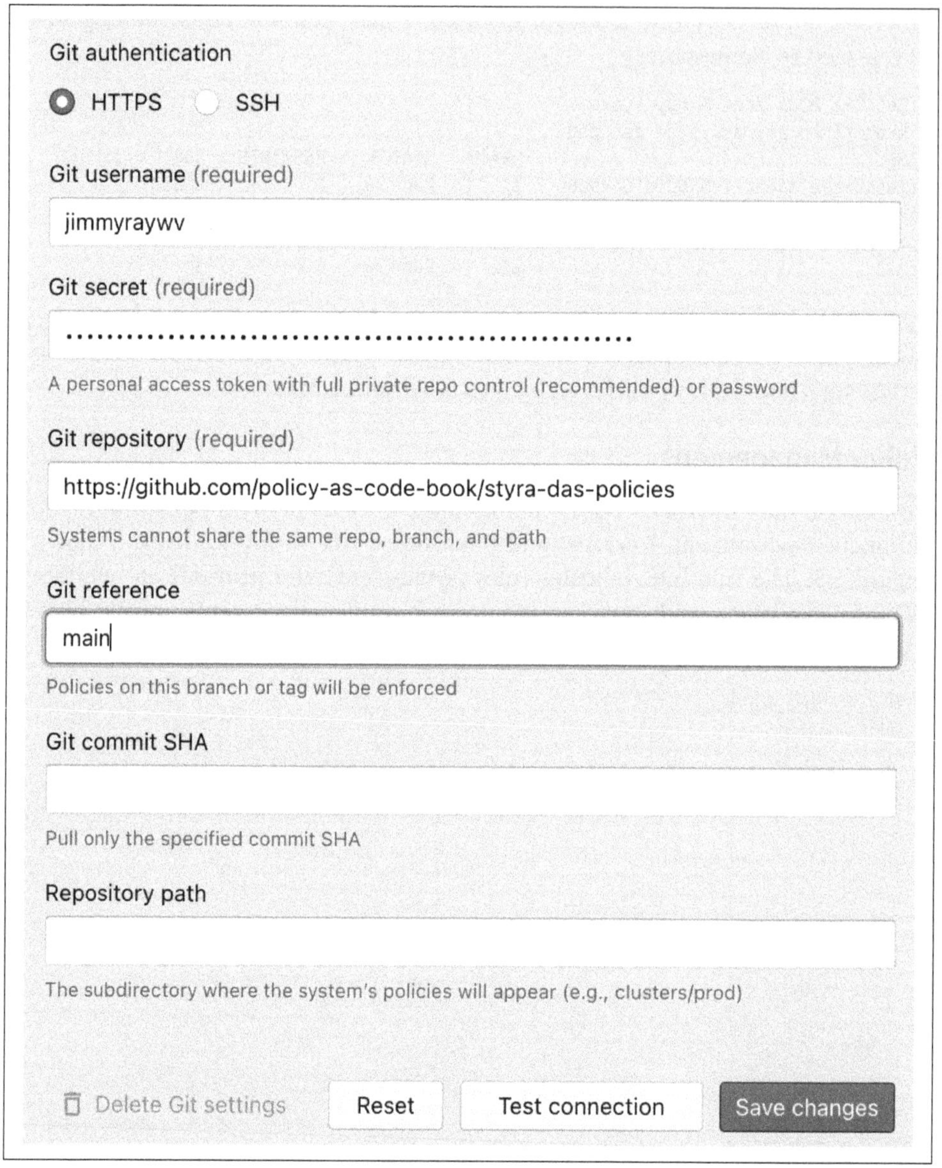

Figure 5-4. Styra DAS Git client configuration

As seen in Figure 5-4, you can optionally configure DAS to pull only from specific branches or tags with specific Git commit hashes at specific paths.

There are several DAS features that I think directly add value for OPA management, and one of my favorites is related to OPA rules. DAS offers Compliance Packs that group policies and best practices. Using predefined groups of policies focused on specific security, governance, and compliance areas is easier than trying to start from scratch. According to the Styra DAS documentation (*https://oreil.ly/ci_G4*), Compliance Packs are only supported in Kubernetes systems. The following packs are available in the DAS free version:

- Kubernetes Best Practices (available in free version)
- CIS Benchmarks (available in free version)
- MITRE ATT&CK
- PCI DSS v3.2
- Pod Security Policies (available in free version)

Publishing the rule created an OPA bundle that was then downloaded to my local OPA agents. I also downloaded the bundle from my workspace and extracted the contents from the bundle tarball. There is a wealth of Rego knowledge to be had in those files. The bundle deployments can be seen in my Styra DAS workspace in Figure 5-5.

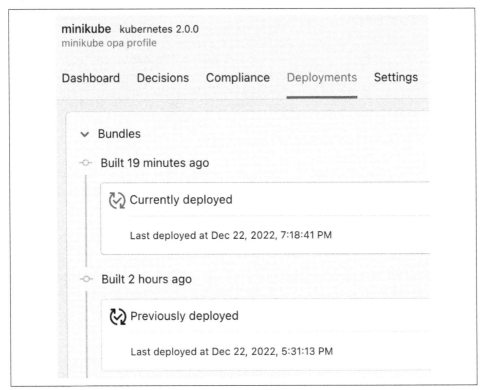

Figure 5-5. Styra DAS bundle deployments

With the bundle now deployed locally, I can test the `deny-all` rule I created in Styra DAS:

```
# Test deny-all policy
$ kubectl -n test apply -f 1-test-pod.yaml
Error from server: error when creating "mutating/test/1-test-pod.yaml":
admission webhook "validating-webhook.openpolicyagent.org" denied the
request: Enforced: Request object: "{\"apiVersion\": \"v1\", \"kind\":
\"Pod\"...
```

In Figure 5-6, you can see the centralized logging that is part of the Styra DAS OPA management features.

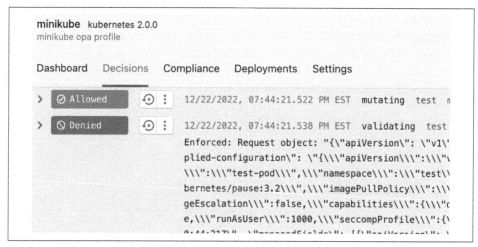

Figure 5-6. Styra DAS centralized OPA decision logs

Using Styra DAS with Kubernetes provides centralized tools to manage and deliver policies, data, and logs to and from multiple OPA agents across multiple clusters.

Before we wrap up, let's walk through uninstalling Styra DAS.

Uninstalling Styra DAS

To uninstall the Styra DAS OPA resources, I can use the uninstall commands made available to me in my workspace with the following automation script I built with the commands I received from Styra DAS:

```
# Uninstall Styra DAS
$ ./down-styra.sh
  % Total    % Received % Xferd  Average Speed   Time    Time     Time  Current
                                 Dload  Upload   Total   Spent    Left  Speed
100 20412    0 20412    0     0  23633      0 --:--:-- --:--:-- --:--:-- 23762
namespace "styra-system" deleted
secret "opa-server" deleted
```

```
configmap "opa-config" deleted
secret "das-slp-token" deleted
clusterrolebinding.rbac.authorization.k8s.io "opa-viewer" deleted
service "opa" deleted
statefulset.apps "opa" deleted
secret "styra-access" deleted
configmap "datasources-agent-config" deleted
clusterrole.rbac.authorization.k8s.io "read-all-global" deleted
clusterrolebinding.rbac.authorization.k8s.io "datasources-agent-read-all"
deleted
deployment.apps "datasources-agent" deleted
validatingwebhookconfiguration.admissionregistration.k8s.io
"opa-validating-webhook" deleted
mutatingwebhookconfiguration.admissionregistration.k8s.io
"opa-mutating-webhook" deleted
No resources found
namespace/kube-system unlabeled
```

Once the OPA resources are removed from my local minikube cluster, I can see
related errors in my Styra DAS minikube-system Deployments screen, shown in
Figure 5-7. These errors indicate a connection issue between my Styra workspace and
my local OPA agent.

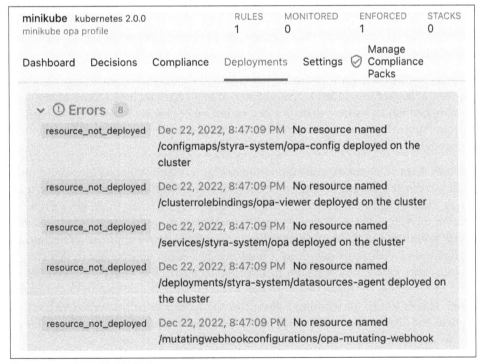

Figure 5-7. Styra DAS deployment errors

The errors in Figure 5-7 should be used to troubleshoot connectivity issues between Styra and remote OPA agents. With Styra DAS, you have a centralized view of your connected OPAs.

Summary

The most important aspect about OPA that I want readers to recognize is that OPA is a very mature solution to policy-enable Kubernetes mutation and validation use cases. Moreover, it has evolved as Kubernetes has evolved. In this chapter, I used tools from three to four years ago—shell scripts and GitHub projects—that still function with the latest versions of OPA. To me, this means that OPA maturity has not sacrificed backward compatibility. While I referred to OPA in this chapter as *OPA classic*, that term is not meant to denigrate OPA. OPA's maturity has led to several enhancements as well as tools that make OPA easier to learn and more viable for enterprise adoption.

OPA was the first PaC solution that I used with Kubernetes, and I still find myself measuring some of the other solutions against it. While the PaC landscape has changed over the years, I think that OPA for Kubernetes is sometimes underrated. As a programmer, I find OPA appealing for its flexibility and extensibility. There are several points—within OPA and the surrounding Kubernetes configuration—where OPA can be modified to fit your needs, such as defining the main entry-point paths for webhook connectivity.

When it comes to OPA policies for Kubenetes, we barely scratched the surface with the few examples I included in this chapter. While I have included more in the companion GitHub repository, there is a vast collection of policies in the OPA-Kubernetes community; when you decide to use OPA, you can tap into years of experience and an abundance of Rego in the wild.

Usually, I am all about demonstrating the easiest way to install, configure, and uninstall Kubernetes resources. In the case of OPA, that was definitely accomplished using Styra DAS integration. However, the kube-mgmt Helm chart may be a preferred option for you, if you (1) want or need a package-management approach to Kubernetes resources and (2) would rather have a more declarative automation beyond my Makefile and shell-script solutions. I used my shell-script approaches in this chapter because they expose how the OPA installation—the hard way—really works. I believe that learning this approach better prepares you for troubleshooting an OPA installation. This is similar to learning Kubernetes the hard way (*https://oreil.ly/EJa9c*). Of course, the Styra DAS solution also offers Helm installation as well as kustomize for those users and organizations that have standardized on those tools.

When it comes to OPA, Rego was somewhat challenging for me at first, but now I am comfortable with its lexicon and syntax. I think that OPA users with programming backgrounds have an easier time with some of Rego's features, such as packages and building and importing libraries for reuse—like my *helpers* library. That being said, this is another area where Styra DAS can help. The rich IDE inside the DAS interface can be augmented with libraries of reusable snippets—business logic and data—as well as the Compliance Packs. And if you have already been using the Rego Playground, as I routinely do for prototyping and troubleshooting, the preview feature of the DAS rules IDE should feel familiar.

With the kube-mgmt sidecar, you can configure policies and data—configmaps and replicated Kubernetes resources—to be loaded into OPA. This adds data, beyond that in the input context, to better support API server request evaluations. We can also apply AuthZ best practices to prevent unwanted access to OPA.

When we return to the PaC Solution Selection Scorecard from Chapter 1, OPA again checks several of the boxes for Kubernetes use cases. As we move forward with other PaC solutions, some of the most prominent differentiators between PaC solutions—with some notable exceptions—will lean more toward matching organizational capabilities and less toward core feature sets.

In Chapter 6, we will explore MagTape for use inside Kubernetes. Like some of the tooling exposed in this chapter, MagTape leverages the strength of OPA and Rego but enhances it with layers of UX features and business logic.

MagTape and Kubernetes

In this chapter, I am going to focus on MagTape (*https://github.com/tmobile/magtape*), an OSS PaC project, originally from T-Mobile, that is underpinned by OPA and Rego. MagTape wraps and extends OPA. In the context of design patterns (*https://www.gofpattern.com*), MagTape applies the Decorator design pattern to give additional functionality to OPA without changing the underlying OPA implementation.

The purpose of MagTape's extensions is to add business workflows, including a notification layer that integrates to Slack via webhooks. As a decorator or a wrapper of OPA, MagTape operates between the Kubernetes API server and the OPA service, like a proxy. MagTape configures a layer of indirection using init containers for OPA service integration.

According to the project insights, most of the contributions to the MagTape project were made in 2020. There were also some in 2021 and 2022, but the project doesn't seem to be too active. This is further evidenced by the relatively older versions of OPA and kube-mgmt that the MagTape install is currently set to use. That being said, I included MagTape in this book to expose some interesting ideas and best practices for using OPA in Kubernetes. So let's get started by exploring how MagTape is installed and configured.

Installing and Uninstalling MagTape

MagTape is easy to install and uninstall via the following install YAML file:

```
# Download install YAML
$ curl -O \
https://raw.githubusercontent.com/tmobile/magtape/v2.4.0/deploy/install.yaml
```

Although instructions for installing and uninstalling MagTape can be found in the project *README.md*, I opted to download the install manifests and modify them for my needs.

MagTape is an older project, with the last update being more than two years ago. Given the PaC solution selection criteria that I gave in Chapter 1, that should be an immediate red flag for readers, and I agree. In fact, after pulling the latest MagTape container from Docker Hub, I ran docker scout quickview (*https://oreil.ly/pXhxz*) to get an idea of CVEs in this outdated container image. I wasn't surprised by the following output:

```
# Docker scout quickview of MagTape container image
$ docker scout quickview tmobile/magtape:v2.4.0
    ✓ Image stored for indexing
    ✓ Indexed 93 packages

    Target                   |  tmobile/magtape:v2.4.0  |  1C   33H   20M   1L
      digest                 |  e545b933cb3c            |
    Base image               |  python:3-alpine         |  1C    9H    4M   0L
    Refreshed base image     |  python:3-alpine         |  0C    1H    1M   0L
                             |                          |  -1    -8    -3
    Updated base image       |  python:3.9-alpine3.18   |  0C    2H    2M   0L
                             |                          |  -1    -7    -2
```

As you can see in the preceding output, several CVEs are listed, including some with high and critical severities. As I said, I expected this from this outdated project.

However, the reason I am sharing MagTape in this book—albeit in a shorter chapter—is because it challenges the traditional Kubernetes PaC deployment scheme. As we will see later in the section "Proxying OPA with MagTape" on page 185, the MagTape application runs between the Kubernetes API server and OPA. This arrangement enables MagTape to deliver organizational-specific business logic that is not part of OPA or other PaC solutions, out of the box.

I experienced a few issues during the install, no doubt because of the age of the project; I encountered multiple errors that I needed to fix. The first error was due to an outdated API version for PodDisruptionBudget (PDB) resources; I am running a Kubernetes 1.29.1 cluster:

```
# Outdated API version error
error: resource mapping not found for name: "magtape-pdb" namespace:
"magtape-system" from "install.yaml": no matches for kind "PodDisruptionBudget"
in version "policy/v1beta1" ensure CRDs are installed first
```

To fix the issues, I edited the downloaded install YAML and updated the PDB to version 1. Then, I updated the OPA and kube-mgmt container images to *openpolicy-agent/opa:0.62.1-static* and *openpolicyagent/kube-mgmt:8.5.5*, respectively. I also set the `--namespaces=magtape-system` on the kube-mgmt container so that kube-mgmt could find and ingest policy ConfigMap resources. Finally, I reset the Validating WebhookConfiguration rules to use the value `apiVersions=v1`, as shown in the following YAML snippet; without that `v1` value, the webhook would not fire:

```
#  ValidatingWebhookConfiguration rules
rules:
  - apiGroups:
    - '*'
    apiVersions:
    - v1  ❶
    operations:
    - CREATE
    - UPDATE
    resources:
    - deployments
    - statefulsets
    - daemonsets
    - pods
    - poddisruptionbudgets
```

❶ The `apiVersions` must be set to `v1` to support explicitly defining multiple resources.

When it comes to ValidatingWebhookConfiguration rules, you need to pay attention to how the `apiVersions` are specified when you explicitly define multiple resources. In the preceding rules, a wildcard (*) would not have worked and would have rendered the webhook unresponsive. When it comes to webhook rules, I keep to the following guidelines:

```
# Explicitly defined multiple resources do not work with an apiVersion wildcard value
rules:
  - operations: ["CREATE", "UPDATE"]
    apiGroups: ["*"]
    apiVersions: ["*"]
    resources: ["pods","deployments","services"]

# Pods alone work with an apiVersion wildcard value
rules:
  - operations: ["CREATE", "UPDATE"]
    apiGroups: ["*"]
```

```
    apiVersions: ["*"]
    resources: ["pods"]

# All wildcard values (apiGroups, apiVersions, resources) work
rules:
  - operations: ["CREATE", "UPDATE"]
    apiGroups: ["*"]
    apiVersions: ["*"]
    resources: ["*"]

# Explicitly defined multiple resources work with an apiVersion v1 value
rules:
  - operations: ["CREATE", "UPDATE"]
    apiGroups: ["*"]
    apiVersions: ["v1"]
    resources: ["pods","deployments","services"]
```

 When troubleshooting nonworking ValidatingWebhookConfiguration, especially when the webhook doesn't seem to fire when it should, the three issues I first search for are:

- Incorrect opt-in or opt-out Namespace labeling

- Resources not included in rules

- apiVersions not congruent with explicitly defined multiple resources

At that point, MagTape installed successfully:

```
# Use downloaded and edited install.yaml to install MagTape
$ make up
./up.sh 2>&1
namespace/magtape-system created
clusterrole.rbac.authorization.k8s.io/magtape-write created
clusterrole.rbac.authorization.k8s.io/magtape-read created
clusterrolebinding.rbac.authorization.k8s.io/magtape-write-crb created
clusterrolebinding.rbac.authorization.k8s.io/magtape-read-crb created
role.rbac.authorization.k8s.io/magtape-ops created
rolebinding.rbac.authorization.k8s.io/magtape-ops-rb created
serviceaccount/magtape-sa created
configmap/magtape-env created
configmap/magtape-vwc-template created
configmap/magtape-opa-default-main created
configmap/magtape-opa-entrypoint created
service/magtape-svc created
poddisruptionbudget.policy/magtape-pdb created
deployment.apps/magtape created
horizontalpodautoscaler.autoscaling/magtape created
configmap/policy-emptydir-check created
configmap/policy-host-path-check created
configmap/policy-host-port-check created
```

```
configmap/policy-liveness-probe-check created
configmap/policy-node-port-range-check created
configmap/policy-pdb-check created
configmap/policy-port-name-mismatch created
configmap/policy-privileged-pod-check created
configmap/policy-readiness-probe-check created
configmap/policy-resource-limits-check created
configmap/policy-resource-requests-check created
configmap/policy-singleton-pod-check created
namespace/policy-test created
namespace/policy-test labeled
```

Once MagTape was installed, I performed the normal checks to make sure it was working and was installed into my minikube cluster. For demo purposes, I set the replica count to 1. I accomplished this by directly editing the MagTape Deployment resource with the following command:

```
# Edit MagTape Deployment resource
$ kubectl -n magtape-system edit deployment magtape
```

Changing the spec.replicas element allowed me to set the number of replicas, and it caused the Deployment to replace the currently running Pod with a new one. I routinely do this when I am testing or prototyping solutions. Having only one replica makes it easier to track down log entries. Editing the downloaded *install.yaml* file before applying it with kubectl would have been another means to set the replicas:

```
# Check that MagTape pods are running
$ kubectl -n magtape-system get pods
NAME                      READY   STATUS    RESTARTS   AGE
magtape-5b45bc79df-vfmc2  1/1     Running   0          4m47s

# Get validatingwebhookconfiguration configuration
$ kubectl get validatingwebhookconfiguration
NAME             WEBHOOKS   AGE
magtape-webhook  1          169m
```

As you can see, a ValidatingWebhookConfiguration was created. The settings of the webhook configuration are in the following YAML:

```
# Get validatingwebhookconfiguration YAML
$ kubectl get validatingwebhookconfiguration magtape-webhook -oyaml

# validatingwebhookconfiguration yaml
apiVersion: admissionregistration.k8s.io/v1
kind: ValidatingWebhookConfiguration
metadata:
  labels:
    app: magtape
  name: magtape-webhook
webhooks:
- admissionReviewVersions:
```

```
  - v1
  clientConfig:
    caBundle: LS0…  ❶
    Service:
      name: magtape-svc
      namespace: magtape-system
      path: /
      port: 443
  failurePolicy: Fail
  matchPolicy: Equivalent
  name: magtape.webhook.k8s.t-mobile.com
  namespaceSelector:
    matchLabels:
      k8s.t-mobile.com/magtape: enabled
  objectSelector: {}
  rules:
  - apiGroups:
    - '*'
    apiVersions:
    - 'v1'
    operations:
    - CREATE
    - UPDATE
    Resources:  ❷
    - deployments
    - statefulsets
    - daemonsets
    - pods
    - poddisruptionbudgets
    scope: '*'
  sideEffects: None
  timeoutSeconds: 10
```

❶   The TLS caBundle allows the webhook to call the service.

❷   These resources will be monitored by this webhook.

The webhook configuration is similar to those we have already seen, except the preceding webhook will pay attention to only a subset of Kubernetes resources, and only from Namespaces that are opted into the MagTape review with the defined label. I have labeled the policy-test Namespace to be reviewed by MagTape:

```
# Create policy-test namespace
$ kubectl apply -f - <<EOF
apiVersion: v1
kind: Namespace
metadata:
  name: policy-test
EOF
namespace/policy-test created
```

```
# Label policy-test namespace to opt-in to validation
$ kubectl label ns policy-test k8s.t-mobile.com/magtape=enabled
namespace/test labeled

# Get namespaces by the k8s.t-mobile.com/magtape=enabled label/value
$ kubectl get namespaces -l k8s.t-mobile.com/magtape=enabled
NAME          STATUS   AGE
policy-test   test     Active    2d5h
```

 Most Kubernetes PaC solutions in this book use an opt-out or
ignore option, via Namespace labels. MagTape uses an opt-in
approach, maybe for organizational-specific requirements.

When using PaC to control unwanted changes to Kubernetes clusters, opt out is a better model. You simply cannot control unwanted
behaviors when your tenants don't have to follow the rules. Moreover, the ability for tenant Namespaces to opt out of PaC review
should be tightly controlled. In Chapter 7, I write about how Gatekeeper controls the ability for opting out by preventing unauthorized labeling of Namespaces that would cause the webhook to
ignore the operations within those Namespaces.

Four containers run in the MagTape Pod:

- MagTape init (init-container)
- MagTape
- OPA
- kube-mgmt

You should be familiar with the OPA and kube-mgmt containers from Chapter 5 as
well as with how to configure a validating admission webhook.

Several ConfigMap resources are created as part of the MagTape install. As we
learned in Chapter 5, the kube-mgmt container loads the policies from the configmaps into OPA if the configmaps are labeled with `openpolicyagent.org/policy:
rego`:

```
# Policy configmap with OK status
kind: ConfigMap
metadata:
  annotations:
    openpolicyagent.org/policy-status: '{"status":"ok"}'
  labels:
    app: opa
    openpolicyagent.org/policy: rego
  name: magtape-opa-entrypoint
  namespace: magtape-system
data:
```

```
magtape.rego: |-
  package magtape

  # This acts as an entrypoint to call all policies under "kubernetes.admission"

  decisions[{"policy": p, "reasons": reasons}] {
    data.kubernetes.admission[p].matches
    reasons := data.kubernetes.admission[p].deny
  }
```

I also used the debugger Pod from Chapter 5 to see what's going on with the OPA instance running inside the MagTape Pod:

```
# Run debugger pod
$ kubectl -n magtape-system run -it debugger \
--image jimmyraywv/debugger:v0.1.0 --restart=Never
/ # curl -k https://10.244.0.10:8443/v1/data/magtape
{"result":{"decisions":[]}}
```

I found the MagTape Pod IP address—used in the preceding command—with the following command that gets the MagTape Pod and uses a JSONPath expression to get the podIP address field value:

```
# Get MagTape Pod IP address
$ kubectl -n magtape-system get po magtape-686748447d-mqb88 \
-o jsonpath='{.status.podIP}'
podIP: 10.244.0.10
```

Now that we've seen the outcome of the install, let's check out the work that the init container does.

MagTape init

As we have already learned, TLS secrets are needed to allow the Kubernetes API server to send HTTPS requests to the webhook services. This requirement is managed by the MagTape init container. MagTape init—written in Python—takes care of the TLS settings that are needed for the webhook to call the MagTape application. The following console output contains the logs from the init container:

```
# Read magtape inti container logs
$ kubectl -n magtape-system logs -l app=magtape -c magtape-init
[2024-03-09 06:33:25,549] INFO: Waiting for certificate approval
[2024-03-09 06:33:25,550] INFO: Found approved certificate
[2024-03-09 06:33:25,551] INFO: Creating secret "magtape-tls" in namespace
"magtape-system"
[2024-03-09 06:33:25,554] INFO: New secret created
[2024-03-09 06:33:25,554] INFO: Writing cert and key locally
[2024-03-09 06:33:25,557] INFO: Existing VWC "magtape-webhook" found
[2024-03-09 06:33:25,563] INFO: Found MagTape webhook defined in the VWC
template
```

```
[2024-03-09 06:33:25,564] INFO: Comparing existing VWC to template
[2024-03-09 06:33:25,564] INFO: Existing VWC matches template
[2024-03-09 06:33:25,564] INFO: Done
```

The MagTape init container also verifies if the ValidatingWebhookConfiguration.mag tape-webhook resource is correct; if it is found to be incorrect, the init application will update it.

In the next section, we will explore how MagTape decorates and improves the OPA user experience.

Proxying OPA with MagTape

The MagTape web application is written in Python using the Flask microframework (*https://oreil.ly/flask*) and Gunicorn (*https://oreil.ly/gunicorn*). MagTape acts as a proxy server in front of OPA. This means that the Kubernetes API server posts requests to the MagTape service, and then MagTape makes POST requests to the OPA container using OPA's v0 REST API endpoint. Figure 6-1 illustrates the architecture behind this concept.

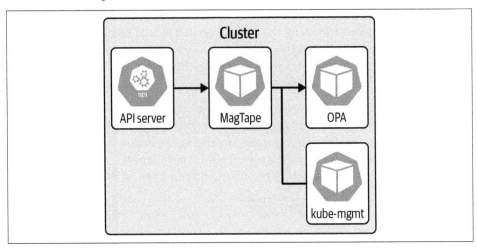

Figure 6-1. MagTape OPA proxy

The OPA v0 REST API endpoint (*https://oreil.ly/qr2pm*) is used because this endpoint is designed to be used when your OPA request payload already has predefined request/response formats. In other words, it doesn't wrap the inbound request with an input document like the v1 endpoint does. This is the case when MagTape intercepts the AdmissionReview request from the Kubernetes API server, forwards it to the OPA server, and then receives the AdmissionReview object as a response back from OPA.

As you can see in Figure 6-1, while MagTape fronts OPA—using the Python Web Server Gateway Interface (WSGI)—kube-mgmt is still in the background to load policies and data into OPA.

If we review the logs of the MagTape container, we can see the Gunicorn WSGI components start and that MagTape is listening on port 5000:

```
# Read magtape container logs
$ kubectl -n magtape-system logs -l app=magtape -c magtape
[2024-03-09 06:33:26 +0000] [1] [INFO] Starting gunicorn 20.1.0
[2024-03-09 06:33:26 +0000] [1] [INFO] Listening at: https://0.0.0.0:5000 (1)
[2024-03-09 06:33:26 +0000] [1] [INFO] Using worker: gthread
[2024-03-09 06:33:26 +0000] [6] [INFO] Booting worker with pid: 6
[2024-03-09 06:33:26 +0000] [7] [INFO] Booting worker with pid: 7
```

Next, let's explore how we can better control the volume of denied requests without modifying policies.

Controlling Deny Volumes

When the Kubernetes API server sends a request to MagTape for a resource to be validated and that resource fails OPA validation, MagTape receives the failed validation but doesn't necessarily deny the API server request. Whether MagTape denies the request is based on the MAGTAPE_DENY_LEVEL environment variable, found in the magtape-env ConfigMap. Environment variables from this ConfigMap are loaded into the magtape container via the envFrom element.

During my testing, I edited the magtape-env ConfigMap and then bounced the MagTape Pod so that my edits would load into a new Pod. In Kubernetes, bouncing a Pod backed by a Deployment resource is done by deleting the Pod so that the Deployment and ReplicaSet resources will start a new Pod. In this scenario, starting a new Pod loaded settings from the ConfigMap resources, including my recent edits:

```
# Environment variables resource reference
envFrom:
- configMapRef:
    name: magtape-env
```

The MagTape policies, loaded into OPA, contain severity levels—LOW, MED, HIGH—and error codes.

 If we consider the GRC Controls Traceability Matrix from Table 1-1 in Chapter 1, it's easy to see that we could add business information to this matrix, such as severity and error codes like those provided in the MagTape solution.

In the following kubectl response, you see specific MagTape error codes and levels applied to the OPA failed validation via the ingested policies. However, since the `MAGTAPE_DENY_LEVEL` is set to OFF, the client receives warnings as the API server request succeeds. The test Deployment YAML came directly from the MagTape GitHub project:

```
# Run tests defined in MagTape GitHub project
$ kubectl -n policy-test apply -f \
https://raw.githubusercontent.com/tmobile/magtape/master/testing/\
deployments/test-deploy02.yaml
Warning: [FAIL] HIGH - Found privileged Security Context for container
"test-deploy02" (MT2001)
Warning: [FAIL] LOW - Liveness Probe missing for container "test-deploy02"
(MT1001)
Warning: [FAIL] LOW - Readiness Probe missing for container "test-deploy02"
(MT1002)
Warning: [FAIL] LOW - Resource limits missing (CPU/MEM) for container
"test-deploy02" (MT1003)
Warning: [FAIL] LOW - Resource requests missing (CPU/MEM) for container
"test-deploy02" (MT1004)
deployment.apps/test-deploy02 created   ❶
```

❶ Even though OPA returned several warnings, the MagTape `MAGTAPE_DENY_LEVEL` setting of OFF prevents the OPA violations from stopping the Deployment from being applied to the cluster.

The preceding output highlights the additional business logic added to the OPA validation via policy metadata and MagTape business logic.

The following example MagTape policy includes the `severity` and `errcode` elements in the `policy_metadata`. OPA uses this policy to evaluate a POST request. The Kubernetes resources that are evaluated by the following Rego policy are defined in the `targets` element; they consist of Pods and some of the resources that create Pods:

```
# MagTape Rego policy to detect privileged Pods
package kubernetes.admission.policy_privileged_pod

policy_metadata = {   ❶
        # Set MagTape Policy Info
        "name": "policy-privileged-pod",
        "severity": "HIGH",
        "errcode": "MT2001",
        "targets": {"Deployment", "StatefulSet", "DaemonSet", "Pod"},
}

servicetype = input.request.kind.kind

matches {
        # Verify request object type matches targets
        policy_metadata.targets[servicetype]
```

```
}

deny[info] {
        # Find container spec
        containers := find_containers(servicetype, policy_metadata)

        # Check for Privileged SecurityContext in container spec
        container := containers[_]
        name := container.name
        container.securityContext.privileged
        msg = sprintf("[FAIL] %v - Found privileged Security Context for " +
    "container \"%v\" (%v)", [
                policy_metadata.severity,
                name, policy_metadata.errcode,  ❷
        ])
        info := {"name": policy_metadata.name, "severity":
    policy_metadata.severity, "errcode": policy_metadata.errcode, "msg": msg}
}

# find_containers accepts a value (k8s object type) and returns the container
# spec
find_containers(type, metadata) = input.request.object.spec.containers {
        type == "Pod"
} else = input.request.object.spec.template.spec.containers {
        metadata.targets[type]
}
```

❶ Policy metadata object to be used later in returned AdmissionReview object.

❷ Return message includes policy metadata.

MagTape receives the response from OPA and checks its internal `MAGTAPE_DENY_LEVEL` to decide if the API server request should be allowed or denied. In the current example, since the `MAGTAPE_DENY_LEVEL` is set to OFF, MagTape will return true to the API server, allowing the request.

If we change the `MAGTAPE_DENY_LEVEL` to LOW, the OPA failure is evaluated by Mag-Tape logic, and `allowed=false` is sent back to the API server, preventing the request from succeeding:

```
$ kubectl -n test apply -f ./testing/deployments/test-deploy02.yaml
Warning: [FAIL] HIGH - Found privileged Security Context for container
"test-deploy02" (MT2001)
Warning: [FAIL] LOW - Liveness Probe missing for container "test-deploy02"
(MT1001)
Warning: [FAIL] LOW - Readiness Probe missing for container "test-deploy02"
(MT1002)
Warning: [FAIL] LOW - Resource limits missing (CPU/MEM) for container
"test-deploy02" (MT1003)
Warning: [FAIL] LOW - Resource requests missing (CPU/MEM) for container
"test-deploy02" (MT1004)
```

```
Error from server: error when creating ❶
"./testing/deployments/test-deploy02.yaml": admission webhook
"magtape.webhook.k8s.t-mobile.com" denied the request: [FAIL] HIGH -
Found privileged Security Context for container "test-deploy02" (MT2001),
[FAIL] LOW - Liveness Probe missing for container "test-deploy02" (MT1001),
[FAIL] LOW - Readiness Probe missing for container "test-deploy02" (MT1002),
[FAIL] LOW - Resource limits missing (CPU/MEM) for container "test-deploy02"
(MT1003), [FAIL] LOW - Resource requests missing (CPU/MEM) for container
"test-deploy02" (MT1004)
```

❶ Multiple error messages returned, each including the policy metadata, such as name, severity, and error code.

In the preceding output, we can still see all of the previous warnings, but we can also see that now the API server request was denied by MagTape. In the next section, we will explore how MagTape controls the volume of denials.

The Deny Volume Knob

MagTape uses a combination of the severity and errcode elements from the policy_metadata and the threshold set by the MAGTAPE_DENY_LEVEL environment variable. The deny-level threshold logically acts like a deny volume knob. The deny-level settings in Table 6-1 are inversely related to the security levels that are blocked.

Table 6-1. MagTape severity blocking

Deny level	Severities blocked by MagTape
OFF	None
LOW	HIGH severities only
MED	HIGH and MED severities
HIGH	All severities (HIGH, MED, LOW)

In the preceding example, when the deny level was set to LOW, it correlated to a low volume of blocked requests. So MagTaple actually blocked only the HIGH-level severities, even though OPA sent denials for all of the policies that failed. Setting the deny level to HIGH would increase the volume of possible denials, preventing all severities from progressing.

With this logical "volume knob," MagTape increases or decreases the volume of possible denials. This approach is valuable as the maturity of platforms and users increases over time or if you want different levels of enforcement across different environments, like production and nonproduction.

Now that we have seen how to adjust the volume of denials, let's see how easy it is to enable notifications from MagTape.

Slack Notifications

One of my favorite features of MagTape is how easy it is to configure Slack notifications. If we examine the magtape-env configmap, we can see the Slack settings that are used to enable and configure Slack notifications:

```
kind: ConfigMap
apiVersion: v1
metadata:
  name: magtape-env
  namespace: magtape-system
  labels:
    app: magtape
data:
  FLASK_ENV: "production"
  PYTHONUNBUFFERED: "TRUE"
  MAGTAPE_CLUSTER_NAME: "test-cluster"
  MAGTAPE_LOG_LEVEL: "INFO"
  MAGTAPE_DENY_LEVEL: "LOW"
  MAGTAPE_K8S_EVENTS_ENABLED: "TRUE"
  MAGTAPE_SLACK_ENABLED: "TRUE" ❶
  MAGTAPE_SLACK_PASSIVE: "FALSE"
  MAGTAPE_SLACK_WEBHOOK_URL_DEFAULT: "https://hooks.slack.com/…"
  MAGTAPE_SLACK_USER: "mtbot"
  MAGTAPE_SLACK_ICON: ":rotating_light:"
  OPA_BASE_URL: "http://127.0.0.1:8181"
  OPA_K8S_PATH: "/v0/data/magtape"
```

❶ Slack integration settings are configured to send failure messages from MagTape to a specific Slack workspace and channel via a predefined Slack webhook.

> You can find more information about configuring Slack webhooks in the MagTape project *README.md* (*https://oreil.ly/6jaHR*) and from Slack's official documentation (*https://oreil.ly/RRijC*).

With the preceding Slack settings, denials sent back to the Kubernetes API server were also forwarded to my Policy as Code Book Slack workspace, to the #pac channel. To make this work, I had to install a webhook application into my Slack workspace and then use the configured webhook URL in the magtape-env configmap. Once this was configured, I was able to receive Slack notifications from MagTape, as shown in the following MagTape log output and Figure 6-2:

```
# Logs entries for Slack integration
[2022-12-24 22:59:30,063] INFO in magtape: K8s Event are enabled
[2022-12-24 22:59:30,071] INFO in magtape: Slack alerts are enabled
[2022-12-24 22:59:30,402] INFO in magtape: Slack Alert (default) was
```

```
successful (200) ❶
[2022-12-24 22:59:30,403] INFO in magtape: Sending Response to K8s API Server
```

❶ Logs indicate that alerts were successfully sent to Slack.

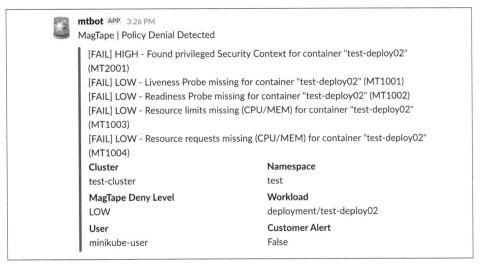

Figure 6-2. Slack notification from MagTape

The log output indicates that the Slack webhook call was successful, with an HTTP 200 status code.

As Figure 6-2 shows, I received the Slack alert from the mtbot user, which included all the warning messages from OPA—passed through MagTape—as well as information about the resource under change. The Slack alert was customized with the rotating_light emoji as a means of signaling a possible error message. This level of integration, available to millions of Slack users, is compelling functionality that is made easier by the MagTape configuration.

Summary

MagTape is not necessarily the most active project. However, MagTape has several features that I think should be considered as best practices and examples of UX benefits for PaC solutions. The idea of using a business-logic layer between the PaC solution and the Kubernetes API server is novel and should be explored more. This layer of indirection precludes the need to add such specific logic to actual PaC solutions. I would love to see this become a reusable pattern, regardless of implementation details.

I like the idea of repeatable policy structure. For example, including a `policy_meta data` element in each policy implements a reusable approach to identifying policies, defining policy targets, and providing information for downstream business logic. The `severity` and `errcode` elements could easily be sourced from business documents, such as the Controls Traceability Matrix that I introduced in Chapter 1.

I also like the whole WSGI approach used in the MagTape Python implementation. In fact, I think that other PaC solutions—including OPA—could benefit from an architecture that uses pluggable business-logic modules.

The "Deny Volume Knob" concept improves the UX by allowing you to reuse policies across multiple environments. You can adjust the denial volume based on the needs of each cluster. For example, production-level policies may not make sense for non-production environments. Turning the volume down to LOW and still receiving the warnings—without denying requests—does make sense when you want to introduce new controls without impeding productivity. We saw a similar pattern in Chapter 5 with the Styra DAS rule modes Ignore, Monitor, and Enforce. As you progress further in this book and explore additional PaC solutions, you will see similar patterns for policy and rule modes.

MagTape's Slack-notification functionality provides immediate benefits to Slack users and teams. Given the adequate Slack workspace permissions, it was very easy to configure MagTape to send alerts to my Slack channel.

When we consider the PaC Solution Selection Scorecard, MagTape makes us think about business logic and notification functionality that we would like to see in our PaC solutions. That said, the two aspects of MagTape that give me pause are lack of activity in the OSS project and lack of mutating webhook support. MagTape is also another service in the chain that is called by the Kubernetes API server, via the validating webhook. In my limited testing, I saw noticeable lag, and that additional component and its effect on the system should not be ignored during load testing. However, as I said before, MagTape introduces several ideas for how our PaC solutions should work for us, to help us better align with business needs.

In Chapter 7, we are going to explore OPA/Gatekeeper—a.k.a. Gatekeeper. Like MagTape, it uses OPA and Rego. Gatekeeper is a mature and very active graduated CNCF project that improves the UX of OPA, thereby increasing adoption of OPA and Rego for PaC while at the same time reducing the amount of Rego coding.

OPA/Gatekeeper and Kubernetes

When it comes to PaC solutions for Kubernetes API server requests, OPA/Gatekeeper—a.k.a. Gatekeeper—is one the most popular solutions. Gatekeeper (*https://oreil.ly/gatekeeper*) is underpinned by OPA; however, it is designed to use native Kubernetes CRDs to build policies for mutation and validation. Using the CRDs and the Constraint Framework—covered later in this chapter—promotes the expressiveness and reusability of Gatekeeper policies.

Gatekeeper is a very mature OSS project with a strong and active community of developers and users. The following links will help you gain more information about Gatekeeper:

- GitHub project (*https://oreil.ly/gatekeeper*)
- Documentation website (*https://oreil.ly/DkVjK*)
- Policy library (*https://oreil.ly/0ekPn*)
- Slack community (*https://slack.openpolicyagent.org*): #opa-gatekeeper

In this chapter, we will explore Gatekeeper, examining how it is installed and used. Along the way, I will cover topics like policies, the Constraint Framework, and different modes of operation. Finally, I will describe three features that were recently added to ease adoption of Gatekeeper: external data providers, policy expansion, and the gator CLI.

Let's begin with installing and configuring Gatekeeper to operate—and play nice—in your clusters.

Installation

There are multiple ways to install Gatekeeper:

- kubectl
- Helm
- make

Since multiple resources are installed at the cluster level and at the Namespace level, I prefer to use the package-manager approach of Helm:

```
# Add helm repo
$ helm repo add gatekeeper \ https://open-policy-agent.github.io/gatekeeper/charts
"gatekeeper" has been added to your repositories

# Update helm repos
$ helm repo update
Hang tight while we grab the latest from your chart repositories...
...Successfully got an update from the "gatekeeper" chart repository
…

# Install gatekeeper
$ helm install gatekeeper gatekeeper/gatekeeper \
    --namespace gatekeeper-system --create-namespace \
    --values values.yaml

NAME: gatekeeper
LAST DEPLOYED: Mon Dec 26 22:07:02 2022
NAMESPACE: gatekeeper-system
STATUS: deployed
REVISION: 1
TEST SUITE: None
```

I used the following Helm values file to supply the configuration parameters:

```
# Helm values file
logDenies: true
replicas: 1
version: v3.15.0
controllerManager:
  exemptNamespaces: ["kube-system"]
enableGeneratorResourceExpansion: true
enableExternalData: true
externaldataProviderResponseCacheTTL: 0
```

For demo purposes, I reduced the replica count for the Gatekeeper controller manager to one; it defaults to three. One replica makes it easier for me to review logs during development.

The current release of Gatekeeper is assumed to be compatible with the currently supported Kubernetes releases, as per the Kubernetes Supported Versions policy (*https://oreil.ly/dQknm*). I installed Gatekeeper v3.15.0 into a 1.28.3 Kubernetes cluster. The install creates two Deployment resources in the `gatekeeper-system` Namespace:

```
# Check Deployments
$ kubectl -n gatekeeper-system get deployment
NAME                             READY   UP-TO-DATE   AVAILABLE   AGE
gatekeeper-audit                 1/1     1            1           24h
gatekeeper-controller-manager    1/1     1            1           24h


# Check Pods
$ kubectl -n gatekeeper-system get po
NAME                                             READY   STATUS    RESTARTS   AGE
gatekeeper-audit-7c7494fc77-l4mr2                1/1     Running   0          24h
gatekeeper-controller-manager-78b4bdc4bf-46fc7   1/1     Running   0          24h
```

Once Gatekeeper was installed, I performed my customary postinstallation checks, which involved reviewing logs, installed CRDs, and Gatekeeper-system resources. Then, I installed a Gatekeeper deny-all-pods policy and tested the policy with the following command and output:

```
# Install deny-all constraint-template
$ kubectl apply -f ./examples/validating/deny/constraint-templates/0-denyall.yaml
constrainttemplate.templates.gatekeeper.sh/k8sdenyall created


# Install deny-all-pods constraint
$ kubectl apply -f ./examples/validating/deny/constraints/0-denyall-pods.yaml
k8sdenyall.constraints.gatekeeper.sh/deny-all-pods created


# Create policy-test namespace
$ kubectl apply -f ./examples/validating/deny/0-ns.yaml
namespace/policy-test created


# Apply test Pod
$ kubectl -n policy-test apply -f ./examples/validating/deny/1-test-pod.yaml
Error from server (Forbidden): error when creating "1-test-pod.yaml":
admission webhook "validation.gatekeeper.sh" denied the request:
[deny-all-pods] INPUT: {"parameters": {}, "review": {"dryRun": false, "kind":
{"group": "", "kind": "Pod", "version": "v1"}, "name": "test-pod",
"namespace": "policy-test", …
```

During the Gatekeeper install, three webhook configurations are installed—two validating webhooks and one mutating webhook—as seen in the following console outputs:

```
# List validating webhook configurations
$ kubectl get validatingwebhookconfigurations \
gatekeeper-validating-webhook-configuration
NAME                                            WEBHOOKS   AGE
gatekeeper-validating-webhook-configuration     2          3h10m
```

```
# List mutating webhook configurations
$ kubectl get mutatingwebhookconfiguration gatekeeper-mutating-webhook-configuration
NAME                                          WEBHOOKS   AGE
gatekeeper-mutating-webhook-configuration     1          3h11m
```

Two of the three webhook configurations are set to ignore failures—a.k.a. fail open. The mutating webhook and validating webhook are set to fail open with a `failure` `Policy: Ignore` setting. The third webhook, which checks if a Namespace may be labeled to be ignored, is set to fail closed: `failurePolicy: Fail`. This means that the webhooks that handle resource mutation and validation will fail open and allow resources to be created, even if the webhook service fails to respond within the allotted time. This is the safest setting, as setting the `failurePolicy` to `Fail` could cause your cluster API server to stop responding to API requests.

Once I was satisfied that Gatekeeper was executing policies correctly, I checked if Namespace selection was working. To that end, let's look at how the third webhook is used to control which Namespaces are and can be ignored.

Ignoring Namespaces

In my experience, it is usually a good idea to exempt certain Kubernetes system Namespaces from validating webhooks. Gatekeeper enabled this configuration with a two-part process. The installation installed two validating webhook configurations: one to perform API server request validation and the other to check if Namespaces can be labeled to be ignored. The two webhooks were configured in the same Kubernetes resource:

```
# Check that two validating webhooks are configured
$ kubectl get validatingwebhookconfiguration
NAME                                          WEBHOOKS   AGE
gatekeeper-validating-webhook-configuration   2          12m
```

The *check-ignore-label.gatekeeper.sh* webhook is used to prevent unauthorized labeling of Namespaces that would cause the webhook to ignore the operations within those Namespaces. The `admission.gatekeeper.sh/ignore` label is used to allow the *validation.gatekeeper.sh* to ignore Namespaces:

```
# Namespace selector
...
  namespaceSelector:
    matchExpressions:
    - key: admission.gatekeeper.sh/ignore
      operator: DoesNotExist
```

Gatekeeper just checks for the existence of the `admission.gatekeeper.sh/ignore` label, so the value is not important. That said, you could use the label value to indicate who added the label or why the label was added.

When you try to label a Namespace that is not configured as exempt in Gatekeeper, you will receive the following error from the *check-ignore-label.gatekeeper.sh* webhook:

```
# Try to label Namespace to be ignored
$ kubectl label ns policy-test admission.gatekeeper.sh/ignore=jimmy
Error from server (Only exempt namespace can have the
admission.gatekeeper.sh/ignore label): admission webhook
"check-ignore-label.gatekeeper.sh" denied the request: Only
exempt namespace can have the admission.gatekeeper.sh/ignore label
```

Even if a Namespace cannot have the `admission.gatekeeper.sh/ignore` label, policy constraints can be configured to include or exclude Namespaces.

In my Helm install command, I configured the `kube-system` Namespace to be "exempt":

```
# Helm set parameter for exempting Namespaces
--set "controllerManager.exemptNamespaces={kube-system}"

# Gatekeeper controller manager arguments
  containers:
  - args:
  …
    - --exempt-namespace=gatekeeper-system
  …
    - --exempt-namespace=kube-system
```

When a Namespace is included as "exempt" by the Gatekeeper controller manager, you can then successfully label it to be ignored. This check is meant to prevent unauthorized users from circumventing Gatekeeper policies. Of course, this only works when you tightly control access to the Gatekeeper configuration.

I wrapped my Helm install command in a shell script and a Makefile so that after Helm installed and configured Gatekeeper, the shell script labeled the `kube-system` Namespace to be ignored:

```
# Install Gatekeeper shell script
#!/usr/bin/env bash

# error handling
set -e
trap 'catch $? $LINENO' ERR
catch() {
  if [ "$1" != "0" ]; then
    echo "Error $1 occurred on $2"
  fi
}

KUBECTL="kubectl"
```

```
helm install gatekeeper gatekeeper/gatekeeper \
    --namespace gatekeeper-system --create-namespace \
    --set logDenies=true --set replicas=1 --set version=v3.15.0 \
    --set "controllerManager.exemptNamespaces={kube-system}"

LABEL=$(${KUBECTL} get ns kube-system -oyaml | \
{ grep admission.gatekeeper.sh/ignore || true; })
if [[ "$LABEL" == "" ]]
then
  ${KUBECTL} label ns kube-system admission.gatekeeper.sh/ignore=jimmy
  ${KUBECTL} get ns kube-system -oyaml | grep admission.gatekeeper.sh/ignore
Fi
```

Helm eased the Gatekeeper installation. Makefiles and shell scripts—as usual—provided me with reproducible automation. During the install, I configured Gatekeeper to exempt Namespaces so that I could label them to be ignored by Gatekeeper operations. This two-step process provides a security checks-and-balances mechanism to prevent unauthorized users from erroneously exempting Namespaces.

In the next section, we will explore how excluding Namespaces can also be done by dynamic configuration after Gatekeeper starts.

Config: Alpha Feature

Gatekeeper has included a config feature (*https://oreil.ly/5D-A3*)—still in alpha at the time of this writing—that allows you to exclude Namespaces, sync Kubernetes data, and configure debugging traces. *Tracing* is a software-debugging technique used for troubleshooting that allows programmers to follow the execution path of programs and isolate issues.

The following config resource is based on the *configs.config.gatekeeper.sh* CRD and can be used to exclude Namespaces:

```
# Exclude Namespaces config
apiVersion: config.gatekeeper.sh/v1alpha1
kind: Config
metadata:
  name: config
  namespace: "gatekeeper-system"
spec:
  match:
    - excludedNamespaces: ["policy-test"]
      processes: ["*"]
```

The preceding config excludes the `policy-test` Namespace from all processing with the wildcard in the `processes` field. Wildcards are also usable in the `excludedNames paces` array. Using the config resource does not require Gatekeeper controller manager arguments or the `admission.gatekeeper.sh/ignore` label.

There is a considerable caveat to the config solution. Unlike the label/argument solution, which excludes Namespaces at the webhook config level via labels and results in the API server never calling Gatekeeper, this config solution still results in the API server calling Gatekeeper. The decision to process or exclude Namespaces is made by Gatekeeper—instead of the webhook config—based on the config resource.

The difference in how Namespace exclusion functions may seem negligible on the surface, but if you exclude a sensitive Namespace using the config resources approach, and for some reason Gatekeeper is not responding, you could compromise the operation of your cluster. For that reason, I would never use the config resource solution to exclude processing of the kube-system Namespace.

With Gatekeeper configured and executing correctly, let's see how I uninstalled Gatekeeper.

Uninstalling Gatekeeper

My approach to uninstall Gatekeeper—like my install—is shell script and Helm based. I used the following shell script to uninstall Gatekeeper:

```
# Uninstall script
#!/usr/bin/env bash

# error handling
set -e
trap 'catch $? $LINENO' ERR
catch() {
  if [ "$1" != "0" ]; then
    echo "Error $1 occurred on $2"
  fi
}

KUBECTL="kubectl"

helm uninstall gatekeeper    ❶

${KUBECTL} delete crd -l gatekeeper.sh/system=yes    ❷
${KUBECTL} delete ns gatekeeper-system
${KUBECTL} label ns kube-system admission.gatekeeper.sh/ignore-    ❸
```

❶ Uninstall the Gatekeeper Helm installation.

❷ Explicitly uninstall the CRDs installed by Gatekeeper.

❸ Unlabel the kube-system Namespace.

The shell script must uninstall the Gatekeeper CRDs; by design, the Helm 3 client will not. When the CRDs are deleted, related items are also deleted via Kubernetes garbage collection (*https://oreil.ly/91Gwb*).

Now, let's look at how Gatekeeper uses OPA and its Constraint Framework.

Policies

Even though Gatekeeper is underpinned by OPA and uses Rego for policies, the Gatekeeper policy engine is substantially different from the one used by OPA classic. As we will explore further in this chapter, Gatekeeper installs Kubernetes CRDs—10 at last count—to build mutating and validation policies and associated functionality.

Instead of a single policy that is ingested via configmaps or pushed in via HTTP methods, Gatekeeper policies are authored using compound resources that provide a means to house and execute Rego while extending policy reach and focus.

In this section, we'll explore how Gatekeeper policies are constructed and used to solve mutation and validation use cases.

OPA Constraint Framework

Gatekeeper runs OPA internally but does not expose OPA outside of Gatekeeper's application boundary. To interface policies with OPA, you must create at least two resources: the ConstraintTemplate and the Constraint. How you build Constraint-Templates and Constraints is underpinned by the OPA Constraint Framework (OPA CF) (*https://oreil.ly/constraint*).

OPA CF is a set of Golang libraries defining several components used by Gatekeeper:

ConstraintTemplate
    Used to declare new constraint types and contains policy Rego

Constraint
    Declaration that a system must meet, given a set of requirements

Enforcement points
    Places where constraints can be enforced

Targets
    Represent a coherent set of objects sharing a common identification and/or selection scheme, such as a Kubernetes admission webhook

As an enforcement point, Kubernetes must be able to support the following actions:

- Add/remove templates
- Add/remove constraints

- Add/remove cached data
- Submit an object for a review
- Request an audit of the cached data

Obviously, not all enforcement points implement these actions in the same way. For example, creating a template in Kubernetes involves creating a CRD. The OPA CF client type handles this implementation detail.

OPA CF defines the format of the Rego rule schema used in Gatekeeper Constraint-Templates. For instance, the violation rule must be formatted as the following example, where `msg` is a required string containing the message or reason why a violation occurred, and `details` is optional, with no defined schema:

```
# Rego rule
violation[{"msg": msg, "details": {}}] {
  # rule body
}
```

In summary, the OPA CF is the library that enables Gatekeeper and allows users to manage policies and data. Now, let's start with Gatekeeper validation policies and see how the OPA CF is utilized at the Kubernetes level.

Validation Policies

Gatekeeper validating policies use Rego, but they are not authored in the same way as OPA. While OPA (classic) policies are Rego files that can import other Rego files, Gatekeeper policies are composed of two Kubernetes resources: ConstraintTemplates and Constraints. ConstraintTemplates are based on the *constrainttemplates.templates.gatekeeper.sh* CRD. Creating resources based on this CRD actually creates additional CRDs for each ConstraintTemplate.

Rego in ConstraintTemplates can import OPA libraries like *future.keywords.in*; however, reusing user-supplied libraries—like we did with OPA in Chapter 5—requires that you add those libraries in each ConstraintTemplate as an additional target under the `targets` element. This is by design, based on this GitHub issue: #1204 (*https://oreil.ly/1204*).

The following console output lists the CRDs installed with Gatekeeper, along with one ConstraintTemplate that I added:

```
# Get CRDs by name
$ kubectl get crd -o=custom-columns='NAME:.metadata.name'
NAME
assign.mutations.gatekeeper.sh
assignmetadata.mutations.gatekeeper.sh
configs.config.gatekeeper.sh
constraintpodstatuses.status.gatekeeper.sh
```

```
constrainttemplatepodstatuses.status.gatekeeper.sh
constrainttemplates.templates.gatekeeper.sh
eniconfigs.crd.k8s.amazonaws.com
expansiontemplate.expansion.gatekeeper.sh
k8sdepregistry.constraints.gatekeeper.sh    ❶
modifyset.mutations.gatekeeper.sh
mutatorpodstatuses.status.gatekeeper.sh
providers.externaldata.gatekeeper.sh
Securitygrouppolicies.vpcresources.k8s.aws
```

❶ The kind I created with the ConstraintTemplate.

If we look at my ConstraintTemplate source YAML, we can see that it's based on *constrainttemplates.templates.gatekeeper.sh*, and it defines the Rego for the policy as well as the schema that is used to define the Constraint parameters. When the Constraint is created, it is created as a K8sDepRegistry resource:

```
# Constraint template
apiVersion: templates.gatekeeper.sh/v1
kind: ConstraintTemplate    ❶
metadata:
  name: k8sdepregistry
  labels:
    policy.jimmyray.io/gatekeeper: template
spec:
  crd:
    spec:
      names:
        kind: K8sDepRegistry    ❷
      validation:
        # Schema for the `parameters` field
        openAPIV3Schema:
          type: object
          Properties:    ❸
            allowedOps:
              type: array
              items:
                type: string
            allowedRegistries:
              type: array
              items:
                type: string
            errMsg:
              type: string
  targets:
    - target: admission.k8s.gatekeeper.sh
      rego: |    ❹
        package k8sdepregistry

        violation[{"msg": msg, "details": {}}] {
          input.review.operation = input.parameters.allowedOps[_]
          image = input.review.object.spec.template.spec.containers[_].image
```

```
                not reg_matches_any(image,input.parameters.allowedRegistries)
                msg = sprintf("%v: %v image is not sourced from an authorized " +
                "registry. Resource ID (ns/name/kind): %v/%v/%v",
                [input.parameters.errMsg,image,
                input.review.object.metadata.namespace,
                input.review.object.metadata.name,input.review.kind.kind])
            }

            reg_matches_any(str, patterns) {
              reg_matches(str, patterns[_])
            }

            reg_matches(str, pattern) {
              contains(str, pattern)
            }
```

❶ The kind is a ConstraintTemplate.

❷ The name of the new type created by this ConstraintTemplate is `K8sDepRegistry`.

❸ Properties define the parameters that will be used in the downstream Constraint.

❹ The `rego` target contains the Rego policy for this policy.

> You may notice that the input of the Gatekeeper policy—from the Kubernetes API server AdmissionReview object—is different from that in OPA:
>
> - OPA = input.**request**.object
> - Gatekeeper = input.**review**.object
>
> Given that difference, you may need to refactor—at least partially—to move Rego between OPA and Gatekeeper.

When the Constraint is created, it is created as a K8sDepRegistry resource type. The following kubectl commands illustrate the relationship between ConstraintTemplates and Constraints:

```
# List CRDs with new k8sdepregistry constraint template CRD
$ kubectl get crd -o=custom-columns='NAME:.metadata.name,KIND:kind'
NAME                                        KIND
constrainttemplates.templates.gatekeeper.sh CustomResourceDefinition
...

k8sdepregistry.constraints.gatekeeper.sh    CustomResourceDefinition ❶
...
```

❶ New Kubernetes type created by applying the ConstraintTemplate

```
# List of constrainttemplate resources
$ kubectl get constrainttemplate -o=custom-columns='NAME:.metadata.name,KIND:kind'
NAME            KIND
k8sdepregistry  ConstraintTemplate

# List of constraint resources
$ kubectl get constraint -o=custom-columns='NAME:.metadata.name,KIND:kind'
NAME                      KIND
deployment-allowed-registry   K8sDepRegistry  ❶
```

❶ New Constraint is typed by the new CRD created by the ConstraintTemplate

```
# List of k8sdepregistry resources
$ kubectl get k8sdepregistry -o=custom-columns='NAME:.metadata.name,KIND:kind'
NAME                      KIND
deployment-allowed-registry   K8sDepRegistry
```

The following K8sDepRegistry Constraint YAML sets the parameters used by Rego in the ConstraintTemplate:

```
# Constraint
apiVersion: constraints.gatekeeper.sh/v1beta1
kind: K8sDepRegistry  ❶
metadata:
  name: deployment-allowed-registry
  labels:
    policy.jimmyray.io/gatekeeper: constraint
spec:
  enforcementAction: deny
  match:
    kinds:
      - apiGroups: ["*"]
        kinds: ["Deployment"]  ❷
    namespaces:
      - "policy-test"  ❸
  parameters:
    allowedOps: ["CREATE","UPDATE"]  ❹
    allowedRegistries: ["GOOD_REGISTRY","VERY_GOOD_REGISTRY"]
    errMsg: "INVALID_DEPLOYMENT_REGISTRY"
```

❶ The ConstraintTemplate name is used as the Constraint kind.

❷ This Constraint only applies to Deployment resources.

❸ This Constraint only applies to resources in the policy-test Namespace.

❹ The Constraint parameters—defined in the ConstraintTemplate as properties—allow the Constraint author to specify the Kubernetes operations as well as the allowed registries and the error message.

As you can see, the Constraint parameters are based on the `openAPIV3Schema.proper` `ties` field in the ConstraintTemplate. The parameters defined in the Constraint are accessed within the Rego—in the ConstraintTemplate—via the `input.parameters` field. The target resources for this policy were set in the `spec.match.kind` fields as Deployment resources, regardless of API version. The values in the `spec.match.name` `spaces` field targets only resources in the `policy-test` Namespace.

If we consider the MagTape examples from Chapter 6, where each Rego policy defined a `policy_metadata` element, we can easily see that items like `policy_metadata.severity` and `policy_meta` `data.errcode` could be added to the ConstraintTemplate as properties and Constraints as parameters.

The end result would be that Constraints could define metadata, like error codes and violation severities that would be returned by the Rego. This is incredibly flexible and makes the Gatekeeper Constraint a customization point for business-aligned data.

Instead of defining the target resources and operations in Rego, Gatekeeper Constraints and ConstraintTemplates can be used to reduce the amount of Rego coded and provide an expressive, declarative means of targeting resources for validation. Rego resides in the ConstraintTemplate. Also within the ConstraintTemplate are the Constraint parameter schemas. Matching and parameter arguments are set in the Constraints.

Constraints are related to ConstraintTemplates similarly to how objects are related to classes in Java. As seen in Figure 7-1, ConstraintTemplates are used to define the structure and behavior of Constraints. Conversely, Constraints are instances of ConstraintTemplates, and multiple Constraints can reference the same Constraint Template. This lets you set different parameters and matching criteria without having to modify any Rego. This separation could also be modeled organizationally, with different developers or teams responsible for Constraints versus ConstraintTemplates.

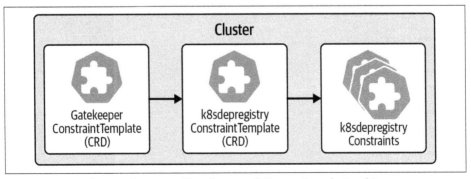

Figure 7-1. Gatekeeper ConstraintTemplates and Constraint relationships

In the ConstraintTemplate-to-Constraint relationship, Constraints specialize the general implementation of a ConstraintTemplate and enable the policy. Without a Constraint, the ConstraintTemplate accomplishes nothing. Given the deny-all policy I used during installation, the ConstraintTemplate was open to all resource kinds:

```
# Deny-all ConstraintTemplate
apiVersion: templates.gatekeeper.sh/v1beta1
kind: ConstraintTemplate
metadata:
  name: k8sdenyall
  labels:
    policy.jimmyray.io/gatekeeper: template
spec:
  crd:
    spec:
      names:
        kind: K8sDenyAll
    targets:
    - target: admission.k8s.gatekeeper.sh
      rego: |
        package k8sdenyall
        violation[{"msg": msg}] {
          msg := sprintf("INPUT: %v", [input])
        }
```

The deny-all-pods Constraint specialized the k8sDenyAll ConstraintTemplate and enabled the overall policy to deny all Pod resources:

```
# Deny-all-pods Constraint
apiVersion: constraints.gatekeeper.sh/v1beta1
kind: K8sDenyAll
metadata:
  name: deny-all-pods
  labels:
    policy.jimmyray.io/gatekeeper: constraint
spec:
  match:
    kinds:
      - apiGroups: [""]
        kinds: ["Pod"]
    namespaces:
      - "policy-test"
```

This Constraint-driven specialization is also seen in the preceding deployment-allowed-registry Constraint. When a test Deployment resource is applied into the `policy-test` Namespace, the API server request is denied, and the following errors are returned to the API server client—in this case, kubectl (the `BAD_REGISTRY` was not included in the specified `allowedRegistries` parameter):

```
# Apply Deployment with bad registry
$ kubectl -n policy-test apply -f \
./examples/validating/tests/11-dep-reg-allow.yaml
Error from server (Forbidden): error when creating
"tests/11-dep-reg-allow.yaml": admission webhook
"validation.gatekeeper.sh" denied the request: [deployment-allowed-registry]
 INVALID_DEPLOYMENT_REGISTRY: BAD_REGISTRY/read-only-container:v0.0.1 image
 is not sourced from an authorized registry. Resource ID (ns/name/kind):
 policy-test/test/Deployment
```

If we take this good/bad registry example further, we could use region-specific image registries in the `allowedRegistries` parameter of the deployment-allowed-registry Constraint. This would enforce that only region-specific image registries are used. Beyond that approach, we could also add mutating policies to—seen in the section "Mutation Policies" later in this chapter—change the registry before it is validated.

Next, let's look at how we control how Constraints are enforced.

Enforcement Actions

As seen in the preceding K8sDepRegistry Constraint, the `spec.enforcementAction` is set to deny. This field is actually optional and defaults to deny. I could also set the value to warn or dryrun. In warn mode, the Constraint would surface any violations but only as a warning; the request would proceed, as shown in the following example:

```
# Constraint warn mode
$ kubectl -n policy-test apply -f \
./examples/validating/tests/11-dep-reg-allow.yaml
Warning: [deployment-allowed-registry] INVALID_DEPLOYMENT_REGISTRY:
BAD_REGISTRY/read-only-container:v0.0.1 image is not sourced from an
authorized registry. Resource ID (ns/name/kind): policy-test/test/Deployment
deployment.apps/test created
```

If the value is set to dryrun, then no warnings or errors are returned to the Kubernetes API server, and the resource request proceeds. Any violations are logged in the Gatekeeper controller logs if log-denies is enabled:

```
// Log entry for log-denies for dryrun
{"level":"info","ts":1672626971.8814828,"logger":"webhook","msg":
"denied admission","process":"admission","event_type":"violation",
"constraint_name":"deployment-allowed-registry","constraint_group":
"constraints.gatekeeper.sh","constraint_api_version":"v1beta1",
"constraint_kind":"K8sDepRegistry","constraint_action":"dryrun",
```

```
"resource_group":"apps","resource_api_version":"v1","resource_kind":
"Deployment","resource_namespace":"policy-test","resource_name":"test",
"request_username":"minikube-user"}
```

Additionally, violations are logged in the status field of the Constraint, as shown in the following console output:

```
# Constraint status field dryrun log
  totalViolations: 1
  violations:
  - enforcementAction: dryrun
    group: apps
    kind: Deployment
    message: 'INVALID_DEPLOYMENT_REGISTRY: BAD_REGISTRY/read-only-container:v0.0.1
      image is not sourced from an authorized registry. Resource ID (ns/name/kind):
      policy-test/test/Deployment'
    name: test
    namespace: policy-test
    version: v1
```

Violations are added here using Gatekeeper audit mode, which we will explore later in this chapter.

 In addition to the example Gatekeeper policies that I included in the GitHub companion repository (*https://oreil.ly/wzGmt*) for this chapter, there is a large collection of policies in the Gatekeeper Policy Library (*https://oreil.ly/UBSuL*).

With validation policies and enforcement actions under our belt, let's now explore mutation policies.

Mutation Policies

To get started with Gatekeeper mutation policies, I modified the Gatekeeper Helm install to log mutations and add resource annotations by adding the `--set logMuta tions=true` and `--set mutationAnnotations=true` parameters. Both parameters apply to the Gatekeeper controller manager and are optional, but they are helpful when testing or prototyping, or when compliance requirements require additional logs and metadata. The Gatekeeper controller manager was then started with the following mutation arguments:

```
# Gatekeeper controller managed arguments for mutation
- args:
  …
    - --log-mutations=true
    - --mutation-annotations=true
  …
```

```
- --operation=mutation-webhook
...
```

 To discover Gatekeeper settings, like the ones I used during the Gatekeeper installation, you should refer to the Gatekeeper Helm chart values file (*https://oreil.ly/tEMat*).

Now when mutation policies are applied, I can review the Gatekeeper controller logs for mutation entries, as shown in the following JSON log entry:

```
// Mutation log entries
{
    "level": "info",
    "ts": 1672262677.1373708,
    "logger": "mutation",
    "msg": "Mutation applied",
    "process": "mutation",
    "Mutation Id": "2e223bf5-73bb-4e55-8e75-d778d5b32cbc",
    "event_type": "mutation_applied",
    "resource_group": "",
    "resource_kind": "Pod",
    "resource_api_version": "v1",
    "resource_namespace": "policy-test",
    "resource_name": "test-pod",
    "iteration_0": "AssignMetadata//label-billing:1,
    AssignMetadata//label-env:1, AssignMetadata//label-owner:1"
}
```

Gatekeeper uses four mutator CRDs, which mutation policies are based on:

assign.mutations.gatekeeper.sh
    These policies mutate any change outside the metadata section of a resource.

assignmetadata.mutations.gatekeeper.sh
    These policies mutate metadata of resources.

modifyset.mutations.gatekeeper.sh
    These policies modify list entries.

assignimage.mutations.gatekeeper.sh
    These policies mutate the container image string.

Starting with the AssignMetadata mutator, I wrote policies to add metadata labels for test Pods. I tested the following policy:

```
# label-owner mutation policy, using the AssignMetadata mutator
apiVersion: mutations.gatekeeper.sh/v1
kind: AssignMetadata
metadata:
```

```
        name: label-owner  ❶
spec:
  match:
    scope: Namespaced  ❷
    kinds:
    - apiGroups: ["*"]
      kinds: ["Pod"]  ❸
    namespaces: ["policy*"]  ❹
  location: "metadata.labels.owner"  ❺
  parameters:
    assign:
      value: "jimmy"  ❻
```

❶ The policy `metadata.name` identifies the policy.

❷ This policy is Namespace scoped.

❸ This policy works on Pods only.

❹ This policy impacts resources in Namespaces whose names start with the `policy*` string.

❺ This policy mutates the `metadata.labels.owner` label.

❻ This policy assigns the `jimmy` string to the label.

To dissect the preceding policy, you should know that the Gatekeeper mutation policy specification is divided into three sections:

extent of changes
What is to be modified (Kinds, Namespaces, etc.)?

intent
What are the path and value of the modification?

conditional
What are the conditions under which the mutation will be applied?

In the preceding policy, the `spec` fields set the following policy characteristics:

- The policy is Namespace scoped (extent).
- The policy is applied to Pod resources (extent).
- The policy is applied to resources in Namespaces whose names begin with "policy" (extent).

- The policy would assign the value of jimmy to the "owner" label (intent).

- Conditional elements were not used.

To test this policy, I applied a Pod resource to the `policy-test` Namespace and then checked the newly applied labels and annotations; the annotations are simply markers to stamp the resource with information about the Gatekeeper mutations:

```
# Pod yaml for testing mutation policy
apiVersion: v1
kind: Pod
metadata:
  name: test-pod
  namespace: policy-test
  labels:
    app: test
spec:
  containers:
    - name: test
      image: gcr.io/google-containers/pause:3.2
      imagePullPolicy: Always
      securityContext:
        allowPrivilegeEscalation: false
        runAsUser: 1000
        readOnlyRootFilesystem: true
        runAsNonRoot: true
        capabilities:
          drop: ["ALL"]
        seccompProfile:
          type: "RuntimeDefault"

# Apply Pod resource
$ kubectl -n policy-test apply -f ../mutating/2-test-pod.yaml
pod/test-pod created

# Verify labels
$ kubectl -n policy-test get pods test-pod -o=jsonpath='{.metadata.labels}'
{"app":"test","billing":"lob-cc","env":"dev","owner":"jimmy"}

# Verify annotations
$ kubectl -n policy-test get pods test-pod \
-o=jsonpath='{.metadata.annotations}'
{"gatekeeper.sh/mutation-id":"2e223bf5-73bb-4e55-8e75-d778d5b32cbc",
"gatekeeper.sh/mutations":"AssignMetadata//label-billing:1,
AssignMetadata//label-env:1, AssignMetadata//label-owner:1",...
```

The Assign mutator example that I wrote used the same Pod YAML from earlier, but this time I removed the seccompProfile to instead set it with a Assign mutation policy:

```
# Pod yaml missing seccompProfile element
…
spec:
  containers:
    - name: test-pod
      image: gcr.io/google-containers/pause:3.2
      imagePullPolicy: Always
      securityContext:
        allowPrivilegeEscalation: false
        runAsUser: 1000
        readOnlyRootFilesystem: true
        runAsNonRoot: true
        capabilities:
          drop: ["ALL"]
```

The Assign policy used a conditional section to first verify that the seccompProfile path was not present, as I did not want to overwrite it. As a rule, the spec .parameters.pathTests.subPath field must be a "prefix" of the spec.location field. In other words, the location field must start with the subPath field value. If not, then the Gatekeeper policy validator will throw the following error:

```
# Error log entry
Error from server: error when applying patch:
…
Resource: "mutations.gatekeeper.sh/v1, Resource=assign", GroupVersionKind:
"mutations.gatekeeper.sh/v1, Kind=Assign"
Name: "add-seccomp", Namespace: ""
for: "../mutating/0-add-pod-labels.yaml": error when patching
"../mutating/0-add-pod-labels.yaml": admission webhook
"validation.gatekeeper.sh" denied the request: all subpaths must be a
prefix of the `location` value of the mutation: subpath
"spec.containers[name: *].securityContext.seccompProfile" is not a
prefix of location
"spec.containers[name: test].securityContext.seccompProfile.type"
```

The spec.match.scope field is not defined, as it defaults to "*"; cluster-scoped or Namespace-scoped resources are matched. I could have included it, set to Name spaced, and the policy would have still functioned as expected:

```
# Mutation policy to assign seccompProfile
apiVersion: mutations.gatekeeper.sh/v1
kind: Assign
metadata:
  name: add-seccomp
spec:
  applyTo:
  - groups: [""]
    kinds: ["Pod"]
    versions: ["v1"]
  match:
    namespaces: ["policy*"]
```

```
location: "spec.containers[name: *].securityContext.seccompProfile.type"
parameters:
  pathTests:
  - subPath: "spec.containers[name: *].securityContext.seccompProfile"
    condition: MustNotExist
  assign:
    value: RuntimeDefault
```

Using kubectl explain

As we saw in Chapter 4, the `kubectl explain` command is very useful for understanding the API specifications for different Kubernetes APIs. The following command is for the `Assign.spec.match.scope` field:

```
# Using kubectl explain for API information
$ kubectl explain Assign.spec.match.scope
KIND:     Assign
VERSION: mutations.gatekeeper.sh/v1

FIELD:    scope <string>

DESCRIPTION:
     Scope determines if cluster-scoped and/or namespaced-scoped resources are
     matched. Accepts `*`, `Cluster`, or `Namespaced`. (defaults to `*`)
```

Being able to derive API information from current cluster APIs is vital when you are trying to learn or verify an API. The `kubectl explain` command also works for CRDs created by you when you create your ConstraintTemplates from Gatekeeper CRDs:

```
# Drill-down with kubectl explain
$ kubectl explain k8sdepregistry.constraints.gatekeeper.sh.spec.parameters
KIND:     K8sDepRegistry
VERSION: constraints.gatekeeper.sh/v1beta1

RESOURCE: parameters <Object>

DESCRIPTION:
     <empty>

FIELDS:
    allowedOps <[]string>

    allowedRegistries <[]string>

    errMsg <string>
```

Once the test Pod was applied, I verified that the mutations were successful:

```
# Get mutated Pod annotations as JSONPath
$ kubectl -n policy-test get pods another-test-pod \
-o=jsonpath='{.metadata.annotations}'
{"gatekeeper.sh/mutation-id":"f2bda7be-609a-4da4-ba8b-ee3d0cc4b00f",
"gatekeeper.sh/mutations":"Assign//add-seccomp:5,
AssignMetadata//label-billing:1, AssignMetadata//label-env:1,
AssignMetadata//label-owner:1",...
```

The preceding four mutations—three labels and one seccompProfile—were applied to the Pod before it was validated. We can verify the seccompProfile setting with the following command:

```
# Get seccompProfile
$ kubectl -n policy-test get pods another-test-pod \
-o=jsonpath='{.spec.containers[].securityContext.seccompProfile}'
{"type":"RuntimeDefault"}
```

I wrote no Rego in the proceeding mutation policy; unlike the validating policies, the mutation policies were all defined with YAML.

If you consider the Kubernetes API server request flow that we explored in Chapter 4, you should remember that the validation step follows the mutation step. It is very important that if you are mutating resources—for proper configuration and subsequent operation—you should follow those mutations with relative validations to ensure that your desired mutations were correctly applied. To better illustrate this concept, let's now explore a use case where mutation and validation policies work together to achieve desired outcomes.

Use Case: Multitenancy Isolation

In Kubernetes multitenancy use cases, resource isolation is a desired goal. The degree of isolation needed depends on the isolation factors—data classification, application type, environment, and so on—of your workloads. In my example, I am trying to isolate workloads into their own Namespaces, with each Namespace isolated to its own Kubernetes nodegroup, as shown in Figure 7-2.

To achieve the isolation depicted in Figure 7-2, I used a combination of node taints and Pod tolerations, node labels and Pod-to-Node affinities, and mutation and validation policies.

Node taints repel unwanted Pods from running on tainted nodes. Kubernetes routinely uses taints to stop the scheduler from scheduling Pods on specific nodes. Tolerations—added to Pods—allow the Pods to tolerate specific taints, run on tainted nodes. Pod-to-Node affinities are used to attract Pods to specifically labeled nodes. So taints will repel unwanted Pods while affinities will attract wanted Pods, and we will achieve Namespace-to-nodegroup isolation.

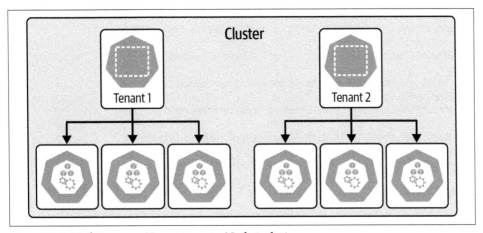

Figure 7-2. Multitenancy Namespace-to-Node isolation

To make all of this work, I followed these steps:

1. Create a Kubernetes cluster with multiple nodegroups.

2. Taint the nodes in a target nodegroup.

3. Label the nodes in the same target nodegroup.

4. Write a mutation policy to add a node affinity to Pods inbound to a target Namespace.

5. Write a mutation policy to add a toleration to Pods inbound to a target Namespace.

6. Write a validation policy to ensure that the inbound Pods to a target Namespace have the correct node affinity.

7. Write a validation policy to ensure that the inbound Pods to a target Namespace have the correct toleration.

8. Write a validation policy to prevent Namespaces, other than the target Namespace, from using target toleration.

9. Perform positive and negative testing.

Once the cluster was running and Gatekeeper was installed, I verified that the target nodes were labeled and tainted:

```
# Get labeled nodes
$ kubectl get nodes -l tenant=tenant1 -o=custom-columns='NAME:.metadata.name'
NAME
ip-10-0-10-77.us-east-2.compute.internal
ip-10-0-16-19.us-east-2.compute.internal
ip-10-0-38-245.us-east-2.compute.internal
```

```
# Get node taints
$ kubectl get nodes ip-10-0-10-77.us-east-2.compute.internal \
-ojsonpath='{.spec.taints}'
[{"effect":"NoSchedule","key":"tenant","value":"tenant1"}]

$ kubectl get nodes ip-10-0-16-19.us-east-2.compute.internal \
-ojsonpath='{.spec.taints}'
[{"effect":"NoSchedule","key":"tenant","value":"tenant1"}]

$ kubectl get nodes ip-10-0-38-245.us-east-2.compute.internal \
-ojsonpath='{.spec.taints}'
[{"effect":"NoSchedule","key":"tenant","value":"tenant1"}]
```

Then I added the Assign mutators for the Pod node affinity and toleration:

```
# Adds a node affinity to all Pods in a specific Namespace
...spec:
  applyTo:
  - groups: [""]
    kinds: ["Pod"]
    versions: ["v1"]
  match:
    namespaces: ["tenant1"]
  location: >
        "spec.affinity.nodeAffinity."
        "requiredDuringSchedulingIgnoredDuringExecution.nodeSelectorTerms"
  parameters:
    assign:
      value:
        - matchExpressions:
          - key: "tenant"
            operator: In
            values:
            - "tenant1"


# Adds a toleration to all Pods in a specific Namespace
...spec:
  applyTo:
  - groups: [""]
    kinds: ["Pod"]
    versions: ["v1"]
  match:
    namespaces: ["tenant1"]
  location: "spec.tolerations"
  parameters:
    assign:
      value:
      - key: "tenant"
        operator: "Equal"
        value: "tenant1"
        effect: "NoSchedule"
```

Next came the validation policies to verify that the toleration and node affinity were added. The following snippets from the ConstraintTemplates and Constraints construct the policy:

```
# ConstraintTemplate Rego to validate node affinity
package k8srequirednodeaffinity

import data.lib.k8s.helpers as helpers

violation[{"msg": msg, "details": {"missing":missing}}] {
  helpers.review_operation == input.parameters.ops[_]
  provided := {x | x := input.review.object.spec.affinity.nodeAffinity}
  required := {x | x := input.parameters.nodeAffinity}
  missing := required - provided
  count(missing) > 0
  msg := sprintf("%v: Resource missing correct node affinity. Provided node " +
  "affinity: %v, Required node affinity: %v. Resource ID (ns/name/kind): %v",
  [input.parameters.errMsg,provided,required,helpers.review_id])
}

# Constraint to validate node affinity
…spec:
  match:
    kinds:
      - apiGroups: [""]
        kinds: ["Pod"]
    namespaces:
      - "tenant1"
  parameters:
    ops: ["CREATE","UPDATE"]
    errMsg: "INVALID_POD_NODEAFFINITY"
    nodeAffinity:
      requiredDuringSchedulingIgnoredDuringExecution:
        nodeSelectorTerms:
        - matchExpressions:
          - key: tenant
            operator: In
            values:
            - tenant1

# Constraint template Rego to validate toleration
package k8srequiredtolerations

import data.lib.k8s.helpers as helpers

violation[{"msg": msg, "details": {"missing":missing}}] {
  helpers.review_operation == input.parameters.ops[_]
  provided := {x | x := input.review.object.spec.tolerations[_]}
  required := {x | x := input.parameters.tolerations[_]}
  missing := required - provided
  count(missing) > 0
  msg := sprintf("%v: Resource missing correct toleration(s). " +
```

```
    "Provided toleration(s): %v, Required toleration(s): %v. " +
    "Resource ID (ns/name/kind): %v", [input.parameters.errMsg,provided,
    required,helpers.review_id])
}

# Constraint to validate toleration
spec:
  match:
    kinds:
      - apiGroups: [""]
        kinds: ["Pod"]
    namespaces:
      - "tenant1"
  parameters:
    ops: ["CREATE","UPDATE"]
    tolerations:
    - effect: NoSchedule
      key: tenant
      operator: Equal
      value: tenant1
    errMsg: "INVALID_POD_TOLERATIONS"
```

Finally, I added a validation policy that prevented unauthorized Namespaces from using the `tenant1` toleration:

```
# ConstraintTemplate Rego
package k8srequiredtolerations

import data.lib.k8s.helpers as helpers
import future.keywords.in

violation[{"msg": msg, "details": {"missing":missing}}] {
  helpers.review_operation == input.parameters.ops[_]
  provided := {x | x := input.review.object.spec.tolerations[_]}
  required := {x | x := input.parameters.tolerations[_]}
  missing := required - provided
  count(missing) <= 0
  not (helpers.review_namespace in input.parameters.namespaces)
  msg := sprintf("%v namespace cannot use tolerations: %v",
  [helpers.review_namespace,input.parameters.tolerations])
}

# Constraint
spec:
  match:
    kinds:
      - apiGroups: [""]
        kinds: ["Pod"]
    excludedNamespaces: ["tenant1"]
  parameters:
    ops: ["CREATE","UPDATE"]
    namespaces: ["tenant1"]
```

```
    tolerations:
    - effect: NoSchedule
      key: tenant
      operator: Equal
      value: tenant1
    errMsg: "INVALID_NS_TOLERATIONS"
```

I created a Pod in the `tenant1` Namespace so that I could perform positive testing. I then verified that the correct toleration and node affinity were applied and that the Pod ran on the correctly labeled and tainted nodes:

```
# Check toleration
$ kubectl -n tenant1 get po tenant-test-pod -ojson | \
jq -r '.spec.tolerations[] | select (.key=="tenant")'| jq -r tostring
{"effect":"NoSchedule","key":"tenant","operator":"Equal","value":"tenant1"}

# Check node affinity
$ kubectl -n tenant1 get po tenant-test-pod -ojsonpath='{.spec.affinity}'
{"nodeAffinity":{"requiredDuringSchedulingIgnoredDuringExecution":
{"nodeSelectorTerms":[{"matchExpressions":[{"key":"tenant","operator":
"In","values":["tenant1"]}]}]}}}

# Match pod node to labeled nodes
$ kubectl get nodes -l tenant=tenant1 \
-o=custom-columns='NAME:.metadata.name'| \
grep $(kubectl -n tenant1 get po tenant-test-pod -ojsonpath='{.spec.nodeName}')
ip-10-0-38-245.us-east-2.compute.internal
```

For negative testing, I created a Pod in the `default` Namespace and verified that the node affinity and tolerations were not applied. I completed a second negative test by adding a Pod to the `default` Namespace, with a toleration only allowed in the `tenant1` Namespace:

```
$ kubectl -n default apply -f test/70-test-pod.yaml
Error from server (Forbidden): error when creating "test/70-test-pod.yaml":
admission webhook "validation.gatekeeper.sh" denied the request:
[toleration-ns-check-pod] default namespace cannot use tolerations:
[{"effect": "NoSchedule", "key": "tenant", "operator": "Equal", "value":
"tenant1"}]
```

When mutating resources for an operational reason, it's normally a best practice to follow mutation policies with validation policies. In my multitenancy isolation use case, I mutated inbound requests for specific Namespaces to land Pods onto specific nodes. I validated the mutations and prevented unwanted Pods from reusing the target tolerations.

Virtual clusters are another Kubernetes multitenancy solution. The OSS vCluster (*https://oreil.ly/vcluster*) project provides a virtual cluster solution. Loft Labs (*https://loft.sh*), the creator of vCluster, offers an enterprise vCluster solution with vCluster Pro (*https://www.vcluster.com/pro*).

So far, we have explored mutation and validation of Kubernetes API server requests. Next, let's see how Gatekeeper audits existing resources outside of the API server request flow.

Audit Mode

Not all policy evaluations are triggered by Kubernetes API server requests. When implementing PaC in Kubernetes, you need to consider the possibility that some resources may not be evaluated during the threshold of the webhook timeouts or when policies are in place to perform the evaluations.

Gatekeeper Audit (*https://oreil.ly/fuwr2*) is designed to evaluate preexisting resource configurations with Constraints. Preexisting resources could be the result of resources that existed before Constraints were added or resources that were not caught by webhook processes. With audit functionality, we are shifting to the Gatekeeper Audit Pod. I used the following settings to configure audit functionality, with the only nondefault setting in bold:

```
# Gatekeeper settings (snippet)
- args:
  - --audit-interval=60
  - --log-level=INFO
  - --constraint-violations-limit=20
  - --audit-from-cache=false
  - --audit-chunk-size=500
  - --audit-match-kind-only=false
  - --emit-audit-events=true
  - --operation=audit
  - --operation=status
  - --operation=mutation-status
  - --logtostderr
  - --health-addr=:9090
  - --prometheus-port=8888
  - --enable-external-data=false
  - --enable-generator-resource-expansion=false
  - --metrics-backend=prometheus
  - --disable-cert-rotation=true
```

When the Audit controller starts, with no Constraints configured, the following log entries are emitted every 60 seconds:

```
// Gatekeeper log entries when no constraints
{"level":"info","ts":1672433592.7277467,"logger":"controller","msg":
"no constraint is found with apiversion","process":"audit","audit_id":
"2022-12-30T20:53:12Z","constraint apiversion":
"constraints.gatekeeper.sh/v1beta1"}
{"level":"info","ts":1672433592.7278154,"logger":"controller","msg":
"auditing is complete","process":"audit","audit_id":"2022-12-30T20:53:12Z",
"event_type":"audit_finished"}
```

Once a Gatekeeper policy—ConstraintTemplate and Constraint—is added to the cluster, the audit process uses that policy to detect violations, as seen in the JSON log entry:

```
// Audit policy log entries
{"level":"info","ts":1672434373.4897652,"logger":"controller","msg":
"constraint status update","process":"audit","audit_id":"2022-12-30T21:06:12Z",
"object":{"apiVersion":"constraints.gatekeeper.sh/v1beta1","kind":
"K8sPSPSeccomp","name":"psp-seccomp"}}
{"level":"info","ts":1672434373.4930406,"logger":"controller","msg":
"handling constraint update","process":"constraint_controller","instance":
{"apiVersion":"constraints.gatekeeper.sh/v1beta1","kind":"K8sPSPSeccomp",
"name":"psp-seccomp"}}
{"level":"info","ts":1672434373.4934077,"logger":"controller","msg":
"updated constraint status violations","process":"audit","audit_id":
"2022-12-30T21:06:12Z","constraintName":"psp-seccomp","count":3}
```

I used the K8sPSPSeccomp policy from the Gatekeeper policy library. Once audits began, I was able to review the status information from the k8spspseccomp resource:

```
# Get status with violations
$ kubectl get k8spspseccomp -ojsonpath='{.items[].status}'
…"totalViolations":3,"violations":[{"enforcementAction":"deny","group":"",
"kind":"Pod","message":
"Seccomp profile 'not configured' is not allowed for container 'coredns'.
Found at: no explicit profile found. Allowed profiles: {\"RuntimeDefault\",
\"docker/default\"...
```

 Only the most recent instances of audit violations are stored in the Constraint status field so as to not overwhelm Kubernetes storage limits. And there is a limit on how many different violations can be stored. However, the totalViolations field will continue to increase. This storage limit can be set via the constraintViola tionsLimit Helm chart value; it defaults to 20.

Similar information is also logged in the Gatekeeper Audit controller logs, and since we enabled events to be emitted, events—like the one shown in Figure 7-3—are seen in the gatekeeper-system Namespace.

Event: coredns-565d847f94-7llxm.1735aea35f8564a0	✏️ 🗑️ ✕
Created	124m 53s ago 2022-12-30T16:14:13-05:00
Name	coredns-565d847f94-7llxm.1735aea35f8564a0
Namespace	gatekeeper-system
Message	(combined from similar events): Timestamp: 2022-12-30T23:17:28Z, Resource Namespace: kube-system, Constraint: psp-seccomp, Message: Seccomp profile 'not configured' is not allowed for container 'coredns'. Found at: no explicit profile found. Allowed profiles: {"RuntimeDefault", "docker/default", "runtime/default"}
Reason	AuditViolation
Source	gatekeeper-audit
First seen	124m ago (2022-12-30T16:14:13-05:00)
Last seen	97s ago (2022-12-30T18:17:29-05:00)
Count	23
Type	Warning

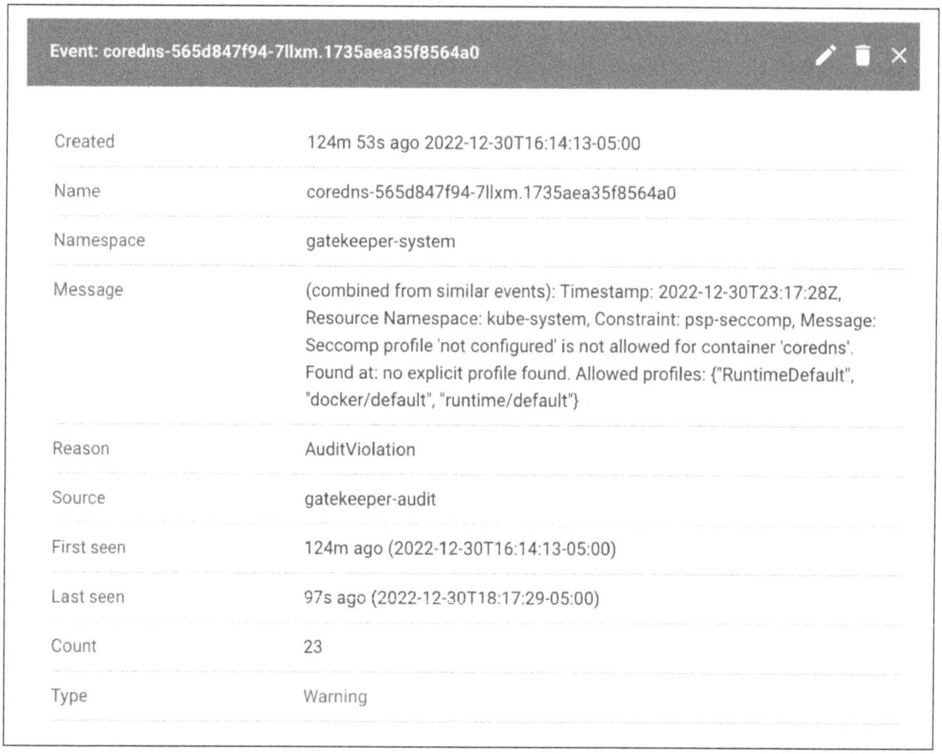

Figure 7-3. Audit event (seen in OpenLens (https://oreil.ly/lens)) produced by Gatekeeper Audit

As you see in Figure 7-3, the event refers to a coredns Pod in the gatekeeper-system Namespace. While we excluded the kube-system Namespace in the controller manager, we didn't exclude the gatekeeper-system Namespace for the audit controller. To exclude Namespaces from audit, you must add them to the excludedNamespaces list (array) in the actual Constraint processed by the audit process or in the *configs.config.gatekeeper.sh* resource. The following example illustrates how I exclude Namespaces via Constraint settings:

```
# Exclude gatekeeper-system namespace
apiVersion: constraints.gatekeeper.sh/v1beta1
kind: K8sPSPSeccomp
metadata:
  name: psp-seccomp
spec:
  match:
```

```
  kinds:
    - apiGroups: [""]
      kinds: ["Pod"]
  excludedNamespaces: ["kube-system","gatekeeper-system"]
parameters:
  allowedProfiles:
  - runtime/default
  - docker/default
```

Not all Constraints can be used with the audit process. Although I didn't include examples, the following fields can't be populated by the audit process and shouldn't be relied upon to detect audit violations:

- `review.userInfo`
- `review.operation`
- `review.uid`

Constraints using those fields are not auditable. That also means that functionality that leverages the Audit API, like logging violations to constraints on dry run, may also not work correctly if policies use the preceding fields. ConstraintTemplate authors should take care to handle the situation where violation decisions are based, at least in part, on those fields and make sure to handle the situation when the data is not available. Failing to do so may result in false violations.

In the next section, we will explore Gatekeeper's new external data feature.

External Data Providers

External data (*https://oreil.ly/cheYm*) is a Gatekeeper feature that allows you to write Rego that can call services outside of Gatekeeper to retrieve data for policy decisions. This is useful in scenarios when the data needed by policies is not part of the request's AdmissionReview object or existing Kubernetes objects. This feature uses a data-provider model that extends the reach of Gatekeeper beyond Kubernetes. Data providers are configured as shown in the following YAML:

```
# External data provider config
apiVersion: externaldata.gatekeeper.sh/v1beta1
kind: Provider   ❶
metadata:
  labels:
    app: answers
    billing: lob-cc
    env: dev
    owner: jimmy
  name: answers-provider
spec:
  caBundle: LS0t…   ❷
```

```
    timeout: 1
    url: https://answers.answers.svc/provide  ❸
```

❶ The `Provider` specifies configuration for external data sources.

❷ The `spec.caBundle` is used to make TLS calls to the external data source service.

❸ The `spec.url` points to the external data source service.

As seen in the preceding configuration, the answers-provider points to the Answers service in the `answers` Namespace. Gatekeeper uses the `caBundle` field—which contains the Answers server TLS authority certificate—to call the service that uses a self-signed TLS key and certificate. This is similar to how I configured OPA in Chapter 5.

While the Gatekeeper docs explain how to configure TLS—and mutual TLS (mTLS)—for external data providers, I just reused the approach that I showed you in Chapter 5, with slight modifications, as seen in the following shell script:

```
# TLS for external data connectivity
#!/usr/bin/env bash

# error handling
set -e
trap 'catch $? $LINENO' ERR
catch() {
  if [ "$1" != "0" ]; then
    echo "Error $1 occurred on $2"
  fi
}

OWNER="jimmy"
ENV="dev"
BILLING="lob-cc"
KUBECTL="kubectl"
CA_BUNDLE=""
CONFIGS_DIRECTORY="generated/configs"
SECRETS_DIRECTORY="generated/secrets"
TEMPLATES_DIRECTORY="templates"

if [ ! -d "$TEMPLATES_DIRECTORY" ]; then
  echo "$TEMPLATES_DIRECTORY not found, install aborted"
  exit 99
fi

if [ ! -d "$CONFIGS_DIRECTORY" ]; then
  mkdir -p $CONFIGS_DIRECTORY
fi

if [ ! -d "$SECRETS_DIRECTORY" ]; then
  mkdir -p $SECRETS_DIRECTORY
```

```
fi

rm -f $CONFIGS_DIRECTORY/*
rm -f $SECRETS_DIRECTORY/*

openssl genrsa -out $SECRETS_DIRECTORY/answers-ca.key 2048
openssl req -x509 -new -nodes -sha256 -key $SECRETS_DIRECTORY/answers-ca.key \
-days 365 -out $SECRETS_DIRECTORY/answers-ca.crt -subj /CN=admission_ca 2>&1
openssl genrsa -out $SECRETS_DIRECTORY/answers-server.key 2048
openssl req -new -key $SECRETS_DIRECTORY/answers-server.key -sha256 -out \
$SECRETS_DIRECTORY/answers-server.csr -subj /CN=answers.answers.svc -config \
$TEMPLATES_DIRECTORY/server.conf 2>&1
openssl x509 -req -in $SECRETS_DIRECTORY/answers-server.csr -sha256 -CA \
$SECRETS_DIRECTORY/answers-ca.crt -CAkey $SECRETS_DIRECTORY/answers-ca.key \
-CAcreateserial -out $SECRETS_DIRECTORY/answers-server.crt -days 100000 \
-extensions v3_ext -extfile $TEMPLATES_DIRECTORY/server.conf

cat $TEMPLATES_DIRECTORY/ns-template.yaml | sed -e \
"s/__OWNER_VALUE__/${OWNER}/g" | sed -e "s/__ENV_VALUE__/${ENV}/g" | \
sed -e "s/__BILLING_VALUE__/${BILLING}/g" > "$CONFIGS_DIRECTORY/ns.yaml"
${KUBECTL} apply -f $CONFIGS_DIRECTORY/ns.yaml

echo "Trying to delete \"answers-server\" secret..."
${KUBECTL} -n answers delete secret answers-server --ignore-not-found 2>&1
${KUBECTL} -n answers create secret tls answers-server \
--cert=$SECRETS_DIRECTORY/answers-server.crt \
--key=$SECRETS_DIRECTORY/answers-server.key

cat $TEMPLATES_DIRECTORY/answers-app-template.yaml | sed -e \
"s/__OWNER_VALUE__/${OWNER}/g" | sed -e "s/__ENV_VALUE__/${ENV}/g" | \
sed -e "s/__BILLING_VALUE__/${BILLING}/g" > \
"$CONFIGS_DIRECTORY/answers-app.yaml"
${KUBECTL} apply -f $CONFIGS_DIRECTORY/answers-app.yaml

CA_BUNDLE="$(base64 -i $SECRETS_DIRECTORY/answers-ca.crt)"
cat $TEMPLATES_DIRECTORY/provider-template.yaml | sed -e \
"s/__OWNER_VALUE__/${OWNER}/g" | sed -e "s/__ENV_VALUE__/${ENV}/g" | \
sed -e "s/__BILLING_VALUE__/${BILLING}/g" | sed -e \
"s/__CA_BUNDLE_VALUE__/${CA_BUNDLE}/g" > \
"$CONFIGS_DIRECTORY/answers-provider.yaml"
${KUBECTL} apply -f $CONFIGS_DIRECTORY/answers-provider.yaml
```

The diagram in Figure 7-4 illustrates the components involved in the external data provider solution.

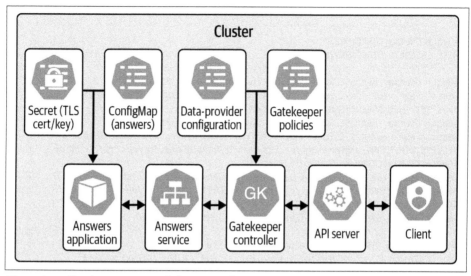

Figure 7-4. Gatekeeper external data provider components

As shown in Figure 7-4, Gatekeeper receives Kubernetes API server requests and forwards them to the Answers external data provider. Responses are sent back to Gatekeeper, where decisions are made. Gatekeeper then responds to the API server, which in turn responds to the Kubernetes client—in this case, a user using the kubectl client.

The Answers application is a simple Golang HTTP server that answers requests similarly to how the Magic 8 Ball toy (*https://oreil.ly/Xr31y*) behaves. If you pass the correct request, you might get a useful answer:

```
// Request payload - request.json
{
    "apiVersion": "externaldata.gatekeeper.sh/v1beta1",
    "kind": "ProviderRequest",
    "request": {
        "keys": [
            "gcr.io/google-containers/pause:3.2",
            "gcr.io/google-containers/pause:3.3"
        ]
    }
}

# Send curl request to answers application
$ curl -vX POST http://localhost:8080/provide \
-d @request.json \
--header "Content-Type: application/json"
HTTP/2 200
content-type: application/json
content-length: 195
date: Wed, 04 Jan 2023 01:13:02 GMT
```

```
// Response payload
{"apiVersion":"externaldata.gatekeeper.sh/v1beta1","kind":"ProviderResponse",
"response":{"idempotent":true,"items":[{"key":
"gcr.io/google-containers/pause:3.2","value":"Outlook not so good.:N",
"error":"Outlook not so good.:N:DENIED"},{"key":
"gcr.io/google-containers/pause:3.3","value":"Outlook not so good.:N","error":
"Outlook not so good.:N:DENIED"}]}}
```

I wrote this application to test my Gatekeeper external data policies. As with the
Magic 8 Ball toy, its responses are random. After all, who hasn't worked with Kubernetes and sometimes thought that the behavior was random during troubleshooting
sessions? The following ConstraintTemplate references the answers-provider external
data provider; I took inspiration from the Gatekeeper project:

```
# Answers provider template
apiVersion: templates.gatekeeper.sh/v1
kind: ConstraintTemplate
metadata:
  name: k8sanswerverification
  annotations:
    description: >-
      Calls external data provider answers app.
spec:
  crd:
    spec:
      names:
        kind: K8sAnswerVerification
  targets:
    - target: admission.k8s.gatekeeper.sh
      rego: |
        package k8sanswerverification

        violation[{"msg": msg}] {
          # build a list of keys containing images
          images := [img | img = input.review.object.spec.containers[_].image]

          # send external data request
          response := external_data({"provider": "answers-provider", "keys": images})

          response_with_error(response)

          msg := sprintf("invalid response: %v", [response])
        }

        response_with_error(response) {
          count(response.errors) > 0
          errs := response.errors[_]
          contains(errs[1],"DENIED")
        }

        response_with_error(response) {
```

```
        count(response.system_error) > 0
    }
```

The Rego in the preceding ConstraintTemplate sends Pod image URIs to the Answers application via the external data provider. If the service replies with a system error or `item.error`, then the validation fails, and the response is returned to the calling client. For security purposes, it might be a better idea to hide the response object details and return a message that belies the implementation details of the external data response.

The corresponding Constraint is shown in the following YAML:

```yaml
# Answers Constraint
apiVersion: constraints.gatekeeper.sh/v1beta1
kind: K8sAnswerVerification
metadata:
  name: pod-answers
spec:
  match:
    kinds:
      - apiGroups: [""]
        kinds: ["Pod"]
    namespaces:
      - "policy-test"
```

The Constraint is similar to what we have already seen and doesn't indicate that the policy uses an external data call. The logic is set up to allow the request only if the Magic 8 Ball message is favorable: yes. If the Magic 8 Ball replies with a negative response or maybe, then the request is denied. The following command and output illustrate the deny case:

```
$ kubectl apply -f ./examples/external-data-provider/test/3-test-pod.yaml
Error from server (Forbidden): error when creating "test/3-test-pod.yaml":
admission webhook "validation.gatekeeper.sh" denied the request: [pod-answers]
invalid response: {"errors": [["gcr.io/google-containers/pause:3.2",
"Don't count on it.:N:DENIED"]], "responses": [], "status_code": 200,
"system_error": ""}
```

The request and failure responses are shown in the following JSON outputs:

```
// Request
{"apiVersion":"externaldata.gatekeeper.sh/v1beta1","kind":"ProviderRequest",
"request":{"keys":["gcr.io/google-containers/pause:3.2"]}}

// Failure response
{"apiVersion":"externaldata.gatekeeper.sh/v1alpha1","kind":"ProviderResponse",
"response":{"idempotent":true,"items":[{"key":
"gcr.io/google-containers/pause:3.2","value":"Don't count on it.:N","error":
"Don't count on it.:N:DENIED"}]}}
```

Again, it doesn't matter what's in the request payloads; this is a Magic 8 Ball.

The valid response is shown in the following JSON:

```
// Success response
{"apiVersion":"externaldata.gatekeeper.sh/v1alpha1","kind":"ProviderResponse",
"response":{"idempotent":true,"items":[{"key":
"gcr.io/google-containers/pause:3.2","value":"It is certain.:Y"}]}}
```

Good luck!

Now, let's explore use cases for external data. Mutation and validation policies are supported by the external data feature. Most of the use cases—of which I'm aware so far—revolve around mutating and validating container images. These use cases are included and discussed in more detail in the Gatekeeper external data documentation (*https://oreil.ly/ZJyEB*).

When I started integrating PaC with Kubernetes, I mutated and validated labels and other metadata elements. If you consider external data providers, there is a great use case to call out to APIs that validate your manifests against live data, such as configuration management database (CMDB) data. Another use case could be to check your manifests against upstream software supply chain attestations. We will look more at PaC and the software supply chain in Chapter 14.

Regardless of use case, it's important to realize that external data policies can be called in the Gatekeeper Audit process. If this process executes every 60 seconds—the default—then the external data provider is also called every 60 seconds. Some use cases make network calls outside of the Kubernetes cluster when called by the external data policy.

To avoid unnecessary network traffic, it may be necessary for applications called by external data policies to cache data. Furthermore, to accommodate the time needed for the external data round trips, you may need to tune both the external data provider timeout—default is one second—as well as the Gatekeeper timeout—default is three seconds. It is also a good idea to design your external data applications to handle the timeout period. An example of this design written in Golang can be found in the tag-to-digest provider (*https://oreil.ly/tC4Nf*).

Gatekeeper has also added a cache that invalidates by default every three minutes. This external-data cache, added to Gatekeeper in version 3.13.0, is keyed by data sent to the external data provider and eliminates unnecessary round trips to external data sources. During my testing, I needed to see immediate—noncached—responses, so I disabled the cache with the following setting added to Gatekeeper in version 3.13.1:

```
# Disable Gatekeeper external data provider cache time-to-live (TTL)
externaldataProviderResponseCacheTTL: 0
```

Now, let's explore how we can use Pod policies to expand and handle workloads that create Pods.

Policy Expansion

The majority of Pods created in Kubernetes are the result of applying workload resources: Deployments, DaemonSets, and so on. Up until now, if you wrote a Pod policy for mutation or validation, you had to write others to perform similar operations on workloads. Part of this issue is due to the path differences in specifications. For example, to get at the containers in a Pod, you would use the *input.review. object.spec.containers* path, but in a Deployment resource, you would need to use *input.review.object.spec.template.spec.containers*.

There is also a UX improvement here. If you only write policies for Pods but deploy Pods mostly through workloads, then the UX is difficult. The workload may apply successfully—with no negative client signal—but Pod policies could still prevent the Pods from starting. You would need to follow up with Pod checks and then look at the workload statuses to see why the Pods never started.

Gatekeeper has introduced a new feature—still in beta at the time of this writing—that "expands" Pod policies to cover other workloads that create Pods. This "policy expansion" is made possible by the new ExpansionTemplate CRD. With this new CRD, policies written for Pods are expanded to cover workloads as well. The following example ExpansionTemplate resource is from the Gatekeeper documentation (*https://oreil.ly/6u6S_*):

```
# Policy expansion example
apiVersion: expansion.gatekeeper.sh/v1alpha1
kind: ExpansionTemplate
metadata:
  name: expand-deployments
spec:
  applyTo:
    - groups: ["apps"]
      kinds:
        - "DaemonSet"
        - "Deployment"
        - "Job"
        - "ReplicaSet"
        - "ReplicationController"
        - "StatefulSet"
      versions: ["v1"]
  templateSource: "spec.template"
  enforcementAction: "warn"
  generatedGVK:
    kind: "Pod"
    group: ""
    version: "v1"
```

To enable the use of the ExpansionTemplate, Gatekeeper must be started with the `enableGeneratorResourceExpansion` flag, as shown in the following YAML configuration:

```
# Helm install with policy expansion setting
$ helm install gatekeeper gatekeeper/gatekeeper \
    --namespace gatekeeper-system --create-namespace \
    --set logDenies=true --set replicas=1 --set version=v3.10.0 \
    --set "controllerManager.exemptNamespaces={kube-system}" \
    --set enableGeneratorResourceExpansion=true
```

To test this new feature, I added the ConstraintTemplate and Constraint for the deny-all-pods policy. Then I applied a Deployment resource to the `policy-test` Namespace. While the Deployment was applied, the Pod was never started; Gatekeeper sent the API server warning for the client request. Changing the `enforcementAction` field to `deny` would actually deny the Deployment, but the UX is very helpful with `warn` as well:

```
# Policy expansion test
$ kubectl -n policy-test apply -f ../validating/tests/11-dep-reg-allow.yaml
Warning: [deny-all-pods] [Implied by expand-deployments] INPUT:
{"parameters": {}, "review": {"kind": {"group": "", "kind": "Pod", "version":
"v1"}, "namespace": "policy-test", "object": {"apiVersion": "v1", "kind":
"Pod",...
```

So how does Gatekeeper apply Pod policies to workloads? It's all about the GVKs. In Kubernetes parlance, GVK stands for *group, version, kind*. The workload GVKs are defined in the preceding ExpansionTemplate `spec.applyTo` field. This means that this expansion will be applied to those GVKs. However, workload specs do not include Pod specs. In fact, Pods are created by downstream processes. For example, Deployments result in ReplicaSet resources, and Pods come from those ReplicaSets.

So again, how is the missing Pod resource evaluated by the Pod policy? As it turns out, Gatekeeper mocks the Pod resources as part of the workload resource validation and then validates the mocked Pod resource. Any violations are then "aggregated" onto the parent resource. The `templateSource` field tells the expansion where to find the source for the mock, and the `generatedGVK` field indicates what GVK should be created by the mock. To achieve this, Gatekeeper creates a "mock resource" for the Pod, runs validation on it, and aggregates the mock resource's violations onto the parent resource (the Deployment in this example).

Even as a beta feature, being able to expand the context of Pod policies to workloads—without having to author or manage the workload policies—is an interesting proposition that could save time and effort.

Now, let's quickly explore how we can verify Gatekeeper policies using a CLI.

Policy Testing

The gator (g8r) CLI (*https://oreil.ly/O2VC7*) is primarily used for Gatekeeper policy verification—that is, verifying policies, not Kubernetes resources. At the time of this writing, g8r transitioned to beta from alpha. To test this CLI, I used the `gator verify` command, as shown in the following console output:

```
# Gator verify test suite
$ gator verify suite.yaml
ok      suite.yaml      0.011s
PASS
```

As seen in the preceding command, `verify` uses a test-suite YAML file. The following example test-suite file configures the gator test:

```
# Gator test suite spec
kind: Suite
apiVersion: test.gatekeeper.sh/v1beta1
tests:
- name: allowed-repos
  template: template.yaml
  constraint: constraint.yaml
  cases:
  - name: allowed
    object: review-good.yaml
    assertions:
    - violations: no
  - name: disallowed
    object: review-bad.yaml
    assertions:
    - violations: yes
```

The idea here is to define tests and test cases that use ConstraintTemplates and Constraints against resource files or mocked AdmissionReview objects. The purpose of g8r is to verify Gatekeeper policies—ConstraintTemplates and Constraints, so you should use known-good and known-bad resource files—as well as purpose-built AdmissionReview mocks to elicit the desired violations.

If the policy or review object mocks were incorrect, then I would see a failure like the one in the following example:

```
# Gator violations did not match expectations
$ gator verify suite.yaml
    --- FAIL: allowed    (0.003s)
        unexpected number of violations: got 1 violations but want none: got
        messages [INVALID_DEPLOYMENT_REGISTRY:
        BAD_REGISTRY/read-only-container:v0.0.1 image is not sourced from an
        authorized registry. Resource ID (ns/name/kind): NOT_FOUND/NOT_FOUND/]
--- FAIL: allowed-repos (0.011s)
FAIL    suite.yaml      0.011s
```

```
FAIL

Error: FAIL
```

In my example test-suite file, I defined one test, allowed-repos, that defines two test cases: allowed and disallowed. The test cases define the resource files—*good.yaml* and *bad.yaml*—that are used in the test. The ConstraintTemplate and Constraint are defined at the test level. G8r also supports expansion with the `gator expand` command.

G8r can use AdmissionReview mocks as input to the test suite instead of Kubernetes resources. The following example AdmissionReview mock sets up a failure scenario:

```
# Admission review mock for bad registry
kind: AdmissionReview
...
        spec:
          containers:
          - name: test
            image: BAD_REGISTRY/read-only-container:v0.0.1

# Admission review mock for good registry
kind: AdmissionReview
...
        spec:
          containers:
          - name: test
            image: GOOD_REGISTRY/read-only-container:v0.0.1
```

To use this mock, you simply need to reference the YAML file in the test case object field, just like it was a resource file.

I imagine that the g8r CLI would be included as part of a CI automation process, providing attestations for new or modified Gatekeeper policies before they are applied to clusters.

 The traditional—and still valid—means of testing Rego, like that found in Gatekeeper ConstraintTemplates, is to write Rego test cases (*https://oreil.ly/cU-Zi*).

Summary

I see Gatekeeper as a decorator and facade over OPA. As a facade, Gatekeeper hides the details of its usage of OPA, and users cannot directly call OPA. Underpinned by the OPA Constraint Framework, Gatekeeper decorates OPA with new functionality to create policies with a mixture of YAML and Rego. The Gatekeeper CRDs define APIs that extend Kubernetes to perform actions like configuration, expansion, audit, mutation, and validation. The idea that Constraints can be used to target Kubernetes resources—extending a single ConstraintTemplate CRD—adds extensibility and expressiveness to Kubernetes policies. We still get Rego, which is arguably a powerful policy language; however, we also get the ability to decouple Rego from how we apply policies and the parameters that we can change.

Like OPA, Gatekeeper is a mature OSS and a CNCF graduated project. And if we again consider the PaC Solution Selection Scorecard from Chapter 1, like OPA, Gatekeeper satisfies several of the items for Kubernetes use cases. That said, the general consensus is that if you want an OPA/Rego-based Kubernetes PaC solution, then Gatekeeper is the go-to choice. If you also want policy and data management tools—like status logs, decision logs, and bundles—then you would want to consider OPA.

Using Gatekeeper, we still have the strength of Rego, but now we also have the flexibility and acceptance of YAML as well as the relationship that permits multiple Constraints to reference the same ConstraintTemplate. So, depending on how we write our Rego, in the ConstraintTemplates we can cover multiple resources—GVKs—by how we configure our Constraints.

Our Gatekeeper policies can mutate and validate inbound API server requests, and with Gatekeeper Audit, we can apply policies to existing resources to detect existing violations as well as those violations that may have slipped by our webhook process, which is set to fail open.

With Gatekeeper, we get three new features that make it easier to use and manage Kubernetes policies:

- External data providers
- Policy expansion
- Gator CLI

To be transparent, OPA does support going after external data with its own `http.send` function. However, OPA doesn't recommend using `http.send` to effect changes in remote systems, as internal OPA policy optimizations will not guarantee that the `http.send` will actually be called from a policy evaluation. Moreover, in my experience, it's rarely used during Kubernetes mutation and validation evaluations. Gatekeeper external data providers make it easier to instrument Gatekeeper policies with services—external to Gatekeeper—that provide additional data and even act as proxies to reach outside the cluster.

Policy expansion promises to reduce the need for Gatekeeper users to manage semi-duplicative policies for workload resources that create Pods. With policy expansion, users can write Pod policies and then expand them into workload policies with expansion templates—never needing to actually write the workload policies.

Finally, the gator CLI is a good tool to integrate into your CI processes to perform manual and automated testing on Gatekeeper policies, using Kubernetes resource manifests and mocked API server AdmissionReview objects.

Throughout this book, I have written considerably about OPA and related tools. Chapter 8 is the first in a series devoted to non-OPA PaC solutions that, like Gatekeeper, are built solely—or at least primarily—for use with Kubernetes.

Kyverno and Kubernetes

Kyverno, Greek for *govern*, is a mature OSS—incubating CNCF—policy-engine project that is designed specifically for Kubernetes. With Kyverno, you can policy-enable your Kubernetes clusters and DevOps pipelines to control cluster behavior and validate policies before use. As we will see in this chapter, Kyverno integrates to Kubernetes via the same dynamic admission controllers, similar to previous Kubernetes solutions that we have already explored and that we will see in subsequent chapters.

The Kyverno project, created by Nirmata (*https://nirmata.com*), enjoys a very active community of contributors and users. The following links will help you gain more information about Kyverno:

- Core GitHub project (*https://github.com/kyverno/kyverno*)
- Documentation website (*https://kyverno.io/docs*)
- Policy library (*https://kyverno.io/policies*)
- Kyverno Slack community (*https://oreil.ly/95iD_*)
- CNCF page (*https://www.cncf.io/projects/kyverno*)

Unlike the Kubernetes PaC solutions that we have discussed so far, Kyverno is not underpinned by OPA or Rego. Kyverno policies are written using YAML. YAML syntax is used widely throughout Kubernetes, so Kyverno adoption does not require learning a new policy-language syntax. The learning curve for Kyverno includes the Kyverno YAML lexicon. As we will see later in this chapter, an additional JSON query language—JMESPath (*https://jmespath.org*)—can be used to apply fine-grained selection logic in Kyverno policies.

Let's get started by installing Kyverno in minikube.

Installation

Kyverno can be installed using Helm or via kubectl and YAML resources. As a Kyverno user, I prefer the Helm install. The Helm chart is far more capable of being tweaked and configured than the YAML manifest.

Kyverno uses a compatibility matrix (*https://oreil.ly/_IzkZ*) to ensure a match between Kyverno versions and Kubernetes versions.

As I did with previous PaC installs, I used a Makefile and shell script to automate the install. The Helm command I used during the install is shown in the following console output:

```
# Helm command
$ helm install kyverno kyverno/kyverno -n kyverno --create-namespace \
--values values.yaml
```

In the following install output, I liked that the output included the Helm chart version and the Kyverno version; I consider it a best practice to include that information:

```
# Kyverno install
$ make up
./up.sh
NAME: kyverno
LAST DEPLOYED: Sat Mar 16 20:24:20 2024
NAMESPACE: kyverno
STATUS: deployed
REVISION: 1
NOTES:
Chart version: 3.1.4
Kyverno version: v1.11.4

Thank you for installing kyverno! Your release is named kyverno.

The following components have been installed in your cluster:
- CRDs
- Admission controller
- Reports controller
- Cleanup controller
- Background controller


WARNING: Setting the admission controller replica count below 3 means Kyverno
is not running in high availability mode.  ❶

WARNING: Generating reports from ValidatingAdmissionPolicies require a
Kubernetes 1.27+ cluster with `ValidatingAdmissionPolicy` feature gate and
```

`admissionregistration.k8s.io` API group enabled.

Note: There is a trade-off when deciding which approach to take regarding
Namespace exclusions. Please see the documentation at
https://kyverno.io/docs/installation/#security-vs-operability to understand
the risks. ❸

❶ The Kyverno installation checks your replica count and warns you when your
    settings are not optimal for production configurations.

❷ When you enable policy reports for ValidatingAdmissionPolicies, the install
    warns you about the feature gates that need to be enabled.

❸ Kyverno also makes you aware of the trade-offs of ignoring Namespaces.

As with previous PaC installs, I stayed with one replica and ignored the kube-system
and PaC solution—kyverno, in this case—Namespaces. In production, you would
want multiple replicas. In fact, as seen in the preceding output, the Kyverno Helm
install—using Helm notes (*https://oreil.ly/_ngLN*)—warned me about my single-
replica choice.

Like most Kubernetes applications, you should follow best practices to ensure high
availability (HA) is configured, if needed. Since PaC solutions can directly affect cluster operations, you should use appropriate HA settings in a production environment.

Finally, it seems to take at least five seconds—in a small minikube cluster—for
Kyverno webhook configurations to propagate after Helm reports a successful install.

I also used the following command to detect when mutating resources were ready:

```
# Get mutating webhook configurations, watch for changes
$ kubectl get mutatingwebhookconfiguration --watch
NAME                                      WEBHOOKS   AGE
kyverno-policy-mutating-webhook-cfg       1          0s
kyverno-resource-mutating-webhook-cfg     0          0s
kyverno-verify-mutating-webhook-cfg       1          0s
```

The --watch argument keeps the command open, watching for changes. This can be
stopped by the Ctrl+c key sequence.

The Kyverno installation installed 13 CRD resources as well:

```
# Get Kyverno CRD
$ kubectl get crd -l app.kubernetes.io/part-of=kyverno-crds
NAME                                        CREATED AT
admissionreports.kyverno.io                 2024-03-08T00:28:01Z
backgroundscanreports.kyverno.io            2024-03-08T00:28:01Z
cleanuppolicies.kyverno.io                  2024-03-08T00:28:01Z
clusteradmissionreports.kyverno.io          2024-03-08T00:28:01Z
clusterbackgroundscanreports.kyverno.io     2024-03-08T00:28:01Z
```

```
clustercleanuppolicies.kyverno.io          2024-03-08T00:28:01Z
clusterpolicies.kyverno.io                  2024-03-08T00:28:01Z
clusterpolicyreports.wgpolicyk8s.io         2024-03-08T00:28:01Z
policies.kyverno.io                         2024-03-08T00:28:01Z
policyexceptions.kyverno.io                 2024-03-08T00:28:01Z
policyreports.wgpolicyk8s.io                2024-03-08T00:28:01Z
updaterequests.kyverno.io                   2024-03-08T00:28:01Z
```

 As we saw in prior chapters, you can easily discover the purpose of the CRDs—extending the Kubernetes API—via the following kubectl explain command:

```
$ kubectl explain updaterequests.kyverno.io | \
grep DESCRIPTION -A2
DESCRIPTION:
    UpdateRequest is a request to process mutate and
    generate rules in background.
```

With a successful install, let's look at how Kyverno is configured to ignore sensitive Namespaces to ensure smooth cluster operation.

Ignoring Namespaces

With any Kubernetes PaC solution that is used to intercept API server requests before they reach etcd, it is a good idea to understand how you can avoid processing resources in sensitive, system-level Namespaces. Incorrectly configured, a Kubernetes PaC solution can compromise cluster operations and integrity. The trade-off of ignoring so-called sensitive Namespaces is documented well in Kyverno's Security vs. Operability (*https://oreil.ly/J48Bc*) documentation. In short, policy may not be applied to those Namespaces in the future.

During the Kyverno install, I specified a local *values.yaml* file with custom settings that I wanted for the Kyverno install:

```
# Values YAML file
config:
  webhooks:
  - namespaceSelector:
      matchExpressions:
      - key: kubernetes.io/metadata.name
        operator: NotIn
        values:
        - kube-system
replicaCount: 1
image:
  pullPolicy: Always
  tag: v1.11.4
```

Even if I didn't include the preceding values, I could have edited the kyverno Config Map in the kyverno Namespace and included the kube-system Namespace to be ignored by the webhook:

```
# Webhook settings to ignore Namespaces
webhooks: '[{"namespaceSelector":{"matchExpressions":[{"key":
"kubernetes.io/metadata.name","operator":"NotIn","values":["kube-system"]},
{"key":"kubernetes.io/metadata.name","operator":"NotIn","values":
["kyverno"]}],"matchLabels":null}}]'
```

The end result is that the webhooks—mutating and validating—were set to ignore Namespaces I specified:

```
# Namespaces to ignore in webhook configuration
...
  namespaceSelector:
    matchExpressions:
    - key: kubernetes.io/metadata.name
      operator: NotIn
      values:
      - kube-system
    - key: kubernetes.io/metadata.name
      operator: NotIn
      values:
      - kyverno
...
```

If I decided to edit the aforementioned kyverno ConfigMap and remove the kube-system Namespace from the webhooks configuration, the Kyverno resources mutating and validating webhook configurations would be automatically modified to remove the Namespace from their configurations.

Now, let's look at how Kverno reduces API server traffic with dynamic webhook configurations.

Dynamic Webhook Configurations

After the install, I noticed something different about Kyverno that I did not see in previous PaC installs. Not all of the webhook configurations were provisioned:

```
# Mutating admission webhook
$ kubectl get mutatingwebhookconfiguration
NAME                                    WEBHOOKS    AGE
kyverno-policy-mutating-webhook-cfg     1           98s
kyverno-resource-mutating-webhook-cfg   0           98s  ❶
kyverno-verify-mutating-webhook-cfg     1           98s


# Validating admission webhook
$ kubectl get validatingwebhookconfiguration
NAME                                    WEBHOOKS    AGE
kyverno-cleanup-validating-webhook-cfg  1           102s
```

```
kyverno-exception-validating-webhook-cfg    1           101s
kyverno-policy-validating-webhook-cfg       1           101s
kyverno-resource-validating-webhook-cfg     0           101s ❷
kyverno-ttl-validating-webhook-cfg          1           102s
```

❶ The mutating webhook for Kubernetes resources was created but not configured with any webhooks connection back to Kyverno.

❷ The validating webhook for Kubernetes resources was created but not configured with any webhooks connection back to Kyverno.

In the preceding kubectl outputs, you should notice that neither the resource mutating or validating webhooks were fully configured. In fact, they are not configured until mutating or validating policies—respectively—are added to Kyverno. Per Kyverno documentation, this has been done on purpose since version 1.5.0 to dynamically manage webhooks, thereby "preventing unnecessary admission requests being forwarded to Kyverno." If we consider how dynamic admission controllers can impact API server operations, reducing unnecessary admission control traffic makes perfect sense.

The Kyverno Helm chart *values.yaml* file includes a set of resource filters (*https://oreil.ly/oKOck*) that configure Kyverno to skip processing of certain resources. You use resource filters when you need to exclude certain resources from being processed by policies. The resource filters are a list of lists, wrapped in single quotes. Each list is comprised of three elements:

- Kubernetes kind
- Namespace
- Name

In the following `resourceFilters` element, the first list item filters out Event resources, regardless of Namespace or name. Additionally, the last element does the same for Node resources. Kyverno policies will not apply to these resources, regardless of the Namespace or name. The remaining resource-filter list items shown filter out all resources, regardless of kind or name, that are the listed Namespaces: `kube-system`, `kube-public`, and `kube-node-lease`:

```
# Resource filters
  resourceFilters:
    - '[Event,*,*]' ❶
    - '[*,kube-system,*]' ❷
    - '[*,kube-public,*]'
    - '[*,kube-node-lease,*]'
    - '[Node,*,*]' …
```

❶ Event resources, regardless of Namespace or name, are filtered out and not processed.

❷ All resources in the kube-system Namespace, regardless of type or name, are filtered out and not processed.

As you can see from the preceding resourceFilters lists, each resource filter list element can be a wildcard, though it would be a bad idea to add three wildcards as all resource kinds, in all Namespaces regardless of resource name, would be skipped by Kyverno. This would render policies ineffective.

Using resource filters is not the same as ignoring Namespaces by the webhook configuration. Resource filters will still result in calls to Kyverno, and then, internal Kyverno logic will "skip" resource processing. Depending on webhook settings, this could still result in cluster issues if Kyverno cannot be reached.

With Kyverno installed and configured, we can now explore how to uninstall it.

Uninstalling Kyverno

Uninstalling Kyverno is also easy with the following Helm command:

```
# down.sh
#!/usr/bin/env bash
# error handling
set -e
trap 'catch $? $LINENO' ERR
catch() {
  if [ "$1" != "0" ]; then
    echo "Error $1 occurred on $2"
  fi
}

KUBECTL="kubectl"

${KUBECTL} config set-context --current --namespace=kyverno

helm uninstall kyverno

${KUBECTL} delete ns kyverno --ignore-not-found

# Uninstall command and output
$ make down
./down.sh
Context "kyverno" modified.
release "kyverno" uninstalled
namespace "kyverno" deleted
```

So far, Kyverno is very easy to install, configure, and uninstall. Next, we will explore how Kyverno policies are built and used.

Policies

The two best ways to get started with Kyverno policies are to explore the policy library (*https://kyverno.io/policies*) in the Kyverno documentation and to try policies against resources in the new Kyverno Playground (*https://playground.kyverno.io*). The policy library includes a handy navigation-filter user interface, shown in Figure 8-1.

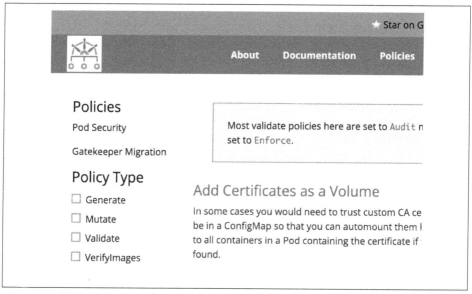

Figure 8-1. Kyverno policy library filters

The left-side navigation filters, shown in Figure 8-1, make it easy to select Kyverno policies for specific use cases. Filter selections include:

Policy type
    CleanUp, Generate, Mutate, Validate, VerifyImages

Policy category
    Use cases like AWS, pod security, and multitenancy

Minimum version
    The minimum Kyverno version for the related policy

Subject
    Related subjects, such as Kubernetes, Argo, and KubeVirt resources

The Kyverno Playground, shown in Figure 8-2, helps you learn Kyverno policies by allowing you to run policies against resources via a web interface.

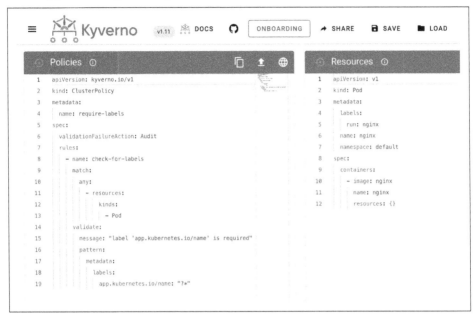

Figure 8-2. Kyverno Playground

In Figure 8-2, the left pane contains the require-labels policy applied to the Pod resource in the right pane. The Start button—not pictured—applies the policy to the resource. Since the Pod resource does not contain the `app.kubernetes.io/name` label, the resource fails validation, as shown in Figure 8-3.

Figure 8-3. Kyverno Playground resource-validation failure

As shown in Figure 8-3, the policy can be easily copied to the clipboard for use elsewhere. The Kyverno Playground is great for prototyping and troubleshooting new policies.

Now that we know where to find Kyverno policies and how to try them out in the Kyverno Playground, let's look deeper into the Kyverno policy lexicon.

Policy Lexicon

As I mentioned earlier in this chapter, Kyverno policies are written in YAML, so there is no new policy language to learn. However, Kyverno does use two advanced features as part of the policy lexicon that must be understood to effectively read and write policies. In this section, we will explore how Kyverno uses JMESPath and YAML anchors.

JMESPath (*https://jmespath.org*)—pronounced "james-path"—is the JSON query language behind Kyverno. In Kyverno policies, JMESPath expressions are used to perform more complex selections of fields and values as well as conditions. The Kyverno CLI, discussed later in this chapter, also uses JMESPath to query data from supplied YAML files.

The Kyverno JMESPath documentation (*https://oreil.ly/7JRlL*) explains the usage and provides several examples to help you understand how to use this powerful query language. The following snippet is from a best practices example for checking deprecated Kubernetes APIs (*https://oreil.ly/beOzJ*):

```
# JMESPath snippet
rules:
  - name: validate-v1-25-removals
    match:
      any:
      - resources:
          kinds:
          - batch/*/CronJob
          - discovery.k8s.io/*/EndpointSlice
          - events.k8s.io/*/Event
          - policy/*/PodDisruptionBudget
          - node.k8s.io/*/RuntimeClass
    preconditions:
      all:
      - key: "{{ request.operation || 'BACKGROUND' }}"
        operator: NotEquals
        value: DELETE
      - key: "{{request.object.apiVersion}}" ❶
        operator: AnyIn
        value:
        - batch/v1beta1
        - discovery.k8s.io/v1beta1
        - events.k8s.io/v1beta1
        - policy/v1beta1
        - node.k8s.io/v1beta1
    validate:
      message: >-
        {{ request.object.apiVersion }}/{{ request.object.kind }} is
```

```
    deprecated and will be removed in v1.25. ❷
    See: https://kubernetes.io/docs/reference/using-api/deprecation-guide/
  deny: {}
```

❶ This JMESPath expression is used to match Kubernetes apiVersions.

❷ This JMESPath expression is used to build messages from the AdmissionReview object in the API server request.

In the preceding policy snippet, JMESPath is used to match inbound Kubernetes API AdmissionReview objects using request operations and request-object API versions. If the precondition is matched, then JMESPath is again used to construct the message sent back to the API server client. JMESPath expressions make Kyverno policies more expressive.

Another advanced feature that you should learn is how Kyverno uses YAML anchors (*https://oreil.ly/HqaBo*). In its simplest form, a YAML anchor is used to apply DRY methodology to YAML data. With an anchor, you can write YAML values and alias those values if they are needed later in YAML documents. The following example illustrates the basics of YAML anchors and aliases:

```
# Using YAML anchors and aliases
spec:
  containers:
    - name: test-pod
      imagePullPolicy: &imagePullPolicy Always  ❶
    - name: test-pod2
      imagePullPolicy: *imagePullPolicy  ❷

# Parsed YAML
spec:
  containers:
   - name: test-pod
     imagePullPolicy: Always
   - name: test-pod2
     imagePullPolicy: Always
```

❶ Anchors are created to share YAML data across elements.

❷ The alias is used to reference anchored data.

In the preceding example, the & operator is used to prefix the value with an anchor label. Then that label is used as an alias with the * operator to get at the actual value. This is similar to how pointers are referenced and dereferenced in Golang. This syntax creates an alias in the test-pod2 Pod for the imagePullPolicy element, referencing the like value anchored in the test-pod Pod.

Kyverno uses custom YAML anchors (*https://oreil.ly/HqaBo*) for conditional process‐
ing. The following is an example from a Kyverno policy (*https://oreil.ly/S8_7o*)
written to prevent Windows containers from using the `hostProcess` field:

```
# Kyverno YAML anchor example
pattern:
  spec:
    =(ephemeralContainers):  ❶
      - =(securityContext):
          =(windowsOptions):
            =(hostProcess): "false"
    =(initContainers):
      - =(securityContext):
          =(windowsOptions):
            =(hostProcess): "false"
    containers:
      - =(securityContext):
          =(windowsOptions):
            =(hostProcess): "false"
```

❶ Custom anchor tags configure conditional logic where processing continues as
   long as the fields and nested fields exist.

The use of custom anchors in this preceding policy performs an "if-then" evaluation
on the fields such that if a parent field is specified, it should evaluate its child fields
for existence or value.

The `pod.spec.containers.securityContext.windowsOptions.hostProcess` field is
a boolean field that can allow a Windows container to run as a host process. To pre‐
vent this, the policy uses the preceding snippet to ensure that if the nested fields exist,
then the last field should be evaluated. If the logic makes it to the `hostProcess` field
and it exists in a container specification, the field must be set to `false`. This policy
prevents Windows containers from getting elevated host access.

Now that we've seen how JMESPath and YAML anchors are used to express Kyverno
policy conditions and to match and query data, let's explore how Kyverno policies are
composed.

Policy Composition

Kyverno policies are composed of rules, patterns, and actions. Rules contain patterns
and actions. Patterns are used to match the policy to Kubernetes resources as well as
to elements within the resources. Actions define what the policy will do when it
matches resources. The following policy specification specifies policy settings as well
policy rules, thereby controlling how the policy matches resources, and it is executed
by the policy engine to control Kubernetes cluster behavior:

```
# Validation policy specification
spec:
  background: true ❶
  failurePolicy: Fail ❷
  rules: ❸
  - match:
      any:
      - resources:
          kinds:
          - Pod
    name: check-seccomp
    validate: ❹
      message: |
            Use of custom Seccomp profiles is disallowed. The fields
            spec.securityContext.seccompProfile.type,
            spec.containers[*].securityContext.seccompProfile.type,
            spec.initContainers[*].securityContext.seccompProfile.type, and
            spec.ephemeralContainers[*].securityContext.seccompProfile.type
            must be unset or set to `RuntimeDefault` or `Localhost`.
      pattern: ❺
        spec:
          =(ephemeralContainers):
          - =(securityContext):
              =(seccompProfile):
                =(type): RuntimeDefault | Localhost
          =(initContainers):
          - =(securityContext):
              =(seccompProfile):
                =(type): RuntimeDefault | Localhost
          =(securityContext):
            =(seccompProfile):
              =(type): RuntimeDefault | Localhost
          containers:
          - =(securityContext):
              =(seccompProfile):
                =(type): RuntimeDefault | Localhost
    validationFailureAction: Enforce ❻
```

❶ The background setting controls if rules are applied to existing resources during a background scan.

❷ The failurePolicy setting defines how unexpected policy errors and webhook response timeout errors are handled.

❸ Rules is a list of rule instances. A policy can contain multiple rules, and each rule can validate, mutate, clean up resources, generate resources, or verify images.

❹ Used to validate matching resources.

❺ Pattern used to check resources.

❻ Should rule violation block the admission review request (`Enforce`) or allow (`Audit`) and report it? The default is Audit.

The preceding policy specification is from the restrict-seccomp ClusterPolicy installed via the kyverno/kyverno-policies Helm chart (*https://oreil.ly/3bqqL*). This chart installs the Pod Security Standard policies from the Kyverno library. However, all these policies—and many more—can be had directly from the library. A similar policy—restrict-seccomp-strict (*https://oreil.ly/qXpdC*)—can be found in the Kyverno policy library as well.

The check-seecomp rule in this policy matches all Pod requests, passed to Kyverno via the webhook configuration. The YAML anchors in the `policy.spec.rules.vali date.pattern` field match the `securityContext.seccompProfile.type` field for each container type—ephemeral, init, and regular—and make sure that the value is either `RuntimeDefault` or `Localhost`. Again, the use of custom anchors performs an "if-then" evaluation on the fields such that if a parent field is specified, it then should evaluate its child fields.

Kyverno uses policy metadata to set useful information about how policies are used. For example, In the following metadata, you see the supported Kyverno and Kubernetes versions for this policy. You also see the subject—Pod—of the policy as well as the medium severity. To be clear, most of the annotations shown in the following example are used for the policy listing on the Kyverno web site, are entirely optional, and control no Kyverno functionality:

```
# Policy metadata
metadata:
  name: add-default-resources
  annotations:
    policies.kyverno.io/title: Add Default Resources
    policies.kyverno.io/category: Other
    policies.kyverno.io/severity: medium
    kyverno.io/kyverno-version: 1.6.0
    policies.kyverno.io/minversion: 1.6.0
    kyverno.io/kubernetes-version: "1.23"
    policies.kyverno.io/subject: Pod
    policies.kyverno.io/description: >-
      DESCRIPTION HERE
```

The category, severity, and scored items are used in policy reporting, which we will explore later in this chapter, as well as policy results.

Now that we have looked at policy composition, let's examine the different Kyverno policy types.

Policy Types

In previous chapters, we explored the Mutate and Validate policy types, so you should be familiar with them. The CleanUp, Generate, and VerifyImages policies are new and are specific to Kyverno. We will look at all five types in this section.

Regardless of type, Kyverno policies are primarily scoped as cluster-wide policies or Namespaced policies. In Kyverno, ClusterPolicy resources—shortname *cpol*—are based on the clusterpolicies.kyverno.io CRD, and Namespace-scoped policy resources—shortname *pol*—are based on the policies.kyverno.io CRD.

As we explore Kyverno policy types, we will also see how they can be scoped to cluster or Namespace.

Mutate policies

As with previous PaC solutions, Kyverno mutation policies are used to mutate inbound API server requests before they are validated. The following simple example shows how a mutating policy adds labels to multiple resource types:

```
# Add labels
spec:
  mutateExistingOnPolicyUpdate: true
  rules:
  - name: add-labels
    match:
      any:
      - resources:
          kinds:
          - Pod
          - Service
          - ConfigMap
          - Secret
    mutate:
      patchStrategicMerge:
        metadata:
          labels:
            owner: jimmy
            billing: lob-cc
            env: dev
```

With this policy in place, we can test by submitting a Pod request with this metadata:

```
# Pod metadata with missing labels
metadata:
  labels:
    app: test
```

The metadata of the created Pod includes the new labels:

```
# Applied Pod resource with added labels from mutation policy
metadata:
  labels:
    app: test
    billing: lob-cc
    env: dev
    owner: jimmy
```

The next example policy—add-default-resources (*https://oreil.ly/HxGby*)—can be found in the Kyverno policy library. This example is a little more involved, as it uses JMESPath to check operations and YAML anchors for fields and values:

```
# Example mutation policy spec
spec:
  rules:
  - name: add-mesh-annotations
    match:
      any:
      - resources:
          kinds:
          - Namespace      ❶
    mutate:
      patchStrategicMerge:
        metadata:
          annotations:
            +(linkerd.io/inject): enabled      ❷
            +(config.linkerd.io/proxy-await): enabled
```

❶   This policy patches Namespace resources.

❷   This policy adds the Linkerd annotations to Namespaces using the "add if not present" anchor.

In the preceding policy spec, the add-default-requests mutation rule is used to mutate inbound Pod requests where the CREATE or UPDATE operation is used. The Kyverno "add if not present" anchor (*https://oreil.ly/W7uPz*) is used to add the memory and CPU requests if they don't already exist in the Pod spec.

The following policy replaces the k8s.gcr.io registry with the registry.k8s.io registry:

```
# Example mutation-policy spec that replaces image registry
spec:
  rules:
  - name: change-deprecated-containers
    match:
      any:
      - resources:
          kinds:
          - Pod
```

```
preconditions:
  all:
  - key: "{{request.operation}}"
    operator: AnyIn
    value:
    - CREATE
    - UPDATE
  - key: k8s.gcr.io
    operator: AnyIn
    value: "{{ images.containers.*.registry[] || `[]` }}"
mutate:
  foreach:  ❶
  - list: "request.object.spec.containers"
    patchStrategicMerge:
      spec:
        containers:
        - name: "{{ element.name }}"
          image: >
              registry.k8s.io/{{ images.containers."{{element.name}}".
              path}}:{{images.containers."{{element.name}}".tag}}
```

❶ In this policy, the `foreach` element enables iteration over containers within the Pod matched by this policy.

The preceding policy spec uses the predefined `image` variables (*https://oreil.ly/B3CHt*) automatically created by Kyverno to make them available in policy rules.

The preceding policy uses a new `foreach` Kyverno feature (*https://oreil.ly/n2rS_*) that enables the iteration over list objects. The `foreach` expressions must contain a `list` field and may contain an `order` field to control ascending or descending iteration order. Multiple and/or nested `foreach` elements may be defined.

Mutation policies are usually added to respond to inbound API server requests. However, Kyverno mutation policies can also be used to modify existing Kubernetes resources, triggered by mutating policy CREATE or UPDATE operations. Furthermore, mutation policies can be used to mutate a different resource than that which triggers the behavior. For example, the observation of an UPDATE event on a Deployment can result in the mutation of an existing service.

The following policy uses the `mutateExistingOnPolicyUpdate` field in the policy spec to update existing Namespaces after the policy is applied:

```
# Mutate new and existing Namespaces with PSA/PSS labels
spec:
  mutateExistingOnPolicyUpdate: true
  rules:
  - name: label-privileged-namespaces
    match:
      any:
      - resources:
```

```
     kinds:
     - Namespace
mutate:
  Targets:    !❶
    - apiVersion: v1
      kind: Namespace
  patchStrategicMerge:
    metadata:
      <(name): "!kube-system"
      labels:
        pod-security.kubernetes.io/enforce: privileged
        pod-security.kubernetes.io/audit: baseline
        pod-security.kubernetes.io/warn: baseline
```

❶   The `mutate.Targets` field configures which resources will be mutated.

In the preceding policy, `mutateExistingOnPolicyUpdate: true` is used to tell the Kyverno policy engine to use this policy to mutate new and updated Namespaces as well as existing Namespaces when I apply this policy. This policy affects all Namespaces except the `kube-system` Namespace, as configured in the rule, and any Namespace already ignored by the mutating webhook configuration.

To clarify, mutate-existing rules are not bound by either the webhook configuration or the resource filters when it comes to mutation of existing resources. Both of these elements only influence the triggering resource as specified in the `match` block; triggers always come in from the admission side. For example, if the `kube-system` Namespace is excluded in webhooks (and/or the resource filters), then an UPDATE operation on that Namespace could not result in mutation of an existing resource because Kyverno would receive no triggering notification from this event. Mutation of existing resources is always initiated by some triggering event, either on the policy itself or on some other resource as named in the rule.

It's important to understand that while mutation policies—with this spec—can mutate existing resources, there are limits (*https://oreil.ly/sqYcL*) imposed by Kubernetes. Any mutation policy that mutates existing resources will be bound by these Kubernetes limits. For example, you cannot use this approach to modify `name` and `namespace` fields in the Pod metadata, but you could change `container[*].image` fields in the Pod specification.

Writing mutation rules in Kyverno—with YAML, JMESPath, and anchors—is easy and a welcome change from previous rules I have authored in this book. It's useful to be able to mutate existing resources, not just new or updated ones.

Now, let's explore how we write validation rules and policies.

Validate policies

Validation policies are the most common policy type used in Kubernetes PaC solutions. In Kyverno, validation policy specifications start with the action that will be taken by Kyverno when a violation occurs. Kverno validation policies are written with multiple rule types. Once Kyverno was installed, I used the `kubectl explain` command to see all the rule types supported by Kyverno validation policies:

```
$ kubectl explain policy.spec.rules.validate
GROUP:     kyverno.io
KIND:      Policy
VERSION:   v1

FIELD: validate <Object>

DESCRIPTION:
    Validation is used to validate matching resources.

FIELDS:
  anyPattern    <Object>
    AnyPattern specifies list of validation patterns. At least one of the
    patterns must be satisfied for the validation rule to succeed.

  cel   <Object>
    CEL allows validation checks using the Common Expression Language
    (https://kubernetes.io/docs/reference/using-api/cel/).

  deny  <Object>
    Deny defines conditions used to pass or fail a validation rule.

  foreach       <[]Object>
    ForEach applies validate rules to a list of sub-elements by creating a
    context for each entry in the list and looping over it to apply the
    specified logic.

  manifests     <Object>
    Manifest specifies conditions for manifest verification

  message       <string>
    Message specifies a custom message to be displayed on failure.

  pattern       <Object>
    Pattern specifies an overlay-style pattern used to check resources.

  podSecurity   <Object>
    PodSecurity applies exemptions for Kubernetes Pod Security admission by
    specifying exclusions for Pod Security Standards controls.
```

In the following example, the `validationFailureAction` field indicates that violations of this policy will be audited and available in downstream reports, but they will not block any actions; to block actions with violations, change this field to `Enforce`:

```
# Validation policy spec
spec:
  validationFailureAction: Audit   ❶
  background: false
  rules:
  - name: check-privileged
    match:
      any:
      - resources:   ❷
          kinds:
            - Namespace
          selector:
            matchLabels:
              pod-security.kubernetes.io/enforce: privileged
    exclude:
      any:
      - clusterRoles:
        - cluster-admin   ❸
    validate:
      message: >
            Only cluster-admins may create Namespaces that allow setting the
            privileged level.
      deny: {}
```

❶ This policy will Audit—create a PolicyReport—but will not stop the cluster change that triggered the policy.

❷ Namespaces that are labeled with the PSA enforce mode and PSS privileged profile should be selected and reported.

❸ This policy will not affect changes made by users with the cluster-admin ClusterRole.

PolicyReports are explained later in this chapter.

The preceding policy integrates Kubernetes PSA/PSS and audits, or reports, violations when users other than cluster administrators try to provision Namespaces that are privileged. This policy is our first example of using the exclude block along with the match block.

In addition to enforcing or auditing violations, Kyverno validation policies can deny requests based on certain conditions. The following example uses a JMESPath expression to create a deny message and a condition with a JMESPath expression to deny delete operations, except for—again—cluster administrators:

```
# Deny request example
spec:
  validationFailureAction: Enforce
  background: false
  rules:
```

```
- name: block-deletes-for-kyverno-resources
  match:
    any:
    - resources:
        selector:
          matchLabels:
            app.kubernetes.io/managed-by: kyverno  ❶
  exclude:
    any:
    - clusterRoles:
      - cluster-admin   ❷
  validate:
    message: >
          Deleting {{request.oldObject.kind}}/
          {{request.oldObject.metadata.name}} is not allowed
    deny:  ❸
      conditions:
        any:
        - key: "{{request.operation}}"   ❹
          operator: Equals
          value: DELETE   ❺
```

❶   This policy is triggered by changes to resources labeled as managed by Kyverno.

❷   Changes triggered by clients with the cluster-admin ClusterRole will not be blocked.

❸   This policy includes a deny rule.

❹   Deny rules use tripartite expressions (key-operator-value).

❺   The policy focuses on and only denies DELETE operations.

The preceding policy could be used to prevent Kyverno policies from being deleted, ensuring security, compliance, governance, or best practices are not circumvented. A better approach would be to control access to policies via Kubernetes RBAC. The preceding policy could be used as complementary control. Kyverno policy CREATE/ UPDATE/DELETE operations are highly privileged acts and should be performed only by a select few individuals with privileged access.

   Understanding paths to Kubernetes vulnerabilities is a large part of Kubernetes threat modeling. Using policies to eliminate paths that introduce unwanted cluster changes is the promise of PaC. With this approach, PaC becomes an additional layer of a defense-in-depth strategy to secure clusters. We saw a similar approach in Chapter 7 where Namespaces could not be ignored with labels unless they were first marked as exempt during installation.

Now that we understand how validating policies are created, managed, and used, let's look at how we can augment the policy management UX by reducing the load on policy administrators.

Policy Auto-Gen. In Kubernetes PaC solutions, when writing validation policies for Pod resources, we also need to consider that Pods are mostly created by other workload resources. It is not good enough just to validate Pod requests. For example, Deployments are mostly used to run application Pods. If we have only Pod validation policies, then the UX is difficult. The Deployment will succeed even though the Pod(s) will not. Users would have to query the Deployment status to see why the Pod(s) didn't start. This is similar to how PopSecurityPolicies used to work before they were removed from Kubernetes v1.25. I also discussed a similar user experience in Chapter 4, when I wrote about the PSA enforce mode only working with Pods.

As we have seen, Kubernetes PaC solutions routinely rely on paths to fields within resources to locate values. The paths to Pod specifications differ between Pods and the workloads that create Pods. In Chapter 7, we explored a new Gatekeeper policy expansion feature that expands Pod policies into the policies that also validate workloads that create Pods. Kyverno has had this feature—Auto-Gen Rules for Pod Controllers (*https://oreil.ly/dSxPj*)—for a few years, and it was just updated to also support ReplicaSets and ReplicationControllers.

With Kyverno Auto-Gen, we need to write only the Pod rule, and Auto-Gen will generate the other rules that find the Pod specifications in each workload type. For example, consider the following policy spec:

```
# Pod policy rule
spec:
  background: false
  rules:
  - match:
      any:
      - resources:
          kinds:
          - Pod
    name: check-for-labels
    preconditions:
      any:
      - key: '{{ request.operation }}'
        operator: Equals
        value: CREATE
    validate:
      message: The label `app.kubernetes.io/name` is required.
      pattern:
        metadata:
          labels:
```

```
            app.kubernetes.io/name: ?*
  validationFailureAction: Enforce
```

When a Pod request violates this rule, the following error message is returned to the client:

```
# Pod required labels violation message
$ kubectl apply -f 2-test-pod.yaml
Error from server: error when creating "2-test-pod.yaml": admission webhook
"validate.kyverno.svc-fail" denied the request:

resource Pod/policy-test/test-pod was blocked due to the following policies

require-labels:
  check-for-labels: >
                    validation error: The label `app.kubernetes.io/name` is
                    required. rule check-for-labels failed at path
                    /metadata/labels/app.kubernetes.io/name/'
```

Alone, this rule, when applied as policy or ClusterPolicy, would prevent any Pod from starting if the Pod resource metadata did not include the required app.kuber netes.io/name label. However, after this Pod rule is applied to the cluster, the following Pod controller rules are auto-generated by Kyverno:

```
# Auto-generated Pod controller rules
status:
  autogen:
    rules:
    - exclude:
        resources: {}
      generate:
        clone: {}
        cloneList: {}
      match:
        any:
        - resources:
            kinds:
            - DaemonSet
            - Deployment
            - Job
            - StatefulSet
            - ReplicaSet
            - ReplicationController
        resources: {}
      mutate: {}
      name: autogen-check-for-labels
      preconditions:
        any:
        - key: '{{ request.operation }}'
          operator: Equals
          value: CREATE
      validate:
```

```
          message: The label `app.kubernetes.io/name` is required.
          pattern:
            spec:
              template:
                metadata:
                  labels:
                    app.kubernetes.io/name: ?*
  - exclude:
      resources: {}
    generate:
      clone: {}
      cloneList: {}
    match:
      any:
      - resources:
          kinds:
          - CronJob
        resources: {}
    mutate: {}
    name: autogen-cronjob-check-for-labels
    preconditions:
      any:
      - key: '{{ request.operation }}'
        operator: Equals
        value: CREATE
    validate:
      message: The label `app.kubernetes.io/name` is required.
      pattern:
        spec:
          jobTemplate:
            spec:
              template:
                metadata:
                  labels:
                    app.kubernetes.io/name: ?*
```

While Auto-Gen is very useful, there are times when it may not be wanted or needed for all workloads that create Pods. By using the `pod-policies.kyverno.io/autogen-controllers` annotation on a policy, you can restrict how Auto-Gen is applied. The following example sets Auto-Gen to create rules only for Deployments:

```
# Restrict auto-gen to Deployment only
apiVersion: kyverno.io/v1
kind: ClusterPolicy
metadata:
  name: time-bound-policy
  annotations:
    pod-policies.kyverno.io/autogen-controllers: "Deployment"
...
```

When you use the annotation to restrict Auto-Gen, you will see a Kverno warning like the one in the following console output:

```
Warning: Policies that match Pods apply to all Pods including those created
and managed by controllers excluded from autogen. Use preconditions to
exclude the Pods managed by controllers which are excluded from autogen.
Refer to https://kyverno.io/docs/writing-policies/autogen/ for details.
```

The Kyverno Auto-Gen feature makes Kyverno policies more expressive by auto-generating the rules and paths for workloads that create and manage Pods. This reduces the need to write and manage multiple policies and rules to handle Pods and the workloads that create Pods. It also improves the UX for workloads that create Pods; the user or cluster administrator doesn't have to troubleshoot why the workload successfully created but the Pods did not start.

Next, we will explore how policies can be set to apply only during specified times.

Time-bound policies. Time-bound policies (*https://oreil.ly/E1k8j*) are used when you want to set policies to be active during specified times. For example, you could use the following policy spec to set a specific time that this policy will deny CREATE and UPDATE Pod operations in the `policy-test` Namespace:

```
# Time-bound policy specification
spec:
  validationFailureAction: Enforce
  background: false
  rules:
    - name: no-pods-during-maintenance
      match:
        any:
        - resources:
            kinds:
            - Pod
            namespaces:
            - policy-test
      preconditions:
        all:
          # Get the hour of the current time
        - key: "{{ time_now_utc().time_to_cron(@).split(@,' ') | [1].to_number(@) }}"
          operator: AnyIn
          # Only operate during business hours, 8am-5pm EST, in UTC
          value: 1-10
        - key: "{{request.operation}}"
          operator: AnyIn
          value:
          - CREATE
          - UPDATE
      validate:
        message: "No pods during maintenance window."
        deny: {}
```

With time-bound policies, you can use maintenance windows to control when policies are active. Time is UTC, so you may need to adjust the values for your time zone.

Common expression language policies. I introduced Common Expression Language (CEL) (*https://oreil.ly/cel-spec*) in Chapter 4 when I wrote about the new Kubernetes Validating Admission Policy (VAP) (*https://oreil.ly/aT2k7*) in-tree PaC solution. Kyverno validation policies can also use the CEL expressions. The following ClusterPolicy spec (snippet) is an example (*https://oreil.ly/RTP36*) of how to use CEL expressions in Kyverno policies. This example restricts seccomp settings (*https://oreil.ly/sejOs*) at the Pod and container levels:

```
# Validation policy spec (snippet) using CEL expressions
spec:
  background: true
  validationFailureAction: Audit
  rules:
    - name: check-seccomp
      match:
        any:
        - resources:
            kinds:
              - Pod
      validate:
        cel:
          Expressions:
            - expression: >-   ❶
                !has(object.spec.securityContext) ||
                !has(object.spec.securityContext.seccompProfile) ||
                !has(object.spec.securityContext.seccompProfile.type) ||
                object.spec.securityContext.seccompProfile.type ==
                'RuntimeDefault' ||
                object.spec.securityContext.seccompProfile.type ==
                'Localhost'
              message: >-
                Use of custom Seccomp profiles is disallowed. The field
                spec.securityContext.seccompProfile.type must be unset or
                set to `RuntimeDefault` or `Localhost`.

            - expression: >-   ❷
                object.spec.containers.all(container,
                !has(container.securityContext) ||
                !has(container.securityContext.seccompProfile) ||
                !has(container.securityContext.seccompProfile.type) ||
                container.securityContext.seccompProfile.type ==
                'RuntimeDefault' ||
                container.securityContext.seccompProfile.type ==
                'Localhost')
              message: >-
                Use of custom Seccomp profiles is disallowed. The field
```

```
         spec.containers[*].securityContext.seccompProfile.type must
         be unset or set to `RuntimeDefault` or `Localhost`.
```

❶ CEL expression to restrict seccomp profiles in the Pod-level `securityContext`
   element.

❷ CEL expression to restrict seccomp profiles at the container-level `security
   Context` element.

The preceding policy ensures that the seccomp profile exists and restricts its type to
`RuntimeDefault` or `Localhost`.

We explored mutating and validating policies, how to auto-generate validating policies for Pod workloads, and how to control when policies are active. Now, we are
going to look at a relatively new type of policy to verify container images.

VerifyImages policies

VerifyImages policies (*https://oreil.ly/tJuej*) enhance Kubernetes security by ensuring
that only OCI (*https://opencontainers.org*) images with verified signatures are allowed
in your clusters. These policies are part of a broader effort to secure the overall software supply chain by verifying the provenance of container images with cryptographic signatures. Kyverno supports verifying image signatures using Sigstore
Cosign (*https://oreil.ly/27-8L*) and CNCF Notary (*https://oreil.ly/-MBxL*). The following ClusterPolicy example, from the Kyverno documentation, demonstrates how to
use the VerifyImages policies with OCI images signed using Cosign:

```
# VerifyImages policy for OCI images signed with Cosign
apiVersion: kyverno.io/v1
kind: ClusterPolicy
metadata:
  name: verify-image
  annotations:
....
spec:
  validationFailureAction: enforce
  background: false
  rules:
    - name: verify-image
      match:
        any:
        - resources:
            kinds:
              - Pod
      verifyImages:  ❶
      - imageReferences:
        - "ghcr.io/kyverno/test-verify-image*"
        mutateDigest: true  ❷
        attestors:  ❸
```

```
  - entries:
    - keys:
        publicKeys: |
          -----BEGIN PUBLIC KEY-----
          MFkwEwYHKoZIzj0CAQYIKoZIzj0DAQcDQgAE8nXRh950IZbRj8Ra/N9sbqOPZrfM
          5/KAQN0/KjHcorm/J5yctVd7iEcnessRQjU917hmKO6JWVGHpDguIyakZA==
          -----END PUBLIC KEY-----
```

❶ The `verifyImages` rule types are used to verify image signatures and replace image tags with image digests.

❷ `mutateDigest` is used for replacement of image tags with digests and defaults to `true`.

❸ Attestors define the authority used to attest or verify the OCI image. In the case of this example, a public key is used as that authority. The private key was used to sign the OCI image after the image was stored in the OCI repository.

The `verifyImages.type` field is not shown in the preceding example. This field specifies the verification method for the `verifyImages` rules. It defaults to `Cosign` but can be set to `Notary` for that verification method.

> Image digests are unique and immutable identifiers for container images. Just as the latest versions of container images should never be used, it is a best practice to pull images using the image digest instead of an image tag. Image digests are created using the SHA-256 secure hash algorithm (*https://oreil.ly/RZLdD*).
>
> Image digests are used to ensure the integrity of an image. The smallest change to an image may still result in the same image tag, unless tag immutability is enabled on the OCI repository. Consumers cannot ensure that image repositories use tag immutability; moreover, tag-based container image signing does not usually work with repository-level tag immutability.
>
> To ensure integrity of images, image digests are used as the digest changes, regardless of the size of the change to the underlying image change.

Instead of a public key as an attestor authority, Kyverno VerifyImages policies configured to use Notary (*https://oreil.ly/3Ss4n*) use a certificate. This AWS Containers blog post (*https://oreil.ly/euptw*)—to which I contributed—provides more information about the Notary approach, along with a Kyverno example.

Now that we have seen how to use Kyverno to verify container images, let's see how Kyverno generate policies are used to generate Kubernetes resources.

Generate policies

Beyond mutation and validation policies, Kyverno policies can create new resources. For example, when creating Namespaces, it's a good idea to also lock down the network for Pods running in each Namespace. To that end, you can use Kyverno generation policies (*https://oreil.ly/tNbEh*) to generate NetworkPolicy resources every time a Namespace is created.

Since NetworkPolicy rules are cumulative and Pods can communicate to other Pods by default, it is a best practice to create a deny-all policy—egress and ingress—to prevent all network traffic in the new Namespace. Then, you open egress and ingress traffic that is needed to allow the Pod to function.

The following ClusterPolicy from the Kyverno policy library creates a NetworkPolicy resource in the Namespace that was just created:

```
# Generation Policy specification
spec:
  #generateExisting: true        ❶
  rules:
  - name: deny-all-traffic
    match:
      any:
      - resources:
          kinds:
          - Namespace        ❷
    exclude:
      any:
      - resources:
          Namespaces:        ❸
          - kube-system
          - default
          - kube-public
          - kyverno
    Generate:
      kind: NetworkPolicy        ❹
      apiVersion: networking.k8s.io/v1
      name: deny-all-traffic
      namespace: "{{request.object.metadata.name}}"
      data:
        spec:
          # select all Pods in the namespace
          podSelector: {}
          policyTypes:
          - Ingress
          - Egress
```

❶ The `generateExisting` field defaults to `false`. When set to `true`, this sets the policy to apply to existing resources that match. This means that the policy will scan for matching resources and apply the changes without waiting for a CREATE or UPDATE event.

❷ This policy applies to Namespace resources.

❸ This policy excludes Namespaces in this list.

❹ The policy creates a deny-all network policy, which is a best practice for new Kubernetes Namespaces.

The following NetworkPolicy—generated by the preceding Kyverno generation policy—requires a network policy engine operating in the cluster to control traffic:

```
# NetworkPolicy created by generation policy
apiVersion: networking.k8s.io/v1
kind: NetworkPolicy
metadata:
  creationTimestamp: "2023-03-07T02:58:32Z"
  generation: 1
  labels:
    app.kubernetes.io/managed-by: kyverno
    kyverno.io/background-gen-rule: deny-all-traffic
    kyverno.io/generated-by-kind: Namespace
    kyverno.io/generated-by-name: policy-test
    kyverno.io/generated-by-namespace: ""
    policy.kyverno.io/gr-name: ur-66lmm
    policy.kyverno.io/policy-name: default
    policy.kyverno.io/synchronize: disable
  name: deny-all-traffic
  namespace: policy-test    ❶
  resourceVersion: "16287"
  uid: 22cdbe8f-0963-49a4-a152-cf5e7f703fc1
spec:
  podSelector: {}    ❷
  policyTypes:
  - Ingress
  - Egress
status: {}
```

❶ The NetworkPolicy was created in the `policy-test` Namespace.

❷ The empty `podSelector` field means that this policy will apply to all Pods.

Kyverno generation policies can be configured to link generated resources to the resources that triggered the generation. As of Kyverno v1.10, this linking is accomplished via the `generate.synchronize=true` configuration.

For example, I might want to create a PodDisruptionBudget (PDB) resource when I create a Deployment. If I use the `synchronize: true` directive, then the PDB will be linked to the Deployment. If the Deployment is deleted, the PDB will also be deleted. It's important to point out that if you want the generated resource to be editable independently of the generating resource, then you should not use `synchronize: true`.

Depending on what your generation policy does, you may need to grant the kyverno-background-controller more permissions. For example, when I tried to apply the following generation ClusterPolicy to create a PodDisruptionBudget, triggered by a Deployment operation, I received an error:

```
# Generation policy to create PodDisruption budget triggered by Deployment resource
apiVersion: kyverno.io/v1
kind: ClusterPolicy
metadata:
  name: create-default-pdb
spec:
  generateExisting: true
  rules:
  - name: create-default-pdb    ❶
    match:
      any:
      - resources:
          kinds:
          - Deployment    ❷
    exclude:
      resources:
        namespaces:
        - local-path-storage
    generate:
      apiVersion: policy/v1
      kind: PodDisruptionBudget    ❸
      name: "{{request.object.metadata.name}}-default-pdb"
      namespace: "{{request.object.metadata.namespace}}"
      synchronize: true
      data:
        spec:
          minAvailable: 1
          selector:
            matchLabels:
              "{{request.object.metadata.labels}}"
```

❶ The rule name indicates that it will create a PodDisruptionBudget resource.

❷ This rule is triggered by Deployment operations. Generate policies are triggered by CREATE and UPDATE operations.

❸ The `generate` field contains the resource YAML to create a PodDisruption Budget resource.

```
# Error thrown when kyverno-background-controller didn't have permissions
# to create PodDisruptionBudget
$ kubectl apply -f pdb-policy.yaml
Error from server: error when creating "pdb-policy.yaml": admission webhook
"validate-policy.kyverno.svc" denied the request: path:
spec.rules[0].generate..:
system:serviceaccount:kyverno:kyverno-background-controller
does not have permissions to 'create'
resource policy/v1/PodDisruptionBudget//{{request.object.metadata.namespace}}.
Grant proper permissions to the background controller
```

To fix this issue, I created the following ClusterRole with permissions to manage Pod DisruptionBudget resources:

```
# ClusterRole with permissions to manage PodDisruptionBudget resources.
apiVersion: rbac.authorization.k8s.io/v1
kind: ClusterRole
metadata:
  labels:  ❶
    app.kubernetes.io/component: background-controller
    app.kubernetes.io/instance: kyverno
    app.kubernetes.io/part-of: kyverno
  name: kyverno:create-pdbs
rules:  ❷
- apiGroups:
  - "policy"
  resources:
  - poddisruptionbudgets
  verbs:
  - create
  - update
  - patch
  - delete
  - list
```

❶ Labels used for ClusterRole aggregation

❷ Rules added to permit PodDisruptionBudget resource management

The preceding ClusterRole uses specific labels that are used for ClusterRole aggregation (*https://oreil.ly/fqx7C*). This is a Kubernetes RBAC feature that aggregates permissions from multiple ClusterRoles into a single ClusterRole. The following aggregated ClusterRole includes the new PodDisruptionBudget permissions:

```
$ kubectl get clusterrole kyverno:background-controller -oyaml
aggregationRule:  ❶
  clusterRoleSelectors:
  - matchLabels:
      app.kubernetes.io/component: background-controller
      app.kubernetes.io/instance: kyverno
      app.kubernetes.io/part-of: kyverno
```

```
apiVersion: rbac.authorization.k8s.io/v1
kind: ClusterRole
metadata:
...
  name: kyverno:background-controller
...
- apiGroups:  ❷
  - policy
  resources:
  - poddisruptionbudgets
  verbs:
  - create
  - update
  - patch
  - delete
  - list
```

❶ The ClusterRole `aggregationRule` configures how ClusterRoles will be selected.

❷ The permissions for PodDisruptionBudget management were aggregated from the `kyverno:create-pdbs` ClusterRole.

Generation policies also support the idea of data sources. The following example from the Kyverno documentation (*https://oreil.ly/huHJA*) shows how to use data—embedded in the rule—to create a ConfigMap:

```
# Generation policy generate element
generate:
  synchronize: true
  apiVersion: v1
  kind: ConfigMap
  name: zk-kafka-address
  # generate the resource in the new namespace
  namespace: "{{request.object.metadata.name}}"
  data:
    kind: ConfigMap
    metadata:
      labels:
        somekey: somevalue
    data:
      ZK_ADDRESS: "192.168.10.10:2181,192.168.10.11:2181,192.168.10.12:2181"
      KAFKA_ADDRESS: "192.168.10.13:9092,192.168.10.14:9092,192.168.10.15:9092"
```

Finally, cloning existing resources is also supported. The following example from the Kyverno documentation shows how to supply a list of resources from the `staging` Namespace to clone, based on the `allowedToBeCloned` label:

```
# Generation policy specification to clone resources
spec:
  rules:
  - name: sync-secret
```

```
match:
  any:
  - resources:
      kinds:
      - Namespace
exclude:
  any:
  - resources:
      namespaces:
      - kube-system
      - default
      - kube-public
      - kyverno
generate:
  namespace: "{{request.object.metadata.name}}"
  synchronize: true
  cloneList:
    namespace: staging
    kinds:
      - v1/Secret
      - v1/ConfigMap
    selector:
      matchLabels:
        allowedToBeCloned: "true"
```

A cool use case is to store cloneable resources in a central Namespace. Maybe you populate and update those centralized resources via GitOps. When new Namespaces that need the same resource content—stored in the central Namespace—are created, generation policies could be used to clone those resources into each Namespace. This is particularly useful for resources that can be accessed only by workloads, if they are located in the same Namespace, such as ConfigMaps and Secrets.

Kyverno generation policies are a powerful tool to reduce policy-management overhead while also delivering a means to automate default security and compliance. The event-based and automated approach augments security, compliance, and best practices by controlling what gets generated through policies.

Now, let's shift gears and see how Kyverno policies can be used to clean up Kubernetes resources.

CleanUp policies

As of Kyverno v1.9.0, CleanUp policies (*https://oreil.ly/BMBI-*) have been added to automate some housekeeping processes at the cluster and Namespace levels.

Cleanup policies are triggered by CronJob resources and are not event-based from the API server. As such, CleanUpPolicy rules cannot use certain items in the `match` and `exclude` blocks. For example, since the context of the API server request is not present in the CronJob execution, items such as subjects, roles, and ClusterRoles are among those that cannot be used in the rule `match` blocks.

The following ClusterCleanupPolicy example from the Kyverno documentation uses a JMESPath expression to identify Deployments with fewer than two replicas:

```
# ClusterCleanupPolicy example
apiVersion: kyverno.io/v2beta1
kind: ClusterCleanupPolicy
metadata:
  name: clean-deploys
spec:
  match:
    any:
    - resources:
        kinds:
          - Deployment    ❶
        selector:
          matchLabels:
            canremove: "true"    ❷
  conditions:
    any:
    - key: "{{ target.spec.replicas }}"    ❸
      operator: LessThan
      value: 2
  schedule: "*/5 * * * *"    ❹
```

❶ This ClusterCleanupPolicy applies to Deployments.

❷ The `canremove=true` label must be present on the Deployment resource so that the Kyverno Cleanup Controller reaps them.

❸ The cleanup condition is a Deployment with fewer than two replicas.

❹ This policy runs every five minutes.

This CronJob would run every five minutes, looking for Deployments with fewer than two replicas. Once found by this policy, the target Deployments are "cleaned up," as shown in the following logs:

```
# cleanup logs
I0313 01:15:00.755977        1 handlers.go:51] cleanup "msg"="cleaning up..."
"policy"="cleandeploy"
I0313 01:15:00.760420        1 handlers.go:168] cleanup "msg"="resource
matched, it will be deleted..." "name"="test" "namespace"="admission-test"
"policy"="cleandeploy"
I0313 01:15:00.762534        1 handlers.go:61] cleanup "msg"="done"
"policy"="cleandeploy"
I0313 01:15:00.762657        1 event.go:294] "Event occurred"
object="cleandeploy" fieldPath="" kind="ClusterCleanupPolicy"
```

```
apiVersion="kyverno.io/v2alpha1" type="Normal" reason="PolicyApplied"
message="successfully cleaned up the target resource
Deployment/admission-test/test"
```

Similar to the preceding Generate policy example, I used a new ClusterRole and the aggregation:

```
apiVersion: rbac.authorization.k8s.io/v1
kind: ClusterRole
metadata:
  name: kyverno-cleanup-deploys
  labels:
    app.kubernetes.io/component: cleanup-controller
    app.kubernetes.io/instance: kyverno
    app.kubernetes.io/name: kyverno-cleanup-controller
rules:
  - verbs:
      - get
      - watch
      - list
      - delete
    apiGroups:
      - "apps"
    resources:
      - deployments
```

As before, using ClusterRole aggregation eliminates the need to modify existing ClusterRoles when new permissions are needed, and it helps Kyverno implement least-privileged access for its controllers.

With ClusterRole aggregation, a Kubernetes controller running in the cluster control plane watches for new ClusterRoles and adds rules from my new ClusterRole to the aggregated kyverno:cleanup-controller ClusterRole. Without the new permissions, I could not have even applied the new CleanUp policy, as seen in the following error:

```
Error from server: error when creating "deploys.yaml": admission webhook
"kyverno-cleanup-controller.kyverno.svc" denied the request: cleanup
controller has no permission to delete kind Deployment
```

Another use case for cleanup policies is to remove orphaned Pods not created by other workloads. The orphaned Pods—a.k.a. loner-Pods—are used sometimes for automated testing, troubleshooting, and cluster maintenance. Often, they are forgotten and left behind, leading to "cluster cruft." The following policy would be used to periodically remove Pods with no `metadata.ownerReferences` values, meaning they were not associated with other workloads; using a policy in this way provides necessary cluster hygiene:

```
# Policy specification to clean-up left-over Pods
spec:
  match:
```

```
any:
 - resources:
     kinds:
         - Pod
conditions:
  all:
   - key: "{{ target.metadata.ownerReferences[] || `[]` }}"
     operator: Equals
     value: []
schedule: "*/5 * * * *"
```

In the preceding policy, I purposefully prevented the Auto-Gen controller from creating policy rules for workloads that create Pods; after all, I am interested only in Pods. And as I did before, I had to create a ClusterRole to aggregate the needed permissions for the cleanup controller:

```
# ClusterRole rules for Pod cleanup
rules:
  - verbs:
      - get
      - watch
      - list
      - delete
    apiGroups:
      - ""
    resources:
      - pods
```

With CleanUp policies, you can automate cluster housekeeping tasks and remove the cruft that accumulates in your clusters with a least-privilege approach. This resembles the work for which we used to write Kubernetes operators, so CleanUp policies promise to reduce our workload as well as cluster attack surfaces.

Now, let's expand upon policy exclusions and see how we can create first-class policy exceptions.

Policy exceptions

Kyverno policy rules already support the ability to exclude resources. For example, the following policy rule from the Kyverno documentation excludes resources in the kube-system Namespace using the spec.rules[*].exclude block:

```
# Policy specification exclusion rules
spec:
  rules:
    - name: match-pods-except-admin
      match:
        any:
         - resources:
             kinds:
               - Pod
```

```
    exclude:
      any:
      - resources:
          namespaces:
          - policy-excluded-namespace  ❶
```

❶   The exclude rule uses a list of Namespaces that are excluded from processing.

These exclusions are also done dynamically by maintaining a list of Namespaces in a ConfigMap and then referencing that list in policy rules. The following rule example from the Kyverno documentation uses this dynamic exclusion technique:

```
# Policy specification with dynamic exclusion
spec:
  validationFailureAction: Audit
  background: true
  rules:
  - name: exclude-namespaces-dynamically
    context:
      - name: namespacefilters
        configMap:
          name: namespace-filters
          namespace: default  ❶
    match:
      any:
      - resources:
          kinds:
          - Pod  ❷
    preconditions:
      all:
      - key: "{{request.object.metadata.namespace}}"
        operator: AnyNotIn
        value: "{{namespacefilters.data.exclude}}"  ❸
    validate:
      message: >
        Creating Pods in the {{request.namespace}} Namespace,
        which is not in the excluded list of Namespaces
        {{ namespacefilters.data.exclude }},
        is forbidden unless it carries the label `foo`.
      pattern:
        metadata:
          labels:
            foo: "*"
```

❶   The exclusions come from the namespace-filters ConfigMap in the default Namespace.

❷   This policy applies to Pods.

❸ The policy uses a precondition that uses the Namespace list from the namespace-filters ConfigMap.

The preceding example uses the namespace-filters ConfigMap—in the `default` Namespace—to dynamically manage a list of Namespaces to exclude via precondition logic.

 Excluding Namespace resource processing at the policy-rule level still means that the Kyverno webhook will be called for Namespace resource processing. To prevent the webhook calls altogether, you should use the techniques I presented in the section "Ignoring Namespaces" on page 240.

With its 1.9.0 release, Kyverno has introduced an alpha feature—policy exceptions—that allows you to create exception resources to exclude processing of certain resources. Since this is an alpha feature, I had to enable it via the following install flags:

```
# Enable policy exception with Helm flags
$ helm install kyverno kyverno/kyverno -n kyverno --create-namespace \
--values values.yaml \
--set "extraArgs={-v=4,--dumpPayload=true,--enablePolicyException=true}"
```

Without these settings, I would see the following error when I tried to apply a policy exception resource:

```
# PolicyException warning
Warning: PolicyException resources would not be processed until it is enabled.
policyexception.kyverno.io/policy-test-exception created
```

Once enabled, I tested the solution with the following registry validation policy, which was created to prevent resources from using deprecated registries:

```
# Image registry validation policy specification
spec:
  validationFailureAction: Enforce
  background: true
  rules:
  - name: detect-deprecated-registry
    match:
      any:
      - resources:
          kinds:
          - Pod
    validate:
      message: >
            The \"k8s.gcr.io\" image registry is deprecated.
            \"registry.k8s.io\" should now be used.
        foreach: ❶
```

```
      - list: "request.object.spec.[initContainers,
                                    ephemeralContainers,
                                    containers][]"
    deny:
      conditions:
        all:
          - key: "{{ element.image }}"
            operator: Equals
            value: "k8s.gcr.io/*"
```

❶ Use the `foreach` rule to iterate through all containers in the Pod.

The preceding rule is for a ClusterPolicy to prevent the use of deprecated container image registries. However, to allow a Namespace to still use these registries without changing the policy rules, I wrote the following policy exception, applied to the `policy-test` Namespace:

```
# PolicyException
apiVersion: kyverno.io/v2alpha1
kind: PolicyException
metadata:
  name: policy-test-exception
  namespace: policy-test
spec:
  exceptions:
  - policyName: restrict-image-registries
    ruleNames:
    - detect-deprecated-registry
    - autogen-detect-deprecated-registry
  match:
    any:
    - resources:
        kinds:
        - Pod
        - Deployment
        namespaces:
        - policy-test
        names:
        - test
        - test-pod
```

The `exceptions` element in the preceding policy exception points to the detect-deprecated-registry and autogen-detect-deprecated-registry rules that will be applied to Pod and Deployment resources—named test and test-pod—in the `policy-test` Namespace. I had to include the auto-generated rules explicitly. Without this explicit addition, the exception would not apply to the auto-generated Deployment rules.

Policy exceptions are a new Kyverno resource that allows users to create exceptions to specific policies and rules without having to modify Namespace labels, webhook settings, or policy-rules `exclude` blocks. Additionally, policy exceptions can be paired with generation and cleanup policies. For example, you may only want policy exceptions to be temporary. To accomplish this, you could use generation policies to create cleanup policies when policy exceptions are applied. The cleanup policies would remove the policy exception at a scheduled time. This solution is outlined further in this blog post by Chip Zoller (*https://oreil.ly/Be8s7*).

Now that we have explored the different types of Kyverno policies and how they are written and used, let's look at how we can use policy reporting to view results of Validate and VerifyImages Policy and ClusterPolicy types.

Policy Reporting

I first introduced PolicyReports in Chapter 4. As a reminder, PolicyReports are human- and machine-readable artifacts that describe the execution of policies against resources. These reports are based on CRDs and the open format published by the CNCF Kubernetes Policy WG (*https://oreil.ly/BYlPV*). The following PolicyReport is a result of a validation policy with the following settings:

```
# ClusterPolicy specifications
spec:
  validationFailureAction: Enforce
  background: true


# PolicyReport resource
$ kubectl -n policy-test get polr b9d4352c-4c38-4948-bcc6-8cd849c22f1f -oyaml
apiVersion: wgpolicyk8s.io/v1alpha2
kind: PolicyReport  ❶
metadata:
...
  name: b9d4352c-4c38-4948-bcc6-8cd849c22f1f  ❷
  namespace: policy-test
  ownerReferences:  ❸
  - apiVersion: v1
    kind: Pod
    name: test-pod
    uid: b9d4352c-4c38-4948-bcc6-8cd849c22f1f
...
results:
- message: 'validation error: The label `app.kubernetes.io/name` is required. rule
    check-for-labels failed at path /metadata/labels/app.kubernetes.io/name/'
  policy: require-labels  ❹
  result: fail
  rule: check-for-labels
  scored: true
  severity: medium  ❺
  source: kyverno
  timestamp:
    nanos: 0
    seconds: 1710644178
Scope:
```

```
  apiVersion: v1
  kind: Pod
  name: test-pod
  namespace: policy-test
  uid: b9d4352c-4c38-4948-bcc6-8cd849c22f1f
summary:
  error: 0
  fail: 1  ❻
  pass: 0
  skip: 0
  warn: 0
```

❶ The PolicyReport is related to Namespace-scoped resources and stored in the Namespace that contains the resource with the detected issue.

❷ The PolicyReport name is derived from the UID element of the Pod with the detected issue.

❸ The ownerReferences element links the PolicyReport to the resource evaluated—in this case, the test-pod Pod. When the test-pod Pod is deleted, Kubernetes will also delete the linked PolicyReport.

❹ The PolicyReport provides the ClusterPolicy that performed the evaluation.

❺ The PolicyReport includes the severity that was annotated on the ClusterPolicy.

❻ The PolicyReport indicates one detected failure.

As you can see in the preceding PolicyReport, the check-for-labels rule in the require-labels policy detected the medium-severity failure for missing labels. Of note is the fact that this Namespace-scoped PolicyReport is the result of a ClusterPolicy. This is because the PolicyReports are Namespaced by the element reported—in this case, a Pod. The PolicyReport was created as a result of a Kyverno background scan, discussed in the next section.

The following console output contains namespaced PolicyReports, retrieved using kubectl:

```
# PolicyReport listing
$ kubectl get polr -A \
-o=custom-columns=Namespace:.metadata.namespace,Name:.metadata.name,\
Kind:.scope.kind,PASS:summary.pass,FAIL:summary.fail, \
WARN:.summary.warn,ERROR:.summary.error
Namespace          Name         Kind       PASS   FAIL   WARN   ERROR
...
policy-test        c7a9948e…    Pod        0      1      0      0
...
```

As a point of reference, ClusterPolicyReports are created when issues are detected with cluster-wide resources, and these reports are stored in the `default` Namespace.

Policy reports create auditable artifacts that can be used for compliance. To help with compliance reporting, Kyverno has created the Policy Reporter (*https://oreil.ly/WfXbV*) project, shown in Figure 8-4, which provides a handy user interface to view policy reports, policies, and Kyverno compliance reports.

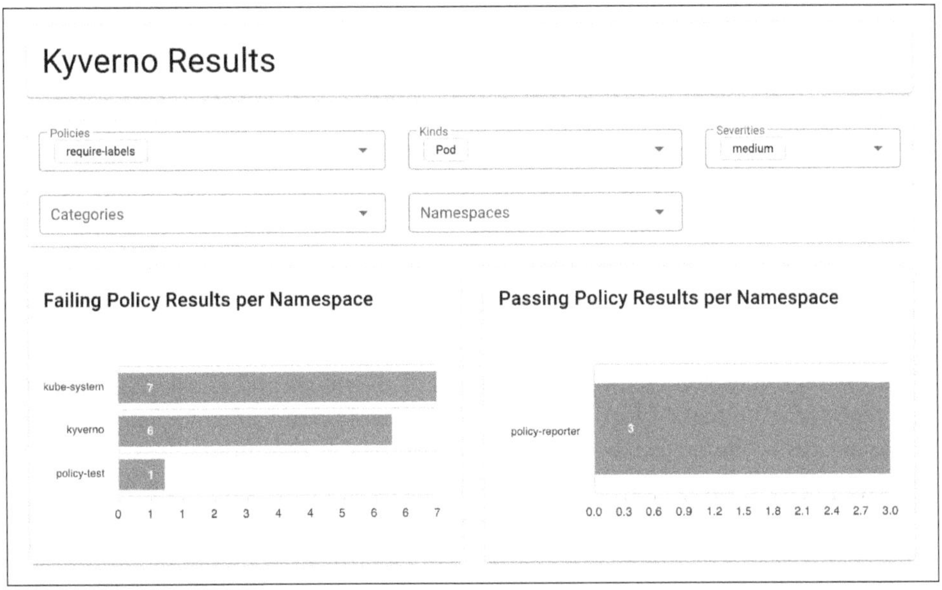

Figure 8-4. Kyverno Policy Reporter

Now that we have seen how to create and review PolicyReports, let's explore how Kverno background scans function.

Background Scans

When we think about PaC in Kubernetes, we normally think about how the API server request flow uses policy engines—like Kyverno—to respond to mutating and validating webhook requests. However, Kyverno also includes background scanning. Background scanning is enabled by default in validation and verify-image policies. It can be disabled at the policy level with the following `spec.background` setting:

```
# Specification to disable background scanning
spec:
  validationFailureAction: Enforce
  background: false
```

Background scans can be used to apply policies to existing resources that are already in the cluster when a new policy is introduced. Background scans can also be used to periodically reapply all policies to all resources and to recalculate policy reports as an additional layer of security while producing auditable artifacts. These policy types can handle changes in external data, like a vulnerability scan report that includes new findings or a validation policy on a resource that exceeds a budget.

By default, Kyverno background scans are set to run every hour, but this can be changed by setting the `backgroundScanInterval` flag during installation, as I've done in the following Helm command:

```
# Helm install with specific background scan interval
$ helm install kyverno kyverno/kyverno -n kyverno --create-namespace \
--values values.yaml --set "extraArgs={backgroundScanInterval=30m}"
```

With background scans, the Kubernetes API server request flow is not involved in the policy trigger. Just like other policy scenarios we have reviewed that are not triggered by API server requests, there is information from the AdmissionReview object that cannot be used, such as the `request.userinfo`. Also, as with cleanup policies, the Subject, Role, and ClusterRole fields cannot be used in Kyverno policy rules `match` or `exclude` blocks.

Policy background-scan settings affect how PolicyReports and ClusterPolicyReports are reported. The matrix in Figure 8-5—from the Kyverno documentation (*https:// oreil.ly/kvdFP*)—illustrates the relationship between background scans and policy reports. When background scans are disabled and `validationFailureAction` is set to `Enforce`, report results will still be created for resources that apply to and pass one or more policies. Obviously, resources that fail policy rules are blocked; therefore, no policy report result is created.

Reporting behavior when background: true	New Resource	Existing Resource
validationFailureAction: Enforce	Pass only	Report
validationFailureAction: Audit	Report	Report

Reporting behavior when background: false	New Resource	Existing Resource
validationFailureAction: Enforce	Pass only	None
validationFailureAction: Audit	Report	None

Figure 8-5. Kyverno background-scan reporting behaviors

With background scans, Kyverno policies report on existing resources. This is very useful in the case where a violation is not caught by the webhook operation. As we discussed before, this can happen when the webhook times out and the `failurePolicy` is set to ignore. Another use case is to perform impact analysis on existing cluster resources when releasing new policies. While compensating for failed webhook calls that are configured to fail open is a valid use case, the main value proposition of background scans is for users to be able to introduce a Kyverno policy into an existing cluster (i.e., "brownfield" or "retroactively") and see the results of the policy applied to those resources without causing any impact. Impact analysis of newly introduced policies should always be completed to avoid possible unintended consequences.

Now that we understand how background scanning works with PolicyReports and the various use cases that are solved by these policy types, let's move on to policy testing.

Policy Testing

A lot of policy testing occurs in nonproduction clusters; however, this is suboptimal for CI automation processes. The Kyverno CLI (*https://oreil.ly/F1lfH*) handles testing policies with and without a Kubernetes cluster.

You can install the Kyverno CLI via a kubectl krew plug-in or as a standalone binary. I have used both methods, and I prefer the standalone binary. The following command gets the version of the Kyverno CLI:

```
# Kyverno version command
$ kyverno version
Version: 1.11.4
```

I first used the Kyverno CLI to test policies. For that to work, I created the following Kyverno test configuration to deterministically configure how I wanted to test my policy:

```
# Kyverno Test configuration
apiVersion: cli.kyverno.io/v1alpha1
kind: Test
metadata:
  name: kyverno-test
policies:
  # - registry-mutate.yaml      ❶
  - registry-validate.yaml      ❷
resources:
  - resources.yaml      ❸
results:
- policy: restrict-image-registries      ❹
  isValidatingAdmissionPolicy: true
  rule: restrict-image-registries
  resources:
```

```
  - policy-test/test-pod-bad
  kind: Pod
  result: fail
- policy: restrict-image-registries      ❺
  isValidatingAdmissionPolicy: true
  rule: restrict-image-registries
  resources:
  - policy-test/test-pod-good
  kind: Pod
  result: pass
```

❶ Configure the test to include applying a mutating policy.

❷ Configure the test to include applying a validating policy.

❸ Supply the Kubernetes resources.

❹ Define the test scenario for a failure, including the policy type, rule, resource, and fail result.

❺ Define the test scenario for a pass, including the policy type, rule, resource, and pass result.

The actual tests are orchestrated by test cases in a test file—*kyverno-test.yaml*—that is in the following directory tree:

```
# Directory tree of files used in my test scenario
$ tree
.
├── 2-test-pod.yaml
├── 3-test-deploy.yaml
├── 4-good.yaml
├── kyverno-test.yaml
├── registry-mutate.yaml
├── registry-validate.yaml
└── resources.yaml
```

I used the following resources file for the test, referenced by the test configuration:

```
# Test resources
apiVersion: v1
kind: Pod
metadata:
  name: test-pod-bad
  namespace: policy-test
  labels:
    app: test-bad
spec:
  containers:
    - name: test
```

```
      image: k8s.gcr.io/pause:3.9    ❶
---
apiVersion: v1
kind: Pod
metadata:
  name: test-pod-good
  namespace: policy-test
  labels:
    app: test-good
spec:
  containers:
    - name: test
      image: registry.k8s.io/pause:3.9    ❷
```

❶ This manifest defines the known deprecated container image registry.

❷ This manifest defines the known valid container image registry.

I tested the following ClusterPolicy with the subsequent Kyverno CLI test command:

```
apiVersion: kyverno.io/v1
kind: ClusterPolicy
metadata:
  name: restrict-image-registries    ❶
...
spec:
  validationFailureAction:    Enforce
  background: true
  rules:
  - name: restrict-image-registries    ❷
    match:
      any:
      - resources:
          kinds:
          - Pod
          namespaces:
          - policy-test
          operations:
          - CREATE
          - UPDATE    ❸
    validate:
      message: >
            The "k8s.gcr.io" image registry is deprecated.
            "registry.k8s.io" should now be used.
      foreach:
        - list: "request.object.spec.[initContainers,
                                      ephemeralContainers,
                                      containers][]"
          deny:
            conditions:
              all:
```

```
        - key: "{{ element.image }}"
          operator: Equals
          value: "k8s.gcr.io/*"  ❹
```

❶ I tested the restrict-image-registries ClusterPolicy.

❷ The restrict-image-registries ClusterPolicy defined the restrict-image-registries rule.

❸ The rule defined the match to Pod resources in the `policy-test` Namespace during CREATE and UPDATE operations.

❹ The deny conditions matched to container images that contained the `k8s.gcr.io` string.

```
# Run Kyverno policy test
$ kyverno test .
Loading test  ( kyverno-test.yaml ) ...
  Loading values/variables ...
  Loading policies ...
  Loading resources ...
  Applying 1 policy to 2 resources ...
  Checking results ...
```

The preceding policy test used the *kyverno-test.yaml* file in the parent directory to apply one policy to two resources. Both tests passed because the policy validation passed and failed as per the test configuration. Table 8-1 shows the output from the successful test.

Table 8-1. Kyverno ClusterPolicy test output

ID	Policy	Rule	Resource	Result	Reason
1	restrict-image-registries	restrict-image-registries	policy-test/Pod/test-pod-bad	Pass	OK
2	restrict-image-registries	restrict-image-registries	policy-test/Pod/test-pod-good	Pass	OK

```
Test Summary: 2 tests passed and 0 tests failed
```

After the successful test execution, I changed the test configuration to also apply the following mutating policy:

```
# Deprecated image registry mutation ClusterPolicy spec
spec:
  rules:
  - name: change-deprecated-containers
    match:
```

```
    any:
    - resources:
        kinds:
        - Pod  ❶
  preconditions:
    all:
    - key: "{{request.operation}}"  ❷
      operator: AnyIn
      value:
      - CREATE
      - UPDATE
    - key: k8s.gcr.io  ❸
      operator: AnyIn
      value: "{{ images.containers.*.registry[] || `[]` }}"
  mutate:
    Foreach:  ❹
    - list: "request.object.spec.containers"
      patchStrategicMerge:
        spec:
          containers:
          - name: "{{ element.name }}"
            image: >
                registry.k8s.io/{{ images.containers."{{element.name}}".
                path}}:{{images.containers."{{element.name}}".tag}}
```

❶ This mutation policy affects only Pod resources.

❷ This mutation policy affects only CREATE and UPDATE operations.

❸ This mutation policy looks for the `k8s.gcr.io` string in the container registry value.

❹ Once conditions are met, the policy replaces the registry in each container image.

I modified the test configuration to now include the mutating policy. Then, I reran the test, as shown in Table 8-2:

```
...
policies:
  - registry-mutate.yaml
  - registry-validate.yaml
...

# Second test run, with the mutation policy added
$ kyverno test .
Loading test ( kyverno-test.yaml ) ...
  Loading values/variables ...
  Loading policies ...
  Loading resources ...
  Applying 2 policies to 2 resources ...
  Checking results ...
```

Table 8-2. Test run with added mutating ClusterPolicy

ID	Policy	Rule	Resource	Result	Reason
1	restrict-image-registries	restrict-image-registries	policy-test/Pod/test-pod-bad	Pass	Want fail, got pass
2	restrict-image-registries	restrict-image-registries	policy-test/Pod/test-pod-good	Pass	OK

Test Summary: 2 tests passed and 0 tests failed

The new test configuration applied both the mutating and validating ClusterPolicies during the test. This resulted in two passes, even though the mutating policy was applied and changed the deprecated registry before validation. I was expecting a test failure, but the Kyverno CLI marked the result as a pass, with the comment, "Want fail, got pass."

Beyond testing policies, I used the Kyverno CLI to apply policies in dry-run mode against resources outside and inside a cluster. The following command applied the policy against a known bad Deployment resource:

```
# Apply validation policy in dry-run against know bad Deployment
$ kyverno apply registry-validate.yaml --resource 3-test-deploy.yaml

Applying 3 policy rule(s) to 1 resource(s)...

pass: 0, fail: 1, warn: 0, error: 0, skip: 0
Error: exit as fail or error count > 0
```

Applying this policy elicited the expected response. Even though the original policy was written for Pods, the Kyverno Auto-Gen feature worked in the Kverno CLI and created the related Deployment validation policies.

I also dry ran the policy against existing cluster resources. The following command performed the dry run with a PolicyReport as an output:

```
# Dry-run ClusterPolicy against cluster resources and output PolicyReport
$ kyverno apply registry-validate.yaml --cluster -p
Applying 3 policy rule(s) to 11 resource(s)...

# PolicyReport from Kyverno CLI policy dry-run against existing cluster
# resource
-----------------------------------------------------------------------
POLICY REPORT:
-----------------------------------------------------------------------
apiVersion: wgpolicyk8s.io/v1alpha2
kind: ClusterPolicyReport
metadata:
  creationTimestamp: null
  name: merged
```

```
Results:
- category: Best Practices
  message: >
        validation failure: The "k8s.gcr.io" image registry is deprecated.
        "registry.k8s.io" should now be used.'
  policy: restrict-image-registries
  resources:
  - apiVersion: v1
    kind: Pod
    name: test-pod
    namespace: policy-test
    uid: 9e43d3e3-8c2c-4fbf-b54a-4405dc121dc4
  result: fail
  rule: restrict-image-registries
  scored: true
  severity: medium
  source: kyverno
  timestamp:
    nanos: 0
    seconds: 1710286354
Summary:
  error: 0
  fail: 1
  pass: 0
  skip: 0
  warn: 0
```

Although we have only touched on the Kyverno CLI, it should be apparent how it makes policy testing easier and ready for CI automation. It also can be used to evaluate, or dry run, policies against existing clusters and resources, which is a good way to test as well as a good reporting tool for policy-impact analysis when introducing new policies to your clusters.

Summary

Throughout this chapter, I focused on the Kyverno features and characteristics that:

- Differentiate it from other PaC solutions
- Solve relative and poignant Kubernetes use cases
- Ease policy creation and management across multiple resources and use cases

I consider the fact that Kyverno does not use a separate, new language for policy syntax to be one of its biggest value propositions. Using YAML—instrumented and decorated with JMESPath and YAML anchors—eases adoption. While there is a learning curve for Kyverno, users can concentrate on policy use cases without a new language to learn. Kyverno also offers a large, searchable policy library, which I used throughout this chapter, to help users get up to speed quickly. The Kyverno Playground is a great setting in which to prototype and troubleshoot policies.

By now, mutation and validation policies may seem like table stakes. However, the ability to mutate existing resources when policies are created or updated is a game changer. Policy auto-generation and time-bound policies for validation reduce the overhead involved with policy management and provide scheduled policy enforcement.

Generate and CleanUp policies equip users with the ability to create automated compliance and housekeeping policies for better cluster management. Policy exceptions surface a deterministic and less intrusive means by which to exclude resources from policy processing. Kyverno extends use cases with VerifyImages policies, allowing you to use emerging industry standards and helping you determine OCI image provenance. Finally, background scans allow users to perform impact analysis of new policies while providing a defense-in-depth approach for catching resource violations that may not have been caught by validating webhook operations.

Beyond policies, human- and machine-readable policy reporting provides auditable artifacts that are available in the cluster as a result of webhook operation and background scanning of existing resources. These reports are also available as a result of policy testing triggered outside the cluster. The Kyverno CLI improves policy testing through test-case execution and dry-run operations, and it can be integrated into automated CI processes.

I have barely touched on the utility and expressiveness of the Kyverno solution; however, I think it's clear that the effectiveness and UX of Kyverno are worth exploring. As I stated at the beginning of this chapter, Kyverno is a policy engine designed for Kubernetes. If we again consider the PaC Solution Selection Scorecard from Chapter 1, Kyverno scores very well. It's a mature project with a large and helpful community as well as considerable momentum. Its policy language is simple, expressive, and extensible.

Kyverno covers the traditional Kubernetes use cases very well, and it expands to other use cases not covered by other PaC solutions. With more than a billion downloads and a vast policy library, Kyverno usage is well represented in the Kubernetes community and is still growing. I have personally collaborated with the creators and some of the maintainers of Kyverno, and I am always impressed by their openness and bias toward action.

Although Kyverno is a mature OSS project, it is still well supported by its creator, Nirmata. Nirmata offers enterprise solutions for those customers who require long-term support with service-level agreements for CVEs and critical fixes as well as additional enterprise tooling for collaboration and integrations. If I were to recommend a call to action, it would be to explore Kyverno for your Kubernetes PaC needs.

Coming up in Chapter 9, we will explore—yet again—a new PaC solution for Kubernetes: jsPolicy. jsPolicy promises to reduce the need to learn new policy languages by using JavaScript with Kubernetes PaC.

jsPolicy and Kubernetes

In Chapter 1, I introduced the idea of selecting PaC solutions based on factors and criteria, and I gave you a scorecard to help with PaC selection. The first three selection criteria of that scorecard are used for organizational alignment. In this chapter, I focus on matching a solution's underlying technology, such as policy language, to organizational capabilities, strategies, and standards. Aligning technology to organizational capabilities minimizes negative disruptions that a new solution might introduce.

jsPolicy leverages JavaScript to write Kubernetes policies that are effective while being easy to understand and maintain. That's why I chose to write about jsPolicy in this book. JavaScript is everywhere. Sure, it started in the web browser and still is an integral part of web user experiences, but it also runs on servers, like Node.js (*https://nodejs.org/en*).

JavaScript and the languages that compile or transpile to JavaScript, such as TypeScript, are used by many organizations, across many industries. I started using JavaScript more than 20 years ago, and I still find it easy to pick up when I need to. Choosing a PaC solution that leverages that kind of common knowledge and experience helps organizations avoid the learning curve of a new language syntax. Moreover, you are more productive and faster when you can avoid steep learning curves. That is the promise of jsPolicy, a project introduced and still supported by Loft Labs (*https://loft.sh*). The following links will help you gain more information about jsPolicy:

- Core GitHub project (*https://github.com/loft-sh/jspolicy*)
- Documentation website (*https://www.jspolicy.com/docs/quickstart*)
- Policy examples (*https://github.com/loft-sh/jspolicy/tree/main/examples*)
- jsPolicy Slack channel (*https://loft-sh.slack.com*)

jsPolicy is the first PaC solution in this book to use a very well-known programming language—JavaScript—as its native policy language. In this chapter, I will give an overview of jsPolicy similar to those of the preceding Kubernetes PaC solutions while pointing out items specific to jsPolicy.

jsPolicy also uses the V8 JavaScript engine (*https://v8.dev*), an open source JavaScript and WebAssembly engine from Google. The V8 engine is written in C++ (*https://oreil.ly/-B4hi*) and is highly optimized for better performance in web browsers like Chrome, as well as in JSON-based NoSQL databases like Couchbase (*https://www.couchbase.com*).

Let's get started by installing and exercising jsPolicy in Kubernetes 1.26 with minikube.

Installation

To get started with jsPolicy, I followed the jsPolicy Quickstart Guide (*https://oreil.ly/BdqXG*). As I have done in previous chapters, I wrapped jsPolicy commands in shell scripts to be used with a Makefile, making it easier for DevOps automation. The following script installs jsPolicy:

```
#!/usr/bin/env bash
# error handling
set -e
trap 'catch $? $LINENO' ERR
catch() {
  if [ "$1" != "0" ]; then
    echo "Error $1 occurred on $2"
  fi
}

KUBECTL="kubectl"
NS=${1:-jspolicy}

helm install jspolicy jspolicy -n $NS \
--create-namespace --repo https://charts.loft.sh

LABEL=$(${KUBECTL} get ns $NS -oyaml | { grep jspolicy-ignore || true; })
if [[ "$LABEL" == "" ]]
then
  ${KUBECTL} label ns $NS jspolicy-ignore=ignore
  ${KUBECTL} get ns $NS -oyaml | grep jspolicy-ignore
fi

LABEL=$(${KUBECTL} get ns kube-system -oyaml | { grep jspolicy-ignore || true; })
if [[ "$LABEL" == "" ]]
then
  ${KUBECTL} label ns kube-system jspolicy-ignore=ignore
```

```
${KUBECTL} get ns kube-system -oyaml | grep jspolicy-ignore
fi
```

 At the time of writing, jsPolicy does not yet support the Linux/ ARM64 architecture. As I primarily use an ARM64 M2 MacBook Pro and minikube, I had to switch to my older Intel-based machine to run jsPolicy.

Running the preceding install script resulted in the following output:

```
# Make command to install jsPolicy
$ make up
./up.sh
NAME: jspolicy
LAST DEPLOYED: Sat Mar  9 18:25:22 2024
NAMESPACE: jspolicy
STATUS: deployed
REVISION: 1
TEST SUITE: None
NOTES:
Thank you for installing jspolicy.

Your release is named jspolicy.

To learn more about the release, try:

  $ helm status jspolicy -n jspolicy
  $ helm get all jspolicy -n jspolicy

Learn more about using jsPolicy here: https://github.com/loft-sh/jspolicy
namespace/jspolicy labeled
    jspolicy-ignore: ignore
namespace/kube-system labeled
    jspolicy-ignore: ignore
```

After installation, I validated that jsPolicy was running correctly with the following kubectl commands to review the running resources:

```
# jsPolicy Deployments and Pods
$ kubectl -n jspolicy get all
NAME                            READY   STATUS    RESTARTS   AGE
pod/jspolicy-6c695f6bbf-2bpw4   1/1     Running   0          24s
...
NAME                         READY   UP-TO-DATE   AVAILABLE   AGE
deployment.apps/jspolicy     1/1     1            1           24s
...


# jsPolicy controller logs
$ kubectl logs jspolicy-6c695f6bbf-zqnzs
I0607 02:47:18.097502       1 deleg.go:121] controller-runtime:
metrics: Metrics server is starting to listen addr :8080
```

```
I0607 02:47:18.113062       1 logr.go:249] controller-runtime:
webhook: path /policy/: Registering webhook
I0607 02:47:18.113281       1 logr.go:249] controller-runtime:
webhook: path /crds: Registering webhook
I0607 02:47:18.113399       1 deleg.go:121] setup: starting manager
I0607 02:47:18.113478       1 logr.go:249] controller-runtime:
webhook: webhooks: Starting webhook server
```

During the install, jsPolicy also installs five Kubernetes CRDs:

```
# CRDs installed by jsPolicy
$ kubectl get crd
NAME                                     CREATED AT
clusterpolicyreports.wgpolicyk8s.io      2023-06-05T18:00:06Z
jspolicies.policy.jspolicy.com           2023-06-05T18:00:06Z
jspolicybundles.policy.jspolicy.com      2023-06-05T18:00:06Z
jspolicyviolations.policy.jspolicy.com   2023-06-05T18:00:06Z
policyreports.wgpolicyk8s.io             2023-06-05T18:00:06Z
```

CRD Webhook Configuration

During initial installation, jsPolicy installs a single Kubernetes webhook configuration that sends calls to the */crds* endpoint of the jsPolicy controller. This webhook is configured to act only on CREATE and UPDATE operations related to resources in the policy.jspolicy.com Kubernetes API group, created by the jsPolicy CRDs:

```
# CRD webhook configuration to ingest policies
    service:
      name: jspolicy
      namespace: jspolicy
      path: /crds
      port: 443
  failurePolicy: Fail
  matchPolicy: Equivalent
  name: jspolicy.jspolicy.com
  namespaceSelector: {}
  objectSelector: {}
  rules:
  - apiGroups:
    - policy.jspolicy.com   ❶
    apiVersions:
    - v1beta1
    operations:
    - CREATE
    - UPDATE
    resources:
    - '*'
    scope: '*'
```

❶   This webhook will only be used during jsPolicy ingestion.

The purpose of the preceding webhook configuration is to handle jsPolicy policies and prepare—compile, bundle, encode, and compress—them to be used in the Kubernetes clusters. I will dive deeper into the policy ingestion process later in the chapter.

Policy Webhook Configurations

Perhaps we have been conditioned to think that Kubernetes PaC solutions reuse webhook configurations to service multiple policies. Previous PaC solutions have used that pattern. Before PaC, if you wanted to control multiple scenarios not intrinsically monitored and controlled by Kubnernetes in-tree solutions, then you would write and deploy multiple controllers or operators to run within your clusters. I wrote one such controller solution (*https://oreil.ly/9XhHv*) last year to verify container image signatures.

Reusing the same webhook configurations, even for the same controller service, is not a requirement. I have written—and you can also write—multiple webhook configurations that point to the same controller service or even multiple services in your Kubernetes clusters. If you consider all the webhook configuration items (*https:// oreil.ly/AkrME*) available to you when building dynamic admission controller solutions, it's not far-fetched to imagine all the different combinations that are realized by using multiple webhook configurations.

Writing or generating multiple webhook configurations gives you that level of configuration granularity—a layer of indirection, if you will—through which you can configure multiple configuration scenarios to best leverage the controller services at your disposal. jsPolicy embraces that configuration granularity. Unlike the Kubernetes PaC solutions we explored in previous chapters, jsPolicy does not use webhook configurations that handle multiple policies of the same type: mutating and validating. Instead, the Webhook Manager, an architectural component of jsPolicy, registers webhooks for each successfully ingested policy resource. Figure 9-1 illustrates this concept as compared to the baseline that we have come to expect so far.

In Figure 9-1, each policy-based webhook configuration is for a different policy of the same policy type: mutating and validating. All webhook configurations point to the same policy service base URL—*/policy*—and each includes the name of the policy in the last path segment of the `service.path` configuration element.

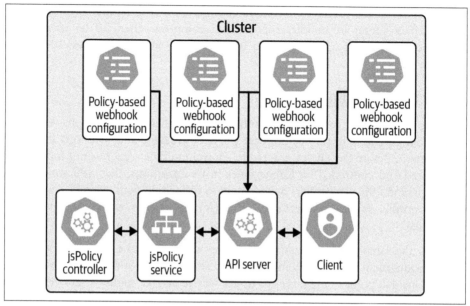

Figure 9-1. Multiple policy-based webhook configurations

In the following output, five policies are listed as ingested by jsPolicy:

```
# Five ingested policies
$ kubectl get jspolicies -oname
jspolicy.policy.jspolicy.com/copy-namespace-annotations.example.com
jspolicy.policy.jspolicy.com/copy-namespace-annotations2.example.com
jspolicy.policy.jspolicy.com/copy-namespace-labels.jimmyray.io
jspolicy.policy.jspolicy.com/dont-create-me.jimmyray.io
jspolicy.policy.jspolicy.com/npol.ns.jimmyray.io
```

These policies are typed as:

- Mutating: three each
- Validating: one each
- Controller: one each

Of the five ingested policies, only four of them actually use webhook configurations. As you will learn later in this chapter, controller policies are cluster-event based and do not participate in the Kubernetes API server request flow; therefore, they do not use webhook configurations. The following lists of mutating and validating webhook configurations indicate the one-for-one cardinality between policies that participate in the Kubernetes API server request flow and their respective webhook configurations:

```
# Get mutating webhook configurations
$ kubectl get mutatingwebhookconfigurations
NAME                                          WEBHOOKS   AGE
copy-namespace-annotations.example.com-ifdea  1          20m
copy-namespace-annotations2.example.com-gjnmi 1          20m
copy-namespace-labels.jimmyray.io-utkfd       1          20m

# Get validating webhook configurations
$ kubectl get validatingwebhookconfigurations
NAME                           WEBHOOKS   AGE
dont-create-me.jimmyray.io-xexyy  1       22m
jspolicy                          1       25m
```

As you can see in the preceding outputs, there are three mutating webhook configurations, each with only one defined webhook, corresponding to the three ingested mutating policies. There are two validating webhook configurations, each with one defined webhook, corresponding to the one ingested validating policy and the base jsPolicy controller webhook configuration that is installed with jsPolicy and is required for policy ingestion and compilation.

The following example shows how the webhook configuration is applied to the Kubernetes cluster by the jsPolicy Webhook Manager for the deny-specific-container-image.example.com policy (*https://oreil.ly/LKYOg*), from the jsPolicy GitHub project example policies:

```
# Policy webhook configuration to apply policy rules to resources
apiVersion: admissionregistration.k8s.io/v1
kind: ValidatingWebhookConfiguration
metadata:
  name: deny-specific-container-image.example.com-faqlb
  ownerReferences:
  - apiVersion: policy.jspolicy.com/v1beta1
    controller: true
    kind: JsPolicy
    name: deny-specific-container-image.example.com
    uid: 2ee42f1e-488b-4a99-bdfe-3c5714780e30
  resourceVersion: "6303"
  uid: 75008e80-7b8d-4a45-97b3-e30766c7b843
webhooks:
- admissionReviewVersions:
  - v1
  clientConfig:
    caBundle: LS0tLS1…
    service:
      name: jspolicy
      namespace: jspolicy
      path: /policy/deny-specific-container-image.example.com    ❶
      port: 443
  failurePolicy: Fail
  matchPolicy: Equivalent
  name: deny-specific-container-image.example.com
```

```
  namespaceSelector: {}
  objectSelector: {}
  rules:
  - apiGroups:
    - '*'
    apiVersions:
    - '*'
    operations:
    - CREATE   .
    resources:
    - pods    ❷
    scope: '*'
  sideEffects: None
  timeoutSeconds: 10
```

❶   The jsPolicy service URL includes the path to the jsPolicy policy.

❷   This webhook will only listen for CREATE operations on Pods.

You can see that the webhook points to the `jspolicy` service in the `jspolicy` Namespace. You can also see that the webhook is set to `Fail` if the configured service does not respond. This webhook is set to only review Pod resources during the CREATE operation.

We'll explore the policy in more detail later in the chapter, but for now, it's important to understand that each policy is underpinned by a Kubernetes webhook configuration, and all the webhooks point to the same underlying Kubernetes service. The webhook granularity enables more focused policies that act on resources with specific Kubernetes API groups and versions, using specific namespace and object selection. While this approach increases the number of webhook configuration resources, it grants policy authors more control over how and when policies are applied. This approach also provides the secondary benefit of not having to centrally manage logic to ignore specific Namespaces, as utilized by previous PaC solutions.

Next, let's explore how to uninstall jsPolicy.

Uninstalling jsPolicy

Uninstalling jsPolicy is easy with the following Helm command, wrapped in my uninstall script:

```
# Uninstall script
#!/usr/bin/env bash
# error handling
set -e
trap 'catch $? $LINENO' ERR
catch() {
  if [ "$1" != "0" ]; then
    echo "Error $1 occurred on $2"
```

```
    fi
}

KUBECTL="kubectl"
NS=${1:-jspolicy}

# ${KUBECTL} config set-context --current --namespace=$NS

helm -n $NS uninstall jspolicy

${KUBECTL} delete ns $NS

${KUBECTL} delete validatingwebhookconfiguration jspolicy
${KUBECTL} delete mutatingwebhookconfiguration jspolicy

${KUBECTL} api-resources --api-group='policy.jspolicy.com' \
-o name | xargs ${KUBECTL} delete crd

${KUBECTL} api-resources --api-group='wgpolicyk8s.io' \
-o name | xargs ${KUBECTL} delete crd

${KUBECTL} label ns kube-system jspolicy-ignore-
```

As far as I could tell, the jsPolicy CRDs persisted beyond the Helm uninstall, so I added lines in the following script to explicitly delete the CRDs:

```
# Make command to uninstall jsPolicy
$ make down
./down.sh
release "jspolicy" uninstalled
namespace "jspolicy" deleted
customresourcedefinition.apiextensions.k8s.io
"jspolicies.policy.jspolicy.com" deleted
customresourcedefinition.apiextensions.k8s.io
"jspolicybundles.policy.jspolicy.com" deleted
customresourcedefinition.apiextensions.k8s.io
"jspolicyviolations.policy.jspolicy.com" deleted
customresourcedefinition.apiextensions.k8s.io
"clusterpolicyreports.wgpolicyk8s.io" deleted
customresourcedefinition.apiextensions.k8s.io
"policyreports.wgpolicyk8s.io" deleted
namespace/kube-system unlabeled
```

So far, jsPolicy is very easy to install, configure, and uninstall. Next, we will explore how jsPolicy policies are built, ingested, and applied to Kubernetes resources.

Policies

By now, it should be evident that regardless of the Kubernetes PaC solution and policy language, policies are introduced into clusters via YAML documents. jsPolicy is no different. However, since jsPolicy uses JavaScript for its policy language, it can leverage the JavaScript ecosystem for building and testing policies. jsPolicy can also use other languages, like TypeScript, that transpile to JavaScript.

 Transpiling (*https://oreil.ly/TlZYH*)—a.k.a. source-to-source compiling—translates one computer language source to another.

jsPolicy policies can be added to Kubernetes clusters in two ways:

Inline policies
Policies created by embedding JavaScript inside the `spec.javascript` field of resources based on the `jsPolicy` kind

Bundled policies
Encoded and compressed JavaScript embedded in the `spec.bundle` field of the `JsPolicyBundle` kind

Let's start our policy journey by exploring inline policies.

Inline Policies

With inline policies, you write the raw JavaScript directly into the jsPolicy YAML document. Inline policies support what jsPolicy calls "vanilla" JavaScript—a.k.a. Java Script ES5 (*https://oreil.ly/WhQ9Z*). The following validating policy applies to Pods being created in Namespaces that opt in to processing using the `policy=enabled` label and where Pods are labeled with the `env=dev` label:

```
# Validating inline policy document
apiVersion: policy.jspolicy.com/v1beta1
kind: JsPolicy
metadata:
  name: "dont-create-me.jimmyray.io"
spec:
  operations: ["CREATE"]
  resources: ["pods"]
  namespaceSelector:
    matchExpressions:
    - key: policy
      operator: In
      values: ["enabled"]  ❶
  objectSelector:
```

```
    matchLabels:
      env: "dev"
  javascript: |    ❷
    print("Incoming request for: " + request.object.metadata?.name)

    if (request.object.metadata?.annotations?.["dont-create-me"]) {
      deny("dont-create-me annotation is not allowed");
    }
```

❶   The `namespaceSelector` configures opt-in for Namespaces by label.

❷   In an inline policy, JavaScript is embedded within the YAML.

The policy logic denies the request if the Pod `metadata.annotations` field contains the `dont-create-me` annotation.

 Since jsPolicy is based on JavaScript, it inherits JavaScript functions and provides its own set of functions, like the `deny()` function (*https://oreil.ly/ZlHie*) from the preceding policy.

In the preceding policy, the `namespaceSelector`, `objectSelector`, `operations`, and `resources` fields are used to match the policy to inbound Kubernetes API server requests that create Pods that are specifically labeled. Again, this is a pattern we have seen in other PaC solutions. First, a match is made, then logic is applied to validate the request.

The embedded JavaScript code is used to deny the request if the specified annotation is present. The JavaScript code uses the *optional chaining* operator `?.` to match object properties and array items. In the preceding code, optional chaining allows the policy code to short-circuit (*https://oreil.ly/UGPbt*) if the `annotations` property doesn't exist in the `metadata` object or if the `dont-create-me` item does not exist in the `meta data.annotations` array property.

With the following Namespace and Pod manifests, we can trigger the jsPolicy violation:

```
# Namespace manifest
apiVersion: v1
kind: Namespace
metadata:
  name: policy-test
  labels:
    policy: enabled

# Pod manifest
apiVersion: v1
```

```
kind: Pod
metadata:
  name: test-pod
  namespace: policy-test
  annotations:
    dont-create-me: stop
spec:
  containers:
    - name: test-pod
...


# Trigger policy violation
$ kubectl apply -f test
namespace/policy-test created
Error from server (Forbidden): error when creating "test/2-test-pod.yaml":
admission webhook "dont-create-me.jimmyray.io" denied the request:
dont-create-me annotation is not allowed
```

Inline policies are the easiest way to get started with jsPolicy. Next, let's look at how inline policies are ingested and processed by jsPolicy.

Policy ingestion

When inline policies are ingested by the jsPolicy controller, the policy compiler (*https://oreil.ly/DX0yu*) prepares the raw JavaScript in the inline policy to be used by the jsPolicy engine. Upon successful compilation, at least two Kubernetes resources are created: jsPolicy and jsPolicyBundle. In the case of mutating and validating policies, which participate in the Kubernetes API server request flow, MutatingWebhook Configuration and ValidatingWebhookConfiguration resources are created.

Examining the jsPolicy resource from our earlier example, you can see the status field that indicates the successful compilation:

```
# Get jsPolicy resource
$ kubectl get jspolicy dont-create-me.jimmyray.io -oyaml

apiVersion: policy.jspolicy.com/v1beta1
kind: JsPolicy
metadata:
  name: dont-create-me.jimmyray.io
spec:
  javascript: "..."    ❶
  namespaceSelector:
    matchLabels:
      policy: enabled
  objectSelector:
    matchLabels:
      env: dev
  operations:
  - CREATE
  resources:
```

```
  - pods
status:
  bundleHash: fc961234b59e07416b806ff0c58bdb764f28c6e250c97dc01d8234843ae01671  ❷
  conditions:
  - lastTransitionTime: "2023-06-08T00:30:07Z"
    status: "True"
    type: Ready
  - lastTransitionTime: "2023-06-08T00:30:07Z"
    status: "True"
    type: BundleCompiled
  - lastTransitionTime: "2023-06-08T00:30:07Z"
    status: "True"
    type: WebhookReady
  observedGeneration: 4
  phase: Synced
```

❶   For brevity, I removed the JavaScript code from this example.

❷   The `bundleHash` element points to the bundle resource.

The jsPolicyBundle resource is a result of the downstream bundling process that gathers Node Package Manager (npm) dependencies (*https://www.npmjs.com*) specified in the JavaScript, via the `spec.dependencies` field. Then, webpack (*https://webpack.js.org*) is used to bundle the scripts into a module:

```
# jsPolicyBundle resource
$ kubectl get jspolicybundle dont-create-me.jimmyray.io -oyaml

# jsPolicy bundle resource
apiVersion: policy.jspolicy.com/v1beta1
kind: JsPolicyBundle
metadata:
  name: dont-create-me.jimmyray.io
  ownerReferences:
  - apiVersion: policy.jspolicy.com/v1beta1
    blockOwnerDeletion: true
    controller: true
    kind: JsPolicy
    name: dont-create-me.jimmyray.io
    uid: 765a6c0b-2317-42b4-9805-27c9d4c846b3
spec:
  bundle: H4sIAAAAAAAA/3SOQUvDQBSE/8q6h7…EAAA==  ❶
```

❶   The `bundle` element contains the compressed and encoded JavaScript code.

Once the module is built, then it is Gzip compressed, base64 encoded, and stored in the `spec.bundle` field. This entire process optimizes the JavaScript to be efficiently processed by the jsPolicy engine.

If there is a coding error, such as a JavaScript syntax error, it is not immediately signaled when the policy resource is applied to the Kubernetes cluster. Instead, users must view the `status` field in the jsPolicy resource to check for successful compile and bundling. The following example includes an error condition introduced via a JavaScript syntax error:

```
# jsPolicy status field with errors
status:
  bundleHash: 5c9a2254965920bababbfb1410584be11245b828e799638975b2d0f68224a65bf
  conditions:
  - lastTransitionTime: "2023-06-25T01:16:40Z"
    message: >
        error bundling javascript: assets by status 563 bytes [cached] 1
        asset\n./index.js 884 bytes [built] [code generated]
        [1 error]\n\nERROR in ./index.js 13:13\nModule parse failed:
        Unexpected token (13:13)\nYou may need an appropriate loader to
        handle this file type, currently no loaders are configured to process
        this file. See https://webpack.js.org/concepts#loaders\n| delete
        request.object.metadata.labels['policy']*/\n| \n> axaxaxadfor
        (var key in request.object.metadata.labels) {\n|    if
        (exclude.includes(key)) {\n|delete request.object.metadata.labels
        [key]\n\nwebpack 5.75.0 compiled with 1 error in 369 ms\n exit
        status 1"
    reason: CompileFailed
    severity: Error
    status: "False"
    type: Ready
```

Finally, as I mentioned before, a separate webhook configuration is created for the successfully ingested policies of type mutating or validating. The following YAML includes a validating webhook configuration:

```
# ValidatingWebhookConfiguration
$ kubectl get validatingwebhookconfiguration \
dont-create-me.jimmyray.io-qbydl -oyaml

# ValidatingWebhookConfiguration for dont-create-me.jimmyray.io policy
apiVersion: admissionregistration.k8s.io/v1
kind: ValidatingWebhookConfiguration
metadata:
  name: dont-create-me.jimmyray.io-qbydl
  ownerReferences:
  - apiVersion: policy.jspolicy.com/v1beta1
    controller: true
    kind: JsPolicy
    name: dont-create-me.jimmyray.io
    uid: 765a6c0b-2317-42b4-9805-27c9d4c846b3
webhooks:
- admissionReviewVersions:
  - v1
  clientConfig:
```

```
    caBundle: LS0tLS1CRUdJT…LS0tCg==...
    service:
      name: jspolicy
      namespace: jspolicy
      path: /policy/dont-create-me.jimmyray.io
      port: 443
failurePolicy: Fail
matchPolicy: Equivalent
name: dont-create-me.jimmyray.io
namespaceSelector:
  matchLabels:
    policy: enabled
objectSelector:
  matchLabels:
    env: dev
rules:
- apiGroups:
  - '*'
  apiVersions:
  - '*'
  operations:
  - CREATE
  resources:
  - pods
  scope: '*'
sideEffects: None
timeoutSeconds: 10
```

Given the latency and tuning topics discussed in Chapter 4 as well as how jsPolicy creates a separate webhook configuration for each mutating and validating policy, it is still important that webhook and API server request timeouts are tuned for optimal API server latency.

The preceding webhook configuration inherits the resource-matching settings from its parent jsPolicy resource to configure the webhook rules as well as the namespace Selector and objectSelector fields. A default timeout of 10 seconds is configured as well as a default failure policy. Finally, the path field—used for calling the service configured by the webhook configuration—includes the parent-policy name.

Now that we have seen a validating policy example, let's review a mutating policy example.

Mutating policies

Inline mutating policies are ingested similarly to validating policies. In the following mutating policy example, the Namespace labels are copied to Pods created in the Namespace:

```
# Mutating inline policy example
apiVersion: policy.jspolicy.com/v1beta1
kind: JsPolicy
metadata:
  name: "copy-namespace-labels.jimmyray.io"
spec:
  namespaceSelector:
    matchExpressions:
    - key: policy
      operator: In
      values: ["enabled"]
  type: Mutating
  operations: ["CREATE"]
  resources: ["pods"]
  javascript: |
    // this webhook will copy the namespace labels to pods
    const namespace = get("Namespace", "v1", request.namespace);
    const excludes = ['pod-security.kubernetes.io/audit',
    'pod-security.kubernetes.io/enforce',
    'pod-security.kubernetes.io/warn','policy','kubernetes.io/metadata.name']

    // copy labels from namespace, remove excluded labels
    request.object.metadata.labels = namespace?.metadata?.labels;  ❶

    for (var key in request.object.metadata.labels) {  ❷
      if (excludes.includes(key)) {
        delete request.object.metadata.labels[key]
      }
    }

    // automatically calculate patch and exit
    mutate(request.object);  ❸
```

❶ Copy Namespace labels to be used later.

❷ Remove irrelevant labels by key.

❸ Perform the mutation operation.

The preceding mutating policy copies labels from the parent Namespace to child Pods. The logic copies all the labels to the inbound request object, then removes specified unwanted labels from the `excludes` array using the JavaScript delete operator on the `request.object.metadata.labels` associative array. The final array of labels does not include the Namespace labels that are irrelevant at the Pod level.

There are many tools out there to help you write JavaScript and TypeScript. The following are a few that I have used for this chapter and other projects:

- JavaScript Playground (*https://playcode.io*)
- JSFiddle (*https://jsfiddle.net*)
- RunJS (*https://runjs.co*)
- TypeScript Playground (*https://www.typescriptlang.org*)

As we saw in the validating inline policy example, the jsPolicyBundle resource is created. And since this is a mutating policy example, a MutatingWebhookConfiguration resource is created with settings similar to the ValidatingWebhookConfiguration resource:

```
# jsPolicy mutating webhook example
$ kubectl get mutatingwebhookconfiguration
copy-namespace-labels.jimmyray.io-kbczr -oyaml

# MutatingWebhookConfiguration for copy-namespace-labels.jimmyray.io
apiVersion: admissionregistration.k8s.io/v1
kind: MutatingWebhookConfiguration
metadata:
  annotations:
    jspolicy.com/apply: |...
webhooks:
- admissionReviewVersions:
  - v1
  clientConfig:
    caBundle: LS0tLS…
    service:
      name: jspolicy
      namespace: jspolicy
      path: /policy/copy-namespace-labels.jimmyray.io
      port: 443
  failurePolicy: Fail
  matchPolicy: Equivalent
  name: copy-namespace-labels.jimmyray.io
  namespaceSelector:
    matchExpressions:
    - key: policy
      operator: In
      values:
      - enabled
  objectSelector: {}
  reinvocationPolicy: Never
  rules:
  - apiGroups:
    - '*'
    apiVersions:
```

```
    - '*'
  operations:
  - CREATE
  resources:
  - pods
  scope: '*'
sideEffects: None
timeoutSeconds: 10
```

Next, we will explore jsPolicy controller policies.

Controller policies

jsPolicy controller policies (*https://oreil.ly/Lat_y*) are different from policies that we have seen so far. Unlike mutating and validating policies, controller policies do not participate in the Kubernetes API server request flow. Instead, controller policy triggers are event based, triggered by the events that are published by Kubernetes as a result of cluster state changes persisted to etcd. Controller policies are designed to watch for and react to Kubernetes cluster-state changes.

jsPolicy controller policies are similar to the Kyverno Generate policies that we explored in Chapter 8. Both solutions create an event-based scheme that reacts to Kubernetes cluster changes. While Kyverno Generate policies are primarily focused on creating resources, jsPolicy controller policies are able to accomplish additional tasks beyond creating resources.

For example, in a multitenant environment isolated by Namespaces, it is considered a good practice by some to automatically create certain related Namespace-scoped resources—network policies, resource quotas, limit ranges, and so on—when tenant Namespaces are created. This practice is done to apply default security and resource settings. This can also be done via GitOps automation; the choice is yours. However, creating resources on the fly, without specific code artifacts backing each resource instance within its specific context, is seen by some to violate GitOps fundamentals. The decision is yours, as is the trade-off.

Even if you opt to not use controller policies and use GitOps best practices instead, I would use PaC within the codebase and automated pipelines to verify that related and needed Kubernetes resource artifacts are present in the source branches observed by GitOps processes before resources are applied to Kubernetes clusters by your GitOps processes. I would also add validating policies in the Kubernetes clusters to ensure that needed Namespace components are present before the Namespaces are turned over to their respective tenants.

The following controller policy creates a deny-all egress and ingress network policy when Namespaces are created and labeled with `npol=enabled`:

```
# example controller policy to create network policy
apiVersion: policy.jspolicy.com/v1beta1
kind: JsPolicy
metadata:
  name: "npol.ns.jimmyray.io"
spec:
  operations: ["CREATE"]
  resources: ["namespaces"]  ❶
  apiGroups: [""]
  type: Controller
  objectSelector:
    matchLabels:
      npol: "enabled"  ❷
  javascript: |
    const npolName = "deny-all"
    const kind = "NetworkPolicy"
    const apiVersion = "networking.k8s.io/v1"
    const npol = get(kind, apiVersion, request.name + "/" + npolName);

    if (!npol) {
      const created = create({
        "kind": kind,
        "apiVersion": apiVersion,
        "metadata": {
          "name": npolName,
          "namespace": request.name
        },
        "spec": {
          "podSelector": {},
          "policyTypes": [
            "Ingress",
            "Egress"
          ]
        }
      });
      if (!created.ok && created.reason !== "AlreadyExists") {
        requeue(created.message);
      } else {
        print(`created ${kind} ${request.name}/${npolName}`);
      }
    }
```

❶ Policy webhook fires when Namespaces are created.

❷ Only Namespaces that are enabled by the `npol=enabled` label will be mutated.

The result is a near-real-time creation of a network policy when the parent Namespace is created. The print(...) statement in the preceding policy creates the following log entry in the jsPolicy controller logs:

```
# jsPolicy controller log
$ kubectl logs jspolicy-6c695f6bbf-2bpw4
...
I0625 03:58:26.800811      1 main.go:173] [npol.ns.jimmyray.io] created
NetworkPolicy test/deny-all
```

The following deny-all network policy was created by the controller policy when the correctly labeled Namespace was created:

```
# created network policy
$ kubectl -n test get networkpolicies deny-all -oyaml

# Network policy resource created by controller policy
apiVersion: networking.k8s.io/v1
kind: NetworkPolicy
metadata:
  creationTimestamp: "2023-06-25T03:58:26Z"
  generation: 1
  name: deny-all
  namespace: test
  resourceVersion: "82153"
  uid: d9ae4070-c64f-4b1c-bf13-5fad1d0e40e1
spec:
  podSelector: {}
  policyTypes:
  - Ingress
  - Egress
status: {}
```

Creating, updating, or deleting Kubernetes resources using controller policies requires that you clearly understand the Kubernetes API, GVK, and the required elements for Kubernetes resources. Given the complexity of Kubernetes, troubleshooting controller policies can also get complex. While syntax errors are caught by the policy compiler and reported in the relative status fields, logic issues are harder to find.

For example, if I used the wrong Kubernetes API version for the network policy resource, I could review the main jsPolicy controller logs, as shown in the following:

```
# jsPolicy controller log errors
$ kubectl logs jspolicy-6c695f6bbf-2bpw4
...
E0625 03:23:31.151463 1 logr.go:265] policy-handler:  Error executing policy
 npol.ns.jimmyray.io: RetrieveObject: no matches for kind "NetworkPolicy"
in version "v1"
```

Additionally, I could review jsPolicyViolation resources to view the possible errors from controller policy execution:

```
# controller policy troubleshooting with policy violations
$ kubectl get jspolicyviolations npol.ns.jimmyray.io -oyaml

# JsPolicyViolations resource
apiVersion: policy.jspolicy.com/v1beta1
kind: JsPolicyViolations
metadata:
  name: npol.ns.jimmyray.io
spec: {}
status:
  violations:
  - action: Controller
    code: 500
    message: 'RetrieveObject: no matches for kind "NetworkPolicy"
in version "v1"'
    requestInfo:
      apiVersion: v1
      kind: Namespace
      name: test
      operation: CREATE
    userInfo: {}
```

I should point out that in the preceding violation, the userInfo field is empty. This is related to how controller policies are not executed as webhook calls in the Kubernetes API server request flow; therefore, user info is not available. The following is an example jsPolicyViolation resource from the earlier example in which the userInfo field is populated:

```
# validating policy violation resource with userInfo
$ kubectl get jspolicyviolations.policy.jspolicy.com \
dont-create-me.jimmyray.io -oyaml

apiVersion: policy.jspolicy.com/v1beta1
kind: JsPolicyViolations
metadata:
  name: dont-create-me.jimmyray.io
  ownerReferences:
  - apiVersion: policy.jspolicy.com/v1beta1
    blockOwnerDeletion: true
    controller: true
    kind: JsPolicy
    name: dont-create-me.jimmyray.io
spec: {}
status:
  violations:
  - action: Deny
    code: 403
    message: dont-create-me annotation is not allowed
```

```
reason: Forbidden
requestInfo:
  apiVersion: v1
  kind: Pod
  name: test-pod
  namespace: default
  operation: CREATE
userInfo:
  username: minikube-user  ❶
```

❶ userInfo is only included when the policy is applied to the API server request
from clients that are trying to change resources.

> Since controller policy violations do not return the userInfo
> element, policy logic cannot be used for user-specific evaluations.

As a point of reference, the jsPolicyViolation resources are deleted when their
associated jsPolicy resources are deleted.

Controller policies watch for specific cluster changes to transpire; this makes controller policies reactive as opposed to proactive or preventive. Conversely, mutating and
validating policies that participate in the Kubernetes API server request flow are considered preventive. Therefore, the use of controller policies as a security or compliance method should be combined with additional logic, such as DevOps automation
and validating logic, to verify that controller policy results occur.

Policy deletion

You may have noticed the metadata.ownerReferences fields in the jsPolicyBundle
and *WebhookConfiguration resources that we discussed earlier. This indicates that
those resources are child resources related to the parent jsPolicy. The ownerReferen
ces field is part of the Kubernetes owners and dependents functionality (*https://
oreil.ly/rGZbW*). Moreover, when the parent jsPolicy resource is deleted, the corresponding child resources are also deleted as part of a Kubernetes garbage-collection
process.

Now that we have explored jsPolicies inline policies, let's move on to compiling and
creating policies outside of jsPolicy.

Bundled Policies

As I mentioned earlier, jsPolicy supports JavaScript and languages that compile or transpile to run in the V8 JavaScript engine. Using the JavaScript ecosystem and tools, like npm, helps policy developers build policy code as they would any other software development project. In this section, we will explore how TypeScript can be used in an npm project to compile and bundle policies before they are applied to Kubernetes.

To get started with bundled policies, I used the jsPolicy SDK (*https://oreil.ly/yiRPM*), and I cloned the example jspolicy-sdk GitHub project (*https://oreil.ly/ZwbGF*). The project shows how to use TypeScript and npm to create jsPolicy modules ready for distribution to the jsPolicy engine running in Kubernetes. I first used the npm install command to install the project dependencies declared in the *package.json* file as node_modules.

During the install of the project dependencies, I noticed that several high and critical vulnerabilities were detected:

```
# vulnerabilities detected during npm install
$ npm install
…
added 794 packages, and audited 795 packages in 15s

49 packages are looking for funding
  run `npm fund` for details

63 vulnerabilities (48 moderate, 12 high, 3 critical)

To address issues that do not require attention, run:
  npm audit fix

To address all issues possible (including breaking changes), run:
  npm audit fix --force

Some issues need review, and may require choosing
a different dependency.

Run `npm audit` for details.
```

To fix the vulnerabilities in the project dependencies, I used the npm audit fix command:

```
# reduce project dependency vulnerabilities with npm audit fix
$ npm audit fix
added 29 packages, removed 78 packages, changed 92 packages,
and audited 746 packages in 14s
…
36 moderate severity vulnerabilities
…
```

With the preceding command, I reduced the vulnerabilities, including remediating all the high and critical vulnerabilities. However, my vulnerability fix introduced breaking changes in the project, and I was unable to successfully compile the policies. I am not an npm or TypeScript SME, so in the interest of demoing the solution, I recloned the project, installed the dependencies, and compiled the policies without fixing the vulnerabilities. I used the `npm run compile` command to compile the policies from the *./src/policies* directory. This created the *./dist* and *./policies* directories. I then installed the jsPolicy and jsPolicyBundle resources from the *./policies* directory into my nonproduction minikube cluster.

I would never recommend that anyone install any resources with known high and critical vulnerabilities into any Kubernetes cluster. I am not recommending that now. However, after examining the example jspolicy-sdk GitHub project, I surmised that there had not been a lot of activity on this project during the last two years. So to demonstrate the jsPolicy features without spending an inordinate amount of time, I proceeded with caution. If you are interested in this solution, I strongly recommend that you refactor the project and fix the breaking changes and vulnerabilities.

After successful compilation, I ran the test suite with the `npm run test` command:

```
# test policies before installation
$ npm run test

> @jspolicy/jspolicy-typescript-starter@0.0.1 test
> jest --env=node --colors --coverage test

 PASS  tests/capabilities.ts
  Test containerSpec.securityContext.capabilities
    ✓ Check containers (2 ms)
    ✓ Check initContainers
    ✓ Check valid request
...
Test Suites: 1 passed, 1 total
Tests:       3 passed, 3 total
Snapshots:   0 total
Time:        0.605 s, estimated 3 s
Ran all test suites matching /test/i.
```

After testing, I installed the jsPolicy and jsPolicyBundle resources:

```
# jsPolicy resource
apiVersion: policy.jspolicy.com/v1beta1
kind: JsPolicy
metadata:
  name: validate-namespace.mycompany.tld
spec:
```

```
  operations: [CREATE]
  resources: ["*"]
  scope: Namespaced

# jsPolicyBundle resource
apiVersion: policy.jspolicy.com/v1beta1
kind: JsPolicyBundle
metadata:
  name: validate-namespace.mycompany.tld
spec:
  bundle: H4sIAAAAAAAAE6VTTY…
```

The jsPolicy resource needed to be installed before the jsPolicyBundle resource; otherwise, the `kubectl apply` command would hang. This is normally handled by kubectl bulk operations.

Creating the jsPolicy resource did not create a jsPolicyBundle resource or Validating WebhookConfiguration resource; there was no `spec.javascript` element in the jsPolicy resource that would have triggered this operation. When I installed the jsPolicy Bundle resource, the jsPolicy engine controller also created the Validating WebhookConfiguration and the `metadata.ownerReferences` field in the Validating WebhookConfiguration resource, linking it back to the jsPolicy resource. However, no such link was created in the jsPolicyBundle resource. This means that the cascading-delete operation that would normally delete the jsPolicyBundle resource does not occur with bundled policies. The jsPolicyBundle resource must be explicitly deleted.

The installed validating policy prevented Pods from being created in the `default` or `kube-system` Namespaces. I tested the policy by trying to create a Pod in the `default` Namespace:

```
# test bundled policy in Kubernetes
$ kubectl apply -f test/3-test-pod.yaml
Error from server (Forbidden): error when creating "test/3-test-pod.yaml":
admission webhook "validate-namespace.mycompany.tld" denied the request:
Request denied because of the following errors:
-Field metadata.namespace is not allowed to be: default | kube-system
```

Notwithstanding the outdated codebase of the TypeScript bundled-policy example, the use case for building policies outside the Kubernetes cluster—using automation and JavaScript ecosystem tooling—provides a strong capabilities match for organizations that use JavaScript or TypeScript. Organizations with mature DevOps or GitOps practices will also benefit from this development approach.

Summary

jsPolicy supports the two main policy types that we have seen in other PaC solutions: mutating and validating. jsPolicy also introduces its controller-policy type, which enables developers to create policies that act as Kubernetes controllers, watching cluster changes. Controller policies provide an event-based mechanism to build policy-based reactive automation to better manage Kubernetes. Controller policies reduce the need for Kubernetes users to be Kubernetes programming experts.

Under the covers, jsPolicy leverages the JavaScript ecosystem and tooling to create and manage Kubernetes policies. Organizations that have adopted or that plan to adopt JavaScript or even TypeScript can continue to leverage their existing tooling, like npm, to build, test, and publish bundled policies with DevOps or GitOps automation. jsPolicy inline policies provide a quick way to prototype policies using traditional Kubernetes YAML resources and embedded JavaScript. Bundled policies extend policy creation and management to tooling and processes that are similar to most software organizations.

Given the ease of use of jsPolicy and reliance on JavaScript tooling, I could easily see how this solution would match organizational capabilities and reduce the overall negative disruption that comes with adopting PaC. However, during my discovery and experimentation of jsPolicy, I couldn't help but notice a couple of issues, and I would be remiss if I did not surface those in this chapter.

My impression of jsPolicy is that with all its PaC sugar, the project is not as mature as some of the other solutions I have evaluated. I base this primarily on the GitHub project participation—number of contributors, number and age of pull requests, and so on—and the limited project releases. This doesn't mean that I would not recommend the solution, but as I stated in Chapter 1, community adoption and project recency are selection criteria that should be considered when choosing an OSS PaC solution. That said, it's up to each organization to apply the appropriate weight to the selection criteria.

Overall, I am cautiously excited about the jsPolicy solution. I like how mutating and validating policies create webhook configurations and how controller policies create event-based workflows. There is no denying that using the JavaScript family of languages makes it easier to surmount the learning curve for traditional PaC solutions. I look forward to the project gaining more momentum in the future.

Coming up in Chapter 10, I will discuss Cloud Custodian—introduced in this book's Preface—and how it can be used as a Kubernetes PaC solution.

Cloud Custodian and Kubernetes

In the Preface, I discussed how I started using PaC solutions for cloud computing infrastructure as a service with Cloud Custodian (*https://cloudcustodian.io*). As it turns out, Cloud Custodian—known as *c7n* among its community members—also supports Kubernetes use cases.

C7n is an open source project written in Python that was created by folks at Capital One in 2016. I was at Capital One then, and we were looking for tools to create guardrails in our AWS accounts. I am not exaggerating when I say that c7n substantially helped our teams prevent unwanted behavior in the cloud. C7n was originally designed to apply compliance and governance controls to our AWS accounts and resources. Support for other cloud providers, such as Microsoft Azure and GCP, followed later, as did Kubernetes support.

Since the c7n project is written in Python, users and developers can take advantage of the rich Python ecosystem. In fact, I used the c7n source to gain a better understanding of Boto3 (*https://oreil.ly/0kM84*), the AWS SDK for Python. The c7n policy language is YAML based, with a rich schema that is accessed similarly to how `kubectl explain` exposes the Kubernetes API.

The following links will help you gain more information about c7n:

- Core GitHub project (*https://github.com/cloud-custodian/cloud-custodian*)
- Documentation website (*https://cloudcustodian.io/docs/index.html*)
- Kubernetes policy examples (*https://oreil.ly/mCVuU*)
- Cloud Custodian Slack channel (*https://oreil.ly/sNw8P*)

Let's get started with the c7n CLI tools for Kubernetes.

CLI Mode

As a Kubernetes PaC solution, c7n includes a rich CLI with which users can interface to Kubernetes clusters. Using the CLI, users apply policies that report on and modify cluster resources. C7n support for Kubernetes also includes a controller mode (*https://oreil.ly/3EayH*) that uses dynamic admission controllers, like we've seen in previous chapters. I will cover controller mode later in this chapter.

Unlike previous solutions that we have explored, where we started by installing the PaC solution into a Kubernetes cluster, we will first examine the CLI tools before exploring the traditional admission control tools provided by the c7n solution. I think this approach provides the best learning path for c7n policies.

Let's get started by installing and exercising the c7n CLI with Kubernetes 1.26.

Installation

Since c7n is underpinned by Python, you must first have the requisite Python tools installed. I am running MacOS:

```
# get Python version
$ python3 --version
Python 3.11.4
```

To use c7n, I followed the recommendation to create a Python virtual environment (*https://oreil.ly/UpdpN*):

```
# create Python virtual environment
$ python -m venv c7n-env
```

Virtual environments allow Python users and developers to isolate their Python configurations so that they can modify settings without stepping on system Python settings or settings for other projects.

The previous command created a Python virtual environment using the venv module underpinned by the new *custodian* directory. The command deposited the needed files for Python to execute in the isolated environment:

```
# display virtual environment directory
$ tree -d -L 1 c7n-env
c7n-env
├── bin
├── include
└── lib
```

After I created the virtual environment, I activated it with the following command:

```
# activate virtual environment
$ source c7n-env/bin/activate
```

When the virtual environment activated, the command prompt was tagged with the name of the virtual environment:

```
# activated virtual environment with command prompt label
(c7n-env) $ …
```

With the c7n-env virtual environment created and activated, I installed the c7n packages. For this install, I used pip (*https://pypi.org/project/pip*)—the Python package installer—within the context of the Python virtual environment. Checking the pip version, I was able to see that pip was connected to the virtual environment I just created and activated:

```
# using pip in the virtual environment
$ pip --version
pip 23.0.1 from /Users/…/c7n-env/lib/python3.11/site-packages/pip
 (python 3.11)
```

I then installed c7n core and the c7n Kubernetes plug-in:

```
# install c7n core
$ pip3 install c7n
Successfully installed argcomplete-3.1.1 attrs-23.1.0
boto3-1.26.157 botocore-1.29.157 c7n-0.9.28 docutils-0.18.1
importlib-metadata-5.2.0 jmespath-1.0.1 jsonschema-4.17.3
pyrsistent-0.19.3 python-dateutil-2.8.2 pyyaml-6.0 s3transfer-0.6.1
six-1.16.0 tabulate-0.9.0 urllib3-1.26.16 zipp-3.15.0


# install c7n Kubernetes
$ pip3 install c7n_kube
Successfully installed c7n_kube-0.2.27 cachetools-5.3.1
certifi-2023.5.7 charset-normalizer-3.1.0 google-auth-2.20.0
idna-3.4 jsonpatch-1.33 jsonpointer-2.4 kubernetes-26.1.0
oauthlib-3.2.2 pyasn1-0.5.0 pyasn1-modules-0.3.0 requests-2.31.0
requests-oauthlib-1.3.1 rsa-4.9 setuptools-68.0.0 websocket-client-1.6.0
```

Installing c7n into the Python virtual environment with pip installed the packages into the virtual environment file system, as shown in the following tree command output:

```
# tree command of installed c7n artifacts
$ tree c7n-env --prune -P 'c7n*' --matchdirs
c7n-env
├── bin
│   └── c7n-kates
└── lib
    └── python3.11
        └── site-packages
            ├── c7n
            ├── c7n-0.9.28.dist-info
            ├── c7n_kube
            └── c7n_kube-0.2.27.dist-info
```

When c7n is installed and the virtual environment is activated, the custodian binary is ready to be used. I created a *c7n* alias to the custodian binary for ease of use with the following UNIX command:

```
$ alias c7n='custodian'
```

Once c7n was installed, I verified that it was functional with the `version` command and that the c7n_kube plug-in was also present and functional:

```
# verify c7n is installed
$ c7n version
0.9.28

# verify c7n_kube installed
$ c7n schema k8s
resources:
- k8s.cluster-role
- k8s.config-map
- k8s.custom-cluster-resource
- k8s.custom-namespaced-resource
- k8s.daemon-set
- k8s.deployment
- k8s.namespace
- k8s.node
- k8s.pod
- k8s.replica-set
- k8s.replication-controller
- k8s.role
- k8s.secret
- k8s.service
- k8s.service-account
- k8s.stateful-set
- k8s.volume
- k8s.volume-claim
```

Now that c7n is installed and working, let's see how we can deactivate and uninstall it.

Cleanup

Once you're done with the custodian virtual environment, you can deactivate it with the `deactivate` command. You can then come back to it and reactivate the environment with the same `activate` command from earlier. After deactivation, cleanup of the virtual environment is as easy as deleting the *c7n-env* directory that was created previously with the `venv` command.

The content in this section was based loosely on the c7n Kubernetes Getting Started (*https://oreil.ly/OlxOU*) documentation as well as on my prior experience with c7n.

Now that we have configured and activated c7n, let's explore how Kubernetes policies work with the custodian CLI.

Policies

As I mentioned in the chapter introduction, c7n policies are written in YAML. The YAML lexicon is based on the c7n Kubernetes schema that we saw in "Installation" on page 316. If we look at the Pod schema, we can see the c7n filters and actions available for Pods:

```
# c7n Kubernetes Pod policy schema
$ c7n schema k8s.pod
k8s.pod:
  actions:
  - auto-label-user
  - delete
  - event-label
  - label
  - patch
  - webhook
  filters:
  - event
  - list-item
  - reduce
  - value
```

At a high level within c7n policies, filters are used to select (filter out or filter in) resources. For example, the following policy, based on c7n documented samples, filters out Pods to select only those with the condition `metadata.labels.test=c7n`; this policy takes no action on selected resources:

```
# collect Pods policy
policies:
  - name: collect-pods
    description: |
      Collects pods with label test:c7n
    resource: k8s.pod
    Filters:  ❶
      - type: value
        key: metadata.labels.test
        value: c7n
```

❶ Pods that are labeled `test=c7n` will be selected.

To test the preceding policy, we can quickly start a pause Pod in the minikube cluster with the following command and then run the policy to collect information about the Pod:

```
# start pause Pod in default namespace
$ kubectl run pause --image=registry.k8s.io/pause:3.1 --labels=test=c7n

# run no-action c7n policy to collect information
$ c7n run --output-dir=output policies/collect-pods.yaml
--cache-period 0 -v
2023-07-02 22:33:16,795: custodian.policy:INFO policy:collect-pods
resource:k8s.pod region: count:1 time:0.04
```

In the preceding c7n run command, the output is verbose, the files generated by c7n are sent to the relative *output* directory, and the c7n cache is disabled.

When c7n runs, it creates three output files, as shown in the following tree command:

```
# c7n output files
$ tree -L 1 output/collect-pods
output/collect-pods
├── custodian-run.log
├── metadata.json
└── resources.json
```

C7n uses a default cache value that is set to 15 minutes to cut down on API calls and data traffic. The -f CACHE, --cache CACHE arguments can set the cache file, and the default path on MacOS is *~/.cache/cloud-custodian.cache*.

While the cache can improve c7n's operational performance, disabling the cache ensures that your policies are working with the latest resources. This is especially important when prototyping and testing policies.

The *custodian-run.log* contains policy run logs. Multiple runs are kept in the run log. The run logs for two of the test runs are shown in the following console output:

```
# c7n run logs
2023-07-02 22:33:16,795 - custodian.policy - INFO -
policy:collect-pods resource:k8s.pod region: count:1 time:0.04
2023-07-02 22:39:14,659 - custodian.policy - DEBUG -
Running policy:collect-pods resource:k8s.pod region:default c7n:0.9.28
2023-07-02 22:39:14,661 - custodian.k8s.client - DEBUG -
connecting to https://127.0.0.1:64679
2023-07-02 22:39:14,700 - custodian.resources.pod - DEBUG -
Filtered from 8 to 1 pod  ❶
2023-07-02 22:39:14,700 - custodian.policy - INFO -
policy:collect-pods resource:k8s.pod region: count:1 time:0.04
2023-07-02 22:39:14,701 - custodian.output - DEBUG -
metric:ResourceCount Count:1 policy:collect-pods restype:k8s.pod
Scope:policy
```

❶ Selected Pods were filtered from eight down to one.

The run log provides the cluster address to which the c7n CLI connected. C7n uses the local kubectl config to connect. The run log also indicates that the filter reduced the collected Pods from eight to one, and the log gives the policy execution duration (time) in seconds.

The *metadata.json* file describes the c7n policy run. This file includes settings from the command line as well as actual properties of the run:

```
// metadata.json file
{
  "policy": {
    "name": "collect-pods",
    "description": "Collects pods with label test:c7n\n",
    "resource": "k8s.pod",
    "filters": [
      {
        "type": "value",
        "key": "metadata.labels.test",   ❶
        "value": "c7n"
      }
    ]
  },
  "version": "0.9.28",
  "execution": {
    "id": "b74ef210-6225-41f2-84cf-7a87fc363958",
    "start": 1688353712.7711701,
    "end_time": 1688353712.8165162,
    "duration": 0.04534602165222168   ❷
  },
  "config": {
    "region": "",
    "regions": [],
    "cache": "~/.cache/cloud-custodian.cache",
...
    "dryrun": false,
...
    "configs": [
      "policies/collect-pods.yaml"
    ],
...
    "verbose": 1,
    "quiet": null,
    "debug": false,
    "skip_validation": false,
    "command": "c7n.commands.run",
...
  "metrics": [
    {
      "MetricName": "ResourceCount",
```

```json
      "Timestamp": "2023-07-02T23:08:32.815644",
      "Value": 1,
      "Unit": "Count"
    },
    {
      "MetricName": "ResourceTime",
      "Timestamp": "2023-07-02T23:08:32.815652",
      "Value": 0.043942928314208984,
      "Unit": "Seconds"
    },
    {
      "MetricName": "ActionTime",
      "Timestamp": "2023-07-02T23:08:32.816502",
      "Value": 3.814697265625e-06,
      "Unit": "Seconds"
    }
  ]
}
```

❶ These filters were used to select Pods.

❷ This object indicates execution time.

The *resources.json* file describes the resources that were selected by c7n based on filter settings supplied in the policy YAML. This file is most familiar to Kubernetes users as it is created by querying the Kubernetes API. The following example is part of an actual file:

```
// resources.json file
[
  {
    "api_version": null,
    "kind": null,
    "metadata": {
      ...
      "labels": {
        "app": "test",
        "billing": "lob-cc",
        "env": "dev",
        "owner": "jimmy",
        "test": "c7n"          ❶
      },
      ...
      "name": "test-pod-1",    ❷
      "namespace": "policy-test",   ❸
      ...
    },
    "spec": {
      ...
      "containers": [
        {
```

```
…
            "image": "registry.k8s.io/pause:3.1",    ❹

…
    "c7n:MatchedFilters": [
      "Metadata.labels.test"      ❺
    ]
…
```

❶ This label was found on the Pod.

❷ The Pod name is test-pod-1.

❸ The Pod namespace is policy-test.

❹ This is the container image.

❺ This filter was used to select the Pod(s).

You may have noticed that while the items in the *resources.json* resemble the Kubernetes API object schema, item names use a more Python-like snake case (*https://oreil.ly/_mjGW*) instead of the traditional Kubernetes camel case (*https://oreil.ly/_Wmb3*).

With no-action policies, you can gather information about resources using the c7n policy language and Kubernetes schema without taking any action. In the past, I have used this approach for reporting. It's also kind of like a dry-run feature. For example, you could craft policies with no actions to help you gauge the impact of new policies by collecting info about resources selected by filters.

Next, let's look at policies with actions.

Policies with Actions

Now that we have seen how c7n uses filters to select resources, we can add actions to mutate resources in a Kubernetes cluster. The following policy is used to delete pods with the metadata.labels.test=c7n filter:

```
# delete Pods policy
policies:
  - name: delete-pods
    description: |
      Deletes pods with label test:c7n
    resource: k8s.pod
    filters:
      - type: value
        key: metadata.labels.test
        value: c7n
    Actions:      ❶
      - type: delete
```

❶ An action to delete selected Pods has now been added.

To test this policy with our existing pause container in the `policy-test` Namespace, we will first use the `dryrun` flag so that no actions are taken against the selected resources; using the `dryrun` flag is another way to determine the impact of new policies:

```
# dry-run of policy to delete Pods
$ custodian run -d --output-dir=output policies/delete-pods.yaml
--cache-period 0 -v    ❶
2023-07-02 23:53:07,904: custodian.resources.pod:DEBUG Filtered
from 8 to 1 pod
2023-07-02 23:53:07,904: custodian.policy:INFO policy:delete-pods
resource:k8s.pod region: count:1 time:0.05
2023-07-02 23:53:07,905: custodian.policy:DEBUG dryrun:
skipping actions    ❷
2023-07-02 23:53:07,905: custodian.output:DEBUG metric:ResourceCount
Count:1 policy:delete-pods restype:k8s.pod scope:policy
```

❶ The command includes -d to run in the dry-run mode.

❷ Actions were skipped in dry-run mode.

In the preceding output, c7n indicated that actions were skipped due to the dry-run setting.

If we remove the dry-run setting, then the policy action will execute and delete the selected Pod(s):

```
# run policy to delete Pods
$ custodian run --output-dir=output policies/delete-pods.yaml
--cache-period 0 -v
```

Now that we have run two policies, we can see how c7n arranges the output files based on our *output* directory setting and policy names:

```
# tree of output files
$ tree output
output
├── collect-pods
│   ├── custodian-run.log
│   ├── metadata.json
│   └── resources.json
└── delete-pods
    ├── custodian-run.log
    ├── metadata.json
    └── resources.json
```

The policy execution applied the filter to select one Pod from eight Pods and then deleted that selected Pod. The following file output indicates that two calls to the cluster were made during the policy execution:

```
# c7n run log
2023-07-03 00:02:03,442 - custodian.policy - DEBUG - Running
policy:delete-pods resource:k8s.pod region:default c7n:0.9.28
2023-07-03 00:02:03,444 - custodian.k8s.client - DEBUG -
connecting to https://127.0.0.1:64679
2023-07-03 00:02:03,495 - custodian.resources.pod - DEBUG -
Filtered from 8 to 1 pod  ❶
2023-07-03 00:02:03,496 - custodian.policy - INFO -
policy:delete-pods resource:k8s.pod region: count:1 time:0.05
2023-07-03 00:02:03,500 - custodian.k8s.client - DEBUG -
connecting to https://127.0.0.1:64679
2023-07-03 00:02:03,526 - custodian.policy - INFO -
policy:delete-pods action:delete resource resources:1
execution_time:0.03
2023-07-03 00:02:03,526 - custodian.output - DEBUG -
metric:ResourceCount Count:1 policy:delete-pods restype:k8s.pod  ❷
```

❶ Selected Pods were filtered from eight down to one.

❷ One Pod was deleted.

With classic c7n policies, Kubernetes users use the c7n CLI to report and take action on Kubernetes resources. Now, let's explore how we can use c7n policies to learn more about how c7n represents different resources.

Discovery with Policies

C7n policies can be used to discover how resource object schemas are represented in c7n. When I was writing this chapter, I reached out to the c7n community about writing a Pod policy that detected when the container securityContext element was missing. I received feedback that reminded me of how I used c7n in previous projects to learn more about the c7n object model for specific resources.

To use this approach, I wrote a Pod policy with no filters or actions. That coarse-grained policy is listed in the following YAML:

```
# coarse-grained Pod policy
policies:
  - name: get-all-pods
    description: |
      Collects all pods.
    resource: k8s.pod
```

The preceding policy includes no filters or actions, and it was simply run to collect resource data about all the disparate Pods in my minikube cluster. Once I had the resources file, then I reviewed the object model to see where the Pod-level and container-level securityContexts were and how they were represented.

As it turns out, as shown in the following listing, the c7n model refers to the Pod securityContext as `spec.security_context` and `spec.containers[].security_context`:

```
// securityContext in c7n k8s.pod
...
    "containers": [
      {
...
        "image": "registry.k8s.io/pause:3.1",
        "image_pull_policy": "IfNotPresent",
...
        "security_context": null,
...
      }
    ],
...
    "security_context": {
      "fs_group": null,
      "fs_group_change_policy": null,
      "run_as_group": null,
      "run_as_non_root": null,
      "run_as_user": null,
      "se_linux_options": null,
      "seccomp_profile": null,
      "supplemental_groups": null,
      "sysctls": null,
      "windows_options": null
    },
...
```

Armed with new information, I was able to craft a policy—again, with help from the c7n community—to detect Pods where the Pod spec and containers did not have a securityContext element. To do this, I needed to know that securityContext was called security_context in the c7n_kube resources schema:

```
# c7n policy to filter on Pod where containers are missing the
securityContext element
policies:
  - name: security-context-pods
    resource: k8s.pod
    filters:
      - type: value
        key: metadata.labels.test     ❶
        value: c7n
      - type: value
        key: spec.security_context     ❷
        value: empty
```

```
- type: list-item    ❸
  key: spec.containers[]
  attrs:
    - type: value
      key: security_context
      value: empty
```

❶ This filter selects Pods by label.

❷ This filter selects Pods missing the securityContext element at the Pod level.

❸ This filter selects Pods missing the securityContext element at the container level.

In Kubernetes, both Pods and containers can have securityContext elements. Some of the Pod securityContext fields overlap the container securityContext fields. When they do, values in the container securityContext override the Pod securityContext values. When checking container securityContexts fields that overlap with Pod securityContext fields, you must check both the Pod and the containers fields. Not checking both may lead to false violations.

With the preceding policy, I selected all the Pods in the cluster where at least one container is missing the securityContext element and the test=c7n label is present. To operationalize this approach, I could add actions and additional policy logic to check not only for missing elements but also for incorrectly configured child elements. I could even add logic to reverse filters:

```
# c7n policy to filter on Pod where containers are not missing the
securityContext element
policies:
  - name: security-context-pods
    resource: k8s.pod
    filters:
      - type: value
        key: metadata.labels.test
        value: c7n
      - type: list-item
        key: spec.containers[]
        attrs:
          - not:
            - type: value
              key: security_context
              value: empty
```

In the preceding policy, I added a logical NOT function to reverse the filter and collect Pods that do not have empty securityContext elements at the container level.

Finally, I added the patch action to the policy to label and annotate the Pods when their containers did not have securityContext elements:

```
# label and annotate Pods with missing container-level securityContext elements
policies:
  - name: security-context-pods
    description: |
      Collects pods with no container securityContext element.
    resource: k8s.pod
    filters:
      - type: value
        key: metadata.labels.test
        value: c7n
      - type: list-item
        key: spec.containers[]
        attrs:
          - type: value
            key: security_context
            value: empty
    actions:
      - type: patch      ❶
        options:
          metadata:
            labels:
              'compliance-issue': 'sec-con-missing'
            annotations:
              'compliance-issue': >
                        One or more containers are missing the
                        securityContext element.'
```

❶ Actions are defined to patch (mutate) the Pod with labels and annotations.

The preceding policy labeled and annotated the Pods as shown in the following console output:

```
# labeled and annotated Pods
$ kubectl -n policy-test get po test-pod-1 -oyaml
apiVersion: v1
kind: Pod
metadata:
  annotations:
    compliance-issue: One or more containers are missing the securityContext element.
  ...
  labels:
    app: test
    billing: lob-cc
    compliance-issue: sec-con-missing
    env: dev
    owner: jimmy
    test: c7n
  ...
```

In this section, we built c7n_kube policies and applied them with the c7n CLI. We examined the files generated by c7n policy runs and used them to learn more about the c7n_kube schema and object model in order to write more policies.

In the next section, we will run c7n policies in controller mode with a traditional Kubernetes dynamic admission controller.

Controller Mode

The controller mode of the c7n Kubernetes provider (c7n-kube) is somewhat different from what we have seen in past solutions. Even though the c7n-kube uses Kubernetes dynamic admission controllers, it uses only the mutating webhook configuration; no validating webhook configuration is installed.

Installation

When I first started to use controller mode, I ran into an issue where the c7n docs seemed to be outdated. I was using the Helm installation, and the example values file in the docs did not match the current JSON schema (*https://oreil.ly/aXDHc*) for the values file, so I used the values file from the GitHub repository with edits of my own:

```
# c7n-kube controller mode helm install values
certManager:
  enabled: yes        ❶
  issuer:
    create: yes
  certificate:
    create: yes
    name: "{{ .Release.Name }}-issuer"

controller:
  annotations: {}
  create: true
  image: cloudcustodian/c7n:0.9.35.0     ❷
  name: "{{ .Release.Name }}
  onException: warn
  port: 8443
  replicas: 1

pod:
  annotations: {}
  labels:
    app: c7n_kube
  name: "{{ .Release.Name }}"

policies:        ❸
  configMap:
    name: "{{ .Release.Name }}-policies"
    policies:
```

```
      - name: 'warn-all-pods'
        resource: 'k8s.pod'
        mode:
          type: k8s-admission
          on-match: warn
          operations:
            - CREATE
            - UPDATE
      - name: missing-required-labels-pods
        mode:
          type: k8s-admission
          on-match: deny
          operations:
            - CREATE
            - UPDATE
        description: |
          The following labels are required on all pods:

          app
          billing
          env
          owner
        resource: k8s.pod
        filters:
          - or:
            - metadata.labels.app: absent
            - metadata.labels.billing: absent
            - metadata.labels.env: absent
            - metadata.labels.owner": absent

  source: configMap

service:
  create: true
  name: "{{ .Release.Name }}"
  port: 8443

webhook:
  create: true
  failurePolicy: Ignore    ❹

  namespaceSelector:       ❺
    matchExpressions:
    - key: policy
      operator: In
      values: ["enabled"]

  rules:
  - apiGroups:
    - '*'
    apiVersions:
    - 'v1'
```

```
operations:
- CREATE
resources:
- pods          ⑥
```

❶ Cert Manager is used to create the TLS certs needed for the secure communication between the Kubernetes API server and the webhook service.

❷ The c7n Kubernetes controller image is defined.

❸ Policies to be loaded with the controller installed are defined.

❹ The webhook is configured to ignore failures and allow changes if the webhook call is not successful.

❺ The Namespace selector is set to an opt-in model using Namespace labels.

❻ This webhook only monitors Pod resources.

Using the preceding values file, I installed two policies:

- *Warn* on all Pods created or updated. This is noisy and really only used for examples.
- *Deny* all Pods that do not have the required labels.

These examples are related to the examples (*https://oreil.ly/k-bfT*) found in the c7n-kube documentation. Both policies use `type: k8s-admission` to use the policy in controller mode.

In my opinion, policies installed with the controller installation should be limited to cluster-wide policies. These policies should be relatively mature and generally needed for all—or at least most—clusters.

The webhook uses a Namespace selector where the webhook will only service API server requests for resources in Namespaces with the `policy=enabled` label. It is also set to a default of 10 seconds, like solutions we have reviewed from previous chapters.

When installing c7n-kube, I had to decide how I would create the TLS certificate and key as well as the webhook certificate authority bundle. In past examples, like in Chapter 5, I created my own TLS artifacts and manually inserted them. This time, I decided to use a more automated approach with cert-manager (*https://cert-manager.io*) and c7n-kube integration. As I have done in previous chapters, I wrapped the install and uninstall processes with shell scripts:

```
# up.sh
#!/usr/bin/env bash

# error handling
set -e
trap 'catch $? $LINENO' ERR
catch() {
  if [ "$1" != "0" ]; then
    echo "Error $1 occurred on $2"
  fi
}

KUBECTL="kubectl"
NS=${1:-c7n-kube}

read -p "Do you wish to install certmanager?" yn
yn=${yn:-n}
case $yn in
    [Yy]* ) ${KUBECTL} apply -f \
    https://github.com/cert-manager/cert-manager/releases/download/\
    v1.12.0/cert-manager.yaml
    sleep 120    ❶
esac

read -p "Do you wish to install/update the namespace?" yn
yn=${yn:-n}
case $yn in
    [Yy]* ) ${KUBECTL} apply -f k8s/0-ns.yaml
esac

helm install c7n-kube c7n/c7n-kube -n $NS \
--create-namespace --values values.yaml
```

❶ Allow cert-manager time to initialize before proceeding.

The preceding *up.sh* shell script automates the installation of the cert-manager application to be used with c7n-kube. I paused the script for two minutes to allow time for the cert-manager to boot up and be ready to issue.

The *down.sh* script uninstalls c7n-kube, with the option to also remove cert-manager:

```
# down.sh
#!/usr/bin/env bash

# error handling
set -e
trap 'catch $? $LINENO' ERR
catch() {
  if [ "$1" != "0" ]; then
    echo "Error $1 occurred on $2"
  fi
}
```

```
KUBECTL="kubectl"
NS=${1:-c7n-kube}

# ${KUBECTL} config set-context --current --namespace=$NS

helm -n $NS uninstall c7n-kube

# ${KUBECTL} delete mutatingwebhookconfiguration c7n-admission

read -p "Do you wish to delete the namespace? " yn
yn=${yn:-n}
case $yn in
    [Yy]* ) ${KUBECTL} delete -f k8s/0-ns.yaml --ignore-not-found
esac

read -p "Do you wish to uninstall cert manager? " yn
yn=${yn:-n}
case $yn in
    [Yy]* ) ${KUBECTL} delete -f \
    https://github.com/cert-manager/cert-manager/releases/download/\
    v1.12.0/cert-manager.yaml --ignore-not-found
esac
```

Now that we can install and uninstall c7n-kube, let's look at running policies.

Validating Policies

Once I installed the c7n-kube controller, I tested the validating policies with the following Namespace and Pod manifests; please note the labels:

```
# test manifests
apiVersion: v1
kind: Namespace
metadata:
  name: policy-test
  labels:
    app: test
    billing: lob-cc
    env: dev
    owner: jimmy
    policy: enabled
---
apiVersion: v1
kind: Pod
metadata:
  name: test-pod-1
  namespace: policy-test
  labels:
    test: c7n
spec:
  containers:
```

```
- name: c1
  image: registry.k8s.io/pause:3.1
  imagePullPolicy: Always
```

The preceding Namespace is labeled with `policy=enabled`, which configures API server requests to be sent to the c7n-kube webhook. This is the opt-in model.

With the two policies installed and the webhook configuration created, tests using the preceding manifests created the following output:

```
# test results
$ kubectl apply -f test
namespace/policy-test created
Warning: warn-all-pods:
Error from server: error when creating "test/k8s-manifest.yaml":
admission webhook "admission.cloudcustodian.io" denied the request:
Failed admission due to policies:[{"name": "missing-required-labels-pods",
"description": "The following labels are required on all
pods:\n\napp\nbilling\nenv\nowner\n"}]
```

As seen in the preceding output, creating a new Pod triggered a warning from c7n-kube, and since the Pod was not labeled correctly, Pod creation was denied. As a point of reference, both policies were applied. And, if you are following closely, you noticed that no validating admission controller was installed and configured. The mutating webhook handled the validating policies. Though nonstandard, it is a clean solution.

Now, let's explore how we can update the c7n-kube controller with mutating policies.

Mutating Policies

As of the time of this writing, c7n-kube does not support all mutating use cases. For example, the patch action that we used earlier in CLI mode is not supported. That being said, I modified the policies originally installed with the c7n-kube controller by editing the c7n-kube-policies configmap in the c7n-kube Namespace:

```
# mutating policies
policies:
  - name: 'auto-label-userinfo'     ❶
    resource: 'k8s.pod'
    mode:
      type: k8s-admission
      on-match: allow
      operations:
        - CREATE
        - UPDATE
    filters:
      - type: value
        key: metadata.labels.test
        value: c7n
    actions:
```

```
      - type: auto-label-user
        key: owner
  - name: 'label-on-op'        ❷
    resource: 'k8s.pod'
    mode:
      type: k8s-admission
      on-match: allow
      operations:
        - CREATE
        - UPDATE
    filters:
      - type: value
        key: metadata.labels.test
        value: c7n
    actions:
      - type: event-label
        labels:
          touched-by: c7n-kube
```

❶   Label Pods with user info.

❷   Label Pods that were touched by c7n-kube.

After replacing the policies in the configmap, I had to recycle the c7n-kube controller
by deleting the controller Pod. This loaded the policy changes into the policy engine.

 Instead of editing the configmap in place and deleting the c7n-kube Pod, I could have edited the *values.yaml* file and reinstalled the c7n-kube application with Helm.

I then ran the same test and updated the touched-by and owner labels in the Pod. The
c7n-kube controller logs indicated that the Pod was mutated with a JSONPatch:

```
# c7n-kube controller logs for mutating with JSONPatch
2023-07-06 02:48:01,466: c7n_kube.server:INFO {"apiVersion":
"admission.k8s.io/v1", "kind": "AdmissionReview", "response":
{"allowed": true, "warnings": ["warn-all-pods:"],
"uid": "941139c2-03a4-4b92-8110-cdac2d6922d5", "status": {"code": 200,
"message": "OK"}, "patchType": "JSONPatch", "patch":
"W3sib3AiOiAiYWR…"}}
```

The applied policy updated labels in the Pod resource as long as the Pod was already
labeled with test=c7n:

```
# mutated Pods with metadata.labels
$ kubectl -n test get po test-pod-1 -o=jsonpath='{.metadata.labels}'
{"owner":"minikube-user","test":"c7n","touched-by":"c7n-kube"}
```

Applying policies in controller mode is similar to CLI mode; filters and actions can be used to select resources and apply changes to selected resources. Controller mode also uses Kubernetes dynamic admission controllers, as we have seen with other PaC solutions.

Next, let's explore c7n-kates, the c7n-kube server that handles Kubernetes API server requests from inside and outside the Kubernetes cluster.

c7n-kates

C7n-kates is the Python-based c7n server that handles Kubernetes API server requests via dynamic admission control webhooks. When I installed the c7n-kube controller into my cluster, the c7n-kube deployment in the `c7n-kube` Namespace specified the `c7n-kates` command in the Pod specification:

```
# c7n-kube Pod specification
...
spec:
  containers:
  - args:
    - --host=0.0.0.0
    - --port=8443
    - --policy-dir=/policies
    - --on-exception=warn
    - --endpoint=/mutation
    - --cert=/cert/tls.crt
    - --ca-cert=/cert/ca.crt
    - --cert-key=/cert/tls.key
    command:
    - c7n-kates
    image: cloudcustodian/c7n:latest
...
```

C7n-kates can actually run outside of Kubernetes. In fact, though I haven't touched on it much in this book, you can point your dynamic admission control webhook configurations to servers external to your cluster. This is usually done when the application connected by the admission control webhook cannot run in the cluster or is already deployed, supporting other use cases outside of the cluster or across multiple clusters. Prototyping and troubleshooting could be another reason why you run an admission-service application outside the cluster. However, given how time-sensitive request execution is for Kubernetes admission control, you usually run an internal (to the cluster) admission control service.

AuthZ decisions—Kubernetes, API services, or otherwise—are usually time-sensitive use cases. For that reason, it is generally a best practice to keep the policy decision point as close to the policy enforcement point as possible. This concept is illustrated in the Distributed Authorization System Netflix Case Study (*https://oreil.ly/U3mpL*).

The following command shows how to launch the c7n-kates server at a command prompt, outside the cluster, to handle admission:

```
# start c7n-kates
$ c7n-kates --host 10.0.2.2 --port 8443 --policy-dir policies \  ❶
--on-exception warn --endpoint https://c7n-admission:8443/mutation \
--cert config/secrets/server.crt \
--cert-key config/secrets/server.key \
--ca-cert config/secrets/ca.crt \
--generate > ext-webhook.yaml  ❷
```

❶ The c7n-kates server is started outside of the Kubernetes cluster.

❷ The optional `generate` flag is used to create the Kubernetes manifest needed to configure the webhook to connect to the c7n-kates server.

The 10.0.2.2 IP address is a special alias to the local loopback address that I introduced in Chapter 3 and that I routinely use when I need to connect something running in a virtual machine to a service running outside of the virtual machine. I had to use this alias to connect the minikube cluster, running in Docker, to the external c7n-kates server running on my local machine, outside of Docker. The *c7n-admission* host name is mapped in my */etc/hosts* file.

Adding the `--generate` command is optional and is used to generate the Kubernetes manifest to configure the API server to call the external c7n-kates server. The following Kubernetes manifest was created:

```
# generated webhook configuration
apiVersion: admissionregistration.k8s.io/v1
kind: MutatingWebhookConfiguration
metadata:
  labels:
    app.kubernetes.io/component: AdmissionController
    app.kubernetes.io/instance: c7n-kates
    app.kubernetes.io/managed-by: c7n
    app.kubernetes.io/name: c7n-kates
    app.kubernetes.io/part-of: c7n_kube
    app.kubernetes.io/version: 0.2.27
```

```
      name: c7n-admission
webhooks:
- admissionReviewVersions:
  - v1
  - v1beta1
  clientConfig:
    caBundle: LS0tLS1CRUdJT…
    url: https://c7n-admission:8443/mutation  ❶
  failurePolicy: Fail
  name: admission.cloudcustodian.io
  rules:
  - apiGroups:
    - ''
    apiVersions:
    - v1
    operations:
    - CREATE
    - UPDATE
    resources:
    - pods
    scope: '*'
  sideEffects: None
```

❶ The c7n-admission host name is used to reach the c7n-kates server and is mapped in the machine's */etc/host* file.

In the preceding webhook config, I had to manually add the `clientConfig` element.

I created the TLS artifacts—self-signed certs—that allow the Kubernetes API server to communicate securely with the c7n-kates server using the following script and server configuration file:

```
# generate-tls.sh
#!/usr/bin/env bash

trap 'catch $? $LINENO' ERR
catch() {
  echo "Error $1 occurred on $2"
}

SERVER_CONF_DIR=${1:-"server"}
SECRETS_DIRECTORY="secrets"

if [ ! -d "$SERVER_CONF_DIR" ]; then
  echo "$SERVER_CONF_DIR not found, process aborted"
  exit 99
fi

if [ ! -d "$SECRETS_DIRECTORY" ]; then
  mkdir -p $SECRETS_DIRECTORY
fi
```

```
rm -f $SECRETS_DIRECTORY/*

openssl genrsa -out $SECRETS_DIRECTORY/ca.key 2048
openssl req -x509 -new -nodes -sha256 -key $SECRETS_DIRECTORY/ca.key \
-days 365 -out $SECRETS_DIRECTORY/ca.crt -subj /CN=admission_ca 2>&1

openssl genrsa -out $SECRETS_DIRECTORY/server.key 2048

openssl req -new -key $SECRETS_DIRECTORY/server.key -sha256 -out \
$SECRETS_DIRECTORY/server.csr -subj /CN=c7n-admission \
-config $SERVER_CONF_DIR/server.conf 2>&1

openssl x509 -req -days 365 -in $SECRETS_DIRECTORY/server.csr -sha256 \
-CA $SECRETS_DIRECTORY/ca.crt -CAkey $SECRETS_DIRECTORY/ca.key \
-CAcreateserial -out $SECRETS_DIRECTORY/server.crt -days 100000 -extensions \
v3_ext -extfile $SERVER_CONF_DIR/server.conf

# server configuration file
[ req ]
prompt = no
req_extensions = v3_ext
distinguished_name = dn

[ dn ]
CN = c7n-admission    ❶

[ v3_ext ]
basicConstraints = CA:FALSE
keyUsage = nonRepudiation, digitalSignature, keyEncipherment
extendedKeyUsage = clientAuth, serverAuth
subjectAltName = DNS:c7n-admission    ❷
```

❶ The TLS common name should match the server's DNS name.

❷ The server's subjectAltName (*https://oreil.ly/jljNV*) is required and is mapped to
   TLS common name and the server's DNS name.

I tested the webhook configuration with connectivity to the external server. The following logs are from c7n-kates, running external to the cluster and applying mutating
policies:

```
# c7n-kates mutation log
10.0.2.2 - - [09/Jul/2023 20:03:27] "POST /mutation?timeout=10s HTTP/1.1"
200 - 2023-07-09 20:03:27,681: c7n_kube.server:INFO {"apiVersion":
"admission.k8s.io/v1", "kind": "AdmissionReview", "response": {"allowed":
true, "warnings": ["warn-all-pods:"], "uid":
"e623ea31-d500-4208-bb16-d7cd5a08088f", "status": {"code": 200, "message":
"OK"}, "patchType": "JSONPatch", "patch": "W3sib3AiOiAiY…"}}
```

With c7n-kates, you can run a server internal or external to Kubernetes to handle
mutating and validating admission control calls from the Kubernetes API server.

Summary

Cloud Custodian (c7n) is a very mature OSS project that has been used as a cloud computing PaC solution for more than seven years. Its Kubernetes solutions are relatively new. However, for those of us who embrace cloud native technologies—straddling cloud computing and Kubernetes—c7n offers solutions that we can leverage without switching tools or languages.

The c7n-kube tool leverages the existing mature CLI tools and Python ecosystem while at the same time introducing a new Kubernetes policy language schema. The new Kubernetes schema is underpinned by the existing policy schemas that reduce the overall learning curve.

The c7n-kube tools are not as mature as the overall c7n project. At times, I struggled with the documentation, which lacked depth and did not match the codebase. However, the c7n community and project contributors are strong, and my requests for help were answered quickly.

C7n-kates supports the dynamic admission controller solution that we saw with other Kubernetes PaC tools. However, c7n-kates can also run external to Kubernetes clusters. This adds an additional degree of freedom for admission control that could actually work across multiple clusters. This is similar to Open Policy Agent, covered in Chapter 5.

Unlike other Kubernetes PaC solutions, and contrary to accepted Kubernetes standards, c7n-kube does not use a separate validating admission controller. Both validating and mutating policy types are handled by the same c7n-kates service by default. That being said, you can change this by installing multiple c7n-kates services in the same cluster and setting the webhook configurations as needed to segment the traffic.

One of the hallmarks of a mature Kubernetes PaC solution is how complete and thorough the project documentation is and how easy it is for users and developers alike to use that documentation to learn about the solution and solve problems with it. Another big part of maturity emerges from the number of examples and the use cases the examples solve. I think this is where c7n for Kubernetes can mature the most.

If we consider the selection criteria given in Chapter 1 again, as a Kubernetes PaC solution, c7n leverages its project maturity and community depth. The learning curve is not as bad as with other solutions if you already have experience with c7n. And the Python codebase is easy to understand. That being said, the Kubernetes policy support has some maturing to do, compared to some of the other solutions we have seen.

I started using c7n more than seven years ago, building controls for AWS cloud computing. Shortly thereafter, I began my Kubernetes journey and stopped using c7n as much. Using c7n for Kubernetes admission control is like working with a colleague you haven't seen in years. I am excited to see how the c7n-kube tools mature and provide the same deep functionality that I have come to appreciate from the c7n cloud computing tools.

Next, in Chapter 11, we are going to leave Kubernetes behind for a while and focus on infrastructure as code and how PaC solutions solve issues in this space.

PaC and Infrastructure as Code

We spent the last several chapters exploring how PaC is used with Kubernetes. We investigated several solutions in the context of the PaC selection criteria I introduced in Chapter 1. My goal in the Kubernetes chapters was to present solutions that you can evaluate and from which you can choose the best fit for your needs. Each solution has pros and cons, and I personally think some solutions are better—more mature and functional—than others. However, the decision is yours, and I have given you a starting point from which to make those decisions.

In this chapter, we start to look past Kubernetes to other PaC use cases, and we will begin with how PaC improves infrastructure as code (IaC) practices. This chapter will primarily focus on IaC in AWS.

Before we completely abandon Kubernetes, I want to make sure that you remember the most important part of Kubernetes PaC solutions: the API server request flow.

The Kubernetes API server request flow—introduced in Chapter 4 and illustrated in Figure 11-1—is the most powerful aspect of Kubernetes PaC solutions, as it provides a native means by which preventive controls are applied to Kubernetes clusters.

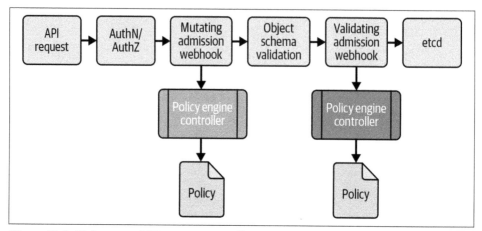

Figure 11-1. Kubernetes API server request flow

With its mutating and validating webhooks integrated to PaC solutions, the Kubernetes API server request flow applies the well-known patterns of data input translation and validation before any data is persisted. These patterns are at least as old as the original client-server models from the 1980s; moreover, I used them when I built Lotus Notes and Domino applications in the 1990s and early 2000s.

While I don't want to belabor the point of input translation and validation, I mean to be purposefully conspicuous about this functionality and how important it is for building preventive (as opposed to detective or reactive) controls. This preventive stance is relatively unique across platforms and systems. As we move forward to explore IaC and how PaC is applied to IaC, we will discuss preventive, detective, and reactive controls as well as how—unlike with Kubernetes—preventive controls in IaC are mostly accomplished with nonnative implementations, upstream from where resources are applied by IaC.

Before we dive into how PaC can be used with IaC, let's define and explore *infrastructure as code* and understand why it is so important to modern infrastructure deployment and management.

Infrastructure as Code

In Chapter 1, I introduced the concept of everything as code (EaC) and described how this concept has transformed how we define and apply resources and policies as machine-readable code artifacts. In doing so, we reuse the successful code-management tools and techniques that we have used for years, such as configuration management and version control systems like Git (*https://git-scm.com*), as we would with other *-as-code artifacts.

IaC (*https://oreil.ly/4mSQG*) enables us to provision and manage datacenter-type resources in a testable, auditable, and reproducible manner as if we were deploying any other application stack. IaC is popular because it is human and machine readable, and it focuses on specific platforms and ecosystems. Although IaC is generally associated with cloud computing and CSPs, it also works with bare-metal resources (*https://oreil.ly/UQ6Ul*). As I mentioned in Chapter 1, there are tools, like Tinkerbell (*https://tinkerbell.org/docs*), that facilitate the provisioning of bare-metal servers.

Now, let's explore one of the best practices of IaC: immutability.

Immutability

IaC both disrupted and transformed how we manage infrastructure, especially cloud computing infrastructure. We now commonly use automated CI/CD and GitOps pipelines and workflows to manage our infrastructure. This transformation allowed us to embrace the known best practice of immutable infrastructure (*https://oreil.ly/BDQgq*), a.k.a. immutability.

When you follow the best practice of immutable infrastructure, you do not change an infrastructure resource once it is deployed. This does not mean that the resource can never be modified—it just shouldn't be modified in place. If a resource needs to be changed, you change the underlying IaC artifacts for the resource, resulting in a new version of the resource. You then use the new version to replace the existing version. This is contrary to infrastructure-management operations we did before, like patching servers in place.

In cloud native computing, we use the concept of immutable infrastructure to detect and prevent unwanted or unauthorized changes, such as drift, primarily brought on by manual changes. For example, before IaC, we used to build servers from the bottom up, starting with the operating system (OS). Then, we would configure the OS, install and configure utilities and libraries, and add the application stack. We then focused on keeping the servers running and patching them as needed.

Before IaC, most of the work was manual. Over time, we automated some tasks with scripts; then, we moved to tools like Puppet (*https://www.puppet.com*) and Chef (*https://www.chef.io*), overlaying additional automation that could be choreographed with DevOps pipelines and server-side scheduling, such as cron (*https://oreil.ly/yfPU3*). The automated processes would use tools like Chef and Puppet or custom scripts to compare current server configurations to previously defined states. Server processes would periodically "wake up" and check configurations. If current configurations drifted from the originally defined configurations, the tools would correct the situation, remediating the drift, and then sleep until the next check interval.

Drift is not just the result of manual changes. Drift can also come from applying incorrect IaC artifacts. Over time, IaC artifacts and tools age and even rot. Tools change, and code becomes outdated. Incorrect changes in the form of outdated and potentially conflicting code can cause unwanted variability, leading to drift.

Complexity of environments can also lead to drift. These environments include not only the stacks for target infrastructure but also the automation tools used to deliver IaC changes. If complexity is not properly managed and segmented or compartmentalized, then unwanted changes can leak across environmental boundaries and lead to drift.

Both the configuration of new servers and the drift detection and correction of existing servers relied on changing server configurations with tools and checking the configuration against target settings. This approach introduced variability and was plagued by outages and server interruptions. We needed a better way, and this led to the realization that baking is better than frying when working with IaC. Let's see why.

Baking Versus Frying

The concept of baking versus frying simplifies the distinction between starting with a known good and complete configuration—in the form of an image or IaC file—and using it to build a new resource, as opposed to creating an incomplete resource and then changing it until the desired configuration state is reached. The idea of starting with the known good image is called *baking*—baking in everything that is needed for the resource. Conversely, *frying* describes the scenario where we start with the minimum needed to provision a resource, and then we add to it until we are satisfied with the outcome. This is like frying a dish and adding ingredients until we are satisfied with the taste. The terms *baking* and *frying* mostly apply to compute and container resources.

Eventually, we matured and documented our practices to use known good and complete images and configurations, thereby reducing the frying we did and relying more on baking. The more frying we were able to eliminate, the more drift and errors we avoided, and the closer to immutability we reached. As we did less frying (local configuration), we realized that compute resources were less important, at least less so than the overall application stack. While in the past we measured success by server uptime metrics, we now measure success by application availability, infrastructure and application performance, security, and reduction of drift and vulnerabilities, all of which lead to better user experiences.

Now that we have explored IaC immutability, let's look at the two types of IaC: imperative and declarative.

Imperative and Declarative IaC

When you define the steps your code will take to change a program's state, which will accomplish a desired goal, you are programming imperatively. In the context of IaC, we imperatively program using programming languages like Java, Go, Python, and TypeScript, underpinned by SDKs. In the context of CSPs, SDKs provide language-specific libraries that call APIs to provision and interrogate CSP infrastructure and build applications.

The following code snippet is an example (*https://oreil.ly/ZiwCa*) of using the AWS Golang SDK to get an Amazon Elastic Container Registry (ECR) client object and then list images from a source ECR repository:

```
# Go SDK ECR Ops
ecrClient := ecr.NewFromConfig(cfg)

input := &ecr.ListImagesInput{
    RepositoryName: aws.String(REPO),
}

resp, err := ecrClient.ListImages(context.TODO(), input)
if err != nil {
    log.Fatal(err)
    return
}

fmt.Println("Listing tags in ", aws.String(REPO))
for _, img := range resp.ImageIds {
    fmt.Println("Digest: ", *img.ImageDigest)

    if img.ImageTag != nil {
        //Added to prevent trying to dereference nil pointer for untagged images
        fmt.Println("Tag: ", *img.ImageTag)
    }
}
```

SDKs are very helpful when you need to build an application in a specific programming language and that application needs to interact with managed services, like those from CSPs.

Declarative programming is often used to manage resource state. When you write your code in a structured data language like JSON or YAML, and you define the desired state of the resources you wish to manage, you are programming declaratively. Programming declaratively requires a processing layer to apply the changes defined in the code.

The following YAML is an example of declarative programming, using code to define the state of an Amazon Elastic Kubernetes Service (EKS) cluster based on the eksctl (*https://eksctl.io*) YAML lexicon:

```
# eksctl cluster definition
---
apiVersion: eksctl.io/v1alpha5
kind: ClusterConfig

metadata:
  name: test-cluster
  region: us-west-2
  version: "1.23"
  tags:
    owner: jimmy
    env: dev
    billing: lob-cc

iam:
  withOIDC: true

secretsEncryption:
  keyARN: "arn:aws:kms:us-west-2:123456789012:key/…" #eks-secrets-uw2

vpc:
  id: "vpc-..."
  cidr: "192.168.0.0/16"
  subnets:
    private:
      private-1:
        id: "subnet-..."
        cidr: "192.168.0.0/20"
        az: us-west-2a
      private-2:
        id: "subnet-..."
        cidr: "192.168.16.0/20"
        az: us-west-2b
      private-3:
        id: "subnet-..."
        cidr: "192.168.32.0/20"
        az: us-west-2c
    public:
      public-1:
        id: "subnet-..."
        cidr: "192.168.48.0/20"
        az: us-west-2a
      public-2:
        id: "subnet-..."
        cidr: "192.168.64.0/20"
        az: us-west-2b
      public-3:
        id: "subnet-..."
        cidr: "192.168.80.0/20"
        az: us-west-2c
  clusterEndpoints:
    publicAccess: true
```

```
    privateAccess: true

cloudWatch:
  clusterLogging:
    enableTypes: ["*"]

addons:
  - name: vpc-cni
    version: latest
    attachPolicyARNs:
      - arn:aws:iam::aws:policy/AmazonEKS_CNI_Policy
  - name: kube-proxy
    version: latest
  - name: coredns
    version: latest
```

The preceding YAML is processed by the eksctl CLI to build an Amazon EKS cluster
with a specific AWS Virtual Private Cloud (VPC) configuration.

> The YAML processed by the eksctl CLI actually results in addi-
> tional AWS CloudFormation (CFN) YAML, which is then pro-
> cessed and applied by the eksctl CLI to AWS CFN to provision
> Amazon EKS cluster resources in an AWS account.

In this section, you have learned that the main difference between imperative and
declarative IaC programming is the idea of how and why state is managed. In imperative programming, program state is managed by defining the steps your code executes. In declarative programming, the state of resources—under management—is
defined in the code and then processed by processors like eksctl and AWS CFN.

> It's important to realize that imperative and declarative program-
> ming models are not always mutually exclusive. With the advent of
> the AWS Cloud Development Kit (CDK) (https://oreil.ly/cdk),
> imperative and declarative programming models are combined to
> manage IaC resources. With the AWS CDK, you write imperative
> code that is then used to output declarative code to be processed by
> the AWS CFN service. For more information on this approach,
> see this blog post (https://oreil.ly/UKXGo) I wrote and this example
> Git repository (https://oreil.ly/SUj0n) I created in support of the
> blog post.

Numerous IaC languages and tools are in use today. Depending on your needs and
the environment in which you are deploying and managing infrastructure, you might
use a declarative approach with JSON or YAML or an imperative approach with your
favorite programming language and SDKs. We use JSON and YAML because of the

human and machine readability of each language as well as the different lexicons that are available when using these languages.

JSON and YAML are also used as substrates for DSLs. DSLs are highly specific languages built to abstract the specialization through lexicons that are focused on specific problem domains. The preceding eksctl YAML is a DSL, as is the lexicon used in AWS CFN templates written in JSON or YAML.

In the next section, I cover another very important reason to use an IaC declarative approach with JSON and YAML. Using declarative JSON and YAML more easily enables IaC validation with PaC solutions.

Applying PaC to IaC

We use PaC to apply controls—security, compliance, governance, FinOps, and best practices—to IaC resources and processes. These controls are usually arranged into three categories:

Detective

Detective controls record and catalog noncompliant issues. These controls are usually aggregated and radiated, and they are used as notifications for awareness and further disposition.

Preventive

Preventive controls are used as "guardrails" and are most effective at stopping noncompliant behaviors and enforcing best practices because they are embedded within the system or platform being controlled, a.k.a. the system under change. Preventive controls are also directly triggered by system events and prevent changes from happening before they change the state of the system.

Reactive

Reactive controls are similar to both preventive and detective controls. They are used to avoid or record noncompliant changes or behaviors, and their application is triggered by internal system events. However, the reactive-control event triggers occur after the system changes have been made and the system state has been modified. Reactive controls become more effective as their time to react to system events decreases. In fact, reactive controls that react within single-digit seconds, or subseconds, can present as preventive controls to end users.

It's important to realize that PaC control types are not always mutually exclusive. For example, a reactive control—reacting to a system event trigger—doesn't have to modify or undo the changes to the system that triggered the event. Instead, the reactive control might just notify system users, maintainers, or incident responders. The reactive control might also radiate the event information by cataloging the event into a centralized security information and event management (SIEM) (*https://oreil.ly/VVmEk*) system. In this mode, the reactive control is functioning as a detective control.

A reactive control might also take very little time to react. If a reactive control responds within two to three seconds or even within subsecond timing, the reactive control acts like a preventive control from a UX perspective. For example, if I implemented a reactive control that terminates a compute instance—created with a public IP address or an unencrypted storage volume—and that control responds with subsecond timing, then the compute instance is terminated in near real time, before users can use it or it can be compromised by bad actors.

As I progress through this chapter, I will primarily focus on preventive controls. Let's start with using OPA for IaC preventive controls.

Preventive Controls

When we use declarative IaC, we can easily apply PaC tools to validate the declarative code artifacts. In fact, regardless of the approach we use, we can use PaC tools to validate any JSON or YAML file. For example, given the preceding eksctl example, we can use the OPA CLI, which I introduced in Chapter 2, to evaluate the eksctl YAML configuration:

```
# eksctl cluster YAML
apiVersion: eksctl.io/v1alpha5
kind: ClusterConfig

metadata:
  name: test
  region: us-east-2
  version: "1.22"
  tags:
    owner: jimmyray
    env: dev
    billing: lob-cc

iam:
  withOIDC: true

secretsEncryption:
  keyARN: "arn:aws:kms:us-east-2:123456789012:key/9e23ba0e…"
```

I wrote the following OPA policy to verify the Amazon EKS version and the AWS Region for cluster creation operation:

```
# eks-cluster.rego
package examples.ch11

import rego.v1

allowed_violations := 0
```

```
allowed_versions := {"1.26", "1.27"}

allowed_regions := {"us-east-1", "us-west-2"}

default allow := false

allow if {
        count(violation_versions) + count(violation_region) <= allowed_violations
}

violation_versions contains msg if {
        input.kind == "ClusterConfig"
        not input.metadata.version in allowed_versions

        msg := sprintf("invalid EKS version, version must be in %q",
    [allowed_versions])
}

violation_region contains msg if {
        input.kind == "ClusterConfig"
        not input.metadata.region in allowed_regions

        msg := sprintf("invalid region, region must be in %q", [allowed_regions])
}
```

In the preceding Rego policy, the `allow` block assignment counts the number of violations from the multiple `violation` block assignments. If the violation count is less than or equal to the `allowed_violations`, the Rego policy sets the `allow` assignment to `true`.

Linting Rego with Regal

To help me write better Rego, I used Styra's Regal tool (*https://oreil.ly/QpS9W*). Regal is the official Rego linter, created by Styra and provided to the community as open source software (*https://oreil.ly/AVt7x*). The preceding policy was linted with Regal and formatted with the `opa fmt` command, mostly because Regal pointed out that I should.

I ran Regal on a previously unlinted version of the preceding policy, and it found the following issues:

```
# Regal lint of eks-cluster policy
$ regal lint policies/unlinted/eks-cluster.rego -c ../.regalcongif.yaml
Rule:          opa-fmt
Description:    File should be formatted with `opa fmt`
Category:       style
Location:       policies/unlinted/eks-cluster.rego
Documentation: https://docs.styra.com/regal/rules/style/opa-fmt
```

```
Rule:          use-contains
Description:   Use the `contains` keyword
Category:      idiomatic
Location:      policies/unlinted/eks-cluster.rego:14:1
Text:          violation[msg] {
Documentation: https://docs.styra.com/regal/rules/idiomatic/use-contains

Rule:          use-contains
Description:   Use the `contains` keyword
Category:      idiomatic
Location:      policies/unlinted/eks-cluster.rego:21:1
Text:          violation[msg] {
Documentation: https://docs.styra.com/regal/rules/idiomatic/use-contains

Rule:          use-if
Description:   Use the `if` keyword
Category:      idiomatic
Location:      policies/unlinted/eks-cluster.rego:10:1
Text:          allow {
Documentation: https://docs.styra.com/regal/rules/idiomatic/use-if

Rule:          use-if
Description:   Use the `if` keyword
Category:      idiomatic
Location:      policies/unlinted/eks-cluster.rego:14:1
Text:          violation[msg] {
Documentation: https://docs.styra.com/regal/rules/idiomatic/use-if

Rule:          use-if
Description:   Use the `if` keyword
Category:      idiomatic
Location:      policies/unlinted/eks-cluster.rego:21:1
Text:          violation[msg] {
Documentation: https://docs.styra.com/regal/rules/idiomatic/use-if

Rule:          use-rego-v1
Description:   Use `import rego.v1`
Category:      imports
Location:      policies/unlinted/eks-cluster.rego:1:1
Text:          package examples.ch11
Documentation: https://docs.styra.com/regal/rules/imports/use-rego-v1

1 file linted. 7 violations found.
```

It's also important to understand that just because Regal can find issues—with many rules enabled by default—you don't have to use those rules; you can ignore them or even lessen their severity. The following Regal config file snippet illustrates how you can set levels—error, ignore, warning—as well as ignore files, like unit-test Rego files:

```
# Regal config file example
rules:
  idiomatic:
```

```
  use-some-for-output-vars:
    level: error
    ignore:
      files:
        - "*_test.rego"
  no-defined-entrypoint:
    level: ignore
style:
  prefer-some-in-iteration:
    level: error
    ignore:
      files:
        - "*_test.rego"
  todo-comment:
    level: warning
  line-length:
    max-line-length: 100
    level: warning
  opa-fmt:
    level: error
    ignore:
      files:
        - "*_test.rego"
```

Regal uses this config file to customize the linting experience. If the file is not found, then Regal defaults are used. As seen in the preceding command example, `-c ../.regal/config.yaml` specifies where to find my Regal configuration file.

Regal also includes IDE support. Figure 11-2 shows three Regal linter indications in VS Code, via the OPA VS Code extension (*https://oreil.ly/rohrT*).

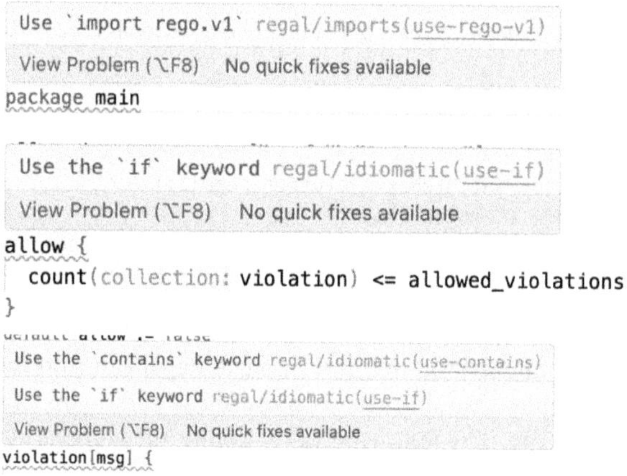

Figure 11-2. Regal support via the OPA VS Code extension

The following OPA CLI exec command validates the OPA input document *eks-cluster.yaml*. It uses the *examples/ch11/allow* decision path, which returns only the result of `true` or `false`:

```
# Apply OPA policy
$ opa exec --bundle policies/linted --decision "examples/ch11/allow" \
iac-resources/eks-cluster.yaml
{
  "result": [
    {
      "path": "iac-resources/eks-cluster.yaml",
      "result": false
    }
  ]
}
```

If I wanted to return more information in the result, like the actual error messages, then I would generalize the OPA exec decision argument by changing the command to omit the */allow* decision path component:

```
# generalizing the decision path to expose more information
$ opa exec --bundle policies/linted --decision "examples/ch11" \
iac-resources/eks-cluster.yaml
{
  "result": [
    {
      "path": "iac-resources/eks-cluster.yaml",
      "result": {
        "allow": false,
        "allowed_regions": [
          "us-east-1",
          "us-west-2"
        ],
        "allowed_versions": [
          "1.26",
          "1.27"
        ],
        "allowed_violations": 0,
        "violation": [
          "invalid EKS version, version must be in \"[\\\"1.26\\\", " +
          "\\\"1.27\\\"]\"",
          "invalid region, region must be in \"[\\\"us-east-1\\\", " +
          "\\\"us-west-2\\\"]\""
        ]
      }
    }
  ]
}
```

With more information in the result, we see that the the JSON output indicates two errors:

- An incorrect Amazon EKS version was specified.
- An incorrect AWS Region was specified.

To get the most value from this validation, the `opa exec` command would execute as part of automation—upstream preventive control—that occurs before the execution of the eskctl command. This implies a shift-left approach in an automated DevSec-Ops pipeline. This shift left is necessary as the IaC declarative code processor—in this case, the eksctl CLI—has little facility for validating user-supplied values in the YAML file. It mostly checks syntax.

As shown in Figure 11-3, the eksctl template validation happens before the eksctl call to AWS CFN—the system under change. While this is technically considered a preventive control, the control decision point is outside of the platform or system under change. This is different from how we used mutating and validating webhooks—preventive controls—in Kubernetes, and this is common to most CSPs.

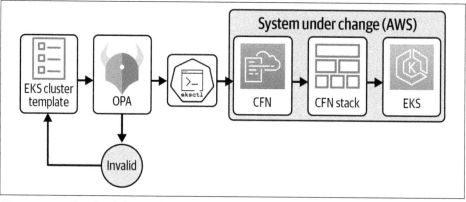

Figure 11-3. Eksctl validation flow

In the next section, we will explore the Conftest solution to simplify the DevSecOps pipeline automation using convention over configuration (*https://oreil.ly/4u-gJ*).

Conftest

While I like the OPA CLI `exec` command for pipeline automation, there is another approach that simplifies the use of OPA policies for this type of validation. Conftest (*https://oreil.ly/conftest*), an OPA project, was built to add convenience when running Rego policies against structured configuration data. When I use Conftest, I try to run it with default conventions, thereby using convention over configuration; this simplifies the use of Rego policies to validate inputs.

If we change the Rego package from *examples.ch11* to just *main*, and we place the policy in the default *policy* directory, we can then simplify the approach using the following example `conftest` command:

```
# conftest using default conventions
$ conftest test iac-resources/eks-cluster.json
FAIL - iac-resources/eks-cluster.json - main - invalid EKS version, version
must be in "[\"1.26\", \"1.27\"]"
FAIL - iac-resources/eks-cluster.json - main - invalid region, region
must be in "[\"us-east-1\", \"us-west-2\"]"

2 tests, 0 passed, 0 warnings, 2 failures, 0 exceptions
```

With default Conftest conventions, we have to specify only the source IaC file to be validated as part of the `conftest test` command. Conftest locates the policy in the default *policy* folder and uses the default *main* package. This convention-over-configuration approach reduces the decisions we need to make when executing the command.

For a better machine-readable JSON output, I added the `-o json` argument:

```
# conftest with JSON output
$ conftest test iac-resources/eks-cluster.json -o json

[
    {
        "filename": "iac-resources/eks-cluster.json",
        "namespace": "main",
        "successes": 0,
        "failures": [
            {
                "msg":
        "invalid EKS version, version...
        ...must be in \"[\\\"1.26\\\", \\\"1.27\\\"]\""
            },
            {
                "msg":
        "invalid region, region must be in...
        ...\"[\\\"us-east-1\\\", \\\"us-west-2\\\"]\""
            }
        ]
    }
]
```

We could still use Conftest without the defaults, using configurations instead of conventions. For example, if we're using OPA policies that are already specifically packaged and pathed, we just need to specify two more arguments. The following console output shows the same command with no defaults:

```
# conftest with no defaults
$ conftest test iac-resources/eks-cluster.json -p policies/linted \
-n examples.ch11 -o json
```

The -n and -p arguments supply the policy namespace (package) and the policy directory path, respectively.

Users choose how they want to run Conftest, via explicit arguments or implicit conventions. This flexibility ensures that Conftest fits multiple use cases and scenarios. Since Conftest is based on OPA, it can validate JSON or YAML. That means that whatever needs to be validated must already exist as, or be converted to, JSON or YAML. In the next section, we will explore another preventive approach that uses Checkov to validate AWS CFN.

Checkov and cfn-lint

According to the project documentation, Checkov (*https://oreil.ly/checkov*) is a static code analysis tool for IaC as well as a software-composition tool. When it comes to validating IaC, Checkov is similar to other PaC tools that can prevent unwanted behaviors. Checkov includes a CLI that makes it compatible with automation.

Checkov is written in Python, and the policies, known as *checks*, are Python based as well. I installed Checkov using Homebrew (*https://brew.sh*). Checkov installed with many policies already included. The Checkov project also includes an index (*https://oreil.ly/tkFsL*) of current policies.

To test the viability of Checkov as an AWS CFN PaC solution, I chose to test the following policy: CKV_AWS_260—Ensure no security groups allow ingress from 0.0.0.0:0 to port 80. At the time of writing, this policy was listed in the AWS policy index (*https://oreil.ly/ZgnbC*).

To test the policy, I wrote a short AWS CFN template to create a VPC and then a SecurityGroup with an ingress that opens the quad-zero IP address—0.0.0.0/0—to HTTP port 80. The following snippet includes the AWS CFN SecurityGroup definition:

```
# SG to allow port 80 inbound from anywhere
  Port80OpenSG:
    Type: "AWS::EC2::SecurityGroup"
    Properties:
      GroupDescription: Allow port 80 inbound from anywhere
      SecurityGroupIngress:
        - CidrIp: 0.0.0.0/0
          Description: Allow port 80 inbound from anywhere
          FromPort: 80
          IpProtocol: tcp
          ToPort: 80
      VpcId: !Ref VPC
```

I then ran Checkov with the following command to scan the *vpc.yaml* file and generate a JSON-formatted report:

```
# validate CFN template with Checkov
$ checkov -c CKV_AWS_260 -f vpc.yaml -o json > vpc-scan.json
```

With the preceding command, the Checkov scan only included the CKV_AWS_260 check. If I had excluded the -c CKV_AWS_260 argument, then the execution would have included the following checks:

```
# AWS CFN default checks
[ kubernetes framework ]: 100%|███████████████|[1/1],
Current File Scanned=vpc.yaml
[ cloudformation framework ]: 100%|███████████████|[1/1],
Current File Scanned=/vpc.yaml
[ secrets framework ]: 100%|███████████████|[1/1],
Current File Scanned=vpc.yaml
```

The following output JSON file indicates a policy failure based on the defined CKV_AWS_260 check:

```
// Checkov JSON output for CKV_AWS_260
{
    "check_type": "cloudformation",
    "results": {
        "passed_checks": [],
        "failed_checks": [
            {
                "check_id": "CKV_AWS_260",
                "bc_check_id": "BC_AWS_NETWORKING_67",
                "check_name":
                "Ensure no security groups allow ingress...
                ...from 0.0.0.0:0 to port 80",
                "check_result": {
                    "result": "FAILED",
                    "evaluated_keys": []
                },
                "code_block": [
                    [
                        251,
                        "  Port80OpenSG:\n"
                    ],
                    [
                        252,
                        "    Type: \"AWS::EC2::SecurityGroup\"\n"
                    ],
                    ...
                ],
                "file_path": "/vpc.yaml",
                "file_abs_path": "vpc.yaml",
                "repo_file_path": "/vpc.yaml",
                "file_line_range": [
```

```
            251,
            261
        ],
        "resource": "AWS::EC2::SecurityGroup.Port80OpenSG",
        "evaluations": {},
        "check_class":
        "checkov.cloudformation.checks.resource.aws.Security...
        ...GroupUnrestrictedIngress80",

        …

        "guideline":
        "https://docs.paloaltonetworks.com/content/techdocs/en_US/...
        ...prisma/prisma-cloud/prisma-cloud-code-security-policy-...
        ...reference/aws-policies/aws-networking-policies/ensure-...
        aws-security-groups-do-not-allow-ingress-from-00000-to-...
        port-80.html",
        "details": [],
        "check_len": null,
        "definition_context_file_path": null
    }
],
"skipped_checks": [],
"parsing_errors": []
},
"summary": {
    "passed": 0,
    "failed": 1,
    "skipped": 0,
    "parsing_errors": 0,
    "resource_count": 26,
    "checkov_version": "2.3.361"
},
"url": "Add an api key '--bc-api-key <api-key>' to see more detailed ...
...insights via https://bridgecrew.cloud"
}
```

With a properly formatted AWS CFN YAML file, Checkov performed as expected. However, I decided to explore what would happen if I had a syntax error in my YAML file. With the syntax error, Checkov did not seem to complete the scan correctly. The following output file indicates an issue: zero passed and zero failed. Obviously, there was an issue with the scan:

```
// Checkov scan results on file with syntax errors
{
    "passed": 0,
    "failed": 0,
    "skipped": 0,
    "parsing_errors": 0,
    "resource_count": 0,
    "checkov_version": "2.3.361"
}
```

Until now, my validations of artifacts with PaC have assumed well-formed JSON or YAML with no syntax errors. However, as we saw in the preceding output, syntax issues can lead to nondeterministic behavior in downstream tools. To avoid this, we need to lint (*https://oreil.ly/r6Vhb*) the artifacts before scanning them with PaC tools.

 We didn't see these issues in the Kubernetes PaC chapters because of the Kubernetes API server request flow depicted in Figure 11-1. That request flow includes an object schema validation step that performs a linting-like validation of the artifacts included in the inbound request.

I chose to use cfn-lint (*https://oreil.ly/cfn-lint*) to lint the AWS CFN template before scanning it for policy violations. I installed cnf-lint with Homebrew. I also had the cfn-lint extension installed in my VS Code instance so that I could detect the syntax error in my code-editing session. I used the following `cfn-lint` command to lint my AWS CFN template:

```
# cfn-lint command
$ cfn-lint -t vpc.yaml -f json

[
    {
        "Filename": "vpc.yaml",
        "Level": "Error",
        "Location": {
            "End": {
                "ColumnNumber": 28,
                "LineNumber": 255
            },
            "Path": null,
            "Start": {
                "ColumnNumber": 27,
                "LineNumber": 255
            }
        },
        "Message": "mapping values are not allowed in this context",
        "Rule": {
            "Description": "Checks for JSON/YAML formatting errors in your template",
            "Id": "E0000",
            "ShortDescription": "Parsing error found when parsing the template",
            "Source": "https://github.com/aws-cloudformation/cfn-python-lint"
        }
    }
]
```

The cfn-lint output indicated that there was an issue on line 255. The YAML syntax error was actually introduced on line 254, but if you have ever worked with YAML linters, you know that the reported line numbers are not always exact. Figure 11-4 is a screenshot of the VS Code showing that the syntax error on line 254 is reported as an error on line 255.

```
251     Port80OpenSG:
252       Type: "AWS::EC2::SecurityGroup"
253       Properties:
254       GroupDescription: Allow port 80 inbound
255 |       SecurityGroupIngress:
256         - CidrIp: 0.0.0.0/0
257           Description: Allow port 80 inbound
258           FromPort: 80
259           IpProtocol: tcp
260           ToPort: 80
261       VpcId: !Ref VPC
```

Figure 11-4. cfn-lint YAML syntax error in VS Code

IaC artifacts should be linted before they are scanned by PaC tools for validation; moreover, it's a best practice to use a separate linter before PaC tools. Even if your PaC tool catches the syntax error, a separate linter specific to the artifact type provides artifact-specific feedback to help you quickly locate and correct the problem. This process is depicted in Figure 11-5.

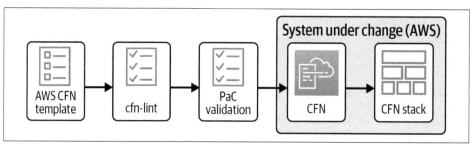

Figure 11-5. Linting IaC artifacts before PaC validation

So far, we have examined IaC PaC solutions for preventive controls that are implemented upstream of the system under change. In the next section, we will explore how we can move the PaC decision to within the system under change with AWS CFN hooks.

Although it's not covered in this chapter, AWS CloudFormation Guard (*https://oreil.ly/xLWcX*) is another AWS CFN–specific PaC tool.

CFN Hooks

If it's not yet clear, it is a best practice to make resource-validation decisions as close to the system under change or management as possible. This is a key driver behind the preventive controls implemented with the Kubernetes mutating and validating webhook functionality. Until 2022, however, the functionality to implement a preventive AWS CFN control as part of the AWS CFN request flow did not exist. Preventive AWS CFN controls involving PaC took place only inside of CI automation, upstream and out-of-band of the AWS CFN service. AWS announced CFN hooks (*https://oreil.ly/gvPXL*) in February 2022, along with a release blog post (*https://oreil.ly/Jnq9b*).

According to the AWS CFN hook user guide (*https://oreil.ly/TjY0y*), hooks are considered proactive controls. Proactive controls are preventive in nature, designed to identify problems and prevent them before they occur. When it comes to PaC, I don't normally differentiate between preventive and proactive controls. However, in its Control Tower controls documentation (*https://oreil.ly/RYaAc*), AWS differentiates between preventive, proactive, and detective controls. For AWS Control Tower, preventive controls are implemented by service control policies (SCPs) (*https://oreil.ly/ek9VU*). SCPs are used to manage AuthZ permissions; they are not used to validate IaC artifacts or events, as we have done in this chapter.

Figure 11-6 shows that the AWS CFN service calls the hook running in the AWS CFN service account. Based on the hook result, the AWS CFN stack either continues to change the AWS environment or is prevented from continuing. Once an AWS CFN stack is prevented from being created, rollback settings will define if the stack is rolled back or left in place, partially finished.

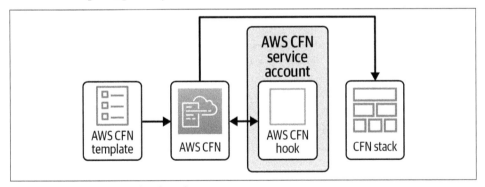

Figure 11-6. AWS CFN hook architecture

As shown in Figure 11-6, the AWS CFN hook is created and run in the AWS CFN service account, not in the AWS customer account. The CloudFormation CLI (*https://oreil.ly/C7Ez5*) is used to develop and upload the hook type to AWS CFN. This AWS blog post (*https://oreil.ly/eAgqx*) explains how to build and use hooks.

In short, the `cfn submit` command builds and registers the hook type with the private AWS CFN registry (*https://oreil.ly/wsbsT*). An example of that command builds and registers the type and sets the default version:

```
# cfn submit command
$ cfn submit --set-default
{'ProgressStatus': 'COMPLETE', 'Description':
'Deployment is currently in DEPLOY_STAGE of status COMPLETED', 'TypeArn':
'arn:aws:cloudformation:<AWS_REGION>:<AWS_ACCOUNT_ID>:type/hook/PaC-Book-Hook',
'TypeVersionArn':
'arn:aws:cloudformation:<AWS_REGION>:<AWS_ACCOUNT_ID>:type/hook/...
...PaC-Book-Hook/00000001', 'ResponseMetadata': {'RequestId':
'13daf344-bd14-4772-a842-fdb879d776d1', 'HTTPStatusCode': 200,
'HTTPHeaders': {'x-amzn-requestid': '13daf344-bd14-4772-a842-fdb879d776d1',
'date': 'Sat, 09 Sep 2023 17:33:23 GMT', 'content-type': 'text/xml',
'content-length': '657', 'connection': 'keep-alive'}, 'RetryAttempts': 0}}
Set default version to
'arn:aws:cloudformation:<AWS_REGION>:<AWS_ACCOUNT_ID>:type/hook/...
...PaC-Book-Hook/00000001
```

Once the hook type is registered with the AWS CFN private registry, you can list the type with the following AWS CLI command:

```
# AWS CLI list CFN types
$ aws cloudformation list-types
{
    "TypeSummaries": [
        {
            "Type": "HOOK",
            "TypeName": "PaC::Book::Hook",
            "DefaultVersionId": "00000001",
            "TypeArn": "arn:aws:cloudformation:<AWS_REGION>:...
            ...<AWS_ACCOUNT_ID>:type/hook/PaC-Book-Hook",
            "LastUpdated": "2023-09-09T17:33:23.094000+00:00",
            "Description": "Hook to prevent unwanted EKS changes"
        }
    ]
}
```

AWS CFN hooks are used for preinvocation of actions on target AWS resources. Hooks support three actions:

- CREATE
- DELETE
- UPDATE

For example, if I wanted to create a hook to validate Amazon EKS cluster resources before they were created, then I might build my hook to handle the CREATE action on the AWS::EKS::Cluster resource. The hook—AWS Lambda—code would handle the `preCreate` invocation, as seen in the following Python example:

```
# Python-based handler for CFN hook preCreate invocation
{
  "additionalProperties": false,
  "description": "Hook to call validate EKS cluster before CFN creation",
  "documentationUrl": "https://example.com/hooks/docs",
  "handlers": {
    "preCreate": {
      "permissions": ["secretsmanager:GetSecretValue"],
      "targetNames": [
        "AWS::EKS::*",
      ]
    }
  }
  },
  ...
  "typeName": "PaC::Book::Hook"
}
```

As you can see, `targetNames` define the AWS resource targets to be handled by the AWS CFN hook handlers. Multiple target names can be specified in each invocation handler: `preCreate`, `preDelete`, and `preUpdate`. Those target names support wildcards (*https://oreil.ly/dqybx*).

In the next section, we'll look at how PaC can be used with AWS CFN hooks.

Using PaC with Hooks

The issue that I see with AWS CFN hooks is that it is too easy to write many custom solutions for different action and resource combinations. One of the promises of PaC is to eliminate the duplicative nature of custom validation solutions. The PaC policy engine handles heavy-lifting and common protocols, using policies to apply the specific validations.

To prevent duplicative custom AWS CFN types, I recommend integrating a general-purpose PaC tool to the hook architecture to build a solution that promotes reusability and reduces duplication. When I think of domain-agnostic and general purpose PaC solutions, I immediately think of OPA to reduce the complexity of AWS CFN hooks.

The OPA pattern is documented in the OPA documentation (*https://oreil.ly/6dkLD*). This solution, depicted in Figure 11-7, uses a centralized OPA server that is called by an AWS CFN hook. This AWS CFN hook is built to handle all three AWS CFN hook invocation actions and all the AWS resources that are supported by AWS CFN hooks. Theoretically, this pattern could be modified to split AWS CFN hook target names and actions across multiple AWS CFN hooks that call the same centralized OPA instance.

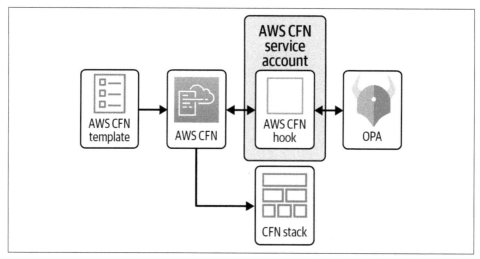

Figure 11-7. AWS CFN hook calling a centralized OPA instance for validation

As shown in Figure 11-7, the AWS hook calls an OPA server instance. In fact, this same central OPA server could serve other validations not related to the AWS CFN service. There is an example project (*https://oreil.ly/OFAXf*) developed by Styra, the creator of OPA, in GitHub for this approach.

This approach greatly reduces the number of custom AWS CFN hooks needed to handle multiple target-name and action combinations. In the past, I have built this solution using Amazon EKS to host my OPA instance so that I could take advantage of possible services offered by Kubernetes, like logging, metrics gathering, high availability, and horizontal scaling.

With a central OPA server that is called by an AWS CFN hook, we need to now consider how the hook will securely call OPA. To secure the calls to OPA, I created a secret in AWS Secrets Manager with the following commands:

```
# commands to opa_auth_token secret
$ UUID=`uuidgen`
$ echo "$UUID"
$ aws secretsmanager create-secret --name opa_auth_token \
--secret-string $UUID
{
    "ARN": "arn:aws:secretsmanager:us-east-2:123456789012:secret:...
    ...opa_auth_token-07DaVf",
    "Name": "opa_auth_token",
    "VersionId": "f040b1a3-b244-4557-89b5-b6bbf01b1b23"
}
```

```
$ export OPA_AUTH_TOKEN_SECRET="arn:aws:secretsmanager:us-east-2:123456789012\
:secret:opa_auth_token-07DaVf"
```

I started the OPA server with the AuthZ settings to use a bearer token (introduced in Chapter 2), as seen in the following console output:

```
# start OPA server with token AuthZ settings
$ opa run -s -l debug --bundle . --authentication=token \
--authorization=basic
```

As part of the bundle passed to the server, I added a simple OPA server AuthZ policy that used the UUID token I stored in AWS Secrets Manager:

```
# simple OPA AuthZ policy
package system.authz

default allow := false

allow if {
        input.identity == "661EBD6A-DB07-4CCF-B921-AB5540F668ED"
}
```

Using the OPA CFN hook project, I used the AWS CFN CLI to register the AWS CFN hook. I then used the following AWS CLI command to set the type configuration for the OPA CFN hook:

```
# set configuration items for OPA CFN hook
$ aws cloudformation --region "$AWS_REGION" set-type-configuration \
  --configuration "{\"CloudFormationConfiguration\":\
  {\"HookConfiguration\":{\"TargetStacks\":\"ALL\",\"FailureMode\":\"FAIL\",\"\
  Properties\":{\"opaUrl\": \"$OPA_URL\",\"opaAuthTokenSecret\":\
  \"$OPA_AUTH_TOKEN_SECRET\"}}}}" --type-arn $HOOK_TYPE_ARN

{
    "ConfigurationArn": "arn:aws:cloudformation:us-east-2:123456789012:...
    ...type-configuration/hook/PaC-Book-Hook/default"
}
```

The preceding command set up the registered AWS CFN hook to point to the OPA server with the opaUrl config item and use the AWS Secrets Manager secret ARN in the opaAuthTokenSecret config item. Given the code from the Styra example project, the AWS CFN hook pulled the stored secret from AWS Secrets Manager and used it as a bearer token for the OPA server. The following Python code snippet from the Styra example project shows how the handler code sets up the call to OPA by setting the Authorization header using a Python f-string expression (*https://oreil.ly/liUDM*):

```
# example project handler code snippet
    headers = {}
    secret = type_configuration.opaAuthTokenSecret
    if secret is not None and secret != "":
```

```
token = get_secret(type_configuration.opaAuthTokenSecret, session)
headers = {"Authorization": f"Bearer {token}"}
```

Leveraging the Styra example project, I applied OPA as a PaC solution to AWS CFN hooks to reduce custom hooks—what I see as the intrinsic custom nature of these AWS Control Tower proactive controls.

In the next section, we are going to switch gears from AWS CFN and use Conftest, underpinned by OPA, to validate Terraform artifacts.

Validating Terraform

HashiCorp's Terraform (*https://www.terraform.io*) is arguably the most popular cross-platform IaC tool used today. With more than a billion downloads, Terraform is used by developers worldwide across multiple CSPs and platforms, including Kubernetes. The vast and active Terraform community has contributed thousands of providers, modules, policies, and third-party integrations. These contributions are easily located by browsing the Terraform Registry (*https://registry.terraform.io*).

Terraform is based on a human- and machine-readable configuration language called HashiCorp Configuration Language (HCL) (*https://oreil.ly/hcl*). I see Terraform as a DSL, based on HCL.

The Terraform DSL

DSLs have their place; they add tremendous value in their supported domains, especially in PaC solutions. By their definitions, DSLs underpinned by programming languages will never be as flexible as the languages on which they are built. Their focus, abstraction, and "noise reduction" compose their value propositions.

While Terraform is a DSL, it's a DSL with considerable momentum, tremendous reach and community support, a rather large library of modules and providers, and a supporting ecosystem with many integrations to modern cloud native environments.

To provide the most value in this book, I have tempered my desire to introduce new concepts and ideas with the need to provide value through the utility of addressing technologies most in use with PaC today. In this chapter and the next, I focused on Terraform because of its popularity, reach, and supportive PaC solutions.

The Terraform HCL files are written into *.tf* files, as seen in the following `tree` output from my example project:

```
# Terraform project tree
$ tree
.
├── main.tf
```

```
├── terraform.tfvars
├── variables.tf
```

In the following HCL example from my project's *main.tf* file, I use a Terraform module to build Amazon EKS clusters:

```
# EKS Terraform module
module "eks" {
  source = "terraform-aws-modules/eks/aws"
  #   version = "~> 18.0"
  version = "18.30.0"

  cluster_name    = var.cluster_name
  cluster_version = var.cluster_version

  cluster_endpoint_private_access = var.cluster_endpoint_private
  cluster_endpoint_public_access  = var.cluster_endpoint_public

  ...
}
```

Now, let's explore using Conftest and Rego policies to do simple Terraform validation.

Terraform and Conftest

JSON and YAML data serialization formats are the easiest types to validate with Rego policies—actually, with PaC in general. HCL is neither JSON nor YAML. To start using OPA and Conftest to validate Terraform, we need to get a compatible output from Terraform or parse HCL into JSON. I'll start with manually parsing JSON from the Terraform plan. I used the following list of commands to generate the JSON output from the Terraform files.

First, I initialized the Terraform project to pull the Terraform modules, providers, and template files from the Terraform registry. I aliased the terraform command with tf to reduce keystrokes:

```
# initialize the project
$ tf init
```

Then, I created a Terraform plan and saved it to a binary output file:

```
# create/save Terraform plan
$ tf plan --out tfplan
```

I used my AWS account credentials in the background; Terraform needed access to my cloud account to create the directed acyclic graph (DAG) (*https://oreil.ly/O6lFz*) in memory. In the Terraform plan, the DAG is used to control how the plan is executed and prevent the cycling of commands that could result in resource duplication.

Once I had the binary Terraform plan file, I used the `terraform show` command to show the plan as JSON output and redirect the output to a *tfplan.json* file:

```
# output binary Terraform plan to JSON file
$ tf show -json tfplan > tfplan.json

$ tree
.
├── main.tf
├── terraform.tfvars
├── tfplan
├── tfplan.json
├── variables.tf
```

In the newly minted *tfplan.json* file, I focused on the Amazon EKS version and the AWS Region. I also decided to verify the Terraform version in the plan:

```
// Terraform plan (snippet) in JSON format
{
    "format_version": "1.2",
    "terraform_version": "1.5.0",
...
        "cluster_version": {
            "value": "1.25"
        },
        ...
        "region": {
            "value": "us-east-2"
        },...
```

I wrote the following OPA policy to match the Terraform plan and verify the Terraform version, the Amazon EKS cluster version, and the AWS Region:

```
# Rego policy to validate terraform JSON plan
package examples.ch11.terraform

import rego.v1

allowed_tf_versions := {"1.5.4"}

allowed_eks_versions := {"1.26", "1.27"}

allowed_regions := {"us-east-1", "us-west-2"}

default allow := false

allow if {
        count(violation) == 0
}

violation contains msg if {
        not input.terraform_version in allowed_tf_versions
```

```
        msg := sprintf("invalid Terraform version, version must be in %q",
    [allowed_tf_versions])
}

violation contains msg if {
        not input.variables.cluster_version.value in allowed_eks_versions

        msg := sprintf("invalid EKS version, version must be in %q",
    [allowed_eks_versions])
}

violation contains msg if {
        not input.variables.region.value in allowed_regions

        msg := sprintf("invalid region, region must be in %q", [allowed_regions])
}
```

Referencing the Rego policy and namespace, I executed the following Conftest command to validate the Terraform plan JSON file:

```
# Conftest command to validate Terraform JSON file
$ conftest test iac-resources/tfplan.json -p policies \
-n examples.ch11.terraform -o json
[
        {
                "filename": "iac-resources/tfplan.json",
                "namespace": "examples.ch11.terraform",
                "successes": 0,
                "failures": [
                        {
                        "msg": "invalid EKS version, version must be in ...
    ...\"[\\\"1.26\\\", \\\"1.27\\\"]\""
                        },
                        {
                        "msg": "invalid Terraform version, version must be in ...
    ...\"[\\\"1.5.4\\\"]\""
                        },
                        {
                        "msg": "invalid region, region must be in ...
    ...\"[\\\"us-east-1\\\", \\\"us-west-2\\\"]\""
                        }
                ]
        }
]
```

As you can see, I wrote the Rego policy—used to validate the Terraform plan JSON output—specifically to match the JSON structure of the Terraform plan. In this case, I focused on the "variables" portion of my plan. I wrote the Rego policy to use multiple violation rules to catch all the possible messages from the failed validations. Using the same name for all of the violation rules allowed me to easily aggregate the rule outputs.

Parsing JSON from the Terraform plan works, but it's laborious and doesn't really take advantage of Conftest's parsing abilities—arguably one of Conftest's biggest strengths. The following command parses the *terraform.tfvars* HCL file:

```
# Parse HCL with conftest
$ conftest parse terraform.tfvars
{
  "ami_type_al2": "AL2_x86_64",
  "cluster_log_types": [
    "audit",
    "api",
    "authenticator",
    "controllerManager",
    "scheduler"
  ],
  "cluster_name": "tf-test",
  "cluster_version": "1.26",
  "mng_al2_name": "tf-test-al2",
  "mng_instance_types": [
    "m5.large"
  ],
  "mng_labels": {
    "billing": "lob-cc",
    "env": "dev",
    "owner": "jimmyray"
  },
  "mng_policies": [
    "arn:aws:iam::aws:policy/AmazonEKSWorkerNodePolicy",
    "arn:aws:iam::aws:policy/AmazonEC2ContainerRegistryReadOnly",
    "arn:aws:iam::aws:policy/AmazonSSMManagedInstanceCore"
  ],
  "mng_tags": {
    "Terraform": "true"
  },
  ...
  "region": "us-east-1",
  ...
}
```

Then, I modified the Rego file to match the simplified output produced by the Conftest parser:

```
# Simplified Rego
package examples.ch11.terraform

import rego.v1

allowed_eks_versions := {"1.26", "1.27"}
```

```
allowed_regions := {"us-east-1", "us-west-2"}

default allow := false

allow if {
        count(violation) == 0
}

violation contains msg if {
        not input.cluster_version in allowed_eks_versions

        msg := sprintf("invalid EKS version, version must be in %q",
    [allowed_eks_versions])
}

violation contains msg if {
        not input.region in allowed_regions

        msg := sprintf("invalid region, region must be in %q", [allowed_regions])
}
```

The following command ran Conftest directly against the *terraform.tfvars* HCL file with an introduced AWS Region error. Conftest detected the file type and correctly parsed it into a JSON object that was then evaluated by the Rego policy:

```
# Using conftest to parse and evaluate HCL, with a github style output
$ conftest test -p policies/hcl.rego terraform.tfvars \
-n examples.ch11.terraform -o github
::group::Testing 'terraform.tfvars' against 2 policies in namespace
'examples.ch11.terraform'
::error file=terraform.tfvars::invalid region, region must be in
"[\"us-east-1\", \"us-west-2\"]"
success file=terraform.tfvars 1
::endgroup::
2 tests, 1 passed, 0 warnings, 1 failure, 0 exceptions
```

Using Conftest's inline parsing is much easier and simpler than manipulating Terraform plans manually. At the time of writing, Conftest format detection and parsing supports more than 20 file formats.

In the next section, we will explore using OPA's built-in Terraform plan features.

OPA tfplan

Of course, there are multiple ways to write Rego policies to handle Terraform—or most JSON and YAML, for that matter. The OPA documentation provides another Terraform example (*https://oreil.ly/AR5x7*) that actually coerces the OPA input document into a Terraform plan type with the following `import` statement:

```
import input as tfplan
```

Once the input document is imported as a Terraform plan, the Rego policy rules and functions can address the hierarchy of the Terraform plan based on the known Terraform HCL structure, implicitly, instead of having to explicitly traverse the generic JSON structure.

In the following example Rego policy, I imported the input JSON document as a OPA tfplan type. With this policy, I denied validation of the plan if it contained aws_iam_policy or aws_iam_role Terraform resource types:

```
# Rego policy to disallow IAM resources in Terraform plan
package examples.ch11.terraform

import input as tfplan
import rego.v1

disallowed_iam_types := {"aws_iam_policy", "aws_iam_role"}

default tfplan_allow := false

tfplan_allow if {
        count(violation_detected_iam) == 0
}

violation_detected_iam contains msg if {
        detected_iam_resources

        msg := sprintf("IAM resources cannot be used in the plan:, %q",
    [disallowed_iam_types])
}

# contributed by srenatus (styra)
detected_iam_resources if {
        some x in disallowed_iam_types
        resources[x]
}

resources contains res.type if {
        some res in tfplan.resource_changes
        res.type in disallowed_iam_types
}
```

The preceding policy uses the Terraform examples from the OPA documentation to access the tfplan document model, thereby removing the need to iterate over the entire JSON document looking for IAM types represented as matching strings. The code requires collections of resource types to select resources to iterate over and resources to trigger violations.

You may have noticed that in the preceding policy, I changed the `allow` assignment to `tfplan_allow`. Since this and prior policies are in the same namespace and would be in the same policies directory in my examples, I changed the name to deconflict any assignment collisions. Without deconflicting the default `allow` setting, I would get the following error:

```
# conflicting multiple default rules for allow
$ conftest test iac-resources/long-tfplan.json -p policies \
-n examples.ch11.terraform -o json

Error: running test: load: loading policies: get compiler: 1 error occurred:
policies/terraform.rego:11: rego_type_error: multiple default rules
data.examples.ch11.terraform.allow found
```

Another option would be to remove the duplicated `default allow := false` expression from all like-namespaced policies; however, I like to keep my example policies free of dependencies on other policies.

Styra DAS Terraform System Type

Styra, the creators of OPA, have also created a Styra DAS Terraform System Type (*https://oreil.ly/JYKPu*) that acts on Terraform **.tf* files without users first needing to convert the files to a plan and then to JSON. Styra DAS handles that input translation for users. With the Styra DAS Terraform System Type, users can either use the Styra CLI or use Terraform Cloud or Terraform Enterprise.

In addition to the Styra offerings, there is the Conftest Policy Packs GitHub project (*https://oreil.ly/CfdNb*), which includes several compliance-as-code examples, including Terraform examples.

Finally, Terraform Cloud (TFC) (*https://oreil.ly/CYbbL*) introduced the ability to use OPA policies for policy enforcement (*https://oreil.ly/ZQvYT*). Depending on your license, you can use policy sets—backed by version-control repositories—to validate tfplan and tfrun artifacts.

I tested the policy against a longer Terraform plan with `conftest test`:

```
# conftest validate no IAM in TF plan
conftest test iac-resources/long-tfplan.json -p policies \
-n examples.ch11.terraform -o json

[
        {
                "filename": "iac-resources/long-tfplan.json",
                "namespace": "examples.ch11.terraform",
                "successes": 3,
                "failures": [
                        {
```

```
                          "msg": "IAM resources detected! The following IAM ...
              ...resources cannot be used in the plan:, ...
              ...\"[\\\"aws_iam_policy\\\", \\\"aws_iam_role\\\"]\""
                      }
              ]
          }
]
```

> The Rego Playground (*https://play.openpolicyagent.org*) is very
> helpful when writing Rego policies to validate Terraform. After
> importing the Terraform plan as a JSON document in the Rego
> policy, I used Rego variables to display the plan—or parts thereof—
> in the Rego Playground Output pane. This approach makes it
> easier to discover and learn the object model of the plan.

When it comes to Terraform and OPA, you have a few choices for policy construction. As with most other policies, you can write your policy to process JSON, ignoring the implicit construction of the Terraform-plan JSON. However, the OPA project and Styra offer additional tools that specifically handle the Terraform-plan object model, thereby reducing the cognitive load of policy authoring.

Summary

IaC transformed the way we manage infrastructure, especially when it comes to cloud computing. Underpinned by IaC, we embraced best practices like immutability and baking rather than frying. These best practices reduced our reliance on individual compute resources, cementing the idea that applications and UX mattered more than individual infrastructure components, like servers that we treated as "indispensable." We now mostly treat these servers as "dispensable."

In this chapter, I focused primarily on declarative IaC, showing only a short example of imperative IaC with an AWS Golang SDK example. I also briefly mentioned the idea of combining declarative and imperative IaC using the AWS CDK. Although I have written about imperative IaC and mixed-mode IaC—declarative with imperative—in my experience, declarative code appears more in modern IaC solutions. To that end, I focused on PaC solutions to control changes made by declarative IaC.

I also introduced the types of controls that are normally seen in IaC use cases: detective, preventive, and reactive. Each control type has its own purpose. Reactive controls can function as both detective and preventive controls, given specific configurations and scenarios.

When it comes to applying PaC to IaC, the general-purpose and domain-agnostic characteristics of OPA make it a good choice for IaC validation. As I introduced in Chapter 2, the OPA exec command is well suited for automation scenarios. Additionally, I introduced you to Confest, which uses OPA's Rego policies and reduces cognitive load through the concept of convention over configuration.

We also looked at Checkov, a solution that is technically known as a static code analysis tool. I showed how it serves as a PaC solution, including many predefined policies. These predefined policies help users get started quickly and overcome the learning curve of the Python-based policies. While exercising Checkov, we discovered that it's a good practice in certain scenarios to lint declarative IaC before validating, especially when PaC validators do not include syntax checks. To that end, we saw how cfn-lint worked well to lint inbound AWS CFN templates and those templates under development in VS Code.

Following the best practice of keeping decision points close to resources being validated—systems under change—we explored AWS CFN hooks and how OPA can reduce the number of custom AWS CFN hooks.

Finally, we started down the path of using Terraform for IaC, again using OPA for validation. There are two ways to validate the exported JSON from a Terraform plan:

- Treating the plan as plain JSON and parsing the JSON with policies built for the specific JSON structure
- Importing the JSON as an OPA tfplan type and using that object model to access the defined resources

Again, Conftest eases the automated validation approach.

Keeping in mind the selection criteria discussed in Chapter 1, I purposely picked tools that I genuinely think are worth researching and that I could easily use to explain concepts. These tools have common functionality that I think fits the needs and capabilities of many organizations when it comes to PaC-based IaC validation.

In this chapter, I focused on IaC in AWS. This should come as no surprise to anyone who knows my background or who read the Preface of this book. However, I honestly think that the PaC approaches I shared are transferable to other CSPs. Coming up in Chapter 12, I will continue applying PaC to IaC, expanding on what I started in this chapter and covering different tools and CSPs.

PaC and Terraform IaC

In Chapter 11, I introduced PaC with IaC. In that chapter, I primarily focused on AWS with AWS CloudFormation and Terraform. Terraform is used beyond AWS, though, and there are other PaC tools that satisfy the requirements for well-managed and secure IaC implementations.

In this chapter, we'll continue looking at how to use Terraform for IaC while expanding PaC options. For initial continuity with Chapter 11, I will start this chapter with another AWS example. Then, I will move to a GCP example with PaC solutions.

Let's start by exploring HashiCorp Sentinel.

HashiCorp Sentinel

You learned in Chapter 11 that OPA is very effective for evaluating the JSON output of a Terraform plan. As you will see later in this chapter, several IaC tools support OPA. However, HashiCorp developed their own PaC language to validate Terraform artifacts.

According to the documentation, HashiCorp Sentinel (*https://oreil.ly/KUJQP*) was designed to be easy to use for programmers and nonprogrammers alike. I have been writing code for almost 30 years, and I find the Sentinel syntax easy to understand. With some exceptions, most languages have simple syntaxes, though; it's the lexicon and libraries that usually prove more challenging. For example, let's look at my simple Hello World example:

```
# sentinel hello world
h = "Hello"
s = " "
w = "World"

func msg(m) {
```

```
    return m + w
}

main = rule {
  print(msg(h + s))
}
```

To understand how this policy evaluates, we must first consider some Sentinel ground rules:

1. Policies are made up of rules, functions, variables, parameters, and so on.

2. All policies must have at least one rule, the `main` rule.

3. The `main` rule must have at least one operand that returns a boolean.

4. True is boolean true, zero, or zero-length collections.

5. Some functions, like `print`, return `true`.

Running the preceding code in the Sentinel Playground (*https://oreil.ly/v2cQh*) generated the following output:

```
# sentinel hello world playground output
Sentinel Result: true

This result means that all Sentinel policies passed and the protected
behavior is allowed.

1 policies evaluated.

## Policy 1: policy.sentinel (advisory)

Result: true

Print messages:

Hello World

policy.sentinel:9:1 - Rule "main"
  Value:
    true
```

The Sentinel Playground is similar to the Rego Playground, which I used in Chapter 2 and Chapter 11, as well as the Kyverno Playground from Chapter 8. The output indicates that all the policies passed and the evaluated behavior was allowed. The output also shows the return of the `main` rule in the policy as well as the `print` statement that returns `true`.

HashiCorp also supplies a Sentinel CLI (*https://oreil.ly/hTGmQ*)—previously known as the Sentinel Simulator—to apply and test Sentinel policies. The Sentinel CLI makes it very easy to use Sentinel locally. The following Sentinel CLI command applies the Hello World policy:

```
# sentinel cli apply command
$ sentinel apply hello-world.sentinel
Pass - hello-world.sentinel
```

The Sentinel CLI output indicates that the policy passed, but not much else. We can get a CLI output that is similar to that of the Sentinel Playground by using the -trace argument:

```
// Using trace for more sentinel policy information, with JSON output
{
  "error": null,
  "policies": [
    {
      "error": null,
      "policy": {
        "enforcement_level": "advisory",  ❶
        "name": "hello-world.sentinel"
      },
      "result": true,
      "trace": {
        "description": "",
        "error": null,
        "print": "Hello World\n",
        "result": true,
        "rules": {
          "main": {
            "desc": "",
            "ident": "main",
            "position": {
              "filename": "hello-world.sentinel",
              "offset": 64,
              "line": 9,
              "column": 1
            },
            "value": true
          }
        }
      }
    }
  ],
  "result": true
}
```

❶ The Sentinel enforcement level is set to advisory; the control is not mandatory.

The preceding output indicates much of the same information returned in the Sentinel Playground output pane. The JSON format was provided by the -json argument.

Now that we have some basics down, we need to go further and explore the Terraform IaC artifacts that we routinely use to manage infrastructure.

Terraform Artifacts

Like other IaC tools, we use Terraform to maintain desired states of our infrastructure. For this chapter, I moved beyond the Terraform CLI to Terraform Cloud (TFC) (*https://oreil.ly/0ZspW*). I made this move to take advantage of some of the key benefits of TFC:

- Integration to GitHub and other platforms
- Automated tools
- Environment configuration
- Referenceable and persistent data

When I created a TFC account, I created a TFC organization that contained a TFC project. The project contained a workspace that was connected to a GitHub repo that contained my IaC.

When working with TFC, you need to be aware of the following four artifacts, their contents, and their purposes:

tfplan
> As mentioned in Chapter 11, the *tfplan* is a binary file that contains the plan for how terraform will maintain state—create, read, update, or delete—IaC resources in the target environment. The tfplan indicates what Terraform is planning to do.

tfconfig
> *Tfconfig* is the data from all the *.tf* files found in your project, including those downloaded during initialization. Data in this artifact represent providers, resources, data sources, modules, and variables.

tfstate
> *Tfstate* is the recorded data that Terraform maintains and reads about infrastructure state. Tfstate is recorded after events, like a Terraform `apply`.

tfrun
> *Tfrun* contains run data from the Terraform runs, made in or connected to TFC. In the tfrun files, you'll find metadata and environment information, such as variables, workspace, and organization information.

You can write Sentinel policies to validate the four previously listed artifacts. That said, the data models for these artifacts are different and can be challenging to reproduce for prototyping and testing purposes. Let's explore how we can mock Terraform data to help us build, run, and test Sentinel policies.

Mocking Data

We write Sentinel policies to validate Terraform artifacts with specific data structures. During policy development and testing, we need a way to build and test the policies against realistic plans. When using the Sentinel Playground, sessions start with an example policy and an example data mock. This is similar to the other playground tools we explored in previous chapters.

Sentinel data mocks (*https://oreil.ly/V4-Z0*) are designed to provide the necessary data to help policy authors write effective policies that match the Terraform artifacts that the policies will be evaluating. Writing data mocks freehand is fine if you are very familiar with the Terraform artifact data structures and the data needed is lightweight. However, freehand data mocks are prone to errors. And when your Terraform artifacts grow in size, you really need a more automated and error-resistant means of generating mocked data.

To build data mocks—needed for policy testing and prototyping—I prefer to use GitHub to store my Terraform IaC, and even policies, integrated with TFC. This approach enables CI processing with TFC and other tools. I followed these steps to use TFC to generate the mock data from an existing Terraform configuration:

1. Store initialized Terraform project in a GitHub account.
2. Create a TFC account (if not already created).
3. Create a project or use the default project.
4. Create a workspace in the project using the "Version control workflow" and connect the workspace to the existing GitHub project from step 1. Use the GitHub Terraform app settings to restrict what GitHub repositories can be accessed by TFC.
5. Configure environment variables needed to access CSP accounts so that Terraform runs can connect. For more information, please see the following tip.
6. From the top-right Actions menu, choose "Start new run" and then choose "Plan only" from the pop-up menu to create only a speculative plan without applying any state changes.
7. Once the run successfully finishes, choose "Download Sentinel mocks" from the bottom left of the run details.

In the preceding example, I used static credentials as environment variables to allow my TFC workspace to access my AWS account. I used MFA for my AWS account, and I activated the key-based credentials only for the duration of my needs. After my TFC workspace no longer needed access to my AWS account, I deleted the credential environment variables and deactivated the related credentials in my AWS IAM service.

For a more secure approach, I recommend that you use TFC dynamic provider credentials (*https://oreil.ly/d9uEW*). This approach reduces the attack-surface left by static credentials. Dynamic provider credentials leverage the CSP AuthN/AuthZ/IAM services and remove a lot of the manual tasks, such as curating and rotating credential keys.

Figure 12-1 is a screenshot of a successful plan-only run I performed for this chapter.

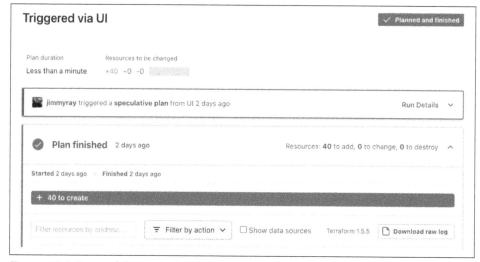

Figure 12-1. Successful speculative plan run

Once I had downloaded the mock data into my Sentinel project, I configured my policy to use the mocks using the *sentinel.hcl* configuration file, shown in the following `tree` output:

```
# Sentinel policy directory structure
$ tree
.
├── eks.sentinel
├── mocks
│   ├── mock-tfconfig-v2.sentinel
│   ├── mock-tfconfig.sentinel
│   ├── mock-tfplan-v2.sentinel
```

```
|    ├── mock-tfplan.sentinel
|    ├── mock-tfrun.sentinel
|    ├── mock-tfstate-v2.sentinel
|    └── mock-tfstate.sentinel
├── sentinel.hcl
```

 Terraform tfplan and mock data may contain sensitive data. For that reason, data should be sanitized—sensitive data removed or masked—before data is stored in code repositories.

I used the configuration file to supply the paths to the mocked data that the policy will need to reference. I also configured the policy that I wanted to execute and the respective settings:

- Policy source file path

- Policy enforcement level

- Parameters supplied to the policy for execution

The *sentinel.hcl* configuration file points to the version of the data mocked for the Terraform artifact types:

```
# sentinel.hsl policy configuration file
mock "tfplan/v2" {
  module {
    source = "./mocks/mock-tfplan-v2.sentinel"
  }
}

policy "eks" {
  source = "./eks.sentinel"
  enforcement_level = "hard-mandatory"
  params = {
    "p_eks_version" = ["1.23"],
    "p_region" = "us-east-1",
    "p_tf_version" = "1.5.5"
  }
}
```

The preceding configuration file provides the path—by version—to mocked data and the policy execution settings used by the `sentinel apply` command. The configuration file also contains configuration for the Sentinel policy, such as the Sentinel enforcement level (*https://oreil.ly/mHknP*), arguments (params) to the policy, and the source policy path.

According to the Sentinel documentation, Sentinel uses three enforcement levels:

Advisory

The policy is allowed to fail. However, a warning should be shown to the user or logged. Advisory is the default enforcement level.

Soft mandatory

The policy must pass unless an override is specified.

Mandatory

The policy must pass no matter what.

These policy enforcement levels should be applied based on the criticality of the control being implemented. Enforcement levels can also change over time as criticality changes or controls are matured, adopted, or retired.

The following policy uses the mocked data for both testing and applying the validation of the tfplan artifact, via the `import` statement:

```
# Sentinel policy using mocked data
import "tfplan/v2" as tfplan

param p_eks_version default ["1.26","1.27"]
param p_region default ["us-east-1","us-west-2"]
param p_tf_version default "1.5.5"

print("Parameters:\np_eks_version =",p_eks_version)
print("p_region =",p_region)
print("p_tf_version =",p_tf_version)
print("\nTFPlan Values:\nEKS Version =",tfplan.variables.cluster_version.value)
print("Region =",tfplan.variables.region.value)
print("Terraform Version =",tfplan.terraform_version)

var_eks_version = rule {
        tfplan.variables.cluster_version.value in p_eks_version
}

var_region = rule {
        tfplan.variables.region.value in p_region
}

tf_version = rule {
        tfplan.terraform_version == p_tf_version
}

eks_clusters = filter tfplan.resource_changes as _, resource_changes {
        resource_changes.type is "aws_eks_cluster" and
        resource_changes.mode is "managed" and
```

```
        (resource_changes.change.actions contains "create" or
            resource_changes.change.actions is ["update"])
}

managed_cluster_version = rule {
    all eks_clusters as _, aws_eks_cluster {
        aws_eks_cluster.change.after.version in p_eks_version
    }
}

managed_clusters = rule {
    length(eks_clusters) > 0
}

main = rule {
        managed_clusters and
        managed_cluster_version and
        var_eks_version and
        var_region and
        tf_version
}
```

The preceding policy uses multiple rules to validate data based on the same Amazon EKS Terraform example I used in Chapter 11. Using the mocked data and the *sentinel.hcl* file, I applied the Sentinel policy with the following sentinel apply command:

```
# sentinel apply
$ sentinel apply
Pass - eks.sentinel
```

It's great that the mocked data passed the policy validation. However, if I wanted more information, I could use the -trace argument as seen in the following example:

```
# sentinel apply with trace
$ sentinel apply -trace
No modules changed since last install

No policies changed since last install

…
Pass - eks.sentinel

Print messages:

Parameters:
p_eks_version = ["1.26"]
p_region = us-east-1
p_tf_version = 1.5.5

TFPlan Values:
EKS Version = 1.26
```

```
Region = us-east-1
Terraform Version = 1.5.5

eks.sentinel:43:1 - Rule "main"
  Value:
    true


eks.sentinel:33:1 - Rule "managed_cluster_version"
  Value:
    true


eks.sentinel:39:1 - Rule "managed_clusters"
  Value:
    true


eks.sentinel:22:1 - Rule "tf_version"
  Value:
    true


eks.sentinel:14:1 - Rule "var_eks_version"
  Value:
    true


eks.sentinel:18:1 - Rule "var_region"
  Value:
    true
```

Using the -trace argument provided additional information, including rule outcomes and print outputs (logs), that would be handy in automated attestations. For a
more machine-readable output, I could replace the -trace argument with a -json
argument.

When writing simple Sentinel policies, rules are fine; however, the Sentinel language
specification (*https://oreil.ly/gSopg*) indicates higher-level support for procedural constructs like functions and loops. In truth, I find functions to be way more powerful
than rules. Rules are simple and elegant but very restrictive.

I rewrote the preceding policy and replaced the managed_cluster_version rule with
the invalid_eks_versions function. I kept the filter to get managed cluster
resources with create and update change actions. The new function uses a for loop to
iterate through the collections of EKS clusters, collects the addresses where the EKS
cluster resources are found in the tfplan and prints information about the failed
clusters:

```
# Sentinel EKS cluster policy using function
import "tfplan/v2" as tfplan

param p_eks_version default ["1.26","1.27"]
param p_region default ["us-east-1","us-west-2"]
param p_tf_version default "1.5.5"
```

```
print("Parameters:\np_eks_version =",p_eks_version)
print("p_region =",p_region)
print("p_tf_version =",p_tf_version)
print("\nTFPlan Values:\nEKS Version =",tfplan.variables.cluster_version.value)
print("Region =",tfplan.variables.region.value)
print("Terraform Version =",tfplan.terraform_version)

var_eks_version = rule {
        tfplan.variables.cluster_version.value in p_eks_version
}

var_region = rule {
        tfplan.variables.region.value in p_region
}

tf_version = rule {
        tfplan.terraform_version == p_tf_version
}

# Validate managed EKS clusters
invalid_eks_versions = func() {
    bads = []

        eks_clusters = filter tfplan.resource_changes as _, resource_changes {
        resource_changes.type is "aws_eks_cluster" and
        resource_changes.mode is "managed" and
        (resource_changes.change.actions contains "create" or
            resource_changes.change.actions is ["update"])
        }

    for eks_clusters as address, e {
        if e.change.after.version not in p_eks_version {
                print("EKS cluster", address, "has invalid version:",
                                e.change.after.version)
                                append(bads, address)
                }
        }

    return bads
}

main = rule {
        length(invalid_eks_versions()) is 0 and
        var_eks_version and
        var_region and
        tf_version
}
```

Using a function allowed me to iterate through each incorrectly versioned cluster resource and print a log statement of the Terraform plan address for the offending cluster resource. I then added the address to a list and returned the list to the `main` rule. The new Sentinel apply output shows the differences with the new function:

```
# updated  sentinel apply output
$ sentinel apply -trace
…

Fail - eks.sentinel

Print messages:

Parameters:
p_eks_version = ["1.28"]
p_region = us-east-1
p_tf_version = 1.5.5

TFPlan Values:
EKS Version = 1.26
Region = us-east-1
Terraform Version = 1.5.5
EKS cluster module.eks.aws_eks_cluster.this[0] has invalid version: 1.26

eks.sentinel:48:1 - Rule "main"
  Value:
    false
```

The output is from a failed validation and shows the short-circuit logic used by Sentinel rules. The `main` rule has several logically ANDed boolean conditions gathered from the function and other rules in the policy. Since the first boolean condition—from analyzing the return for the function—is false, the other logically ANDed conditions don't matter and aren't executed. This logical short circuit leads to better performance.

Now that we have briefly explored locally applying Sentinel policies with mocked data using TFC, let's move on to testing Sentinel policies.

Testing

Multiple testing types apply to Terraform. You should consider the following testing types, depending on the type and size of your Terraform projects. These testing types are listed in the order that they normally appear in development and delivery:

Unit testing
    Unit testing is a form of functional testing that tests the smallest parts of your codebase that can be logically isolated and curated. When it comes to Terraform and Sentinel, the larger the project grows, the more important code modularization becomes. With modularized code, unit tests provide a means of testing isolated components in isolated scenarios.

Integration testing

When code is integrated to larger codebases, new or changed code needs to be functionally tested in the context in which it will execute within and affect the existing codebase. It must correctly work and not break existing code.

Compliance testing

Compliance testing—a.k.a. conformance testing—is a form of nonfunctional testing that ensures that code and configurations comply with and conform to rules and policies you have adopted. Compliance testing keeps your systems running between established guardrails. Compliance testing overlaps end-to-end testing, as compliance policies are applied to infrastructure applied by IaC.

End-to-end (e2e) testing

E2e testing is a form of functional testing that tests the entire system in a separate environment, exercising all defined functionality under nominal and increased loads, as a last check before the new functionality or change is released into production.

In this section, I primarily focus on compliance testing of Terraform artifacts and unit testing of Sentinel policies. However, it's important to understand that when applying the full software development lifecycle (SDLC) to Terraform projects, you will use multiple testing types.

When unit-testing Sentinel policies, I follow these best practices:

- Write policies for specific controls and behaviors.
- Use Sentinel modules (*https://oreil.ly/3E7My*) for DRY practices (*https://oreil.ly/PebVp*) to reuse and deduplicate your code.
- Use both pass and fail Sentinel tests, utilizing different data mocks.
- Use convention over configuration with consistent directory and file structures.

Testing Sentinel policies is made easier by a built-in testing framework (*https://oreil.ly/wJ2T9*) that is similar to what we saw with previous PaC tools like OPA. I usually approach Sentinel testing by simply following the file and directory conventions. In the following `tree` output, I built a typical policy project with mock data and tests:

```
# gcp storage bucket policy and test tree
.
├── common
│   └── functions.sentinel
├── mocks
│   ├── mock-tfconfig-v2.sentinel
│   ├── mock-tfconfig.sentinel
│   ├── mock-tfplan-v2.sentinel
│   ├── mock-tfplan.sentinel
│   ├── mock-tfrun.sentinel
```

```
|     ├── mock-tfstate-v2.sentinel
|     └── mock-tfstate.sentinel
├── required_labels.sentinel
├── sentinel.hcl
└── test
      └── required-labels
            ├── fail.hcl
            ├── mock-tfplan-v2-fail.sentinel
            ├── mock-tfplan-v2-pass.sentinel
            └── pass.hcl
```

Now, let's explore how to connect TFC to GCP using dynamic credentials so that we can start creating and testing policies.

Terraform cloud and GCP

To produce the mock data, I again used TFC; however, this time I used the dynamic credential provider functionality found in the Cloud Foundation Fabric (*https://oreil.ly/x7Wa0*) GitHub project. Specifically, I used a GCP Workload Identity Provider that enables external applications to use short-lived credentials provided by GPC workload identities.

To use this approach, I first logged into GCP for local development with the Application Default Credentials (ADC):

```
# gcloud login
$ gcloud auth application-default login
...
Credentials saved to file:
[/Users/me/.config/gcloud/application_default_credentials.json]

These credentials will be used by any library that requests
Application Default Credentials (ADC).
...
```

Once I logged into GCP, the local credentials were stored for my gcloud and Terraform commands to use:

```
# local credentials
$ cat /Users/me/.config/gcloud/application_default_credentials.json
{
  "client_id": "<CLIENT_ID>",
  "client_secret": "<CLIENT_SECRET>",
  "quota_project_id": "<PROJECT_ID>",
  "refresh_token": "<REFRESH_TOKEN>",
  "type": "authorized_user"
}
```

Then I used the GCP Workload Identity Provider Terraform project to install the needed credentials that would allow my TFC cloud project and workspace to use my GCP project, with the following variable settings:

```
# terraform.auto.tfvars file
billing_account                       = "<GCP_BILLING_ACCT>"
project_create                        = false
project_id                            = "<GCP_PROEJCT_ID>"
parent                                = null
tfc_organization_id                   = "org-..."
tfc_workspace_id                      = "ws-..."
workload_identity_pool_id             = "<GCP_ID_POOL>"
workload_identity_pool_provider_id    = "<GCP_ID_PROVIDER>"
issuer_uri                            = "https://app.terraform.io/"
```

Once I created the resources for external workload identity in my GCP project, I added the environment variables to my TFC workspace, as shown in Figure 12-2.

Workspace variables (5)		
Variables defined within a workspace always overwrite variables from variable sets that have the same type and the same key. Learn more about variable set precedence [link].		
Key	Value	Category
TFC_GCP_PROJECT_NUMBER		env
TFC_GCP_PROVIDER_AUTH	true	env
TFC_GCP_RUN_SERVICE_ACCOUNT_EMAIL		env
TFC_GCP_WORKLOAD_POOL_ID		env
TFC_GCP_WORKLOAD_PROVIDER_ID		env

Figure 12-2. Terraform cloud workspace environment variables

With the TFC workspace environment variables in place, I was able to use the dynamic credential provider to handshake with my GCP project as I ran speculative plans for GCP resources. Figure 12-3 shows the results of a very small plan-only run to create a Google Storage bucket.

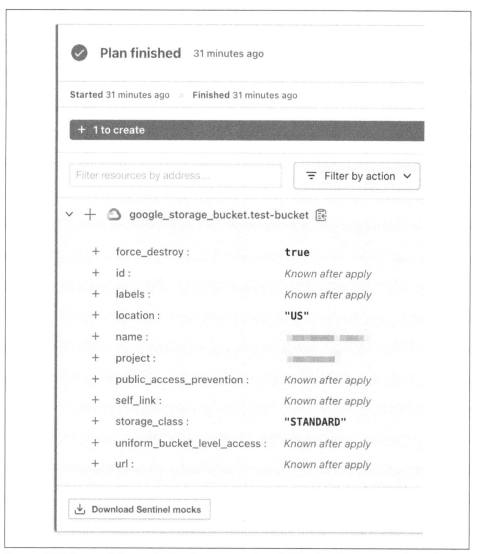

Figure 12-3. Successful speculative plan run against GCP using dynamic credentials

With a successful run, I downloaded the mocked data that the run generated. Based on the mocked data, I wrote the required-labels.sentinel policy:

```
# required-labels policy
import "tfplan/v2" as tfplan
import "types"  ❶
import "common-functions" as cf  ❷

param p_required_labels default ["billing","env","owner"]

print("Parameters:\np_required_labels =",p_required_labels,"\n")

# Validate google storage bucket labels
invalid_buckets = func() {
    bads = []

        buckets = filter tfplan.resource_changes as _, resource_changes {❸
        resource_changes.type is "google_storage_bucket" and
        resource_changes.mode is "managed" and
        (resource_changes.change.actions contains "create" or
            resource_changes.change.actions contains "update") and
        resource_changes.provider_name is "registry.terraform.io/hashicorp/google"
        }

    print("Found",length(buckets),"bucket(s)")

    for buckets as address, b {  ❹
            print("Bucket:",address,"labels =",b.change.after.labels)
        if (types.type_of(b.change.after.labels) is "undefined") or
        (not cf.list_in_list(p_required_labels,keys(b.change.after.labels))) {
            append(bads, address)
        }
    }

    return bads
}

main = rule {
        length(invalid_buckets()) is 0
}
```

❶ The types import allows me to access functions to check for "undefined" types.

❷ The common-functions import allows me to use a function I wrote— list_in_list—to compare list elements.

❸ As in previous policies, I used the filter expression to collect resources I wanted to evaluate.

❹ I then looped through the resources to perform checks.

The following `list_in_list` function checks if all the elements in list 1 are found in list 2; this allows me to check if the required label names for a resource are found in the keys list of the labels map for the changed resource:

```
# list_in_list function
import "types"

list_in_list = func(l1,l2) {
    if types.type_of(l1) is "undefined" {
        print("List 1 is undefined.")
        return false
    }

    if types.type_of(l2) is "undefined" {
        print("List 2 is undefined.")
        return false
    }

    if length(l1) is 0 {
        print("Length of list 1 is 0.")
        return false
    }

    if length(l1) > length(l2) {
        print("Length of list 1 is greater than length of list 2.")
        return false
    }

    for l1 as _, value {
        if l2 not contains value {
            print(value,"not found in list 2.")
            return false
        }
    }

    return true
}
```

The `list_in_list` function is designed with several short-circuit false returns before it has to loop through all the elements in list 1 to check if they exist in list 2. This provides a fast path to failure should the lists not be suitable for comparing.

My *sentinel.hcl* default configuration file sets up the use of the common-functions as well as the mocked data, policy source, policy enforcement level, and policy arguments:

```
# sentinel.hcl configuration file
import "module" "common-functions" {
  source = "./common/functions.sentinel"
}

mock "tfplan/v2" {
  module {
    source = "./mocks/mock-tfplan-v2.sentinel"
  }
}

policy "required-labels" {
  source = "./required-labels.sentinel"
  enforcement_level = "hard-mandatory"
  params = {
    "p_required_labels" = ["billing","env","owner"]
  }
}
```

The preceding Sentinel execution configuration allowed me to cleanly configure the needed settings to deterministically apply the desired policy while including the needed components.

Now, let's move on to testing Sentinel policies.

Building and executing Sentinel tests

I organize tests into respective directories under the *test* directory, and I use specific data mocks to drive each pass or fail test. The test subdirectories match the policy filename without the "sentinel" extension. The only difference between the two data mocks used in testing is the labels map; the pass version has the map with expected label keys and values, and the fail version does not. I used the following two test configuration files:

```
# required-labels/fail.hcl
import "module" "common-functions" {
  source = "../../common/functions.sentinel"
}

mock "tfplan/v2" {
  module {
    source = "./mock-tfplan-v2-fail.sentinel"
  }
}

test {
  rules = {
```

```
    main = false
  }
}

param "p_required_labels" {
  value = ["billing","env","owner"]
}

# required-labels/fail.hcl
import "module" "common-functions" {
  source = "../../common/functions.sentinel"
}

mock "tfplan/v2" {
  module {
    source = "./mock-tfplan-v2-pass.sentinel"
  }
}

test {
  rules = {
    main = true
  }
}

param "p_required_labels" {
  value = ["billing","env","owner"]
}
```

Just as you saw earlier in the *sentinel.hcl* configuration file—used with Sentinel `apply` commands—the pass and fail configuration files must supply any imports and mocks needed by the policy during testing. I don't need to supply the source of the policy if I follow the default directory and file-naming conventions.

From the root project directory, I simply run the `sentinel test` command, and I should see two passing tests: the fail test and the pass test:

```
# sentinel test with pass/fail mocks
$ sentinel test
PASS - required-labels.sentinel
  PASS - test/required-labels/fail.hcl
  PASS - test/required-labels/pass.hcl
1 tests completed in 20.0984ms
```

Wait a minute—the fail test passed? How is that right? Well, the mocks are built to present the fail and pass data scenarios to the respective test configurations; while the pass test is configured to look for a `true` from the `main` policy rule, the fail test is configured to seek a `false` value. Using the `-verbose` flag provides more information:

```
# sentinel test with more information
$ sentinel test -verbose
Installing test modules for test/required-labels/fail.hcl
Installing ...
  - common-functions marked for installation
 installation complete

Installing test modules for test/required-labels/pass.hcl
Installing ...
  - common-functions marked for installation
 installation complete


PASS - required-labels.sentinel
  PASS - test/required-labels/fail.hcl

    logs:
      Parameters:
      p_required_labels = ["billing" "env" "owner"]

      Found 1 bucket(s)
      Bucket: google_storage_bucket.test-bucket labels = undefined
    trace:
      required-labels.sentinel:40:1 - Rule "main"
        Value:
          false

  PASS - test/required-labels/pass.hcl

    logs:
      Parameters:
      p_required_labels = ["billing" "env" "owner"]

      Found 1 bucket(s)
      Bucket: google_storage_bucket.test-bucket labels =
      {"billing": "cc-lob", "env": "dev", "owner": "jimmy"}
    trace:
      required-labels.sentinel:40:1 - Rule "main"
        Value:
          true
1 tests completed in 28.252304ms
```

In this model, Sentinel tests are meant to pass even when the policies under test consume data designed to elicit a `false` return from the respective policy's `main` rule. This convention makes it easier for positive and negative testing scenarios.

Following conventions and slight configurations make Sentinel policy testing easier and ready for automation. To test Sentinel policies in an automated scenario, I could use the `-json` flag to output machine-readable JSON, recording the test data.

When it comes to testing Terraform, I use Sentinel policies to perform compliance testing. Testing Sentinel policies ensures that policies are correctly written to apply the desired controls on Terraform artifacts based on data contained in the artifacts.

 I don't dive deep into Terraform modules (*https://oreil.ly/VtpyP*) in this chapter; however, many organizations use modules to organize Terraform IaC into reusable and shareable components. As of Terraform v1.6.0, HashiCorp made available a new Terraform module testing framework (*https://oreil.ly/0zb5-*). You can find a detailed explanation of how to use it with AWS in this AWS DevOps Blog post (*https://oreil.ly/30OUW*).

Now, let's explore running policies in TFC.

Running Policies in TFC

So far, I have used the local Sentinel CLI to apply and test policies. In tandem with TFC, local development provides the best experience for me. However, my Terraform IaC artifacts are stored in GitHub and accessed via TFC to run speculative plans against GCP and mock data. It just makes sense that I should run policies in TFC as well.

To make that happen, TFC supports policies and policy sets (*https://oreil.ly/Ssuua*) to enable you to use Sentinel or OPA policies to evaluate your Terraform artifacts. Policies and policy sets are created at the TFC organization level. Policies are associated with policy sets, and then policy sets can be applied globally or configured to apply to projects and/or workspaces.

As a test, I created a policy—similar to the GCP bucket labels policy—and associated it with a policy set that was associated with my TFC workspace. I also had the option of loading the policies from a remote code repository, like I did with my Terraform IaC. Figure 12-4 indicates a successful plan run and a subsequent failed Sentinel policy.

Using TFC policies and policy sets unloads some of the local toil for policy execution. TFC also supports loading policies from source control repositories, like I did with Terraform IaC.

Now, let's look at additional Terraform IaC testing and tools that can make our lives easier.

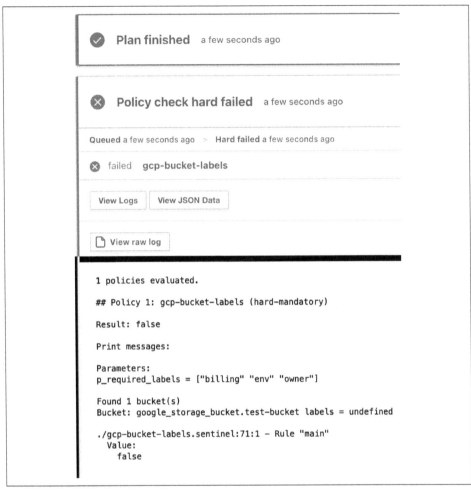

```
✓  Plan finished   a few seconds ago


✗  Policy check hard failed   a few seconds ago

Queued a few seconds ago   >   Hard failed a few seconds ago

✗  failed   gcp-bucket-labels


View Logs      View JSON Data


📄 View raw log


1 policies evaluated.

## Policy 1: gcp-bucket-labels (hard-mandatory)

Result: false

Print messages:

Parameters:
p_required_labels = ["billing" "env" "owner"]

Found 1 bucket(s)
Bucket: google_storage_bucket.test-bucket labels = undefined

./gcp-bucket-labels.sentinel:71:1 - Rule "main"
  Value:
    false
```

Figure 12-4. Failed Sentinel policy after successful plan run in TFC

Additional Terraform Validation

Part of IaC unit, integration, compliance, and e2e testing is determining that new or modified artifacts do not introduce unwanted or unsecured resources or behaviors. With Terraform, some testing requires the Terraform plan and apply commands.

The plan command will run through the entire Terraform plan, connected and authenticated to the target environment, with authorization to apply the resource changes in the plan. One could argue that creating a Terraform plan spans both unit and integration testing, after we apply upstream checks and before we apply additional downstream tools or validation policies. Compliance testing could happen before and after the plan is created.

Going further, Terraform `apply` spans integration and e2e testing. First, the very act of applying the Terraform resource changes exercises the changes in a target environment. Applying is followed by additional validation via PaC or other automated testing to verify that the resultant infrastructure changes are correct. For example, you could use tools like Cloud Custodian (*https://cloudcustodian.io*) and Prowler (*https://oreil.ly/prowler*) to police your CSP environments after an `apply` has occurred. Remember, strategies of shifting compliance left and detecting issues after IaC changes are applied are parts of a comprehensive defense-in-depth security strategy.

There are several additional tools that function upstream of Terraform `plan` and `apply` that could be alternatives or complements to Sentinel. When considering the possible tools, my criteria are:

- OSS
- Easy to install and upgrade via Homebrew, pip, and so on
- Easy to use
- Extensible
- Human- and machine-readable outputs can be produced

Given those criteria, let's look at a few solutions that can help us catch issues with our Terraform IaC before we `plan` or `apply`.

Checkov

In Chapter 11, we explored how Python-based Checkov worked to evaluate AWS CFN templates. Checkov also works on Terraform, and it is really simple to use. I used the following Checkov command to evaluate my GCP storage bucket Terraform IaC:

```
# Checkov for GCP Terraform
$ checkov -d . -o json > checkov-scan.json

# Checkov scan results
$ cat checkov-scan.json
[
    {
        "check_type": "terraform",
        "results": {
            "passed_checks": [],
            "failed_checks": [
                {
                    "check_id": "CKV_GCP_114",
                    "bc_check_id": null,
                    "check_name": "Ensure public access prevention is ...
                    ...enforced on Cloud Storage bucket",
                    "check_result": {
```

```
                    "result": "FAILED",
                    "evaluated_keys": [
                        "public_access_prevention"
                    ]
                },
                "code_block": [
                    [
                        20,
                        "resource \"google_storage_bucket\" ...
                        ...\"test-bucket\" {\n"
...
```

Checkov found the following issues:

- Check: CKV_GCP_114: "Ensure public access prevention is enforced on Cloud Storage bucket"
- Check: CKV_GCP_62: "Bucket should log access"
- Check: CKV_GCP_29: "Ensure that Cloud Storage buckets have uniform bucket-level access enabled"
- Check: CKV_GCP_78: "Ensure Cloud storage has versioning enabled"

As you learned in Chapter 11, you can write new Checkov policies, so Checkov is extensible yet hardy out of the box. You also learned in Chapter 11 that linting IaC sources was a good idea when using Checkov with AWS CFN. To that end, let's look at a linting solution for Terraform.

tflint

Tflint is a Golang-based tool that is actually a framework that uses plug-ins to add features. Out of the box, we can use tflint (*https://oreil.ly/tflint*) to lint Terraform, as seen in the following command and output:

```
# tflint of GCP Terraform IaC
$ tflint
2 issue(s) found:

Warning: terraform "required_version" attribute is required
(terraform_required_version)

  on  line 0:
   (source code not available)

Reference:
https://github.com/terraform-linters/tflint-ruleset-terraform/...
...blob/v0.4.0/docs/rules/terraform_required_version.md

Warning: Missing version constraint for provider "google" in
`required_providers` (terraform_required_providers)
```

```
on provider.tf line 15:
  15: provider "google" {}
```

```
Reference:
https://github.com/terraform-linters/tflint-ruleset-terraform/...
...blob/v0.4.0/docs/rules/terraform_required_providers.md
```

tflint auto-discovered the Terraform IaC artifacts and found two issues that can easily be fixed. There is even a `-f json` argument to produce a machine-readable output.

Let's explore another tool for Terraform IaC: terrascan.

Terrascan

Terrascan (*https://oreil.ly/terrascan*) by Tenable (*https://www.tenable.com*) is a Golang-based tool that performs static code analysis on Terraform IaC using a combination of JSON rule definitions, Rego policy language, and the OPA Golang API libraries. The following `terrascan` command produces a JSON output that indicates missing project components, such as ARM and Docker support, as well a Terraform IaC violation:

```
# terrascan output
$ terrascan scan -o json
2023/08/28 16:44:19 [DEBUG] GET
https://registry.terraform.io/v1/providers/hashicorp/google/versions
{
  "results": {
    "scan_errors": [
      {
        "iac_type": "docker",
        "directory": "/pac-book-tf-gcp",
        "errMsg": "Dockerfile not found in the directory /pac-book-tf-gcp"
      },
...

    "violations": [
      {
        "rule_name": "uniformBucketEnabled",
        "description": "Ensure that Cloud Storage buckets have uniform ...
        ...bucket-level access enabled.",
        "rule_id": "AC_GCP_0234",
        "severity": "MEDIUM",
        "category": "Identity and Access Management",
        "resource_name": "test-bucket",
        "resource_type": "google_storage_bucket",
        "module_name": "root",
        "file": "main.tf",
        "plan_root": "./",
        "line": 20
      }
    ]...
```

Terrascan applied the AC_GCP_0234 (*https://oreil.ly/0gPqS*) rule to detect the "uniform bucket-level access enabled issue" that we have seen before. Terrascan also found the following potential project-level issues:

- Dockerfile not found in the directory
- CFT files not found in the directory
- ARM files not found in the directory
- *kustomization.y(a)ml* file not found in the directory
- No Helm charts found in directory

Next, let's look at a security scanner for Terraform: tfsec.

tfsec

Tfsec (*https://oreil.ly/tfsec*) is an OSS security scanner project for Terraform from Aqua Security (*https://www.aquasec.com*), a pioneer in cloud native security. Tfsec analyzes Terraform IaC, detecting misconfigurations that could possibly lead to security issues. The following command runs tfsec on the Terraform project, including variables, and outputs machine-readable JSON:

```
# tfsec scan with variable file definition and JSON output
$ tfsec -f json --tfvars-file terraform.auto.tfvars
{
        "results": [
                {
                        "rule_id": "AVD-GCP-0066",
                        "long_id": "google-storage-bucket-encryption-customer-key",
                        "rule_description": "Cloud Storage buckets should be ...
                        encrypted with a customer-managed key.",
                        "rule_provider": "google",
                        "rule_service": "storage",
                        "impact": "Using unmanaged keys does not allow for ...
                        proper key management.",
                        "resolution": "Encrypt Cloud Storage buckets using ...
        ...customer-managed keys.",
                        "links": [
                          "https://aquasecurity.github.io/tfsec/v1.28.1/checks/...
                          google/storage/bucket-encryption-customer-key/",
                          "https://registry.terraform.io/providers/hashicorp/...
                          google/latest/docs/resources/storage_bucket#encryption"
                        ],
                        "description": "Storage bucket encryption does not ...
        ...use a customer-managed key.",
                        "severity": "LOW",
                        "warning": false,
                        "status": 0,
                        "resource": "google_storage_bucket.test-bucket",
                        "location": {
```

```
                                    "filename": "/pac-book-tf-gcp/main.tf",
                                    "start_line": 20,
                                    "end_line": 30
                            }
                    },
                    {
                            "rule_id": "AVD-GCP-0002",
                            "long_id": "google-storage-enable-ubla",
                            "rule_description": "Ensure that Cloud Storage buckets...
                            ... have uniform bucket-level access enabled",
                            "rule_provider": "google",
                            "rule_service": "storage",
                            "impact": "ACLs are difficult to manage and often lead...
                            ... to incorrect/unintended configurations.",
                            "resolution": "Enable uniform bucket level access to ...
                            ...provide a uniform permissioning system.",
                            "links": [
                                "https://aquasecurity.github.io/tfsec/v1.28.1/checks/...
                                ...google/storage/enable-ubla/",
                                "https://registry.terraform.io/providers/hashicorp/...
                                ...google/latest/docs/resources/...
                                ...storage_bucket#uniform_bucket_level_access"
                            ],
                            "description": "Bucket has uniform bucket level access ...
                            ...disabled.",
                            "severity": "MEDIUM",
                            "warning": false,
                            "status": 0,
                            "resource": "google_storage_bucket.test-bucket",
                            "location": {
                                    "filename": "/pac-book-tf-gcp/main.tf",
                                    "start_line": 20,
                                    "end_line": 30
                            }
                    }
            ]
}
```

Like the other tools, tfsec supports custom checks (*https://oreil.ly/7FrAl*) and policies using YAML, JSON, or Rego. Tfsec found the following issues on our project:

- Bucket has uniform bucket level access disabled.
- Storage bucket encryption does not use a customer-managed key.

Next, we will explore Snyk and some of its Terraform validation capabilities.

Snyk

Snyk (*https://snyk.io*) is known as a developer security platform, with a value proposition of ease of use. With Snyk, you can quickly detect and fix security vulnerabilities in multiple artifact types throughout your project code, dependencies, and deployment artifacts. As part of the Synk portfolio, the OSS Snyk CLI project (*https://github.com/snyk/cli*) provides tooling that is similar to the tools I just covered.

I created a free Snyk platform (*https://app.snyk.io*) account using my Google credentials. I then installed the Snyk CLI with Homebrew. Once the CLI finished installing, I used the snyk auth command to get platform credentials to use with the Snyk CLI—much the same way I logged into GCP earlier in this chapter.

Once I connected to my Snyk platform organization with the CLI, I used the following command to test the Terraform IaC in my GCP project:

```
# Snyk CLI IaC test
$ snyk iac test .

Snyk Infrastructure as Code

✓ Test completed.

Issues

Low Severity Issues: 3

    [Low] Object versioning is not enabled
    Info:    Object versioning is not enabled. The accidental or malicious changes
             to object will not be reversible
    Rule:    https://security.snyk.io/rules/cloud/SNYK-CC-GCP-271
    Path:    resource > google_storage_bucket[test-bucket] > versioning
    File:    main.tf
    Resolve: Set `versioning.enabled` attribute to `true`

    [Low] Logging is not enabled on storage bucket
    Info:    Logging is not enabled on storage bucket. Usage information will not
             be collected. This may impact ability to determine who accessed data
             stored in the bucket
    Rule:    https://security.snyk.io/rules/cloud/SNYK-CC-GCP-274
    Path:    resource > google_storage_bucket[test-bucket] > logging
    File:    main.tf
    Resolve: Set `logging` block attribute

    [Low] Google storage bucket does not use customer-managed keys to encrypt data
    Info:    Google storage bucket does not use customer-managed keys to encrypt
             data. Google will manage the encryption keys on its servers and could
             access the data without authorization
    Rule:    https://security.snyk.io/rules/cloud/SNYK-CC-TF-185
    Path:    resource > google_storage_bucket[test-bucket] > encryption >
             default_kms_key_name
```

```
File:    main.tf
Resolve: Use encryption keys from self-managed key management service and
         configure the `encryption` block accordingly.

Medium Severity Issues: 1

  [Medium] Uniform bucket-level access disabled
  Info:    Cloud Storage uniform bucket-level access is not enabled. Both bucket
           ACLs and IAM permissions can be used to grant permissions
  Rule:    https://security.snyk.io/rules/cloud/SNYK-CC-TF-240
  Path:    resource > google_storage_bucket[test-bucket] >
           uniform_bucket_level_access
  File:    main.tf
  Resolve: Set `uniform_bucket_level_access` attribute to `true`


-------------------------------------------------------


Test Summary

  Organization: <ORG_NAME>
  Project name: <ORG_NAME>/pac-book-tf-gcp

✓ Files without issues: 2
✗ Files with issues: 1
  Ignored issues: 0
  Total issues: 4 [ 0 critical, 0 high, 1 medium, 3 low ]


-------------------------------------------------------
```

Of course, the snyk iac test command outputs machine-readable JSON, using the
--json flag.

Using the Snyk CLI locally to validate my GCP project IaC is very handy, and there is
a VS Code plug-in that also makes sense. I could also see this CLI technique working
in automated pipelines. However, the real magic emerged when I connected my Snyk
SaaS platform organization to my TFC project and workspace via Snyk integrations
(*https://snyk.io/integrations*).

Once connected, I was able to run a speculative plan in TFC, sourced from my
GitHub project, and add a TFC run task to scan my GCP Terraform IaC with Snyk, as
shown in Figure 12-5.

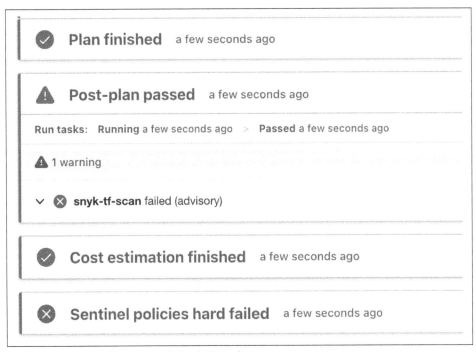

Figure 12-5. TFC plan run with Snyk Terraform scan

As you can see in Figure 12-5, the Snyk scan—via TFC and Snyk platform integration—failed with an advisory level. I then clicked on the far-right Details button (not shown) to open the scan details in the Snyk platform. Figure 12-6 shows the Issues interface in my Snyk organization.

The detected issues in Figure 12-6 align with those we saw in the other Terraform IaC validation tools we covered, and the Snyk and TFC integration provides a solution to help developers quickly detect issues while persisting run and evaluation records. The Snyk CLI together with the Snyk SaaS platform provide a comprehensive solution for local and cloud-based IaC and PaC automation.

This section felt like a lightning round for Terraform validation tools. With minor exceptions, the tools produced the same validation results. While OPA and Sentinel are the heavyweights when it comes to Terraform IaC validation, it's important to realize that there are other tools and frameworks that may also fit your needs and capabilities. And, as you saw, some of the tools we just covered used Rego, OPA's policy language.

Figure 12-6. Snyk Terraform scan results

In Chapter 10, I introduced the new c7n features to perform mutating and validating admission controls in Kubernetes. In Chapter 13, I cover how c7n is used to solve PaC use cases for infrastructure as a service (IaaS) resources in different CSPs.

Stacklet.io introduced the Stacklet IaC Governance (*https://oreil.ly/aT_VU*) product, which provides an enterprise solution for managing and applying Terraform IaC policies. The policy language is based on the OSS c7n project, similar to how c7n was used in Kubernetes in Chapter 10 and is used for IaaS in Chapter 13.

Summary

Notwithstanding recent license changes (*https://oreil.ly/yGf1C*), Terraform is a very popular IaC tool with a huge community of practitioners as well as complementary tools and solutions. One of the major reasons I think Terraform is so popular is because the language on which it is built—HCL—is very close to the widely adopted JSON syntax. While the lexicon, modules, providers, and so forth may be specific to the target of your IaC, the underlying HCL syntax remains common.

HashiCorp Sentinel is a strong solution, underpinned by tools that not only ease development but also increase effectiveness across multiple cloud native environments. Most of the PaC solutions I have written about in this book are based on assertion-based and/or declarative languages as well as DSLs. Sentinel's procedural syntax and modularization appeal directly to my programmer persona. With Sentinel, I can write reusable modules and policies—programs, if you will—that enforce rules and behaviors on Terraform IaC. It is simple and flexible, and it has proven easy for me to learn.

If you use Terraform, then you should investigate using Terraform Cloud (TFC) or Terraform Enterprise (TFE). Either of these solutions should be considered table stakes for organizations that are serious about Terraform use across the enterprise. That said, I really like the SaaS solution offered by TFC. TFC integrates to popular version control systems and multiple CSPs. These features were easy to use and quickly made me more productive while allowing me to use existing systems to manage my IaC artifacts.

TFC also provides automation to build much-needed data mocks, which eases Sentinel policy prototyping. In my experience—and as I tried to show in this chapter—using data mocks leads to more precise and deterministic policy development, which enhances PaC effectiveness with Terraform.

Testing Sentinel policies is made easier by data mocks and by the use of project-level conventions and testing configurations. Positive and negative—pass and fail—testing is designed into Sentinel and expected as part of Sentinel unit testing.

Beyond Sentinel, other PaC tools exist that interrogate Terraform IaC, looking for issues—incorrect syntax, security findings, bad practices, and so on—related to environment-specific infrastructure. While these tools don't use Sentinel, their policies detect similar issues in IaC. Combined with automation, these tools can form a powerful set of guardrails. Snyk takes it further with a platform that directly integrates with TFC.

Because of Terraform's popularity, there are many tools and projects—both OSS and commercial—in use, supporting a variety of use cases and scenarios. In this chapter, I discussed just a few of what I think are the most functional and straightforward PaC solutions for Terraform. Regardless of which tools you select for your Terraform PaC needs, the selection criteria from Chapter 1—or a similar selection framework—should drive your decisions. In fact, the most compelling reason I applied much of my IaC focus to Terraform was because Terraform, even though it's not a PaC solution, satisfied much of the selection criteria that I recommended in Chapter 1.

In Chapter 13, I will discuss using PaC solutions to interrogate IaaS resources downstream of IaC operations.

PaC and Infrastructure as a Service

Throughout this book, I have written about PaC solutions designed to prevent unwanted changes or behaviors in systems and artifacts. In Chapters 4 through 10, I showed you how different PaC solutions could be used to prevent unwanted changes from occurring in Kubernetes. Some of these same solutions could also audit, perform background scans, or execute CLI commands to interrogate existing Kubernetes resources.

In Chapters 11 and 12, I wrote about PaC solutions for IaC, how they detected issues—security and otherwise—and how they prevented the issues found in artifacts from propagating to IaaS resources. These PaC solutions could be used at the command line, included in automation, or be part of SaaS offerings.

PaC is routinely applied to existing IaaS resources as a means of detecting physical issues like drift and unwanted or disallowed resource configurations. Detection is not enough, though. PaC should react to prevent and even correct unwanted, potentially dangerous IaaS configurations. At a minimum, PaC should also notify users of situations found and actions taken. If PaC is not used to correct issues, then PaC should create findings that can be prioritized and remediated. In the case of IaaS in CSPs, PaC could create and radiate findings, using CSP-specific tools as well as external SIEM tools (https://oreil.ly/eJ9J8).

In this chapter, I will introduce two tools that are used to apply policies to existing IaaS resources to detect and potentially react to noncompliant configurations. Prowler detects and reports on unwanted IaaS configurations. Cloud Custodian detects unwanted situations and reacts to correct unwanted behaviors. As we explore these two tools, you should decide which solution—detection only or detection with remediation—best supports your needs.

Let's get started with Prowler.

Prowler

Prowler (*https://oreil.ly/prowler*) is an OSS project written in Python that performs security scans on CSP services and IaaS resources in the following CSPs (listed in order of supported features at the time of writing):

- AWS–290 checks
- GCP–73 checks
- Azure–23 checks

With Prowler, you can perform assessments on existing CSP services and IaaS artifacts. These assessments inform the users on applying security best practices and detecting deviations thereof. When I started with Prowler, I found the official Prowler documentation (*https://docs.prowler.cloud*) to be very helpful.

Since Prowler is a Python tool, I used pip to install it onto my Macbook Pro. I reused the technique that I introduced in Chapter 10, first creating a Python virtual environment in which to install Prowler, activating the environment, and then installing Python-based tools:

```
# create Python virtual environment
$ python -m venv prowler-env

# activate virtual environment
$ source prowler-env/bin/activate

# install prowler
$ pip install prowler
$ prowler -v
Prowler 3.9.0 (it is the latest version, yay!)
```

Using Python virtual environments is a great way to install multiple Python tools without worrying about the collisions that are possible as the multiple installs change common Python settings and libraries.

With Prowler installed, let's explore how policies—known as *Prowler checks*—are built.

Prowler Checks

The means by which Prowler checks are created is somewhat of a departure from the typical PaC solutions about which I have written in this book. However, the approach that the Prowler project follows—with reusable patterns—is effective. Prowler checks are written as a combination of metadata JSON files and Python code. The following metadata JSON file describes an Amazon Elastic Compute Cloud (EC2) check for default Elastic Block Storage (EBS) encryption:

```
// Prowler check metadata - ec2 default ebs encryption
{
  "Provider": "aws",
  "CheckID": "ec2_ebs_default_encryption",
  "CheckTitle": "Check if EBS Default Encryption is activated.",
  "CheckType": [
    "Data Protection"
  ],
  "ServiceName": "ec2",
  "SubServiceName": "ebs",
  "ResourceIdTemplate":
  "arn:partition:service:region:account-id:resource-id",
  "Severity": "medium",
  "ResourceType": "Other",
  "Description": "Check if EBS Default Encryption is activated.",
  "Risk": "If not enabled sensitive information at rest is not protected.",
  "RelatedUrl": "",
  "Remediation": {
    "Code": {
      "CLI": "aws ec2 enable-ebs-encryption-by-default",
      "NativeIaC": "",
      "Other":
      "https://docs.bridgecrew.io/docs/ensure-ebs-default-encryption-is-...
      ...enabled#aws-console",
      "Terraform": "https://docs.bridgecrew.io/docs/ensure-ebs-default-...
      ...encryption-is-enabled#terraform"
    },
    "Recommendation": {
      "Text":
      "Enable Encryption. Use a CMK where possible. It will provide ...
      ...additional management and privacy benefits.",
      "Url":
      "https://aws.amazon.com/premiumsupport/knowledge-center/...
      ...ebs-automatic-encryption/"
    }
  },
  "Categories": [
    "encryption"
  ],
  "DependsOn": [],
  "RelatedTo": [],
  "Notes": ""
}
```

The preceding metadata appears in the Prowler output after execution.

The associated Prowler check for default EBS encryption is implemented as a Python class. This class is then referenced by Prowler to run specific checks based on settings provided to the Prowler CLI command:

```
# Prowler check - ec2 default ebs encryption
from prowler.lib.check.models import Check, Check_Report_AWS
from prowler.providers.aws.services.ec2.ec2_client import ec2_client


class ec2_ebs_default_encryption(Check):
    def execute(self):
        findings = []
        for ebs_encryption in ec2_client.ebs_encryption_by_default:
            report = Check_Report_AWS(self.metadata())
            report.region = ebs_encryption.region
            report.resource_arn = ec2_client.audited_account_arn
            report.resource_id = ec2_client.audited_account
            report.status = "FAIL"
            report.status_extended = "EBS Default Encryption is not activated."
            if ebs_encryption.status:
                report.status = "PASS"
                report.status_extended = "EBS Default Encryption is activated."

            findings.append(report)

        return findings
```

Though checks written as Python classes may stretch the definition of PaC for some, in my opinion, the checks are written as part of a framework of reusable components. The engineered reusability allows checks to be grouped into different collections relative to CSP services, compliance standards, and categories.

Let's move on to the Prowler UX by using the installed CLI.

Prowler CLI

It's easy to get started with the Prowler CLI. For example, I ran all the checks for AWS in the OSS project with a short command: `prowler aws`. The command automatically found the configured AWS credentials and ran against all regions in my AWS test account in a little over five minutes. The Prowler CLI supports many settings, though, and I filtered the execution to only one service in one region and specified the output directory; if I wanted to, I could also use the `--resource-tags` or `--resource-arn` arguments to run the selected checks against only resources with specific tags or with a specific ARN, respectively:

```
# Prowler CLI run for EC2 in us-east-1
$ prowler aws --service ec2 --region us-east-1 -o output/ec2
```

```
|_| the handy cloud security tool
```

```
Date: 2023-09-10 18:10:38

This report is being generated using credentials below:

AWS-CLI Profile: [default] AWS Filter Region: [us-east-1]
AWS Account: [...] UserId: [...]
Caller Identity ARN: [arn:aws:iam::<AWS_ACCOUNT_D>:user/<IAM_PRINCIPAL>]

Executing 38 checks, please wait...

-> Scan completed! |████████████████████████████████████████████| 38/38 [100%]
in 1.8s

Overview Results:

| 26.09% (6) Failed | 73.91% (17) Passed |


Account 296561158246 Scan Results (severity columns are for fails only):
```

Provider	Service	Status	Critical	High	Medium	Low
aws	ec2	FAIL (6)	0	2	4	0

```
* You only see here those services that contains resources.

Detailed results are in:
  - HTML: output/ec2/prowler-output-1234567890-20230910181038.html
  - JSON-OCSF: output/ec2/prowler-output-1234567890-20230910181038.ocsf.json
  - CSV: output/ec2/prowler-output-1234567890-20230910181038.csv
  - JSON: output/ec2/prowler-output-1234567890-20230910181038.json
```

The preceding Prowler command ran just shy of two seconds, executing 38 EC2 checks in the us-east-1 region of my AWS test account. The run created four output files to support human- and machine-readable formats, including the Open Cybersecurity Schema Framework (OCSF) (*https://github.com/ocsf*). With the Prowler CLI, you can control the output mode and filenames or even send data to Slack, like I did in Chapter 6. You can also send the findings to AWS Security Hub (*https://oreil.ly/7ArK-*) or AWS S3.

The following snippet from an OCSF output indicates that the EC2 EBS default encryption is not activated; this is based on the example check in the previous section:

```
// EC2 EBS default encryption security finding
[{
    "finding": {
        "title": "Check if EBS Default Encryption is activated.",
        "desc": "Check if EBS Default Encryption is activated.",
        "supporting_data": {
            "Risk": "If not enabled sensitive information at rest is not ...
            ...protected.",
            "Notes": ""
        },
        "remediation": {
            "kb_articles": [...,
            "https://aws.amazon.com/premiumsupport/knowledge-center/...
            ...ebs-automatic-encryption/"
            ],
            "desc": "Enable Encryption. Use a CMK where possible. It will ...
            ...provide additional management and privacy benefits."
        },
    ...

        {
            "group": {
                "name": "ec2"
            },
            "region": "us-east-1",
    ...
        "status_detail": "EBS Default Encryption is not activated.",
        "compliance": {
            "status": "Failure",
            "requirements": [
                "CISA: your-systems-3, your-data-1",
                "MITRE-ATTACK: T1119",
                "AWS-Foundational-Security-Best-Practices: ec2",
                "HIPAA: 164_308_a_1_ii_b, 164_308_a_4_ii_a, 164_312_a_2_iv, ...
                ...164_312_e_2_ii",
                "GxP-21-CFR-Part-11: 11.10-g, 11.30",
                "AWS-Well-Architected-Framework-Security-Pillar: SEC08-BP02",
                "GxP-EU-Annex-11: 7.1-data-storage-damage-protection",
                "NIST-800-53-Revision-4: sc_28",
                "NIST-800-53-Revision-5: au_9_3, cm_6_a, cm_9_b, cp_9_d, ...
                ...sc_8_3, sc_8_4, sc_13_a, sc_28_1, si_19_4",
                "AWS-Audit-Manager-Control-Tower-Guardrails: 1.0.3",
                "FFIEC: d3-pc-am-b-12"
            ],
            "status_detail": "EBS Default Encryption is not activated."
        },
    ,,,
        "severity": "Medium",
    ...
```

As seen in the preceding output, the finding severity is Medium, and the output includes metadata from the JSON metadata file in the previous section. The output also includes compliance standards to which this check is relevant. In fact, you can run the Prowler CLI to list the available compliance frameworks. The following output is based on my AWS configuration:

```
# list AWS compliance frameworks
$ prowler --list-compliance

- cisa_aws
- soc2_aws
- cis_1.4_aws
- cis_1.5_aws
- mitre_attack_aws
- gdpr_aws
- aws_foundational_security_best_practices_aws
- iso27001_2013_aws
- hipaa_aws
- cis_2.0_aws
- gxp_21_cfr_part_11_aws
- aws_well_architected_framework_security_pillar_aws
- gxp_eu_annex_11_aws
- nist_800_171_revision_2_aws
- nist_800_53_revision_4_aws
- nist_800_53_revision_5_aws
- ens_rd2022_aws
- nist_csf_1.1_aws
- aws_well_architected_framework_reliability_pillar_aws
- aws_audit_manager_control_tower_guardrails_aws
- rbi_cyber_security_framework_aws
- ffiec_aws
- pci_3.2.1_aws
- fedramp_moderate_revision_4_aws
- fedramp_low_revision_4_aws

There are 25 available Compliance Frameworks.
```

The following command ran the `soc2_aws` framework checks in my AWS test account in the us-east-1 region:

```
# soc2 AWS checks with Prowler CLI
$ prowler aws --region us-east-1 --compliance soc2_aws
…
Account 1234567890 Scan Results (severity columns are for fails only):
```

Provider	Service	Status	Critical	High	Medium	Low
aws	acm	FAIL (3)	0	3	0	0
aws	apigateway	PASS (1)	0	0	0	0

aws	cloudtrail	FAIL (3)	0	0	0	3
aws	cloudwatch	FAIL (21)	0	0	21	0
aws	config	FAIL (1)	0	0	1	0
aws	ec2	FAIL (1)	0	1	0	0
aws	guardduty	FAIL (1)	0	0	1	0
aws	iam	FAIL (2)	0	2	0	0
aws	s3	FAIL (15)	1	0	14	0
aws	securityhub	FAIL (1)	0	0	1	0
aws	vpc	FAIL (1)	0	0	1	0

`* You only see here those services that contains resources.`

The one difference between the service-based checks and the compliance-based checks that I noticed was that the output for the compliance-based checks supported only the CSV file format. Although CSV is still machine readable, the parsing is more difficult than with JSON.

With Prowler, I ran checks related to services with filters for regions, tags, and ARNs. The machine-readable output of the Prowler CLI integrates easily to automation. Finally, since Prowler is an OSS project, Python developers can contribute to new and existing checks, making the Prowler solution flexible and extensible.

 A Prowler Pro edition (*https://prowler.pro*) is also available. The Prowler Pro edition is SaaS based and includes features—continuous detection, dashboard, and agentless installations—that make Prowler more suitable for enterprise use.

As shown in Figure 13-1, Prowler can produce HTML reports. These HTML reports are more functional for human review. The reports include parameters used for the run as well as links to additional references to help better understand the individual check results.

As Figure 13-1 shows, the Prowler HTML output includes possible sensitive data— User ID, Caller Identity ARN—that may need to be sanitized, depending on the report audience. That said, the same sensitive data appears in other Prowler outputs, and the AWS Account ID for my AWS runs appeared as part of the output filenames regardless of format.

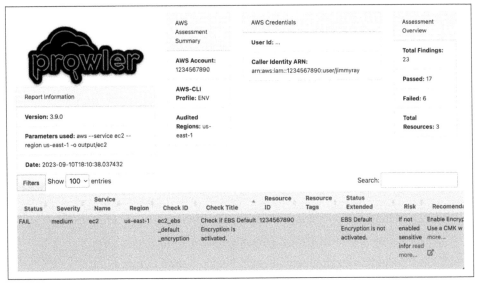

		Service				Resource	Resource	Status		
Status	Severity	Name	Region	Check ID	Check Title	ID	Tags	Extended	Risk	Recomend:
FAIL	medium	ec2	us-east-1	ec2_ebs _default _encryption	Check if EBS Default Encryption is activated.	1234567890		EBS Default Encryption is not activated.	If not enabled sensitive infor read more...	Enable Encryp Use a CMK w more...

Figure 13-1. Prowler HTML output

Prowler, like several of the IaC solutions I covered in Chapters 11 and 12, is a detection and reporting tool. When it comes to evaluating IaC before resources are changed and preventing those changes by creating attestations that indicate invalid code, tools that evaluate, detect, and report solve that IaC use case. Prowler also creates usable intelligence in the form of reports that practitioners can leverage for audits or to determine the overall security posture of the IaaS resources they build and support.

Prowler, and tools like it, can be run locally or in automated pipelines. What's missing in tools like Prowler is the ability to take automated or manual actions to remediate detected issues.

At the time of this writing, Prowler had secured $6 million in seed funding (*https://oreil.ly/KMwxZ*). As a newly formed company, perhaps it will expand its solution to remediation of detected issues.

Starting in the next section, we will explore using c7n to manage cloud resources.

Cloud Custodian

I first introduced c7n in this book's Preface and again in Chapter 10 as a Kubernetes PaC solution. C7n started as a cloud IaaS resource management solution, and in that role, c7n provides the most functionality and utility. With a couple of exceptions—Kubernetes and IaC—c7n focuses primarily on automated cloud compliance across multiple CSPs. This compliance includes monitoring and reporting as well as remediating with corrective actions. C7n policies can operate across multiple CSPs, systems, and environments in multiple modes. I mostly use pull, event-driven, and periodic modes, all discussed later in this chapter.

The following links will help you gain more information about c7n:

- Core GitHub project (*https://github.com/cloud-custodian/cloud-custodian*)
- Documentation website (*https://cloudcustodian.io/docs/index.html*)
- Cloud Custodian community (*https://cloudcustodian.io/community*)

> Stacklet.io (*https://stacklet.io*) offers enterprise support and features for c7n that can help customers execute c7n adoption quickly and more deterministically. Stacklet offers products (*https://oreil.ly/LoDjN*) like the Stacklet Asset DB, the Stacklet Platform, Stacklet Policy Packs, and Stacklet IaC Governance.

Let's start with the c7n installation.

Installation

Some of this will be a refresher from Chapter 10. C7n is written in Python and installed via pip. I am running MacOS with the following Python configuration:

```
# get Python version
$ python3 --version
Python 3.11.4
```

To use c7n, I first created a Python virtual environment:

```
# create Python virtual environment
$ python -m venv c7n
```

After I created the Python virtual environment, I activated it with the following command:

```
# activate virtual environment
$ source c7n/bin/activate
```

With the Python virtual environment running, I installed c7n and then created a c7n alias:

```
# install Cloud Custodian core and create Cloud Custodian alias
$ pip3 install c7n
Successfully installed argcomplete-3.1.1 attrs-23.1.0
boto3-1.26.157 botocore-1.29.157 Cloud Custodian-0.9.28 docutils-0.18.1
importlib-metadata-5.2.0 jmespath-1.0.1 jsonschema-4.17.3
pyrsistent-0.19.3 python-dateutil-2.8.2 pyyaml-6.0 s3transfer-0.6.1
six-1.16.0 tabulate-0.9.0 urllib3-1.26.16 zipp-3.15.0
alias c7n="custodian"
```

The installation created the following file system tree:

```
# Cloud Custodian environment
.
├── README.md
├── c7n
│   ├── bin
│   ├── include
│   ├── lib
│   └── pyvenv.cfg
```

The installation installs the core c7n files and the YAML schema needed to work with AWS. Additional CSP YAML schemas can be installed if needed. For example, the `pip install c7n_azure` command installs the schema needed for Azure.

Once c7n was installed, I verified that it was functional with the `version` command:

```
# verify Cloud Custodian is installed
$ c7n version
0.9.31
```

Before we explore using c7n, let's see how we can remove it from our systems and clean up after an install.

Cleanup

Once you're done with the custodian virtual environment, you can deactivate it with the `deactivate` command that represents a function loaded into memory when the virtual environment is started. You can then come back to it and reactivate the environment with the same `activate` command from earlier. After deactivation, cleanup of the virtual environment is as easy as deleting the *c7n* directory that was created with the earlier `venv` command.

Now that we have configured and activated c7n, and we have learned to easily clean up when we are done, let's explore how c7n policies work.

Cloud Custodian Policies

C7n uses a YAML-based DSL for its policy language. Using this DSL, you can write cloud resource policies for multiple CSPs, with few lexiconic differences. The YAML DSL generalizes the CSP specialization. Under the covers, c7n uses SDKs to interrogate respective CSP APIs. For example, the following policies select compute resources from multiple CSPs using tags:

```
# Get AWS EC2 instances using tags
policies:
  - name: my-compute
    resource: aws.ec2
    filters:
      - type: value
        key: "tag:owner"
        value: "jimmyray"
```

```
# Get Azure VM instances using tags
policies:
  - name: my-compute
    resource: azure.vm
    filters:
      - type: value
        key: "tag:owner"
        value: "jimmyray"
```

In the preceding examples, the c7n policies selected all the AWS EC2 and Azure VM instances that were owned by me. As you can see, only the resource element changed between the two policies. This powerful feature of the c7n policy language helps policy authors leverage policies across multiple CSPs.

The YAML DSL reduces the learning curve of c7n. The reduced learning curve frees policy authors to focus on policies, not the complexity of the underlying CSP APIs. In addition to the DSL syntax, there are lexiconic differences in the DSL between CSPs, but they are minimal. Deeper understanding of the target CSP helps with understanding how to write CSP-specific policies.

C7n policies use the following root-level elements:

Resource
    Sets the resource type for the policy.

Filters
    Used to finely tune the select of resources.

Actions
    Used to specify actions to take against selected resources.

Mode
> Specifies the policy execution mode; pull mode is default.

Conditions
> Sets conditions for when a policy will execute.

Query
> Although not used as much as filters anymore, query permits custom queries for AWS Config operations.

In my experience, there are four main elements to most c7n policies: resources, filters, actions, and mode. Of those four, only the resources element is actually required. You can run a c7n policy without filters or actions. It's not too functional and could actually lead to extended API calls or even throttling in large environments, but it can be done. A policy with resources only or resources and filters—no actions—retrieves data, like a report runner.

Let's start our exploration with resources.

Resources

In c7n policies, the resources element is required. It defines which resources the policy will affect and the actions and filters that can be used. The resources available to c7n policies are based on the schemas installed. A default installation provides the AWS resources. To view the available resources, you run the following schema command:

```
# Cloud Custodian schema - AWS default
$ c7n schema
resources:
- aws.access-analyzer-finding
- aws.account
- aws.acm-certificate
...
```

In my installation, I also installed the Azure and GCP schemas. I viewed the Azure schema with the following schema command:

```
# Cloud Custodian schema - Azure
$ c7n schema azure
resources:
- azure.advisor-recommendation
- azure.aks
- azure.alert-logs
- azure.api-management
...
```

To see the actions and filters—and the occasional example policy—related to specific resources, you run the schema command, specifying the schema you wish to view:

```
# Cloud Custodian - azure.vm actions and filters
$ c7n schema azure.vm
azure.vm:
  actions:
  - auto-tag-date
  - auto-tag-user
  - delete
  …
  filters:
  - advisor-recommendation
  - cost
  - event
  - instance-view
  …
```

New users always often overlook the power of the custodian schema command. When you dig deeper into specific filters and actions, you find the most value. C7n schema will provide sample policies for almost all filters and actions.

Here's an example:

```
# Look-up EC2 filters for AMI Image age
$ custodian schema aws.ec2.filters.image-age

Help
----

EC2 AMI age filter

Filters EC2 instances based on the age of their AMI image (in days)

:Example:

.. code-block:: yaml

    policies:
      - name: ec2-ancient-ami
        resource: ec2
        filters:
          - type: image-age
            op: ge
            days: 90
    …
```

I frequently learn new techniques by digging into the service-specific filters and actions that are constantly being added and updated.

Now that we have reviewed c7n resources, let's look at how filters select resources for policies.

Filters

In the previous section, we saw how c7n arranges actions and filters into schema entries categorized by resource type. While the policy resource element selects the resource type for a policy execution, the filters element acts as the selection criteria for the subset of resources items or instances, much the same way a where clause (*https://oreil.ly/En9nO*) selects specific rows from tables in a SQL query.

The following policy sets the resource to `aws.ec2` and then uses two filters to further narrow the selection to `t2.micro` instance types and instances where the attached EBS volumes are not encrypted:

```
# t2.micro instances with non-encrypted EBS volumes
policies:
  - name: ec2-nonencrypted-ebs-volumes
    resource: aws.ec2
    filters:
      - type: instance-attribute
        attribute: instanceType
        key: "Value"
        value: "t2.micro"
      - type: ebs
        key: Encrypted
        value: false
```

Each filter evaluates the instances, and both filters must be true to select the desired instances in this policy.

When multiple filters are specified, they are logically ANDed by default. If I wanted to select EC2 instances that either are `t2.micro` or have nonencrypted EBS volumes, then I would use an explicit OR element, as in the following policy:

```
# t2.micro or non-encrypted EBS volumes
policies:
  - name: ec2-nonencrypted-ebs-volumes
    resource: ec2
    filters:
      - or:
        - type: instance-attribute
          attribute: instanceType
          key: "Value"
          value: "t2.micro"
        - type: ebs
          key: Encrypted
          value: false
```

Tucking the filters under the OR element applies the logic that either filter can cause a resource selection.

Now let's look at c7n actions.

Actions

As I mentioned previously, policies without actions are really just reports used for detection use cases. Many users build and run policies only to retrieve report data; however, without actions c7n would be like other tools that only detect issues. Instead, c7n provides a large collection of actions that are arranged by the resource types in the installed schemas. These actions allow policy authors to create their own actions as well.

 C7n policies that are run in Pull mode—using the CLI—execute with the permissions of the AWS credentials provided to the user running the command. Whatever you can do, c7n can do much faster, most likely before you can stop it. If you can delete, so can c7n. If your filter is faulty, bad things can happen.

When using the c7n CLI, always use --dryrun until you want to take action and you are sure that the policy has selected the desired resources:

```
# Run Cloud Custodian policy in dry-run mode
$ custodian run -s output --dryrun my-policy.yml
2024-03-16 21:43:06,747: custodian.policy:INFO
policy:s3 resource:aws.s3 region:us-east-1 count:50
time:6.98
```

The following policy selects RDS resources that are not properly tagged and then takes action to notify support. Tags and labels are very important to the operational control of CSP resources. The following policy reports—via email notification—that RDS instances are not properly tagged:

```
# Cloud Custodian policy to report on missing tags
policies:
  - name: rds-tag-compliance
    resource: rds
    filters:
      - or:
        - "tag:billing": absent
        - "tag:env": absent
        - "tag:owner": absent
    actions:
      - type: notify
        template: rds-tag-compliance
        subject: "[custodian] RDS missing tags"
        from: Cloud Custodian <no-reply@example.com>
        to:
          - jimmyray@example.com
        transport:
          type: sqs
          queue: >
```

```
https://sqs.us-east-1.amazonaws.com/1234567890/
cloud-custodian-message-relay
```

The preceding policy determines if any of the mandatory tags—billing, env, owner—are absent from RDS instances. If instances are missing any of the required tags, the policy output is sent to support.

 The rds-tag-compliance policy uses the c7n Mailer (*https://oreil.ly/ gJmjK*) to forward notifications. According to the documentation, messages can be routed to the following systems:

- Email
- Datadog
- Slack
- Splunk
- Webhook

Not all actions take place immediately. Sometimes, you may need to mark a resource for a later operation. For example, if your policy detects a medium- or low-priority issue, you may just want to notify at first and take escalated action later, after you have provided enough time for users to remediate issues. The following policy looks for mandatory tags, and if the tags are not found, the resources are marked for termination:

```
# mark untagged ec2 for termination
policies:
  - name: ec2-mark-term-untagged
    resource: aws.ec2
    filters:
      - or:
        - "tag:billing": absent
        - "tag:env": absent
        - "tag:owner": absent
    actions:
      - type: mark-for-op
        tag: c7n_op
        op: terminate
        days: 4
```

The mark-for-op action uses the c7n_op tag to hold state. Once the resources are marked for the terminate operation, then a second policy is used to complete the workflow:

```
# ec2 marked for termination
policies:
  - name: ec2-term-marked
    resource: ec2
```

```
    filters:
      - type: marked-for-op
        tag: c7n_op
        op: terminate
        tz: utc
    actions:
      - type: terminate
```

In the preceding two policies, I created a workflow when I used the mark-for-op action to set a future date for when resources would be terminated. I then used the marked-for-op filter to select previously marked resources. This workflow resembles a "mark and sweep" garbage-collection algorithm, where I first marked the resources on which I wanted to act and then acted on them at the appointed time.

Mark-for-op workflow is generally run in this order: mark, unmark, take action (like delete). To prevent erroneous actions against resources when issues are corrected before an action is scheduled, periodic policies are run that check for corrected issues, and then resources are unmarked by removing the tag placed on the resource by the mark-for-op action.

The following periodic policy runs every hour to check if the missing tags have been added:

```
# Unmark EC2 when correct tags are added
policies:
  - name: ec2-unmark-tagged
    resource: aws.ec2
    mode:
      type: periodic
      schedule: "rate(1 hour)"
      tags:
        billing: lob-cc
        env: sandbox
        owner: jimmyray
      role: custodian
    description: |
      Unmark ec2 resources that have had tags added
    filters:
      - "tag:billing": present
      - "tag:env": present
      - "tag:owner": present
    actions:
      - type: remove-tag
        tags: ["c7n_op"]
```

If the tags are present, the c7n-op tag is removed, effectively unmarking the resource for action.

The preceding policy was run on a scheduled basis. We will discuss different execution modes later in this chapter.

With actions understood, let's look at how to annotate c7n policies with useful information.

Describing policies

The c7n policy DSL supports three elements that can help you add pertinent information to your policies. The comments and description elements allow you to add bulk text that you can use to describe your policies. As I stated in Chapter 1, policies in PaC solutions should trace back to enterprise standards and policies. In the past, I have used the comments and descriptions to add such information. They are interchangeable, but the description field actually gets propagated to CSP functions—like Lambda—to provide descriptions for the functions. The comments field content stays within the policy.

The metadata field enables you to add custom, machine-readable fields to your policies. When policies are run, all three fields appear in the *metadata.json* file as part of the run's output. The following policy demonstrates how to use the comments, description, and metadata fields:

```
# Adding policy information
policies:
  - name: ec2-mandatory-tags
    resource: aws.ec2
    filters:
      - "State.Name": running
      - or:
        - "tag:billing": absent
        - "tag:env": absent
        - "tag:owner": absent
    metadata:
      severity: high
      author: jimmyray
      control-id: GRC-001
      control-info: EC2 instances must contain required tags [billing, env, owner]
    comments: |
      Lorem ipsum dolor sit amet, consectetur adipiscing elit…
    description: |
      Lorem ipsum dolor sit amet, consectetur adipiscing elit…
```

After the run, the policy metadata field was added to the policy element in the *metadata.json* file as well as the comments and description fields:

```
// Policy metadata from run
{
  "policy": {
    "name": "ec2s",
...
    "metadata": {
      "severity": "high",
      "author": "jimmyray",
```

```
    "control-id": "GRC-001",
    "control-info":
    "EC2 instances must contain required tags [billing, env, owner]"
  },
  "comments": "Lorem ipsum dolor sit …",
  "description": "Lorem ipsum dolor sit …"
}, …
```

Using machine-readable metadata opens multiple possibilities for categorizing and cataloging policies. It provides discrete data that can be used by policy automation. Adding comments and descriptions will improve the intuitive nature of your policies.

Now that you know the basic structure of policies, let's explore policy execution and outputs.

Policy execution

C7n policies run in several different modes, depending on the environment and schemas you are using. In this section, I am going to focus primarily on the pull, Cloud-Trail, and periodic AWS modes. You can use the c7n schema mode command to list the available c7n execution modes:

```
# List c7n schema modes
c7n schema mode
mode:
- pull
- periodic
- phd
- cloudtrail
- ec2-instance-state
- asg-instance-state
- guard-duty
- config-poll-rule
- config-rule
- hub-finding
- hub-action
- azure-periodic
- azure-event-grid
- container-periodic
- container-event
- gcp-periodic
- gcp-audit
- gcp-scc
- k8s-admission
```

You can use dot notation to view specific execution mode details:

```
# View pull mode schema information
c7n schema mode.pull

Help
```

```
----

Pull mode execution of a policy.

Queries resources from cloud provider for filtering and actions.

Schema
------

properties:
type:
enum:
- pull
required:
- type
```

The preceding command retrieved the details for the `pull` mode.

Pull mode policy execution. Pull mode is the easiest way to prototype and run c7n policies. In this mode, you use the c7n CLI run command to execute policies from your desktop to your target environment. The following command runs a policy that detects EC2 instances with nonencrypted EBS volumes:

```
# run policy to detect EC2 instances with non-encrypted EBS volumes
$ c7n run -s output policies/ec2-ebs-nonencrypted.yml
2023-09-27 20:54:40,652: custodian.policy:INFO
policy:ec2-nonencrypted-ebs-volumes resource:ec2 region:us-east-1 count:3
time:1.47
```

The output from the command indicates that it was run against EC2 resources in the us-east-1 region. The policy selected three EC2 resources and took 1.47 seconds to execute.

Besides the command output, the run of the policy created three files in the *output* directory:

custodian-run.log
    Log file that is updated every time the policy executes

metadata.json
    Metadata about the last execution of the policy

resources.json
    Result of selected resources for the last run based on resource type and filters

The *custodian-run.log* file is just that: an ongoing, timestamped update of policy runs showing information similar to what is output from the `run` command.

The *metadata.json* file collects specific metadata from the last successful policy run. The following example shows the policy filters used in the policy as well as configuration data:

```
// policy-run metadata
{
  "policy": {
    "name": "ec2-nonencrypted-ebs-volumes",
    "resource": "ec2",
    "filters": [
      {
        "type": "instance-attribute",
        "attribute": "instanceType",
        "key": "Value",
        "value": "t2.micro"
      },
      {
        "type": "ebs",
        "key": "Encrypted",
        "value": false
      }
    ]
  },
  "version": "0.9.31",
  "execution": {
    "id": "4c2e3059-ad7b-4ac3-9e6b-f39a68d3ec2d",
    "start": 1695862479.174487,
    "end_time": 1695862480.6559172,
    "duration": 1.4814300537109375
  },
  "config": {
    "region": "us-east-1",
    "regions": [
      "us-east-1"
    ],
    "cache": "~/.cache/cloud-custodian.cache",
...
```

The *resources.json* file contains all the data related to the resources selected by the policy. This is a large file with a lot of useful data that I don't always need. Most of the time, I "reshape" this file to parse the most relative data for my use case. The following jq command parses the data I need:

```
# jq to reshape the resources.json data
$ jq '.[]| .["Name"]=(.Tags[]|select(.Key=="Name").Value)|.["Owner"]=\
(.Tags[]|select(.Key=="Owner").Value)|{id:.InstanceId,type:.InstanceType,\
name:.Name,az:.Placement.AvailabilityZone,owner:.Owner}' \
output/ec2-nonencrypted-ebs-volumes/resources.json
{
  "id": "i-0217...",
  "type": "t2.micro",
```

```
  "name": "test-1",
  "az": "us-east-1a",
  "owner": "jimmyray"
}
{
  "id": "i-0d93…",
  "type": "t2.micro",
  "name": "test-2",
  "az": "us-east-1a",
  "owner": "jimmyray"
}
{
  "id": "i-0bbf…",
  "type": "t2.micro",
  "name": "test-3",
  "az": "us-east-1a",
  "owner": "jimmyray"
}
```

I also use the `report` command to reshape the c7n output data. The following command produces a simple report; I first removed all the default fields and then added the fields I needed with my specific column names:

```
# Cloud Custodian simple report
$ c7n report -s output --format simple policies/ec2-ebs-nonencrypted.yml \
--no-default-fields --field id=InstanceId --field type=InstanceType \
--field ip=PrivateIpAddress

id                  type      ip
------------------- --------  -----------
I-02178…            t2.micro  10.41.55.34
I-0d93…             t2.micro  10.41.55.27
I-0bbf…             t2.micro  10.41.55.107
```

When the c7n policy runs locally, data is cached for 15 minutes by default. To avoid this, you can add the `--cache-period 0` argument to not cache data. I routinely disable the cache when I am prototyping and troubleshooting c7n policies.

Beyond output files, you can record policy metrics by using the `--metrics` argument and specifying a Namespace:

```
# create CloudWatch metrics
$ c7n run policies/ec2-ebs-nonencrypted.yml -s output --metrics \
"aws://?namespace=custodian"
```

CloudTrail mode policy execution. While it is helpful to run policies locally, and that approach can be used in automation, c7n supports other modes. One of the most powerful modes of operation for AWS is the CloudTrail mode. In this mode, AWS CloudTrail events trigger policy execution via Amazon EventBridge rules and targets.

The following policy is written to execute as an AWS Lambda triggered by CloudTrail:

```
# CloudTrail triggered Lambda policy
policies:
  - name: ec2-tag-new
    resource: aws.ec2
    description: |
      Policy to tag new ec2 instances with [billing,env,owner]
    mode:
      type: cloudtrail
      tags:
        billing: lob-cc
        env: sandbox
        owner: jimmyray
      role: <ROLE_NAME_OR_ARN>
      events:
        - RunInstances
    actions:
      - type: tag
        tags:
          billing: lob-cc
          env: sandbox
          owner: jimmyray
```

In the preceding policy, I specified the `mode` to be `cloudtrail` and to be triggered by the `RunInstances` event, which is a common shorthand. I supplied a role for the Lambda function that allowed it to tag EC2 instances. I could have used the role name instead of the ARN. While an ARN is more deterministic, using just the name allows for c7n policies to be reused between accounts if AWS IAM roles are like-named.

Before I tried to install the policy into AWS, I validated it with the following `validate` command:

```
# validate policy
$ c7n validate policies/cloudtrail/ct-ec2-tag-new-instance.yml
2023-09-27 22:22:38,263: custodian.commands:INFO Configuration
valid: policies/cloudtrail/ct-ec2-tag-new-instance.yml
```

Validation is also part of the `run` command and can be skipped.

To install the policy as a Lambda in my AWS account, I ran the following run command:

```
# run command to created policy lambda
$ c7n run -s output policies/cloudtrail/ct-ec2-tag-new-instance.yml
2023-09-27 21:54:49,925: custodian.policy:INFO Provisioning policy lambda:
ec2-tag-new region: us-east-1
2023-09-27 21:54:50,281: custodian.serverless:INFO Publishing custodian
policy lambda function custodian-ec2-tag-new
```

As the output indicates, a new Lambda function was published in my AWS account. The command also published an EventBridge rule and target. Figure 13-2 shows the Lambda function in the AWS console with the EventBridge trigger.

Figure 13-2. C7n policy Lambda triggered by EventBridge

Even though the diagram in Figure 13-2 shows that the EventBridge trigger is a CloudWatch event, the rule for this trigger clearly indicates that the source of the event is actually an EC2 API call recorded in CloudTrail:

```
// EventBridge rule
{
  "detail-type": ["AWS API Call via CloudTrail"],
  "detail": {
    "eventSource": ["ec2.amazonaws.com"],
    "eventName": ["RunInstances"]
  }
}
```

This policy tags new EC2 instances immediately upon creation. This is a reactive control, but it reacts fast. In my testing, I created an EC2 instance via the console. When I reviewed the CloudTrail event history, I saw my `RunInstances` API event at 17:49:16. The `CreateTags` event—from my c7n policy Lambda—occurred at 17:49:20. In approximately four seconds, my policy triggered and applied the tags per my policy settings. Given that very short reaction time, I think that this reactive control comes very close to functioning as a preventive control. In past experiences, users saw this quick response as a preventive control and guardrail.

You may be thinking that in AWS, SCPs can be used to implement auto-tagging operations. In my experience, though, not all AWS tenants have access to define SCP resources. In this situation, c7n fills the gap by providing a solution to all users, with the minimal permissions to create and modify resources.

 Azure and GCP also support event-trigger policies as functions. In Azure, the Azure Event Grid is used with Azure Functions, and the response time is about one to two minutes. This seems to be related to when the Azure service publishes events. In GCP, the API Audit Log Events are used with Cloud Functions and react very quickly— more quickly in my testing than the AWS CloudTrail mode with Lambda functions.

To remove the AWS resources—Lambda and EventBridge—created by the run command, I needed to use the *mugc.py* script found in the Cloud Custodian project (*https://oreil.ly/LAz43*). The script needs to run in the same context as the Python virtual environment that I activated for c7n operations:

```
# using mugc.py to remove AWS resources
$ python3 mugc.py -c policies/cloudtrail/ct-ec2-tag-new-instance.yml --present
2023-09-27 22:18:32,542: mugc:INFO Region:us-east-1 Removing
custodian-ec2-tag-new
2023-09-27 22:18:32,863: custodian.serverless:INFO Removing cwe targets and
rule custodian-ec2-tag-new
2023-09-27 22:18:33,064: custodian.serverless:INFO Removing lambda function
```

```
custodian-ec2-tag-new
2023-09-27 22:18:33,277: mugc:INFO Region:us-east-1 Removed
custodian-ec2-tag-new
```

In the preceding policy, `RunInstances` was used in the events element to respond to the CloudTrail event that fires when AWS EC2 instances are started. `RunInstances` is actually a shortcut (*https://oreil.ly/qyelx*) for the following Python code:

```
# RunInstances Shortcut in the CloudWatchEvents class
'RunInstances': {
            'ids': 'responseElements.instancesSet.items[].instanceId',
            'source': 'ec2.amazonaws.com'}}
```

Not all CloudTrail events have shortcuts defined in this class. Without a shortcut in this class, you need to fill out the events, as shown in the following event-based policy:

```
# Example event-based policy with long-hand CloudTrail event definition
policies:
  - name: sg-ingress-ports
    description: |
      Selects security groups with ingress rules that include ports
      open to 0.0.0.0/0
    resource: aws.security-group
    mode:
      type: cloudtrail
      tags:
        billing: lob-cc
        env: sandbox
        owner: jimmyray
      role: custodian
      events:
        - source: ec2.amazonaws.com
          event: AuthorizeSecurityGroupIngress
          ids: "responseElements.securityGroupRuleSet.items[].groupId"
    filters:
    - "tag:Name": c7n-sg-test # added for testing only, remove before flight
    - type: ingress
      IpProtocol: tcp
      Ports: [80,8080,22]
      Cidr:
        value: "0.0.0.0/0"
    actions:
      - type: remove-permissions
        ingress: matched
```

Periodic mode policy execution.   In the preceding policy, the `AuthorizeSecurity` `GroupIngress` event is defined without a shortcut. While using a shortcut would be easier, this approach ensures that you can write policies to react to virtually any CloudTrail event. This policy removes ingress rules that are open to quad-zero CIDRs, based on specific network ports, without removing valid ingress rules.

If I wanted to run a policy Lambda on a scheduled basis, then I could change the mode of the policy to periodic as in the following YAML:

```
# scheduled policy lambda
…
    mode:
      type: periodic
      schedule: "rate(1 hour)"
      tags:
        billing: lob-cc
        env: sandbox
        owner: jimmyray
      role: <ROLE_NAME_OR_ARN>
    filters:
      - "State.Name": running
      - or:
        - "tag:billing": absent
        - "tag:env": absent
        - "tag:owner": absent
    actions:
      - type: tag
        tags:
          billing: lob-cc
          env: sandbox
          owner: jimmyray
```

In the preceding policy, I removed the event-driven elements and added scheduling and filter elements. The preceding policy is scheduled to run every hour, triggered by an EventBridge schedule rule.

The three run modes that I just showed you are not the only options for applying c7n policies; they are really powerful, though. Running policies locally—in pull mode—helps with prototyping, reporting, manual intervention, and automated pipelines. The output files produced provide machine-readable artifacts, and you can even send policy metrics to the cloud.

The two Lambda policy options, CloudTrail and periodic, help you create reactive controls to API events or even scheduled execution. Even though the CloudTrail policy reacts to API events, the reaction time is minimal, making the reactive control experience closer to a preventive control experience.

That's not the end. I could not possibly cover all the possible integrations to AWS, Azure, GCP, and so on or the relative use cases. I hope you continue your discovery of c7n and how it could solve some issues for your projects. Even if you don't own the CSP environments in which you create tenant resources, c7n can help you better manage your resources, operating within needed guardrails to remain secure and compliant.

Now that you have a basic understanding of c7n policies and execution, let's explore how c7n can be used to implement practices in FinOps.

FinOps with Custodian

There are many definitions for *FinOps*. I prefer the FinOps Foundation's definition (*https://oreil.ly/XwLP6*) that references financial operations and DevOps. When I think of correctly managing cloud resources and reducing costs and waste, I see FinOps as part of cloud engineering. As such, I think FinOps should be addressed early in the cloud-engineering process and not just be triggered by high cloud costs.

Cloud FinOps is also a cultural consideration. While FinOps practices and automation may be centralized, the options that teams exercise to increase efficiency and reduce cost and waste work best when they are federated to teams that actually create and manage cloud resources. Federation of knowledge, tools, and best practices creates cultural awareness of cloud cost-consciousness (CCC). CCC drives the practices that individual teams can take to improve their respective financial postures and provides them with levers they can pull to improve their financial effectiveness. CCC that is pervasive throughout an organization doesn't just reduce costs; it prepares the organization for action by ensuring that teams have access to cloud resources when they need them.

Along with the options that teams can use to reduce risks, organizations can use c7n policies to implement FinOps controls. These controls can run in multiple c7n modes.

One of the most pervasive waste situations in cloud computing occurs when compute resources are provisioned and not fully utilized. Stories of overprovisioned yet underutilized compute are legion. When it comes to cloud compute instances, the variable spend model—a.k.a. "pay for what you use"—changes to "pay for what you provision and continue to run." In other words, users routinely provision compute that they don't use. If unused compute continues to run, costs continue to mount. Paying for unused compute is a cardinal sin in cloud computing.

In AWS, some of the most effective policies for reducing compute waste use Amazon CloudWatch metrics to select EC2 instances that are underutilized. The following c7n policy selects EC2 instances where the CloudWatch metrics indicate that CPU utilization is less than or equal to 5% of provisioned resources:

```
# Cloud Custodian FinOps policy for underutilized CPU resources
policies:
  - name: ec2-cpu-metrics
    resource: aws.ec2
    filters:
      - type: metrics
        name: CPUUtilization
        days: 14
        value: 5.0
        missing-value: 0
        op: lte
    actions:
      - stop
      - type: tag
        tags:
          c7n-status: cpu-underutilized
      - type: notify
        to:
          - event-user
          - resource-creator
          - jimmyray@example.com
        owner_absent_contact:
          - backup@example.com
        template: policy-template
        transport:
          type: sqs
          region: us-east-1
          queue: c7n-message-queue
```

The preceding policy takes action on the selected EC2 instance(s) by stopping and tagging the actual instance(s). The policy also sends notifications, via Amazon Simple Queue Service (SQS), to interested parties. The policy could be changed to simply mark the instance(s) for stopping or terminating and still send the notification to warn users that the instance(s) will be stopped in the future.

If I know that the use of large compute instance types usually results in underutilized resources, I might write a policy that proactively acts on large compute instances when I detect them. The following CloudTrail policy does just that, using YAML anchors to supply a list of known suspect large instances on which I want to focus:

```
# Policy to detect large instances and stop them
vars:
  large-instance-types: &large-instance-types
    - m7i.8xlarge
    - m7i.12xlarge
    - m7i.16xlarge
    - m7i.24xlarge
    - m7i.48xlarge

policies:
  - name: ec2-stop-larges
```

```
resource: aws.ec2
mode:
  type: cloudtrail
  tags:
    billing: lob-cc
    env: sandbox
    owner: jimmyray
  role: <ROLE_NAME_OR_ARN>
  events:
    - RunInstances
filters:
  - type: value
    key: InstanceType
    value: *large-instance-types
    op: in
actions:
  - stop
  - type: tag
    tags:
      c7n-status: ec2-too-large
```

Underutilization is also an issue with databases, and the following policy finds AWS Relational Database Service (RDS) instances that are aged at least 14 days and exhibit underutilized CPU metrics:

```
# Policy to find underutilized RDS instances
policies:
  - name: rds-underutilized
    resource: aws.rds
    filters:
      - type: value
        value-type: age
        key: InstanceCreateTime
        value: 14
        op: gt
      - type: metrics
        name: CPUUtilization
        statistics: average
        days: 14
        value: 10
        missing-value: 0
        op: lte
    actions:
      - stop
```

Sometimes, RDS instances go completely unused, and the following policy can detect that situation as well:

```
# Policy to detect unused RDS instances
policies:
  - name: rds-unused
    resource: aws.rds
```

```
filters:
  - type: value
    value_type: age
    value: 14
    op: gte
  - type: metrics
    name: DatabaseConnections
    days: 14
    value: 0
    missing-value: 0
    op: eq
```

Orphaned or unused resources cause waste and hygiene issues that I label as *cloud-cruft*. Regardless of costs, cloud-cruft provides additional security-attack surfaces that have no need to exist if resources are not being used. In that vein, the following policy identifies unused EBS volumes and then snapshots and deletes them:

```
# policy to id and remove unused EBS volumes
policies:
  - name: ebs-volumes-avail-14
    resource: aws.ebs
    filters:
      - Attachements: []
      - type: value
        key: CreateTime
        value_type: age
        op: gte
        value: 14
    actions:
      - snapshot
      - delete
```

The preceding policy looks for EBS volumes that are at least 14 days old and available—they have no attachments—and it creates a snapshot of each volume before deleting the volume.

As a point of reference, the following policy would find orphaned Azure disks:

```
# Policy to select orphaned Azure disks
policies:
  - name: azure-disk-orphan
    resource: azure.disk
    filters:
      - type: value
        key: managedBy
        vaue: null
```

The flipside of orphaned resources is resources that no longer have connections, like load balancers. The following policy finds elastic load balancers (ELBs) that no longer have connected instances:

```
# Policy to locate unused ELBs
policies:
  - name: els-no-instances
    resource: aws.elb
    filters:
      - Instances: []
      - type: value
        key: CreateTime
        value_type: age
        op: gte
        value: 1
```

The preceding policy looks for empty `Instances` arrays in ELBs, indicating that there are no attached instances. It only looks at ELBs that are at least a day old because, as you may know, EC2 attachment is not instantaneous.

Up until now, I've used my FinOps policies to detect underutilized, unused, orphaned, or disconnected resources. However, FinOps also means providing options to teams consuming cloud resources. To that end, the following policies implement off-hours shutdown support to teams that can shut down compute resources when they are not needed:

```
# Off-hour compute shutdown policies
policies:
  - name: offhour-pm-stop
    resource: aws.ec2
    mode:
      type: periodic
      schedule: rate(1 hour)
      role: <ROLE_NAME_OR_ARN>
      tags:
        billing: lob-cc
        env: sandbox
        owner: jimmyray
    filters:
      - type: offhour
        tag: custodian_downtime
        default_tz: et
        offhour: 17
        opt-out: false
      - "tag:aws:autoscaling:groupName": absent
    actions:
      - stop

  - name: offhour-am-start
    resource: aws.ec2
    mode:
      type: periodic
      schedule: rate(1 hour)
      role: <ROLE_NAME_OR_ARN>
      tags:
```

```
      billing: lob-cc
      env: sandbox
      owner: jimmyray
  filters:
    - type: onhour
      tag: custodian_downtime
      default_tz: et
      onhour: 8
      opt-out: false
    - "tag:aws:autoscaling:groupName": absent
  actions:
    - start
```

The preceding policies stop all compute instances tagged with the `custodian_down`
`time` tag that are not part of an autoscaling group at 17:00 US Eastern time and
restart them at 08:00 US Eastern time. Instances are kept off over the weekend. However, users can restart their compute instances as needed. These types of policies can
also be used to suspend, resume, and resize autoscaling groups (ASGs), keeping track
of ASG capacity settings using tags.

FinOps requires a multiprong approach to expose costs and usage trends via reporting, take action against waste, and provide proactive tools for users who create and
manage cloud resources. C7n policies solve all of those use cases. At a minimum, c7n
provides a very functional layer to complement existing solutions and practices.

Summary

In this chapter, I focused on two tools that provide layers of cloud resource management. With Prowler, you can assess your cloud resources and detect unwanted and
potentially insecure resources and situations. Prowler provides hundreds of checks
across multiple CSPs out of the box. Since Prowler is an OSS project written in
Python, you have an opportunity to contribute to the project. The Prowler Pro version offers more enterprise features that can help you execute faster with the Prowler
solution.

The Prowler solution offers many checks for detection, but it provides no solution
with which you can take action on failed checks. While the Prowler project is OSS,
building new checks requires that you know Python and understand how checks are
constructed. I think Prowler makes sense as a possible additional layer in a defense-
in-depth solution. It can be run locally or in automated pipelines.

The second solution that I introduced in this chapter—Cloud Custodian—provides
the ability both to detect issues and to take action on detected issues. C7n is OSS written in Python, so you can also contribute to the project. However, c7n abstracts the
complexity of writing Python code to interact with CSP APIs through its YAML-
based DSL. Most c7n users never have to write Python.

C7n policies work across multiple CSPs, though the lion's share of policies and functionality seems to be for AWS. As you have seen in this and previous chapters, that is not uncommon. And it makes sense given that c7n was initially built to help manage AWS cloud usage. That said, based on my experience, c7n goes beyond many of its competitors with multicloud support. C7n also has a large and active community from whom I have received help multiple times.

The scope of c7n policy language and CSP features—including FinOps policies and notification—provides the most complete solution for a well-managed cloud that I have experienced. If you again consider the PaC solution selection criteria from Chapter 1, c7n meets and exceeds many of the criteria. Its flexibility means that c7n will meet your needs as your organization grows and your cloud usage evolves. Like Prowler, c7n can run locally or in pipeline automation. It can also run in event-driven or periodic modes in the CSP account/subscription/project.

If I had to point out any negatives about the c7n project, I would surface the 1,100 open issues, some dating back to 2016, or some of the 190+ open pull requests (PRs) dating back to 2017. However, there are 2,800+ closed issues, 4,600+ closed PRs, 1,400 forks, and 5,000 stars. While the project could benefit from housekeeping of aged issues and PRs, it is mature and still well supported by maintainers and the community. And that community has been very helpful to me.

Next, in Chapter 14, I will explore how PaC can be used to implement best practices for organizations trying to build and harden their software supply chain.

PaC and the Software Supply Chain

The software supply chain (SSC) includes activities involved in the creation and delivery of software solutions for in-house use, commercial sale, and OSS development. These activities—arranged into processes and automated pipelines—build, test, and maintain software components. As an industry, we have increased our focus over the past several years on securing the SSC and avoiding attacks and exploitations, made possible through known and unknown vulnerabilities.

At the time of this writing, there are many emerging technologies and approaches being used and espoused that promise to improve how we manage SSC. These technologies and approaches come on the heels of some very well-known SSC attacks. I think we need to look at these and similar attacks in general, and imagine how we could help detect or even prevent them with the correct application of PaC solutions.

Attacking Normal

Years ago, when I was surveying Kubernetes security tools, I reviewed a network tool that functioned by first learning the network behavior of Pods. Once Pod network behavior was recorded and characterized, the solution would alert of possible aberrant network behavior and even quarantine Pods found to be "misbehaving." This use case is common in the realm of network security, though it was new to internal Kubernetes cluster networking at the time.

As it turns out, cybersecurity attacks are frequently detected when operations of systems and components stray from their known normal (a.k.a. their baseline). Such was the case with the SolarWinds attack of 2020. This attack first started in 2019 when the SolarWinds Orion product was compromised by the now infamous Sunspot malware. Sunspot compromised the Orion build processes and introduced the Sunburst backdoor (*https://oreil.ly/qDRYE*) into the Orion product. The existence of the malware that introduced the backdoor was not detected in the build processes. Some speculate that the makers of Sunspot hid their tracks well by hiding the differences in the files and by actually removing the malware files from the SolarWinds build systems. This was a very sophisticated attack.

The existence of the Sunburst malware was detected much later, after it had infected instances of Orion being used by customers. Users noticed abnormal behavior and surfaced their concerns, which eventually led to detection and subsequent remediation.

The Log4Shell vulnerability of 2021 is another well-known SSC issue. It was particularly nasty because it allowed remote code execution (RCE) via crafted log payloads, and it required no specific authentication. It was also very widely used though various open source and proprietary software programs, including games. In fact, one of the earliest detections of the vulnerability was made by Minecraft players (*https://oreil.ly/24Gun*), who discovered that adding malicious code in the game's chat feature, being logged by Apache Log4j, would allow them to execute code remotely. Though not initially a result of maliciousness, the Log4Shell vulnerability did enable the possibility of malicious attacks.

Some sources estimate that hundreds of millions of systems needed patching to correct the Log4Shell issues. That is testament to how far some OSS packages can reach across many projects. At the time, I was working with the AWS Kubernetes team in an effort to help Kubernetes customers patch Kubernetes worker nodes using DaemonSets, and I wondered how such a vulnerability could go unnoticed in the codebase for so long.

Both of these major vulnerabilities were SSC issues and were discovered by end users before software maintainers were made aware of the vulnerabilities. Along with other SSC issues, SolarWinds and Log4Shell illustrate the need for improved SSC security.

It is considerably more difficult to detect the abnormal situations upstream in an SSC with many different libraries, components, and build steps. As I have written many times in this book, detecting and preventing abnormal behavior are two of the most important features of PaC solutions. PaC is uniquely positioned to bolster and improve the SSC that is now needed in the software industry.

The purpose of this chapter—as with the entire book—is not to focus on a specific solution so much as to illustrate the possibilities of PaC solutions and how they may fit our problems. Consequently, in this chapter I will build on material and recurring themes from past chapters to apply PaC to the emerging field of SSC. PaC and SSC may have initially evolved independently, but PaC strongly complements the SSC security, compliance, and governance goals toward which many of us are working.

In the next section, I start with some of the different policy enforcement points (PEPs) within a typical SSC.

SSC Policy Enforcement Points

In Chapter 3, I briefly introduced the concept of PEPs and how they integrate to applications and send policy decision requests to policy decision points (PDPs). The boundary between PEP and PDP is a "layer of indirection" that separates the application interface from the policy-engine implementation. The typical SSC contains several PEPs, some of which I list here, along with the PaC use cases:

Codebase
PaC validates actual codebase, such as GitHub actions on a code push.

Pipeline
PaC validates pipeline execution based on evidence from produced artifacts, such as static application security testing (SAST) and software composition analysis (SCA) outputs. Pipeline evidence creates attestations that are evaluated by gates.

Infrastructure as code
As we saw in Chapters 11 and 12, PaC validates IaC before it is applied to environments.

Resource environments
Resource environments include the cloud or datacenters. In cloud computing, PaC validates IaaS resources before and after they are applied.

Execution environments
These can be clusters, like Kubernetes, virtual machines (VMs), or even bare-metal servers. You saw in Chapters 4 through 10 how PaC was used to mutate and validate request payloads before changes were applied.

Applications/APIs
These are the actual functioning applications and interfaces with which users and others systems engage. PaC is applied here to interrogate (mutate and validate) inbound requests, such as the AuthZ use cases seen in Chapter 3.

Figure 14-1 shows a high-level diagram of the SSC PEPs. There are more aspects of the SSC, like OCI registries, not pictured.

Since I have covered some of the SSC PEPs in different chapters, I will not duplicate them here. In this chapter, I provide examples that can be used in codebases and automated pipelines, automating PaC evaluations of code artifacts at both levels. These approaches can be used at the developer desktop or in code repository and pipeline automation.

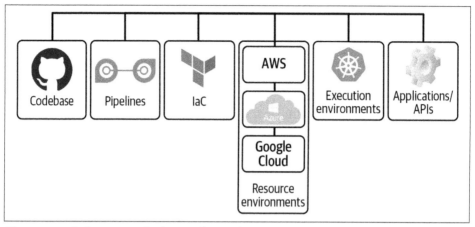

Figure 14-1. Software supply chain policy enforcement points

Codebase and Pipeline PEPs

As you have seen multiple times in this book, PaC generally evaluates structured files—JSON and YAML. However, in Chapter 11 I introduced how Conftest performs inline file format auto-detection and parsing. These Conftest features expand the types of codebase artifacts that are easily scanned without manual parsing and conversion. This is very helpful when we consider the different artifacts found in modern software projects and automation.

For example, many projects result in container images, using the Dockerfile format (*https://oreil.ly/qk8W-*). Many potentially bad behaviors come from how Dockerfiles are misbuilt and the poor user experiences produced by some container tools. Try to spot all of the potentially dangerous settings in the following Dockerfile:

```
# Dockerfile.bad
FROM alpine as builder   ❶

ENV SECRET_KEY=asdsadasdasdasdasda   ❷
ENV AWS_ACCESS_KEY_ID=asdsadasdasdasdasda
ENV AWS_SECRET_ACCESS_KEY=asdsadasdasdasdasda

ADD https://example.com/files/somefile somefile   ❸

FROM alpine:latest   ❹
WORKDIR /
COPY --from=builder somefile somefile

RUN apk add --no-cache curl=8.4.0 \
--repository=https://example.com/curl-repo   ❺

RUN apk add --no-cache curl=1.24.5   ❻
```

```
# WGet some tar file
ARG FILE_LINK="https://example.com/files/somefile.tar.gz"  ❼
ARG TAR_FILE="somefile.tar.gz"
RUN wget -O ${TAR_FILE} ${FILE_LINK} \
 && tar -xzf ${TAR_FILE} \
 && rm ${TAR_FILE}

COPY entrypoint.sh /entrypoint.sh

ENTRYPOINT [ "/entrypoint.sh" ]
```

❶   Container base image version should not be empty.

❷   Secrets should not be in the Dockerfile.

❸   The *example.com* URL should not be used with the ADD command.

❹   Container base image version should not be latest.

❺   The *example.com* URL should not be used with the RUN apk command.

❻   The RUN apk command requires a repository argument.

❼   The *example.com* URL should not be used with the ARG command.

The following Rego policy contains rules that are applied to evaluate the Dockerfiles authored and integrated by developers:

```
# Dockerfile Rego policy
package main

import rego.v1  ❶

places_where_secrets_hide := {
        "secret",
        "apikey",
        "access",
}

bad_domains := {"example.com"}

suspect_runs := {
        "wget",
        "curl",
}

# Deny if secrets found in the ENV command
deny_secrets contains msg if {
        some x in input
        x.Cmd == "env"
```

```
        value := x.Value[0]
        some s in places_where_secrets_hide
        contains(lower(value), s)
        msg := sprintf("secrets found: %q", [value])
}

# Deny if "latest" container image version
deny_latest contains msg if {
        some x in input
        x.Cmd == "from"
        value := x.Value[0]
        endswith(lower(value), "latest")
        msg := sprintf("FROM with latest found: %q", [value])
}

# Deny if no container image version
deny_no_version contains msg if {
        some x in input
        x.Cmd == "from"
        value := x.Value[0]
        count(split(value, ":")) == 1
        msg := sprintf("image with no version found: %q", [value])
}

deny_run_apk_no_repo contains msg if {
        some c in input
        c.Cmd == "run"
        command := c.Value[0]
        subcommand := split(command, " ")[0]
        lower(subcommand) == "apk"
        not contains(lower(command), "--repository")
        msg := sprintf("RUN apk does not specify repo argument, found: %q",
    [command])
}

deny_run_apk_bad_domain contains msg if {
        some c in input
        c.Cmd == "run"
        command := c.Value[0]
        subcommand := split(command, " ")[0]
        lower(subcommand) == "apk"
        contains(lower(command), "--repository")
        some d in bad_domains
        contains(lower(command), d)
        msg := sprintf("RUN apk specifies bad repo domain, found: %q", [command])
}

# Deny if cURL or wget is used with RUN and bad domain
deny_curl_wget contains msg if {
        some x in input
        x.Cmd == "run"
        value := x.Value[0]
```

```
    # print(value)  ❷

    some run in suspect_runs
    contains(lower(value), run)
    some d in bad_domains
    contains(lower(value), d)
    msg := sprintf("RUN with cURL|wget and bad domain, %q, found: %q",
[suspect_runs, value])
}

# Deny if example.com is used with ADD command
deny_add_domain contains msg if {
    some x in input
    x.Cmd == "add"
    value := x.Value[0]
    some d in bad_domains
    contains(lower(value), d)
    msg := sprintf("ADD with bad domain, %q, found: %q", [bad_domains, value])
}

# Deny if example.com is used with ARG command
deny_arg_domain contains msg if {
    some x in input
    x.Cmd == "arg"
    value := x.Value[0]
    some d in bad_domains
    contains(lower(value), d)
    msg := sprintf("ARG with bad domain, %q, found: %q", [bad_domains, value])
}
```

❶ This import is needed for OPA 1.0 compatibility.

❷ The print() statement helps with debugging Rego execution.

While this is a Rego policy that can be used in OPA, this policy is meant to be applied via Conftest. This means that the rule names I used were restricted to deny, viola tion, and warn. Rules used in Conftest Rego policies also support _suffixes. I used this technique to disambiguate the rule names.

When I applied the preceding Rego policy, Conftest detected multiple errors and warnings and displayed the findings:

```
# Test Dockerfile.bad with conftest
$ conftest test -p docker.rego Dockerfile.bad
FAIL - Dockerfile.bad - main - secrets found: "AWS_ACCESS_KEY_ID"
FAIL - Dockerfile.bad - main - secrets found: "AWS_SECRET_ACCESS_KEY"
FAIL - Dockerfile.bad - main - secrets found: "SECRET_KEY"
FAIL - Dockerfile.bad - main - FROM with latest found: "alpine:latest"
FAIL - Dockerfile.bad - main - image with no version found: "alpine"
FAIL - Dockerfile.bad - main - RUN apk does not specify repo argument,
```

```
found: "apk add --no-cache curl=1.24.5"
FAIL - Dockerfile.bad - main - RUN apk specifies bad repo domain,
found: "apk add --no-cache curl=8.4.0
--repository=https://example.com/curl-repo"
FAIL - Dockerfile.bad - main - RUN with cURL|wget and bad domain,
"{\"curl\", \"wget\"}", found: "apk add --no-cache curl=8.4.0
--repository=https://example.com/curl-repo"
FAIL - Dockerfile.bad - main - ADD with bad domain, "{\"example.com\"}",
found: "https://example.com/files/somefile"
FAIL - Dockerfile.bad - main - ARG with bad domain, "{\"example.com\"}",
found: "FILE_LINK=\"https://example.com/files/somefile.tar.gz\""

10 tests, 0 passed, 0 warnings, 10 failures, 0 exceptions
```

 When running Rego against Dockerfiles that use the ARG command, the Dockerfile arguments are not expanded in the Rego execution. That is why I checked for the bad domain—*example.com*—in the ARG command.

The Repo policy works as required, detecting unwanted Dockerfile entries and adhering to Regal linting rules. Next, let's revisit defense in depth in our codebases.

Revisiting defense in depth with codebase PEPs

In Chapter 1, I introduced the concept of defense in depth (DiD) (*https://oreil.ly/_FLpM*) and how PaC can be used to add multiple layers of security and compliance. As you consider codebase PEPs, you can apply DiD with PaC in your codebases. For example, consider Kubernetes admission control, introduced in Chapter 4, with multiple solutions discussed in Chapters 5 through 10. Admission control is used to stop unwanted changes in Kubernetes with execution environment PEPs. Those same changes can be stopped earlier with codebase PEPs, thereby enforcing a DiD strategy.

For example, you can apply a DiD strategy by applying PaC to Kubernetes artifacts in your codebase before they are applied to your clusters. This approach also saves time by identifying issues earlier, before deployment. The following Rego policy tests for the explicit latest version and the implicit latest version (no version) on each image in a Kubernetes Deployment manifest:

```
# Policy for latest versions - deployment.rego
package main

import rego.v1

# latest bad
deny_latest contains msg if {
        some container in input.spec.template.spec.containers
        image := container.image
        endswith(lower(image), "latest")
```

```
      msg = sprintf("Image with latest found: %q", [image])
}

# no version bad
deny_no_version contains msg if {
      some container in input.spec.template.spec.containers
      image := container.image
      count(split(image, ":")) == 1
      msg = sprintf("Image with no version found: %q", [image])
}
```

Beyond PaC validation of Kubernetes manifests, you could use Kubeconform (*https://oreil.ly/kubeconform*) to validate manifests against official Kubernetes schemas. You should do this before PaC is applied to validate actual settings. This is similar to how Kubernetes does it in the API server request flow: schema first, then settings.

DiD is an approach that should be part of every security or compliance strategy. Using codebase PEPs enables DiD and helps detect issues early in your SSC.

Writing and running unit tests are additional PaC—and coding, in general—best practices; let's see how it is done in Rego in the next section.

Don't forget your Rego unit tests

Rego supports a robust and simple unit-testing framework (*https://oreil.ly/CX4bO*). I recommend that Rego authors deliver no Rego without unit tests. Since these policies are applied using Conftest, I used a two-stage process to produce test data and unit test rules:

1. Run `conftest parse` to generate JSON data from known good and bad Dockerfiles.
2. Build unit tests using the parsed JSON data.

In my Dockerfile example, I placed the unit-test Rego file into the same directory as the Dockerfile Rego policy, as seen in the following `tree` output:

```
# Tree of Dockerfile Rego policies
.
├── docker.rego
└── docker_test.rego
```

In the *docker_test.rego* file, I started with the `data_in_bad` variable to hold the parsed JSON:

```
# data_in variable
package main_test
```

```
import rego.v1

data_in_bad := [   ❶
        {
                "Cmd": "from",
                "Flags": [],
                "JSON": false,
                "Stage": 0,
                "SubCmd": "",
                "Value": ["alpine:latest"],   ❷
        },
        {
                "Cmd": "env",
                "Flags": [],
                "JSON": false,
                "Stage": 0,
                "SubCmd": "",
                "Value": [
                        "SECRET_KEY",
                        "Asdsadasdasdasdasda",   ❸
                ],
        },
...
```

❶ The `data_in_bad` object collection provides mock data as JSON, from the parsed Dockerfile, for the Rego test.

❷ The "latest" tag on the alpine image should trigger a test deny or violation.

❸ The secret embedded in the parsed Dockerfile (mocked data) should trigger a deny or violation.

Then, I wrote each unit-test rule to execute its corresponding Rego rule, using the `data_in_bad` variable as the rule input:

```
# Sample unit test rule with data_in_bad variable
test_deny_secrets if {
      main.deny_secrets[msg] with input as data_in_bad
}
```

While it may not be immediately obvious, the `main.deny_secrets[msg]` call matches the rule signature of `deny_secrets contains msg if`. In fact, the signatures were identical before I used the aforementioned Regal linter to correct style and idiomatic Rego issues.

This simple unit-testing approach ensures that your unit tests are correctly written for the data under evaluation.

Rego tests should be defined in a different package then the actual Rego policies under test. Since I placed my policies in the *main* package—for Conftest ease of use—I placed my tests in the *main_test* package. I then prefixed the rules under test with the *main* prefix, so that each unit test in the *main_test* package could locate its respective rule—to be tested—in the *main* package. This is a Regal linter finding.

Using Conftest enforces security, compliance, and governance controls as well as best practices. However, how do you operationalize it to best help your development teams where they work? I would start with deciding when and where you want to expose the policy evaluations to your developers. Spoiler alert: I am a firm believer in the idea of early-and-often exposure. With policies and unit tests written, we can focus on helping developers best use policies where they work.

Enabling developers

As with DevOps and DevSecOps, "early and often" implies that we shift left—read as *upstream*—and that developers use these techniques locally when they are actually coding. For that to work, they should have access to Conftest locally. That is easy enough. They can install the Conftest binary or even run it from a container.

Next, developers need access to centrally curated policies. That is also easy, if you store the policies in a Git repository. Users can download the policies with the `conftest pull` command:

```
# Conftest pull policies from central GitHub repo
$ conftest pull \
git::https://github.com/<GITHUB_ORG>/<GITHUB_PROJECT>.git//<POLICY_FOLDER>/
```

Running the preceding command downloads the policies into a local *policy* folder, relative to a present working directory. As I wrote in Chapter 11, my policies use convention over configuration by namespacing all the conftest Rego policies into *main*. This will make the `conftest` command easier for folks who are not meant to be Conftest or Rego SMEs.

Using the *main* package for all my Conftest Rego is easier for execution, but I sacrifice the organization I would get by arranging my policies into different packages.

However, having developers run tests locally—even with centrally curated Rego policies— works only if the developers choose or remember to follow those practices. We need a better solution, one that employs automation and is triggered by events, like those involved in traditional CI activities. The solution also reduces the cognitive load for developers.

Throughout this book, my projects have been hosted on GitHub. So a GitHub-centric automation solution made the most sense in this context. To that end, I used GitHub actions (*https://oreil.ly/Ll-bw*) to build the needed CI workflows.

I created the CI workflows using GitHub actions, triggered by Git events—the first being push. This workflow configuration is found in my project at the path *.github/workflows/github-actions.yml*. I used the following GitHub action configuration:

```
# On-push GitHub action
---
name: Run Dockerfile Validation
run-name: ${{ github.actor }} pushed a commit   ❶

on:
  push:
    branches:
      - main   ❷

jobs:
  conftest:
    runs-on: ubuntu-latest
    container: openpolicyagent/conftest:v0.47.0   ❸
    steps:
      - name: Checkout   ❹
        uses: actions/checkout@main
      - name: Validate   ❺
        run: |
          conftest test -o github -p policy/docker/docker.rego configs/Dockerfile
```

❶ The run is tied to the GitHub actor.

❷ The action triggers on a push to the main branch.

❸ Use the Conftest container.

❹ Check out the code first.

❺ Validate the code with Conftest.

The preceding configuration runs an action on every push to the *main* branch that launches a GitHub-hosted runner machine, running the Ubuntu OS. The action runs a Docker container based on the pulled *openpolicyagent/conftest:v0.47.0* image. Once the container is running, the action checks out the current codebase head, and then the `conftest` command is executed against the checked-out codebase. The following action logs indicate the same failures and warnings from locally executed tests:

```
# GitHub action conftest logs
Run conftest test -o github -p policy/docker/docker.rego configs/Dockerfile \
--ignore "failing-*"
  conftest test -o github -p policy/docker/docker.rego configs/Dockerfile \
  --ignore "failing-*"
  shell: sh -e {0}
Testing 'configs/Dockerfile' against 10 policies in namespace 'main'
  Error: ADD with bad source, "[\"example.com\"]", found @ line 5
...
```

In Figure 14-2, you can see the run of the GitHub action, with error annotations that reflect Conftest evaluation of the Dockerfiles.

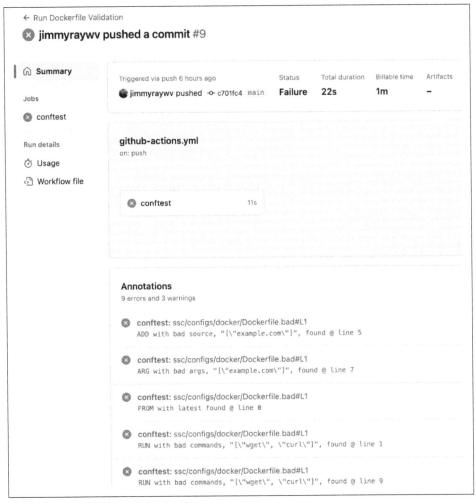

Figure 14-2. GitHub action console output

If running the action on every push to *main* doesn't match requirements, I could change the action or even add another one that runs when a pull request targets a specific branch, like *main*. I would change the on keyword to use the `pull_request` trigger:

```
# GitHub action trigger for PR
on:
  pull_request:
    branches:
      - main
```

Moving the Conftest validation to GitHub means that I can better control when the automated validation occurs, enforcing that it actually occurs while reducing the developer cognitive load. However, code integration still needs to occur for the validation to occur. Performing these checks during integration is not mutually exclusive with performing them while coding. I could also make it easier for local execution by automating the execution with a Makefile, like I have done in previous chapters. In fact, the Makefiles used locally by developers to automate repetitive tasks also work well in CI automation.

The following Makefile works locally for developers and remotely in GitHub actions, providing the same experience and outcome for both PEPs:

```
# PEP-agnostic Makefile to validate Dockerfiles with conftest
.DEFAULT_GOAL := validate-docker

.PHONY: validate-docker

validate-docker:
        docker run --rm -v $(shell pwd):/ssc openpolicyagent/conftest:v0.47.0 \
        test -p /ssc/policy/docker/docker.rego /ssc/configs/docker/ -o github
```

To make the new Makefile approach work, I changed the GitHub action job to call make and no longer explicitly specify the Conftest container in the action:

```
# GitHub action to run make
...
jobs:
  conftest:
    runs-on: ubuntu-latest
    steps:
      - uses: actions/checkout@main
        with:
          fetch-depth: 1
      - name: Run Makefile
        run: make validate-docker
```

By design, the Makefile solution executes across multiple PEPs, providing the same functionality and experience in each. This is not the only means to attain this cross-environment fidelity, but it's a good example to drive the message. Using GitHub actions gives the flexibility to run PaC evaluations triggered by multiple codebase events and control downstream processes with event statuses.

These techniques are suitable for many other types of configuration and code artifacts, including Kubernetes manifests. To that end, please check out the KubeCon Europe 2023 talk by Eve Ben Ezra and Michael Hume titled "Automating Configuration and Permissions Testing for GitOps with OPA Conftest" (*https://oreil.ly/gF_TX*).

Codebase PEPs—local and code repository—are the closest to your developers and should provide the maximum convenience and timely feedback without increasing cognitive load.

In the next section, I explore the Pipeline PEP and using PaC to scan image artifacts.

PaC and Trivy with Container Images

Building artifacts, such as container images, happens in the pipeline—a.k.a. build— PEPs. Once the artifacts are built, automation continues to evaluate the artifacts for correctness, vulnerabilities, and security concerns, such as secrets embedded in artifacts. In the next example, I use the OSS Trivy (*https://oreil.ly/81ynQ*) tool to scan for vulnerabilities and secrets in the container image I built for the Answers example application used in Chapter 7.

Once the image was built and stored in the Docker daemon, I ran Trivy using the following command:

```
# Run Trivy on container image
$ trivy image 3108f1420959 -f json > trivy-answers.json
2024-02-11T09:20:01.528-0500    INFO    Vulnerability scanning is enabled
2024-02-11T09:20:01.528-0500    INFO    Secret scanning is enabled
...
2024-02-11T09:20:01.545-0500    INFO    Detected OS: alpine
2024-02-11T09:20:01.545-0500    INFO    Detecting Alpine vulnerabilities...
2024-02-11T09:20:01.546-0500    INFO    Number of language-specific files: 1
2024-02-11T09:20:01.546-0500    INFO    Detecting gobinary vulnerabilities...
```

As you can see from the preceding output, vulnerability and secret scanning was enabled, and Trivy looked for vulnerabilities in the older Alpine OS as well as the Go binary. The Trivy output was directed to the following *trivy-answers.json* file:

```
// Trivy JSON output snippet
{
  "SchemaVersion": 2,
  "CreatedAt": "2024-02-11T09:20:01.549605-05:00",
  "ArtifactName": "3108f1420959",
  "ArtifactType": "container_image",
  "Metadata": {
    "OS": {
      "Family": "alpine",   ❶
      "Name": "3.17.0"
```

```
      },
    …
    "Results": [
      {
        "Target": "3108f1420959 (alpine 3.17.0)", ❶
        "Class": "os-pkgs",
        "Type": "alpine",
        "Vulnerabilities": [
          {
            "VulnerabilityID": "CVE-2022-3996", ❷
            "PkgID": "libcrypto3@3.0.7-r0",
            "PkgName": "libcrypto3",
            "PkgIdentifier": {
              "PURL":
              "pkg:apk/alpine/libcrypto3@3.0.7-r0?arch=aarch64\...
              ...u0026distro=3.17.0"
            },
    …
```

❶   The output refers to the Alpine image, version 3.17.0.

❷   The vulnerability list contains the CVE information, such as CVE ID, package
    ID, package name, and package URL.

The output indicates vulnerabilities in the Results element. Though I opted to return
all vulnerabilities, Trivy can be configured to look only for HIGH and CRITICAL
vulnerabilities, as seen in the following command:

```
# Restrict trivy output to HIGH and CRITICAL vulnerabilities
$ trivy image 3108f1420959 --severity HIGH,CRITICAL -f json > trivy-answers.json
```

Once the Trivy output file was generated, I applied the following OPA Rego policy to
look for vulnerabilities—with HIGH and CRITICAL severities—reported by Trivy. I
wrote the following policy to surface information related to the vulnerabilities:

```
# Rego policy to interrogate Trivy output
package main

import rego.v1

bad_severities := {"HIGH", "CRITICAL"}

default allow := false

allow if {
        count(violation_high_critical) == 0
}

violation_high_critical contains info if {
        some result in input.Results
        some vuln in result.Vulnerabilities
```

```
        sev := vuln.Severity
        sev in bad_severities
        cve := vuln.VulnerabilityID
        pkg := vuln.PkgID
        info := sprintf("cve: %s, severity: %s, package: %s", [cve, sev, pkg])
}
```

I used the following Conftest command to run the OPA Rego policy:

```
# Evaluate Trivy output for high and critical vulnerabilities
$ conftest test -p trivy.rego trivy-answers.json
FAIL - trivy-answers.json - main - cve: CVE-2022-3996, severity:
HIGH, package: libcrypto3@3.0.7-r0
FAIL - trivy-answers.json - main - cve: CVE-2022-3996, severity:
HIGH, package: libssl3@3.0.7-r0
…
18 tests, 0 passed, 0 warnings, 18 failures, 0 exceptions
```

The policy found 18 vulnerabilities that matched the policy rules.

In the preceding command, I left the output set to the default settings. Depending where the policy runs, I would change the output format to better fit the use case. It's also important to know that I have barely touched on Trivy's capabilities. Trivy has built-in compliance and policies and supports Rego custom policies (*https://oreil.ly/ Xt4mo*) as well.

In the next section, I will switch gears a bit to look at the software bill of materials and how PaC can be used to distill usable intelligence from this emerging standard.

Software Bill of Materials

According to the Executive Order on Improving the Nation's Cybersecurity (*https:// oreil.ly/w3_hV*), a software bill of materials (SBOM) is:

> A formal record containing the details and supply chain relationships of various components used in building software. Software developers and vendors often create products by assembling existing open source and commercial software components. The SBOM enumerates these components in a product.

You can think of SBOMs as structured lists of the ingredients of a software project or artifact, including libraries, modules, licensing, and version information. These ingredients tell you what the software is made of, similar to the list of ingredients on the outside of a bottle of vitamins. In other words, the SBOM provides a certain amount of software transparency. In her book *Software Supply Chain Security* (O'Reilly), Cassie Crossley explains that SBOMs are just one part of software transparency:

> Software transparency is about having visibility into the components or libraries, architectures, design elements, security features, testing results, potential threats and risks, known vulnerabilities, and provenance.

The interesting thing about SBOMs is that they don't just include the comprehensive information about the software ingredients; they also include source information of the ingredients, such as package URL (purl) (*https://oreil.ly/XYCFU*) and Common Platform Enumeration (CPE) information (*https://oreil.ly/R130Z*). They can even include information about how bad ingredients are for you—vulnerabilities.

In their simplest forms, SBOMs are machine-readable, structured-data files that contain a list of components and related data that make up a piece of software. The following SBOM snippet was created using Syft (*https://oreil.ly/syft*); the SBOM format, known as a *schema*, uses the OWASP CycloneDX schema standard (*https://oreil.ly/9skWP*):

```
# OWASP CycloneDX SBOM created by Anchore syft
$ syft 24b080de498b -o cyclonedx-json > syft-sbom.json   ❶
{
    "$schema": "http://cyclonedx.org/schema/bom-1.5.schema.json",
    "bomFormat": "CycloneDX",   ❷
    "specVersion": "1.5",
    "serialNumber": "urn:uuid:5661d77f-754f-4394-a943-6ac1fb325913",
    "version": 1,
    "metadata": {
        "timestamp": "2024-01-31T21:44:09-05:00",
        "tools": {
            "components": [
                {
                    "type": "application",
                    "author": "anchore",
                    "name": "syft",
                    "version": "0.103.1"
                }
            ]
        },
        "component": {
            "bom-ref": "e2c8e2f23265dd51",
            "type": "container",
            "name": "24b080de498b",
            "version": "sha256:1f7b1...9a3e8"
        }
    },
    "components": [
        {
            "bom-ref": "pkg:golang/./build/private@(devel)?package-id=...
            ...b45956558ee71293#bgospace/Go3p-Github-Jmespath-GoJmespath/...
            src/githubcom/jmespath/go-jmespath",   ❸
            "type": "library",
            "name": "./build/private/bgospace/Go3p-Github-Jmespath-...
            ...GoJmespath/src/github.com/jmespath/go-jmespath",
            "version": "(devel)",
            "cpe": "cpe:2.3:a:build:private\\/bgospace\\/...
                ...Go3p-Github-Jmespath-GoJmespath\\/src\\/github.com\\/...
                ...jmespath\\/go-jmespath:\\(devel\\):*:*:*:*:*:*:*",   ❹
```

```
              "purl": "pkg:golang/./build/private@(devel)#bgospace/...
                      ...Go3p-Github-Jmespath-GoJmespath/src/github.com/...
                      ...jmespath/go-jmespath",   ❺
...
```

❶ The `syft` command creates an SBOM from a container image using the
    CycloneDX format and writes it to a JSON file.

❷ The SBOM format is CycloneDX.

❸ The components start with the go-jmespath library.

❹ The CPE is included in the component reference.

❺ The package URL is included in the component reference.

In the next section, I apply PaC using OPA Rego and Conftest to evaluate SBOMs.

Evaluating SBOMs with PaC

Given that this preceding SBOM is a JSON file, PaC can be used to interrogate the
SBOM for certain conditions. For example, if I wanted to know if crypto packages
were being used in the software artifact represented by the previous SBOM example, I
could run a policy to look for that source information. The following example Rego
policy is written to be used with Conftest; it uses a `warn` rule to throw a warning if the
string `crypto` is found in any purl of an included software component, thereby indicating that a cryptography library might be in use in the software represented by this
SBOM:

```
# Example conftest policy to warn on crypto components
package main

import rego.v1

default crypto_found := false   ❶

crypto_found if {
        count(warn_crypto) > 0   ❷
}

warn_crypto contains info if {   ❸
        some component in input.components
        purl := component.purl
        ref := component["bom-ref"]
        contains(lower(purl), "crypto")
        info := sprintf("ref: %s", [ref])
}
```

❶ The default value for `crypto_found` is set to `false`.

❷ Count of `warn_crypto` should be 0.

❸ The `warn_crypto` rule looks into the package URL for the `crypto` string.

 The `ref := component["bom-ref"]` Rego expression replaces the typical dot-notation used in the rest of the policy. This is needed since the field name `bom-ref` is hyphenated. Using dot-notation instead of the field identifier brackets causes errors in the policy execution as well as in `opa fmt` and `regal lint` commands. Rego doesn't like field names containing hyphens.

When Conftest is run using the preceding policy to evaluate the SBOM, it produces the following output:

```
# Warn on crypto components
$ conftest test -p sbom-crypto.rego syft-sbom.json -o stdout
WARN - syft-sbom.json - main - ref:
pkg:golang/golang.org/x/crypto@v0.9.0?package-id=c6477fdfd5c712a7

1 test, 0 passed, 1 warning, 0 failures, 0 exceptions
```

Given the preceding example, it's easy to see how PaC adds security and intelligence gathering to the SBOM process.

Next, I describe how to use PaC with SBOMs to find documented vulnerabilities included within SBOMs.

Detecting Vulnerabilities in SBOMs with PaC

Beyond the various types of SBOM schemas we use to format an SBOM, different use cases call for different SBOM types. In the following example, I use Grype (*https://oreil.ly/grype*) to create an SBOM that contains vulnerabilities found in Grype's database (*https://oreil.ly/ODJTB*):

```
# Scan for vulnerabilities with Anchore grype
$ grype --by-cve -o cyclonedx-json --quiet 24b080de498b > grype-sbom.json
```

The preceding command creates an SBOM that includes vulnerabilities, oriented by CVE (*https://www.cve.org*). The command is similar to using `grype` to evaluate the output of `syft`, as seen in the following piped example:

```
# Piping syft sbom output to grype for vulnerability scanning
$ syft -o cyclonedx-json 24b080de498b | grype -o cyclonedx-json > syft-grype.json
```

The following snippet provides an example of what a vulnerability looks like in the CycloneDX SBOM, created by `grype`:

```
// CycloneDX SBOM vulnerability element, created by Anchore grype
… "vulnerabilities": [
    {
      "bom-ref": "urn:uuid:23ea130c-4ff1-4c94-b632-0a3793121766",
      "id": "ALAS-2023-2203",
      "source": {
        "name": "amazon-distro-amazonlinux-2",
        "url": "https://alas.aws.amazon.com/AL2/ALAS-2023-2203.html"
      },
      "references": [
        {
          "id": "ALAS-2023-2203",
          "source": {
            "name": "amazon-distro-amazonlinux-2",
            "url": "https://alas.aws.amazon.com/AL2/ALAS-2023-2203.html"
          }
        }
      ],
      "ratings": [
        {
          "severity": "high"
        }
      ],
      "description":
      "An initial fix in Amazon Linux ca-certificates package relating to ...
      ...CVE-2022-23491 did not properly remove root certificates from ...
      ...TrustCor from the root store. (CVE-2023-32803)",
      "advisories": [
        {
          "url": "https://alas.aws.amazon.com/AL2/ALAS-2023-2203.html"
        }
      ],
      "affects": [
        {
          "ref":
          "pkg:rpm/amzn/ca-certificates@2021.2.50-72.amzn2.0.4?...
          ...arch=noarch&upstream=ca-certificates-2021.2.50-72.amzn...
          ...2.0.4.src.rpm&distro=amzn-2&package-id=c25306c78c469d90"
        }
      ]
    }, …
```

It's important to understand that not all SBOM schemas include the ability to list documented vulnerabilities within an SBOM output. For example, the SPDX schema (*https://spdx.dev*) makes no mention of including vulnerabilities within an SBOM. The jury seems to still be out on whether or not it is a good idea or a violation of SBOM purity to include vulnerabilities in an SBOM.

Let me weigh in. Personally, I like the idea of being able to enrich an SBOM with vulnerability data on demand. However, some tools create SBOMs on the fly from your codebases and then interrogate them to find vulnerabilities, like Trivy described in the previous section. As a friend and colleague of mine, Christopher Phillips, Senior Software Engineer at Anchore, simply explained it, "Grype just colors in the vulnerability section of the SBOM."

Given the preceding vulnerability-enriched SBOM example, I use a policy to look for vulnerability info. The following example policy evaluates the SBOM, looking for vulnerabilities with either high or critical severities:

```
# OPA Rego policy to find high and critical vulnerabilities in SBOMs, using conftest
package main

import rego.v1

bad_severities := {"high", "critical"}   ❶

default compliant := false   ❷

compliant if {
        count(violation_high_critical) == 0   ❸
}

violation_high_critical contains info if {   ❹
        some vulnerability in input.vulnerabilities
        some rating in vulnerability.ratings
        some affect in vulnerability.affects
        rating.severity in bad_severities
        ref := affect.ref
        id := vulnerability.id
        url := vulnerability.source.url
        info := sprintf("id: %s, ref: %s, url: %s", [id, ref, url])
}
```

❶ The Rego policy will look for high or critical vulnerabilities.

❷ By default, the policy returns noncompliant. This enforces negative evaluation.

❸ The total of high and critical vulnerability severities needs to be zero for this SBOM to pass the policy evaluation.

❹ The rule checks if the vulnerability severity rating is in the list of bad severities.

When the preceding policy is executed with the following `conftest` command, vulnerabilities are listed by the CVE, alphabetically and then numerically:

```
# Using conftest to evaluate SBOM with vulnerabilities
$ conftest test -p sbom.rego sbom.json -o stdout
FAIL - sbom.json - main - id: ALAS-2023-2203, ref:
pkg:rpm/amzn/ca-certificates@2021.2.50-72.amzn2.0.4?arch=noarch&upstream=
ca-certificates-2021.2.50-72.amzn2.0.4.src.rpm&distro=amzn-2&package-id=
c25306c78c469d90, url: https://alas.aws.amazon.com/AL2/ALAS-2023-2203.html
...
66 tests, 0 passed, 0 warnings, 66 failures, 0 exceptions
```

The preceding output includes the CVE ID, the affects references, and the CVE source URL. This type of intelligence helps developers and vulnerability-management practitioners detect and use vulnerability information.

Using vulnerability-enriched SBOMs makes sense for those organizations that want to get more out of their SBOMs. Syft and Grype—complementary tools from Anchore—make it very easy to create and process SBOMs. Even though the Anchore tools can detect and alert for vulnerabilities, PaC adds the ability to evaluate SBOMs via automation for controls and detection.

There are many promises of SBOMs. Let's explore them in the next section.

SBOM Promises

In the context of SSC security, I think that several aspects of SBOMs improve overall security postures. If your SSC regularly produces SBOMs, then you can use the SBOMs for drift detection, as described by this Anchore documentation (*https://oreil.ly/GMA3U*). The CycloneDX sbom-utility project (*https://oreil.ly/Z0wkD*) also provides the ability to execute `diff` operations that could be used in drift use cases.

As I have already shown, you can use SBOMs with PaC to detect components to better understand the possible exposure—blast radius—of suspect packages. Looking back at the Log4Shell vulnerability, we can see that blast radius was very important information we needed to fix our codebases and systems.

As we work to improve the overall security postures of our application codebases by reducing CVEs, it helps to understand which CVEs are the highest priority and which we should focus on. We could rely solely on the Common Vulnerability Scoring System (CVSS) (*https://www.first.org/cvss*) scores and severities—critical, high, and so forth—recorded in the National Vulnerability Database (NVD) (*https://nvd.nist.gov*), or we could look to other sources for scores, such as GitHub Advisories (*https://oreil.ly/7G7H5*) and Red Hat. This tends to work in situations where we have only a few CVEs to remediate. However, I think we are better served by understanding more about the CVEs, especially if we have to manage many CVEs across disparate codebases.

I realize that this might be heresy to some CVE purists, but CVSS scores and severities are not enough. I also want to know about the following CVE aspects:

Patchability
> The availability of and ability to patch a specific CVE within the context of the impacted codebase.

Exploitability
> The actual exploitability of the CVE denoted by the Vulnerability Exploitability eXchange (VEX) (*https://oreil.ly/rlknA*) information and the Known Exploited Vulnerabilities (KEV) Catalog (*https://oreil.ly/hurfT*).

Reachability
> As described by Endor Labs (*https://oreil.ly/qYAnK*), reachability analysis uses "call graphs to show relationships between software functions" to see if functions/methods—outlined in a CVE—are reachable in your codebases.

These CVE aspects are especially important if your teams need to remediate many CVEs. At a minimum, additional and relative intelligence improves risk management.

Beyond PaC, several tools are available that enrich and ingest SBOMs. Two of my favorite tools are Palo Alto Prisma Cloud (*https://oreil.ly/J5WF7*) and SBOM Studio (*https://oreil.ly/ai_Ue*) from Cybeats. They both solve the use case where I want more intelligence about CVEs beyond the CVSS scores and severities.

To mine the intelligence we need from SBOMs or otherwise use them reliably and securely, we must ensure that SBOMs are securely created. This security concept is the foundation of SBOM usability, and we explore it in the next section.

SBOM Authenticity and Integrity

The value of SBOMs—or of any SSC artifact—directly stems from how trustworthy they are. The recurring theme of improving SSC security is how we can attest that produced artifacts are trustworthy. In most cases, this means cryptographically signing and verifying artifacts and attestations and interrogating attestations with PaC. Although there are many tools for this approach, Public Key Infrastructure (PKI) (*https://oreil.ly/faaRH*) is part of the process.

Dan Lorenc of Chainguard (*https://www.chainguard.dev*) penned an easy-to-understand description (*https://oreil.ly/mnJWf*) of how PKI can be used to apply signatures to artifacts and attestations to create cryptographically secure references to artifacts and associated "specific claims" about artifacts, known as *statements*. In fact, attestations can be seen as signed statements about software artifacts. These statements and the provenance thereof are foundational to SSC security. SBOMs are more valuable when we can attest and verify their provenance and that they have not been tampered with between creation and consumption. This nonrepudiation approach (*https://oreil.ly/hUCtR*) helps us ensure the authenticity and integrity of the artifacts produced by our respective SSCs.

SBOMs and SLSA

As we consider how we ensure the authenticity and integrity of SBOMs or other SSC artifacts, we can look at frameworks—emerging standards—that provide the needed functionality:

Supply-chain Levels for Software Artifacts (SLSA) (https://slsa.dev)
SLSA—pronounced "salsa"—is a security framework to "prevent tampering, improve integrity, and secure packages and infrastructure."

In-toto (https://github.com/in-toto/in-toto)
In-toto is "a framework to protect the integrity of the software supply chain."

In-toto attestation framework (https://oreil.ly/attestation)
In-toto attestations provide "a specification for generating verifiable claims about any aspect of how a piece of software is produced."

The SLSA framework, controls, and checklists provide a maturity model that gets progressively more difficult to achieve. For example, in the context of SLSA provenance (*https://oreil.ly/YXvgL*)—ensuring authenticity and integrity—of artifacts, SLSA prescribes the following build levels (*https://oreil.ly/p92ux*):

Level 1
Provenance exists but is easily bypassed or forged.

Level 2
Level 1 plus authenticity and integrity through cryptographic signing and verification. Forging provenance or evading verification is still possible through supply-chain attacks.

Level 3
Level 2 plus tampering is prevented and strong confidence is provided by controlling access to cryptographic materials used to sign artifacts and statements.

With SLSA level 3, you are able to better reach the NIST definition of Separation of Duty (SOD) (*https://oreil.ly/MU1NS*): "no user should be given enough privileges to misuse the system on their own." This also leads to your SSC being more observable and better controlled through the execution of trusted processes and steps and the creation of trusted artifacts.

Provenance with in-toto

To reach SLSA level 3, you can use the in-toto attestation framework to build standard attestations in combination with sigstore/cosign (*https://oreil.ly/cosign*) to cryptographically sign and verify as well as with PaC—like OPA or the CUE Data Constraint Language (*https://oreil.ly/cue*)—to interrogate attestations. Sigstore/rekor (*https://oreil.ly/rekor*) is also used to provide an "immutable tamper resistant ledger" to record the signed attestations.

That's a lot of moving parts; moreover, a discussion on using PaC to secure the SSC could actually fill its own book, or at least a conference. Fortunately, many in the software industry and OSS communities are spearheading these approaches with services and products.

Liatrio (*https://www.liatrio.com*) is one the companies leading the efforts through best practices for SSC security. In fact, it has created a set of GitHub trusted build repositories (*https://oreil.ly/e7A5t*) and a YouTube video (*https://oreil.ly/lnHtu*) to demonstrate how to reach SLSA level 3 with the aforementioned tools and approaches. From the Trusted Build Application repository (*https://oreil.ly/Ms02y*) we can see an example of an in-toto attestation:

```
// in-toto attestation snippet (truncated payload element)
{
  "payloadType": "application/vnd.in-toto+json", ❶
  "payload": "eyJfdHlwZSI6I…J9fX0=", ❷
  "signatures": [
    {
      "keyid": "",
      "sig": "MEUCI...pSx2o=" ❸
    }
  ]
}
```

❶ This attestation contains an in-toto payload.

❷ The payload is Base64 encoded.

❸ The signature is also Base64 encoded.

If we decode the payload, we can see more information about it, including the following verifier information:

```
// in-toto attestation payload snippet - verifier information
...
"predicateType": "https://slsa.dev/verification_summary/v0.2" ❶
...
        "policy": {
            "uri": "https://github.com/liatrio/gh-trusted-builds-policy/...
                    ...releases/download/v1.1.1/bundle.tar.gz" ❷
```

```
    },
    "policy_level": "SLSA_LEVEL_3",  ❸
    "resource_uri": "ghcr.io/liatrio/gh-trusted-builds-app",
    "time_verified": "2023-05-23T17:52:14.186161165Z",
    "verification_result": "PASSED",  ❹
    "verifier": {
        "id": "https://github.com/liatrio/gh-trusted-builds-workflows/...
        ....github/workflows/policy-verification.yaml@refs/heads/main"
    }
...
```

❶   The predicate type refers to the SLSA verification summary.

❷   The OPA policy was sourced from this OPA bundle.

❸   This VSA is for SLSA Level 3.

❹   This VSA indicates a policy pass.

In the snippet, we can see that the attestation predicate type was a SLSA verification summary attestation (VSA) (*https://oreil.ly/ZOLNI*). The VSA indicates "that an artifact has been verified at a specific SLSA level and details about that verification." An attestation predicate is metadata related to the artifact and, in this example, it is a VSA type.

The preceding payload includes verifier information that indicates the workflows that were used as well as the OPA policy bundle. If we follow the link to the *policy-verification.yaml* workflow file, we can see that the SLSA VSA was created as part of this workflow with the following command that calls a custom Go binary, built as part of this effort by Liatrio:

```
# GitHub workflow command to create VSA
...
    - name: Create Verification Summary Attestation
      env:
        GITHUB_TOKEN: ${{ secrets.GITHUB_TOKEN }}
      run: |
        attestation vsa \
          --artifact-uri ghcr.io/${{ github.repository }} \
          --artifact-digest ${{ inputs.digest }} \
          --policy-url \
          "https://github.com/liatrio/gh-trusted-builds-policy/releases/\
          download/v1.4.0/bundle.tar.gz" \
          --verifier-id \
          ${{ github.server_url }}/${{ needs.detect-workflow.outputs.\
          repository }}/${{ needs.detect-workflow.outputs.workflow }}@$\
          {{ needs.detect-workflow.outputs.ref }} \
          --fulcio-url ${{ steps.config.outputs.fulcioUrl }} \
          --rekor-url ${{ steps.config.outputs.rekorUrl }}
```

Finally, the bundle URL in the `policy.uri` element of the in-toto attestation payload indicates the source of the OPA Rego policies.

There are several complexities and components that make up this demonstration, too many to cover in detail in this chapter. I strongly recommend that readers watch the aforementioned Liatrio demo video and explore the demo projects. That said, I think the demo illustrates how to build SLSA level 3 SSCs with OSS components and use PaC to perform the evaluations along the way.

I would be remiss if I didn't mention the use of GitHub reusable workflows (*https:// oreil.ly/Pl6SQ*) in this example. As we look to improve our SSC security, embracing and trying to realize NIST SOD and SLSA level 3, we need a means to separate workflow executions and to prevent unwanted use of sensitive artifacts, like secrets. Along with Github OpenID Connect (OIDC) integration (*https://oreil.ly/ozjMa*), reusable workflows provide that separation and harden the execution of GitHub SSC actions.

Summary

Many practitioners throughout the software industry are focused on improving SSC security. The goal is to prevent SSC attacks before users are affected when the attack starts impeding normal operations. In this chapter, I demonstrated how PaC can be used throughout the SSC, integrated with different tools to address concerns across multiple PEPs. Providing early-and-often detection and controls across multiple PEPs is key to improving security and user experiences.

Figure 14-3 illustrates how PaC is used across multiple PEPs, ultimately providing decisions that improve SSC security:

Desktop
PaC is applied at developers' desktops, providing immediate feedback and enabling developers to fix issues earlier.

Codebase
PaC is applied within codebases for early issue detection, triggered by CI activities.

Pipeline
Pipelines employ PaC to permit execution of steps and to validate pipeline outputs.

I see *pipelines* as a generic description for orchestrated automation, and that is purposely broad. Pipelines are a means to an end, used for eliminating manual steps and potential errors while increasing reliability and deterministic behavior. The pipeline in Figure 14-3 could be composed into various configurations, depending on your needs. Regardless of configuration, PaC remains a central component for validation, verification, and decision making.

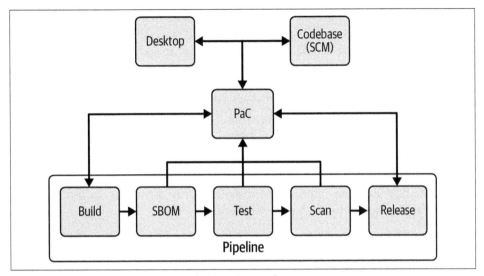

Figure 14-3. PaC is used across multiple policy enforcement points

As we explored how PaC can help us prevent unwanted behaviors and ensure trustworthiness, we looked at SBOMs and some of the value they provide. SBOMs give a list of ingredients included in our software artifacts, including traceable origin information, as well as enrichments that provide much needed intelligence, like vulnerabilities. There are several really good tools out there—Syft, Grype, Trivy—that create and evaluate artifacts, including SBOMs.

SBOMs, combined with tools like Palo Alto Prisma Cloud, Cybeats SBOM Studio, and Endor Labs, can uncover CVE intelligence, like reachability and exploitability, that helps us better decide on which CVEs to concentrate our remediation efforts. This is especially helpful when different CVSS scores emerge from disparate sources, such as GitHub Security Advisory (GHSA), Red Hat, and NVD.

SBOMs, as well as other SSC artifacts, are more valuable when we can attest to their authenticity and integrity. According to SLSA level 3, not only do we need to be able to cryptographically sign and verify artifacts to prove provenance, but we also need to make sure that the steps used to produce, sign, and verify are not forged or evaded.

Reaching—and proving—SLSA level 3 requires considerable rigor and the complex integration of several component technologies, such as in-toto, OPA, sigstore/cosign, sigstore/rekor, and sigstore/fulcio, as well as GitHub reusable workflows and OIDC integration. The latter two are focused on preventing unwanted access as well as enforcing NIST SOD.

As we consider PaC and the SSC, we need to remember that PaC is code as well. PaC artifacts must be securely managed, built, delivered, and verified just like any other SSC output artifact. We would deliver the artifacts to execution environments as signed artifacts and with signed attestations. At a minimum, that would mean that we need admission control in the automated pipelines and the execution environments to verify signatures and attestations. To get to that level of maturity, we need to follow an iterative process, progressively improving.

There is no way a single chapter can address the breadth and depth of the concerns, tools, and processes that exist and that are emerging across the SSC security landscape. I hope that I have whetted readers' appetites to look further into SSC and investigate how PaC can improve the overall security assurance. In fact, as I have shown, PaC is required to reach the levels needed.

## CHAPTER 15

Retrospectives and Futures

When I first started with PaC, almost eight years ago, I was looking for a way to remove the tight coupling between control definition and control implementation. I knew that writing imperative code to implement all the cloud controls we needed was not a sustainable model. That led me to adopt Cloud Custodian in 2016 as part of our AWS cloud migration.

Along the way, I tried Chef InSpec (*https://oreil.ly/5pkX_*) and Puppet (*https://oreil.ly/2OQTC*). While both are viable solutions for what they do, I wasn't satisfied with their approach or syntax for my use cases. I am in no way knocking these solutions. In fact, I used Chef to counter drift in several use cases. I just didn't think they were the best solutions for my need to interrogate our cloud resources and build detective and preventive controls for real-time, near-real-time, or even periodic reactions. And c7n's declarative syntax was very appealing to me.

Two years later, I was searching for a similar solution for building Kubernetes controls; c7n wasn't an option at that time. Instead, I chose OPA and started my Rego adoption. After learning Rego, I found myself writing helper libraries to perform common tasks in Rego Kubernetes policies, like getting Pods, containers, and their respective metadata and settings. I then moved on to more declarative solutions, like Gatekeeper and eventually Kyverno.

Considering the PaC solutions I covered in this book, I think there are a few trends that have led to improved adoption. In this chapter, I discuss the factors that contribute to successful adoption of PaC solutions. Then, I look forward to PaC possibilities and what you may see in the near future.

In the next section, I have summarized the characteristics of successful PaC adoption.

Characteristics of Successful PaC Adoption

OSS projects have some things in common with commercial software. One of those important commonalities is competitiveness. OSS that supports the same or similar use cases as other solutions (OSS and commercial) must compete for market share, driven by adoption. OSS adoption is driven in large part by community need and solution differentiators. Solutions—OSS or otherwise—that want to continually foster adoption and improve market share successfully do so with differentiators that help build a competitive advantage.

With commercial products, "competitive advantage" usually refers to how a company can produce goods or services better or more cheaply than its rivals. With OSS PaC solutions, it is virtually the same, though I think *better* is a relative term, where better is focused on better adoption and market share driven by better tools and technology as well as more use cases supported.

Creating differentiation and competitive advantage is bolstered by—and leads to—project momentum. Let's explore the characteristics of momentum next.

Momentum

Successful PaC projects must expand to support ever-increasing use cases. This expansion requires and contributes to project momentum. For example, I discovered OPA almost a full two years after its inception. And I only discovered it when I was looking for a compliance and governance solution for Kubernetes. In fact, I think the need for a Kubernetes solution and the timeliness of the OPA offering were a boon to the OPA projects. The original Kubernetes solution drew me in. I made the effort to learn Rego as well as to learn more about how Kubernetes worked, especially dynamic admission control.

OPA joining the CNCF helped with the project's momentum. Being part of the CNCF generated project visibility and legitimacy. That visibility and legitimacy led to more participation, both users of and contributors to the project.

Coming on the heels of the original Kubernetes solution, due in part to the steep learning curve of the Rego language, the OPA Gatekeeper project offered a friendlier UX. Gatekeeper also introduced a separation of duties that extended a degree of freedom for folks to build constraints without needing to actually write the Rego found in the constraint templates.

When it comes to momentum, Gatekeeper and OPA classic shared a symbiotic relationship. Gatekeeper enjoyed the momentum of the original OPA project and its CNCF membership. As Gatekeeper matured, it in turn exposed the Rego language and projects to more users. This momentum increased the number of users, contributors, and solved use cases.

The use of DSLs is also a differentiator that has led to better adoption of some PaC solutions. I will discuss DSLs in the next section.

Domain-Specific Languages

As a builder, I never shied away from writing code. I love building and coding to this day, regardless of my employment situation, although as I take on more responsibilities, I get fewer opportunities to build and code. Writing this book has been an enormous undertaking and a huge opportunity to wear my builder hat. However, when building usable and extensible solutions, I have learned to temper my excitement about the solution by grounding it with usability and UX qualities. For this process, I often moved toward more declarative solutions, especially for PaC use cases. Coding can be elegant, but it is usually more elegant to the coder than it is to the consumer. External functionality, performance, and fit trump internal elegance most of the time. After all, who really cares if you built your solution as a monolith or using microservices architecture, as long as it meets functional and nonfunctional requirements? I still love to build and code, and when I think of declarative solutions, DSLs come to mind first.

According to Martin Fowler, a DSL is a "computer language that's targeted to a particular kind of problem." While I am not a fan of DSLs for everything, they have improved my understanding and adoption of solutions—PaC and otherwise. Several solutions in this book use DSLs to give the user a domain-specific lexicon and syntax that ease overall adoption of the respective solution. We use DSLs all the time. For example, most of my automation solutions in this book were implemented with make and Makefiles. The syntax in Makefiles comes from a DSL approach. Structured query language (SQL) is another well-known DSL.

Other DSL approaches use function and method cascading, like the following code example from a blog post I wrote in 2021 (*https://oreil.ly/RAjZN*) about using the AWS CDK with Java:

```
// Java fluent interface example
Bucket.Builder.create(this, "MyFirstBucket")
    .versioned(true)
    .bucketName("cdk-unique-bucket-name")
    .encryption(BucketEncryption.S3_MANAGED)
    .blockPublicAccess(BlockPublicAccess.BLOCK_ALL)
    .removalPolicy(RemovalPolicy.DESTROY)
    .build();
```

The cascading dot-notation makes object creation and configuration easier with a fluent interface (*https://oreil.ly/uJZpF*). This contrasts the traditional constructor and getter/setter approaches used so much in Java.

DSLs are generally categorized as internal or external. Internal DSLs use a host general-purpose language as a base. The preceding fluent-interface example is an internal DSL, using Java as its base language and not requiring a custom parser for the Java syntax.

External DSLs have their own syntax and lexicon, along with a custom parser. Even though the c7n and Kyverno policy languages are examples primarily written in and based on YAML, I would still consider them external DSLs because of their respective parsers. I also consider OPA's Rego language to be an external DSL, as it does not really use a host language. Although Rego is inspired by Datalog, users do not explicitly write Rego-flavored Datalog code and use a Datalog parser. Regardless of their categories, the PaC DSLs are differentiators that lead to solution momentum and adoption.

Next, let's explore how usability helps with solution momentum.

Usability

As it turns out, usability is very important to PaC project momentum for users and contributors. At the same time that OPA and Gatekeeper were tag-teaming Kubernetes and other use cases, other PaC solutions emerged that promised different ways to improve usability.

The k-rail project (*https://oreil.ly/k-rail*) (not covered in this book) used the Go language to build policies. It was a very interesting project, especially to Go developers. Given that Kubernetes is written in Go and most Kubernetes tools are written in Go, k-rail seemed to fit right in. However, for some Kubernetes users trying to surmount the Kubernetes learning curve, also having to become Go programmers in order to write workload policies was a lot to ask of them. Although OPA, Gatekeeper, and other solutions were written in Go, having to write Go to build actual policies seemed counterproductive to momentum. For their policy languages, these projects used DSLs instead of Go. In doing so, their project momentum increased.

 My friend and colleague, Jon Bodner, has written two editions of the book *Learning Go* (O'Reilly). Although I have yet to dive into the second edition, I found the first edition indispensable for my personal journey toward becoming a better Go programmer.

For some in the Kubernetes user community, there was still a strong desire for a more usable solution that did not require learning Rego or Go, something that was more native to Kubernetes, even YAML based. That seemed to be the impetus for Kyverno. From its inception, Kyverno has enjoyed sustained momentum. Kyverno challenged the status quo from the start. You didn't have to learn Rego or Go to write Kyverno policies. Even though Kyverno uses some syntactical sugar—JMESPath and YAML anchors—policies are primarily YAML. That alone greatly reduced the barrier to entry for writing Kyverno policies for Kubernetes compliance and governance.

 Kyverno's success with YAML-based policies mirrors that of c7n. While users and developers of c7n and Kyverno can write Python and Go, respectively, to contribute to the project, they can also contribute to and use the project policies in YAML. They do not need to be Python or Go developers to get value from the respective solutions.

With Kyverno usability came momentum and a healthy competition between Kyverno and other projects. Like other solutions, and aligned with the Kubernetes webhook configurations, Kyverno solved the mutating and validating use cases. However, Kyverno realized the anti-pattern of creating Pods alone—outside of other workloads—so the project added Auto-Gen rules. Auto-Gen rules reduce cognitive load by auto-generating the workload—Deployment, DaemonSets, Job, and so forth—policies while still only requiring users to explicitly write Pod policies. This was a huge win for users, as it reduced the policy-management tasks that other solutions still required.

Kverno went further by adding the ability to set maintenance windows with time-bound policies as well as clean up cluster cruft with CleanUp policies. After listening to the community, Kyverno built VerifyImage policies that support multiple approaches, such as Sigstore Cosign and Notary.

At the same time, the Gatekeeper contributors developed the ability to verify image signatures as well as to use external data sources to feed data—needed for decisions—to policies. This was driven by community needs. Gatekeeper followed up with policy expansion, which provides functionality similar to Kverno's Auto-Gen rules, and jsPolicy added controller policies that listened to cluster events and reacted with policy decisions and actions, like creating new resources, similar to Kyverno Generate policies.

All these innovations were possible because of engaged communities and empowered contributors, under the direction of maintainers that were in tune with their respective communities and the Kubernetes project. Competition helped drive differentiators and project innovations. Project momentum made this possible and then benefited from the project innovations. As in other OSS projects, PaC projects require continuous momentum. This is part of the care and feeding about which I wrote in Chapter 1. These projects need to keep solving new use cases and improving user experiences.

Reuse of existing technologies also improves project adoption and momentum. In the next section, I'll tell you how I think this works.

Project Extensibility and Ecosystem Development

Another way to foster innovation and adoption is to combine efforts through technology reuse, which leads to project extensibility and ecosystem development. Reusing and including technology across multiple solutions builds on and contributes back to existing projects and ecosystems. Extensibility encourages integrations, creates richer ecosystems, and drives adoption.

One could argue that Gatekeeper did this by building on OPA. MagTape did it differently, by proxying OPA to handle API server requests while adding business logic processing between OPA and the Kubernetes API server.

The Kyverno project helped lead as well as adopted the Kubernetes Policy Working Group Policy Report standard, and the project built a UI to review Policy Reports. Kyverno also integrated with multiple image-signing technologies, like Sigstore/Cosign and Notary. Recently, it added CEL policy expressions and syntax.

The jsPolicy project embraced JavaScript and languages that transpile to JavaScript as its policy language. This differentiator helped it gain adoption among users who wanted to stick with JavaScript, a language in which they had already invested considerable resources and time.

Though not included in this book, the Kubewarden project (*https://oreil.ly/EOWQC*) is a CNCF sandbox project where policies are written as WebAssembly (a.k.a. Wasm) binaries, using your favorite programming language that supports Wasm. These Wasm binaries act as plug-in programs that are added to a Kubewarden policy server to evaluate Kubernetes resources.

As I alluded to earlier, I think most Kubernetes users would rather use coarse-grained DSLs to define policies than to write code. So, I was circumspect about the value proposition offered by Kubewarden. However, its reuse of Wasm piqued my interest. As I looked further, I saw that the project used or reused other technologies and approaches from other projects. For example, Kubewarden includes an Audit Scanner feature (*https://oreil.ly/4u3Mg*) that "constantly checks resources in the cluster." This is similar to the audit mode in Gatekeeper as well as background scans in Kyverno. Kubewarden also includes the Policy Reports standard, which I introduced in Chapter 4, as well as the Kyverno Policy Reporter tool from Chapter 8.

In Chapter 2, I introduced the idea of extending OPA with Wasm. Since Kubewarden uses Wasm binaries, it implicitly uses multiple languages—Rust, Go, Rego, and so on—with compilers that can target Wasm binaries. This extensibility—driven by the reuse and inclusion of technologies—will help the Kubewarden project meet policy developers where they work; that should lead to momentum and adoption. In general, technology reuse includes more users and solves more use cases, which leads to more project extensibility, adoption, and momentum.

Now, let's explore how enterprise support contributes to project adoption and momentum.

Enterprise Solutions

OSS projects often benefit from commercial companies that provide enterprise solutions that are based on or include OSS offerings. The following are a few examples of companies offering commercial offerings that use or are based on OSS PaC solutions:

Nirmata (https://nirmata.com)
> Nirmata, the creator and lead maintainer of Kyverno, provides a policy and governance solution powered by Kyverno. The Nirmata Policy Manager (NPM) is designed for cloud native platform teams. It manages policy enforcement across code repositories and pipelines, Kubernetes clusters, and cloud configurations. It provides features for centralized observability and reporting, DevSecOps collaboration workflows like remediation and exception management, and tamper prevention of policies.

Styra (https://www.styra.com)
> Founded by the creators of OPA, Styra enables enterprises to build and manage modern authorization across the entire cloud native stack, from applications to infrastructure, using PaC. Leveraging solutions with both OSS (OPA) and commercial software (the Enterprise OPA Platform) Styra empowers IAM engineering teams, developers, and DevOps teams to mitigate risks, reduce human error, and accelerate application development.

Wiz (https://www.wiz.io)
> Wiz helps organizations rapidly remove the most critical risks in their cloud estate. It connects in minutes, requires zero agents, and automatically correlates the entire security stack to uncover the most pressing issues. Wiz policies leverage OPA for a unified framework across the cloud native stack. Whether for configurations, compliance, or IaC, Wiz enables teams to move faster in the cloud.

Permit.io (https://permit.io)
> Permit.io leverages multiple hybrid approaches for a unique recipe of PaC, supporting multiple policy engines (e.g., OPA, AWS Cedar) through mixing policy models (RBAC, ReBAC, ABAC). Permit.io also provides multiple interfaces that you can use to author policies—no-code UI, high-level API, Terraform (Yes! IaC that generates PaC)—and, of course, to write or mix directly authored "manual" code. You can also use its open source project OPAL to bridge policy as graph from the cloud to Policy as Code at the edge—all with the philosophy of enabling developers to mark authorization as complete and focus on their core products.

Stacklet.io (https://stacklet.io)

> Cofounded by the creator of the Cloud Custodian project, Stacklet provides a full-lifecycle governance-as-code platform that enables your organization to identify and remediate governance issues across cost optimization, security, compliance, and operations. Additionally, it establishes preventive guardrails to avoid future incidents. Extending c7n with advanced features, Stacklet reduces the operational challenges associated with governance tools and accelerates the adoption of governance as code within your organization.

Some companies are reluctant to adopt new tools, especially without enterprise support. Enterprise solutions that use OSS PaC projects help companies gain peace of mind. These enterprise solutions also help drive adoption among folks who need to reduce the risk of adopting OSS by being able to get enterprise support.

I've covered many aspects of PaC in this book, mostly based on my experiential knowledge with multiple solutions and use cases. In the next section, I write about PaC solutions and integrations that I see coming.

PaC Looking Forward

It's not easy to predict what will happen in the world of PaC without my predictions looking more like self-serving ideas based on knowledge that few currently have. In fact, writing and teaching are often based on temporary monopolies of information. As you look forward to the future of PaC, use the solutions and use cases from the rest of this book to help you understand how to evaluate and maybe even embrace the PaC things to come.

In the next section, I start with the emerging use case of combining PaC with the Open Security Controls Assessment Language (OSCAL) standard.

Embracing Standards with OSCAL

Different PaC solutions have different characteristics; moreover, how policies are used from organization to organization also varies. High-severity findings in one organization may be medium or even critical in other organizations. Policies differ greatly among solutions and organizations. It would seem that we need more standardization over how policies are applied and interpreted. This is important if we want to apply and prove uniform compliance across multiple organizations and multiple PaC implementations.

Many PaC adopters also build or utilize prebuilt policy libraries—like the OPA Helper Libraries introduced in Chapter 5—and standards to ease adoption and improve solution expressiveness. Not reinventing or duplicating efforts is foundational to the DRY principle (*https://oreil.ly/oqkFG*) and reduces friction when learning and adopting new solutions.

OSCAL (*https://oreil.ly/8nxf0*) is an emerging standard: a set of formats developed by NIST for the publication, implementation, and assessment of security controls and policies. OSCAL provides machine-readable formats for security and compliance data. This formatted data enables automation of security controls and processes: documentation, implementation, and assessment. Organizations use OSCAL to improve the efficiency and accuracy of their security-compliance efforts. These increases in efficiency and accuracy lead to easier management and communication of security postures and compliance through various standards and regulations.

When it comes to uniformity of compliance, OSCAL can be seen as the universal translator for cybersecurity information. It allows different tools and systems involved in cybersecurity to express data and decisions using the same lexicon.

The OSS Lula project (*https://lula.dev*) has built a demo that combines OSCAL with OPA to apply the uniformity of OSCAL definitions via PaC. In this combination, OPA serves as a provider, applying Rego to evaluate installed components. The OPA provider is defined in the `back-matter` element of the following OSCAL component-definition document:

```
# OSCAL component-definition document
# add the descriptions inline
component-definition:
  uuid: E6A291A4-2BC8-43A0-B4B2-FD67CAAE1F8F
  metadata:
    title: Lula Demo
    last-modified: '2022-09-13T12:00:00Z'
    version: "20220913"
    oscal-version: 1.1.1
    parties:
...
  back-matter:
    resources:
    - uuid: a7377430-2328-4dc4-a9e2-b3f31dc1dff9
      title: Lula Validation
      rlinks:
        - href: lula.dev
      description: >-
        target:
          provider: opa
          domain: kubernetes
          payload:
            resources:
            - name: podsvt # Identifier for use in the rego below
              resourceRule: # Mandatory, resource selection criteria,
                            # at least one resource rule is required
                Group: # empty or "" for core group
                Version: v1 # Version of resource
                Resource: pods # Resource type
                Namespaces: [validation-test] # Namespaces to validate the
                # above resources in. Empty or "" for all namespaces or
```

```
                # non-namespaced resources
        rego: |
          package validate

          import future.keywords.every

          validate {
            every pod in input.podsvt {
              podLabel := pod.metadata.labels.foo
              podLabel == "bar"
            }
          }
```

The `back-matter` element may be found at the end of any OSCAL document and is generally used for external links, citations, attachments, or embedded Images. This makes `back-matter` the place to include non-OSCAL specific content. The Lula demo uses `back-matter` to supply the Rego policy for validating the installed component.

The following command executes the Lula Go binary to perform a validation on the current Kubernetes cluster, based on the supplied OSCAL component-definition document with the Rego policy in the `back-matter` element:

```
# Use Lula to validate Pod in Kubernetes via a OSCAL component-definition
lula validate -f oscal-component.yaml

  NOTE  Saving log file to
        /var/folders/f3/6fbtb6d57csb1jj303jyrp2c0000gq/T/
        lula-2024-03-18-22-28-23-2024900836.log
  • UUID: 62a7b3f7-cb2d-4b45-a69b-8363a7265419
  • Status: not-satisfied
  ✓ Validating Implemented Requirement - 42C2FFDC-5F05-44DF-A67F-EEC8660AEFFD
  • Writing Security Assessment Results to:
    assessment-results-03-18-2024-22:28:23.yaml
```

The Lula execution produced the following assessment-results document, based on the OSCAL Assessments Results Model that is part of the Assessments layer:

```
# Lula validation produced an OSCAL assessment-results document
assessment-results:
  import-ap:
    href: ""
  metadata:
    last-modified: 2024-03-18T22:54:05.271942-04:00
    oscal-version: 1.1.2
    published: 2024-03-18T22:54:05.271942-04:00
    remarks: Assessment Results generated from Lula
    title: '[System Name] Security Assessment Results (SAR)'
    version: 0.0.1
  results:
    - description: |
```

```
          Assessment results for performing Validations with
          Lula version bf5e0e2
findings:
  - description: |
              This control validates that the demo-pod pod in
              the validation-test namespace contains the required
              pod label foo=bar in order to establish compliance.
    related-observations:
      - observation-uuid: 28d7221e-ab15-46f0-8404-3bba2d76f37c
    target:
      status:
        state: not-satisfied
      target-id: ID-1
      type: objective-id
    title: >
        Validation Result - Component:A9D5204C-7E5B-4C43-BD49-
        34DF759B9F04 / Control Implementation: A584FEDC-8CEA-4B0C-
        9F07-85C2C4AE751A / Control:  ID-1'
    uuid: 9fa5f032-fe54-458f-a1fc-4ecb2585a78b
observations:
  - collected: 2024-03-18T22:54:05.24879-04:00
    description: |
      [TEST] ID-1 - a7377430-2328-4dc4-a9e2-b3f31dc1dff9
    methods:
      - TEST
    relevant-evidence:
      - description: |
            Result: not-satisfied
    uuid: 28d7221e-ab15-46f0-8404-3bba2d76f37c
reviewed-controls:
  control-selections:
    - description: Controls Assessed by Lula
      include-controls:
        - control-id: ID-1
  description: Controls validated
  remarks: >
        Validation performed may indicate full or partial satisfaction
  start: 2024-03-18T22:54:05.271942-04:00
  title: Lula Validation Result
  uuid: f7f6d638-2234-49b2-9e63-72d992997013
uuid: 38d6ffa8-5ad9-4885-8d68-e2de6b3d92dc
```

OSCAL's adoption is driven by its value proposition to provide a standard format for expressing the implementation, assessment, and authorization of security controls. OSCAL standardization is a valuable tool for organizations seeking to simplify and refine security and compliance workflows, especially in government and other highly regulated spaces.

Using PaC allows security practitioners to meet the rigorous requirements of OSCAL with solutions that can produce repeatable results. PaC providers mean that OSS projects can be used with OSCAL compliance. This makes OSCAL requirements easier to meet and provides new and expanded use cases for PaC. At the time of writing, the Lula project had an open issue to add Kyverno as another PaC provider.

Next, let's explore how generative artificial intelligence (GenAI) can help you learn and more quickly adopt PaC.

PaC and Generative AI

There is no ignoring the progress that GenAI (*https://oreil.ly/zg3Tc*) has made in the last few years. OpenAI's GPT-3 (*https://openai.com*) ushered in excitement around the possibilities of prompt engineering and large language models (LLMs) (*https://oreil.ly/y9QN_*). Companies are creating new offerings that utilize GenAI, LLMs, and prompt engineering (*https://oreil.ly/n5spj*).

Charles Handler, PhD, wrote an interesting article (*https://oreil.ly/4ShnR*) on GenAI prompt engineering, where it is, and where it is heading. The following are two of my favorite quotes from the article:

"AI's evolution and widespread adoption is built on lowering the friction needed to accomplish complex outcomes."—Charles Handler

"The reality is that prompting AI systems is no different than being an effective communicator with other humans."—Logan Kilpatrick, a developer advocate at OpenAI

In writing this book, I looked at how GenAI can potentially improve how we learn and use PaC solutions. In the next section, I will introduce a GenAI tool that I have used and explore how you can use it to help reduce overall cycle time for learning and troubleshooting.

Learning PaC with GenAI

I have heard—and mostly believe—that different people learn differently. I taught postsecondary courses at the graduate and undergraduate levels, and I witnessed firsthand how different teaching techniques reach students differently. For example, I learn through repetition, reading, and then doing. My oldest son is a visual learner, and my daughter can consume tomes on new topics.

Regardless of how we learn, there is an enormous amount of information to digest. From that enormous amount of information, we must somehow distill the knowledge we need. To write this book, I consumed docs, examples, GitHub projects, posts, and Slack messages. I also spent an inordinate amount of time talking with industry experts. The good news is that you don't have to do that. There is a possible shortcut that will help you mine the most important and relevant PaC content from multiple sources. Distillation of knowledge from many information resources is easier when you use GenAI.

I just recently started—at the beginning of this last chapter—using Cursor (*https://cursor.sh*). Cursor is described as "the AI-first code editor" that helps you "build software faster in an editor designed for pair-programming with AI." I like Cursor because of how it reduces my need to search for items and read through mountains of documentation, trying all the while to isolate relevant content. With Cursor, I just type what I need, and it goes out and finds it for me, using natural language processing (NLP) and prompts to OpenAI's GPT-4 (*https://oreil.ly/SzEKQ*).

Cursor features AI-powered assistance to users. It helps with writing code by suggesting completions and corrections, similar to GitHub Copilot. This feature leverages machine learning models trained on a variety of codebases to predict and suggest the next lines of code or commands that a user might want to write, thereby enhancing productivity and reducing coding errors.

Cursor has three licensing options. I opted for the third option—business—because it afforded me the most so-called fast GTP-4 uses per month and zero data retention at OpenAI:

> Instead of OpenAI's normal policy of retaining data for 30 days for trust and safety, OpenAI will not retain any prompt data for any period of time for business users.

After I installed Cursor, I first pointed it at various documentation sites that I normally used and then I started requesting help. The following request uses the jsPolicy docs that I added to Cursor:

> *Prompt*: @jspolicy Write a policy to enforce seccomp at the container level
>
> *Cursor*: To enforce Seccomp at the container level using JSPolicy, you can create a validating policy that checks if the security context of each container in a Pod has a Seccomp profile defined. If a container does not have a Seccomp profile, the policy will deny the creation or update of the Pod. Here's how you can define such a policy:

```
# policy.yaml
apiVersion: policy.jspolicy.com/v1beta1
kind: JsPolicy
metadata:
  name: "enforce-seccomp.company.tld"
spec:
  operations: ["CREATE", "UPDATE"]  ❶
  resources: ["pods"]
  scope: Namespaced
  javascript: |
    const pod = request.object;
    const containers = pod.spec.containers.concat(pod.spec.initContainers
    || []);  ❷
    for (const container of containers) {
      if (!container.securityContext ||  ❸
```

```
!container.securityContext.seccompProfile) {
      deny(`Container "${container.name}" in Pod "${pod.metadata.name}" `+
      ` does not have a Seccomp profile defined.`);  ❹
   }
}
```

❶ This policy applies to CREATE and UPDATE operations on Pods.

❷ It concatenates the list of init containers (if any) to the list of containers in a Pod to check each container.

❸ It checks if each container has a securityContext defined with a seccompProfile.

❹ If any container does not have a seccompProfile defined in its securityContext, the policy denies the request and outputs a message specifying which container in which Pod is missing the Seccomp profile.

To apply this policy to your Kubernetes cluster, follow these steps:

1. Save the policy code to a file named *policy.yaml*.
2. Apply the policy using kubectl:

   ```
   kubectl apply -f policy.yaml
   ```

This policy ensures that every container in your Kubernetes cluster has a Seccomp profile defined, enhancing the security posture of your cluster by enforcing the use of Seccomp profiles at the container level.

In Figure 15-1, you can see that Cursor used the jsPolicy documentation—to which I pointed it—and it indicated which documents it used for the request.

Figure 15-1. Documents used by Cursor to engineer the prompt to OPenAI's GPT-4

As you can see in the following console output, the jsPolicy created by the Cursor prompt to OpenAI worked as expected:

```
# jsPolicy policy from Cursor prompt to OpenAI worked to prevent Pods from
# being created
$ kubectl apply -f ../test/2-test-pod.yaml
```

```
Error from server (Forbidden): error when creating
"../test/2-test-pod.yaml": admission webhook "dont-create-me.jimmyray.io"
denied the request: dont-create-me annotation is not allowed
```

Next, I requested OpenAI GPT-4—via Cursor—to build for me a Kyverno Generate policy to create a deny-all NetworkPolicy resource for new Namespaces. I told it to exclude a list of Namespaces. You may notice that I misspelled *create* in the following prompt—it didn't matter:

> *Prompt*: @Kyverno Write a Generate policy to **creaet** a deny-all network policy when namespaces are created, exclude the following namespaces: kube-system, kyverno, default, kube-public

> *Cursor*: To create a Kyverno policy that generates a deny-all NetworkPolicy for newly created namespaces, you can use the following YAML definition. This policy matches on any new Namespace creation and generates a NetworkPolicy within that Namespace to deny all inbound and outbound traffic.

```
apiVersion: kyverno.io/v1
kind: ClusterPolicy
metadata:
  name: generate-deny-all-networkpolicy
spec:
  rules:
  - name: generate-deny-all-networkpolicy
    match:
      any:
      - resources:
          kinds:
          - Namespace       ❶
    exclude:
      any:
      - resources:
          Namespaces:       ❷
          - kube-system
          - kyverno
          - default
          - kube-public
    generate:
      kind: NetworkPolicy   ❸
      apiVersion: networking.k8s.io/v1
      name: deny-all
      namespace: "{{request.object.metadata.name}}"   ❹
      synchronize: true
      data:
        spec:
          podSelector: {}   ❺
          policyTypes:
          - Ingress
          - Egress
```

❶ This Generate policy triggers when Namespaces are created.

❷ It excludes the Namespaces in the `exclude` list.

❸ It creates a NetworkPolicy resource.

❹ It pulls the name of the host Namespace and adds it as the `metadata.namespace` value.

❺ The NetworkPolicy selects all Pods for Ingress and Egress to all ports.

While the policy is not perfect—missing the metadata that would be used in Policy-Reports—it functioned fine and created the following NetworkPolicy resource when the `policy-test` Namespace was created:

```
# NetworkPolicy created by Kyverno Generate policy from Cursor prompt to OpenAI
apiVersion: networking.k8s.io/v1
kind: NetworkPolicy
metadata:
  creationTimestamp: "2024-03-19T22:30:39Z"
  generation: 1
  labels:
    app.kubernetes.io/managed-by: kyverno
    generate.kyverno.io/policy-name: generate-deny-all-networkpolicy
    generate.kyverno.io/policy-namespace: ""
    generate.kyverno.io/rule-name: generate-deny-all-networkpolicy
    generate.kyverno.io/trigger-group: ""
    generate.kyverno.io/trigger-kind: Namespace
    generate.kyverno.io/trigger-namespace: ""
    generate.kyverno.io/trigger-uid: 8eaf5630-864b-4fd2-830d-220af0216626
    generate.kyverno.io/trigger-version: v1
  name: deny-all
  namespace: policy-test
  resourceVersion: "2552"
  uid: 1c476e3a-0b78-4aca-ba56-ff30c03bd43b
spec:
  podSelector: {}
  policyTypes:
  - Ingress
  - Egress
```

Next, I tried to use the Cursor IDE pair-programming approach and opened a known bad Rego file:

```
# Rego file has erroneous "===" symbol
package examples.ch2

default hello := false

hello if {
        msg := input.message
```

```
    msg === "world"  ❶
}
```

❶   The three equals signs should be two.

This time, I hovered over the error and let the Cursor IDE make a recommendation
to fix the issue, as shown in Figure 15-2.

```
 ≡ helloworld-bad.rego 1, M  ●

ch2-opa > examples > helloworld-bad >  ≡ helloworld-bad.rego
    1      package examples.ch2
    2
    3      import rego.v1
    4
    5      default h   unexpected eq token  regal/parse(rego_parse_error)
    6                  AI Fix In Chat ⇧⌘E
    7      hello if
    8          msg :   View Problem (⌥F8)   Quick Fix... (⌘.)
    9          msg === "world"|
   10      }
```

Figure 15-2. Hovering over code in Cursor IDE and getting an AI fix in chat

Cursor built the prompt for me and then answered it with the correct recommendation. In the AI prompt, you can see that it's referencing the currently opened file.

As shown in Figure 15-3, the Cursor IDE constructed a specific prompt, including
the desire to receive a concise resolution.

Figure 15-3. Cursor-built prompt to get help with an apparent error

As you can see in Figure 15-4, the Cursor-constructed prompt elicited a solution to fix the extra equals sign in the equality expression.

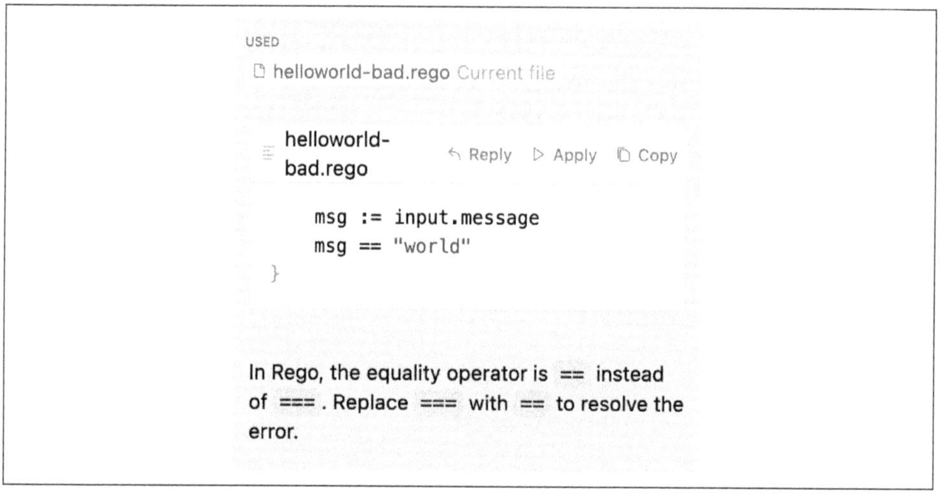

```
USED
 🗋 helloworld-bad.rego Current file


   helloworld-
≣  bad.rego          ↩ Reply  ▷ Apply  ⎘ Copy


      msg := input.message
      msg == "world"
  }



In Rego, the equality operator is == instead
of === . Replace === with == to resolve the
error.
```

Figure 15-4. Cursor response: concise resolution and explanation

Correctly prompted, GenAI can augment your learning as well as your artifact creation and correction. It's not without issues, though. In the next section, I'll review an example of GenAI returning outdated information.

GenAI and outdated data

GenAI responses are not just based on properly engineered prompts but also on data digested in the underlying LLMs. GenAI will return what's at its disposal, even if the LLMs are based on incorrect or outdated data. The following prompt and response indicate an outdated way to write Rego:

> *Prompt*: @Rego Write an ABAC AuthZ policy example
>
> *Cursor*: Here's an example of an Attribute-Based Access Control (ABAC) policy written in Rego, the policy language for Open Policy Agent (OPA). This policy allows or denies access to resources based on attributes of the user and the resource.

```
package abac

❶

# Define a default decision
default allow = false   ❷

# Allow access if the user's role is 'admin'
allow {   ❸
    input.user.role == "admin"
}
```

```
# Allow access if the user is in the same department as the resource and
# the action is read
allow {  ❹
    input.user.department == input.resource.department
    input.action == "read"
}

# Allow access if the user's clearance level is higher than or equal to
# the resource's required clearance
allow {  ❺
    input.user.clearance_level >= input.resource.required_clearance
}
```

❶ This policy is missing the `import rego.v1` import statement, per the Regal linter. Granted, this is a recent addition to the Rego best practices.

❷ Assignment operator (:=) should be used instead of unification operator (=).

❸ The `if` keyword is missing from the rule header.

❹ The `if` keyword is missing from the rule header.

❺ The `if` keyword is missing from the rule header.

 In the preceding Rego example, the `if` keyword is recommended by the Rego linter. In the impending OPA 1.0 release (*https://oreil.ly/cUYAJ*), the `if` keyword is made mandatory. This also has the effect of removing the complexity of single-expression rules by removing the need for curly braces:

```
# Allow access if the user's role is 'admin', no
# curly-braces needed
allow if input.user.role == "admin"
```

How you prompt and how the underlying LLM is constructed and trained have substantial impact on the quality of the GenAI's response. You need to be careful and make sure what you get back is not only correct but also appropriate for your needs and not outdated. GenAI does not absolve you from using good judgment and being at least somewhat versed in the content you are using GenAI to help you with.

Now, let's explore how GenAI can provide us with much-needed insights related to PaC responses.

GenAI insights and explanations

The value we get from GenAI is based on several factors, not the least of which is the data contained within the LLMs for which the GenAI prompts are used. Given enough data and parameters, LLMs can be built to provide valuable insights about PaC-related topics, such as policy evaluation responses, logs, and errors.

Protecting Data When Using GenAI

Before you decide to use GenAI for PaC, you should recognize and limit what information and data you're providing, especially if the LLM underpinning the GenAI solution is outside of your direct control. In particular, asking GenAI to generate security policies may mean you provide it with or grant it access to extra information about your IT and operational technology (OT) environments.

Sharing internal information about your IT and OT environments with external GenAI solutions should be avoided unless you are sure of your control over that information once it leaves your network and is submitted to the GenAI solution. In most cases, your internal IT and OT environment information should never be used to train an LLM to which others outside of your trusted organizational boundaries may have access. The unauthorized sharing of sensitive IT and OT environment data violates the data loss and data exfiltration policies of most organizations.

Unauthorized sharing—accidentally or purposefully—is made easier through the use of uncontrolled GenAI consumption. Controlling how that data is used and who will eventually consume it is more difficult with GenAI. Many product vendors and solution providers are building AI features into their products and solutions, and they regularly have to document how data sent to LLMs under their control will be used. It is common for these vendors to stipulate that customer-supplied data during GenAI feature usage will not be used to train the solution's underlying LLMs.

Many organizations are adopting legal and compliance policies that deter folks from using GenAI solutions outside of said organization's control. It's incumbent upon organizations to understand the sensitivity of their data and classify that data toward approved usage models. Data classification then drives controls, such as data masking, access control, and secure data transmission. Additional data policies, such as data sharing, monitoring, and auditing (legal and compliance), and data minimization, are also based on data classification. Finally, data classification drives the severity and implementation of data loss or exfiltration incident response measures.

Using the Cursor IDE again, I asked OpenAI GPT-4 to analyze the following Rego policy error from Chapter 5:

```
# Rego error for invalid Pod creation attempt in Kubernetes
Error from server (POD_INVALID:
"public.ecr.aws/eks-distro/kubernetes/pause:3.2" image is not
sourced from an authorized registry. Valid registries are
"[\"GOOD_REGISTRY\", \"VERY_GOOD_REGISTRY\"]".
Resource ID (ns/name/kind): "opa-test/test-pod/Pod"):
error when creating "tests/99-test-pod.yaml"
```

Prompt: @opa-k8s-error.txt provide concise insights

Cursor: The error indicates that the Kubernetes Pod creation failed because the image public.ecr.aws/eks-distro/kubernetes/pause:3.2 is not from an authorized registry. Kubernetes, likely through an OPA (Open Policy Agent) policy, is configured to only allow images from the registries listed as GOOD_REGISTRY and VERY_GOOD_REGISTRY. To resolve this issue, you need to use an image from one of the authorized registries or update the OPA policy to include public.ecr.aws as an authorized registry.

Taken alone, this response is not exactly the most insightful. However, consider that PaC solutions are making millions of decisions daily. The data behind those decisions —requests, responses, errors—is quite valuable. A GenAI solution underpinned by LLMs that are trained using PaC request and response data, enhancing LLMs with retrieval-augmented generation (RAG) (*https://oreil.ly/_VpXv*), or even data that represents systems controlled by PaC solutions, would provide valuable insights and recommendations about how to better manage systems and resources.

I believe that PaC solutions that can integrate GenAI to provide users with valuable insights about how to improve overall automated compliance and governance will capture market share and momentum. To that end, Stacklet.io has developed Jun0 (*https://oreil.ly/JwcFf*). According to Stacklet.io:

> Stacklet Jun0 helps you speed up governance tasks, reporting, and initiatives. Stacklet Jun0 can answer and report on complex queries using Stacklet's proprietary database and your tagging structure. Using simple natural language, you can query Stacklet Jun0 for insights or create and validate governance policies.
>
> Stacklet Jun0 allows you to use natural language to generate and validate cloud governance policies. You can also dry-run policies against your cloud platform to test, visualize, and share initial findings.

GenAI can be very powerful to help you learn PaC and write policies. In fact, GenAI can also help you quickly find and retrieve relevant content in large documentation sites or similar content. The Cursor IDE that I used in the preceding examples helps developers with prompt engineering that leads to more effective retrieval of relevant information.

For the record, this chapter is the only chapter in this book where I used GenAI for content, and I used it solely to show readers how GenAI could be used to help users learn PaC faster with AI-assisted tools. As an O'Reilly author, I follow the guidelines set forth in the AI Use Policy for Talent Developing Content for O'Reilly.

In the following sections, I preview a couple of PaC solutions that I did not cover previously. While I didn't have the space to describe these solutions in detail in this book, I think these PaC solutions will have considerable impact on cloud native security as well as on automated compliance and government use cases.

Cedar

In May 2023, AWS made the Cedar policy language (*https://oreil.ly/QV0jb*), authorization engine, and SDK open source. Cedar is written in Rust (*https://oreil.ly/oYUqr*), a memory-safe programming language that was originally built for systems programming use cases. Since Cedar is written in Rust, the execution of its policy evaluation is very fast.

 On April 27, 2023, the National Security Agency (NSA) issued a report (*https://oreil.ly/RpBUk*) on software memory safety, in which it outlined the need for memory-safe programming languages. The report recommended against languages like C and C++ because of the possibility of exploitable vulnerabilities arising from mistakes in memory management. The reports list several so-called memory-safe programming languages, such as Java , C#, Go, Python, and Rust.

According the Cedar documentation, Cedar has the following characteristics:

Expressive
Cedar is a simple yet expressive language that is purpose built to support authorization use cases for common authorization models, such as RBAC and ABAC.

Performant
Cedar is fast and scalable. The policy structure is designed to be indexed for quick retrieval and to support fast and scalable real-time evaluation, with bounded latency.

Analyzable
Cedar is designed for analysis using automated reasoning. This enables analyzer tools capable of optimizing your policies and proving that your security model is what you believe it is.

Cedar policies use a syntax structure based on the PARC model: principal, action, resource, and condition. The condition, expressed with a when clause, is optional. In truth, I routinely think of the PARC model when I am writing policies, regardless of policy language. Cedar policies deny by default, so without an explicit allow, the policy denies.

As shown in the following example, the PARC model helps policy authors build clearly defined policies:

```
# Example Cedar policy with no condition
permit(
        principal == User::"alice",
        action == Action::"view",
        resource in Album::"vacation"
);
```

In the preceding policy, the principal (`User::"alice"`) can perform the action (`Action::"view"`) if the resource is a child of the vacation resource (`Album::"vaca tion"`).

As with other policy languages, the Cedar authorization engine takes in policies, data, and requests. It responds with decisions. The following Go example uses the cedar-go (*https://oreil.ly/cedar-go*) project to use the Cedar authorizer. The Go implementation is still a work in progress, but this example works on policy evaluations:

```
# Evaluate request using entity data and Cedar policy
package main

import (
        "encoding/json"
        "fmt"
        "log"
        "github.com/cedar-policy/cedar-go"
)

const policyCedar = `permit (       ❶
        principal == User::"alice",
        action == Action::"view",
        resource in Album::"vacation"
  );
`
const entitiesJSON = `[        ❷
  {
    "uid": { "type": "User", "id": "alice" },
    "attrs": { "age": 18 },
    "parents": []
  },
  {
    "uid": { "type": "Photo", "id": "VacationPhoto94.jpg" },
    "attrs": {},
    "parents": [{ "type": "Album", "id": "vacation" }]
  }
]`

func main() {
        ps, err := cedar.NewPolicySet("policy.cedar", []byte(policyCedar))   ❸
        if err != nil {
```

```
            log.Fatal(err)
    }
    var entities cedar.Entities
    if err := json.Unmarshal([]byte(entitiesJSON), &entities); err != nil {
            log.Fatal(err)
    }
    req := cedar.Request{  ❹
            Principal: cedar.EntityUID{Type: "User", ID: "alice"},
            Action:    cedar.EntityUID{Type: "Action", ID: "view"},
            Resource:  cedar.EntityUID{Type: "Photo", ID: "VacationPhoto94.jpg"},
            Context:   cedar.Record{},
    }
    ok, _ := ps.IsAuthorized(entities, req)  ❺
    fmt.Println(ok)
}
```

❶ Build the Cedar policy to be used.

❷ Build the data (entities) needed for the evaluation.

❸ Build the policy set with the previously built policy. The policy set will perform the authorization.

❹ Build the Cedar request.

❺ Submit the entities data and the request to the policy set to be authorized.

Cedar is built on Rust to be memory safe and performant. Using the PARC model makes the Cedar policy language expressive. Finally, Cedar was built to be analyzed using automated reasoning so that policy correctness could be proven. Given these characteristics, Cedar emerges as a solution that is both powerful and simple to use for authorization use cases. The ability to mathematically prove policy correctness via automated reasoning is new. I can see this characteristic being used first in highly regulated industries, then later mainstreamed by other organizations for audit purposes.

In the next section, I cover another language that you can use as a PaC solution: Configure, Unify, Execute (CUE).

Configure, Unify, Execute

CUE is an OSS project (*https://oreil.ly/djHOW*) that includes a data validation language and an inference engine; I briefly mentioned it in Chapter 14, when discussing SSC artifact provenance. CUE is very powerful, and I will not do it justice in this single section. In fact, like other solutions in this book, we could write an entire book, or series thereof, on CUE.

According to the CUE documentation (*https://oreil.ly/G21AO*), the primary use cases for CUE are the following:

Data validation
Different departments or groups can each define their own constraints to apply to the same set of data.

Code extraction and generation
Extract CUE definitions from multiple sources (Go code, Protobuf), combine them into a single definition, and use that to generate definitions in another format (e.g., OpenAPI).

Configuration
Values can be combined from different sources without one having to import the other.

CUE is a data-constraint programming language written in and underpinned by Go. CUE is also considered a superset of JSON; moreover, all valid JSON is CUE. You can use CUE to define data structures: schemas, constraints, and values. The following example uses CUE to vet the data of a YAML file:

```
# Data file
policies:
  - Name: Deny-tags
    Tag: deny
  - Name: Warn-labels
    Tag: warn
  - Name: Violate-annotations
    Tag: violate

# CUE File
#Policy: {           ❶
        Name: =~"^[A-Z]{1}[a-z\\-]*$"  ❷
        Tag:  =~"^[a-z]{4,7}$"
}
policies: [...#Policy]    ❸
```

❶ CUE uses the hash (#) for a definition. This is the Policy definition.

❷ Regular Expression (RegEx) optionally can be used for string patterns.

❸ The Policy definition is used to define a collection of policies.

```
$ cue vet policy.cue policy.yaml  ❶
```

❶ The CUE CLI can be used to vet data based on CUE definitions and constraints. If the data file vets OK, then no value is returned from the **vet** command.

In the next example, I used a policy with errors, according to the CUE Policy definition file:

```
# Data file with Policy errors
policies:
  - Name: Deny-2tags  ❶
    Tag: deny
  - Name: Warn-labels
    Tag: warn
    Label: InvalidItem  ❷
  - Name: Violate-annotations
    Tag: "violation"  ❸
```

❶ Number in policy name is not allowed per RegEx.

❷ Label is not a valid member of the Policy definition.

❸ Tag is too long (the string can have quotes or no quotes).

```
$ cue vet file.cue data-bad.yaml
policies.1.Label: field not allowed:
    ./data-bad.yaml:6:5
    ./file.cue:1:10
    ./file.cue:7:12
    ./file.cue:7:15
policies.0.Name: invalid value "Deny-2tags" (out of bound =~"^[A-Z]{1}[a-z\\-]*$"):
    ./file.cue:4:8
    ./data-bad.yaml:2:11
policies.2.Tag: invalid value "violation" (out of bound =~"^[a-z]{4,7}$"):
    ./file.cue:5:8
    ./data-bad.yaml:8:10
```

In the next example, I removed the RegEx for the Policy.Tag field, and I used CUE constraints to constrain the possible Tag value to deny, violate, or warn:

```
# Use CUE string constraint for value
#Policy: {
        Name: =~"^[A-Z]{1}[a-z\\-]*$"
        Tag:  "deny" | "violate" | "warn"  ❶
}
policies: [...#Policy]
```

❶ I changed the RegEx validation to a CUE value constraint.

When I vetted the known bad YAML file with the cue vet command, the following errors appeared in the console output:

```
# CUE constraint validation
$ cue vet policy.cue data-bad.yaml
policies.1.Label: field not allowed:  ❶
    ./data-bad.yaml:6:5
```

```
    ./policy.cue:1:10
    ./policy.cue:7:12
    ./policy.cue:7:15
policies.2.Tag: 3 errors in empty disjunction:  ❷
policies.2.Tag: conflicting values "deny" and "violation":
    ./data-bad.yaml:8:10
    ./policy.cue:5:8
    ./policy.cue:7:12
    ./policy.cue:7:15
policies.2.Tag: conflicting values "violate" and "violation":
    ./data-bad.yaml:8:10
    ./policy.cue:5:17
    ./policy.cue:7:12
    ./policy.cue:7:15
policies.2.Tag: conflicting values "warn" and "violation":
    ./data-bad.yaml:8:10
    ./policy.cue:5:29
    ./policy.cue:7:12
    ./policy.cue:7:15
policies.0.Name: invalid value "Deny-2tags"
(out of bound =~"^[A-Z]{1}[a-z\\-]*$"):  ❸
    ./policy.cue:4:8
    ./data-bad.yaml:2:11
```

❶ Label is not a valid member of the Policy definition.

❷ Each allowed Tag value is compared to the `violation` Tag value.

❸ Number in policy name is not allowed per RegEx.

You can use CUE to to build schemas and use those schemas to create concrete configurations. You use the `cue eval` command to evaluate the concrete configurations and output the configuration to the file format you need. The Kubernetes community is already embracing CUE. In fact, Timoni (*https://timoni.sh*) is a new OSS project aimed at improving distribution and lifecycle management for cloud native applications.

The following example is from the Timoni CUE Features Walkthrough (*https://oreil.ly/s0W0k*) documentation. The example first creates a CUE schema with Kubernetes Service definition. Then, it creates a concrete service based on the schema and Service definition. Finally, it uses the `cue vet` and `cue eval` commands to validate the concrete service against the service schema and output the Kubernetes Service configuration as a YAML:

```
# CUE Kubernetes service schema
package main

#Service: {
    apiVersion: string
```

```
    kind:       string
    metadata: {
        name:       string
        namespace: string
    }
    spec: {
        selector: [string]: string
        ports: [{
            name:       string
            port:       int
            targetPort: int | string
        }]
    }
}

# CUE concrete Kubernetes Service configuration
package main

// Set the schema
nginxSvc: #Service     ❶

// Set the concrete values
nginxSvc: {
    apiVersion: "v1"
    kind:       "Service"
    metadata: {
        name:       "nginx"
        namespace: "default"
    }
    spec: {
        selector: "app.kubernetes.io/name": "nginx"
        ports: [{
            name:       "http"
            port:       80
            targetPort: 80
        }]
    }
}
```

❶ The concrete nginxSvc is linked to the CUE Service definition in the CUE schema.

With the Service definition and the concrete Service configured in CUE, I used the cue eval command to validate the concrete Service against the CUE Service schema:

```
$ cue eval -e nginxSvc --out yaml    ❶
apiVersion: v1
kind: Service
metadata:
  name: nginx
  namespace: default
spec:
```

```
  selector:
    app.kubernetes.io/name: nginx
  ports:
    - name: http
      port: 80
      targetPort: 80
```

❶ The concrete nsginxSvc is linked to the Service definition in the CUE schema, in
    the same package and same directory. So, filenames are not in the `cue eval`
    command.

With CUE, definition and configuration are closer. In the case of Kubernetes manifests, the configuration is actually captured and evaluated in CUE concrete configurations, and YAML or JSON can be output as needed to be applied to Kubernetes
clusters.

Although I barely scratched the surface of CUE's capabilities and solved use cases, I
am excited about the direction the language and tools are taking.

PaC is not done growing or evolving. There are new use cases, technologies, and
approaches being developed as you read this passage. How we use and interact with
PaC solutions is also evolving. While it remains to be seen how PaC will improve how
we control our resources and systems, I think it's safe to assume that PaC solutions
will continue to meet—and, in some instances, exceed—our needs.

Conclusion

Thank you for joining me on my journey to explore PaC and how it has solved and
continues to solve security and automated compliance and governance use cases.
Although I couldn't cover everything, throughout this book I have tried to provide
explanations of different PaC tools, their characteristics, and their use cases.

In Chapter 1, I gave you a gentle intro to PaC and a model to help you decide which
PaC solutions best fit your needs. I hope that I have provided you with a solid foundation from which to learn more about PaC and how the various solutions function.
While there are trade-offs with every decision, knowledge is an equalizer that helps
mitigate decision risk through information and experience.

PaC adoption is increasing. According to the 2023 *State of Policy as Code* research
report from Styra (*https://oreil.ly/8Ubdw*), the creator of OPA, "94% of technical decision makers agree that policy as code is vital for preventative security and compliance
at scale."

At the time of writing, Deloitte goes on to publish (*https://oreil.ly/KZuuR*): "Policy as
Code is transforming the way organizations approach governance by providing a
powerful and flexible way to define, manage and enforce the policies."

No matter how you proceed from here, my hope is that you are now better prepared to provide the security and automated compliance and governance decisions and solutions needed for your organization.

Index

About the Author

Jimmy Ray has over 25 years' experience in technology, specializing in cybersecurity, cloud architecture, containerization, and Policy as Code (PaC). His experience spans multiple industries, including aviation, finance, ecommerce, healthcare logistics, government, semiconductors, and cloud computing.

Jimmy has been writing and speaking for over 20 years, and for the past several years he has focused on providing security, compliance, and governance solutions with PaC in the areas of cloud computing, containerization, and software supply chain. Jimmy is recognized as a subject matter expert in PaC and container supply chain security.

Colophon

The animal on the cover of *Policy as Code* is a *mastiff*. Mastiffs are a powerful but gentle working breed of dog. There are records of their origins in Europe and Asia that date as far back as 3000 BCE. Certain breeds of mastiff (e.g., Cane Coroso) were used as war dogs and guardians. English mastiffs were also sent to ancient Roman arenas to battle against bears, tigers, bulls, lions, other dogs, and gladiators. They also fought in bullbaiting and bearbaiting rings in England.

Mastiffs are heavy-built, large, muscular dogs. They have broad heads with drooping, pendant-shaped ears; broad, short muzzles; and short, coarse coats. Typical coat colors are apricot, silver fawn, and brindled fawn and black. They usually have dark muzzles and ears. Adult mastiffs typically weigh anywhere between 120 and 230 pounds.

Despite their size, mastiffs are affectionate, patient, eager to please, and low-activity dogs. Adults require only about one hour of interactive play or walking per day. They also attempt to be lap dogs despite their massive bodies and are good with families. Due to their size, they require large, soft bedding areas where they can stretch out in order to avoid calluses and bursitis. Mastiffs aren't good in hot climates unless there is ample air conditioning because they overheat.

While mastiffs are not an endangered species, many of the animals on O'Reilly covers are. And all of them are important to the world.

The cover illustration is by Karen Montgomery, based on an antique line engraving from Cassell's *Natural History*. The series design is by Edie Freedman, Ellie Volckhausen, and Karen Montgomery. The cover fonts are Gilroy Semibold and Guardian Sans. The text font is Adobe Minion Pro; the heading font is Adobe Myriad Condensed; and the code font is Dalton Maag's Ubuntu Mono.

Milton Keynes UK
Ingram Content Group UK Ltd.
UKHW052300050724
445127UK00003B/5